French Glossary for Bilingual Secretaries

French-English
English-French

EuroLexus series

i
impact books

First published in Great Britain in 1993 by
Impact Books
151 Dulwich Road, London SE24 0NG

ISBN 1 874687 23 4

Printed and bound by The Guernsey Press, Guernsey

ont contribué/contributors

Patricia Clarke   Jane Goldie
Claudine Rebersat   Carine Lipski

TABLE DES MATIERES
CONTENTS

PRÉFACE
PREFACE

Un(e) secrétaire est appelé(e) à travailler dans une grande diversité de cadres. C'est pourquoi ce lexique renferme un choix étendu et éclectique de termes français et anglais, tels que des termes spécialisés se rapportant aux domaines de la finance, de la comptabilité, du commerce international et autres. Il s'attache également à identifier tout ce qui constitue l'environnement d'un(e) secrétaire - équipement de bureau, ordinateurs, relations avec la clientèle, etc. - et répertorie les mots et expressions utiles s'y rattachant. Enfin, ce lexique offre un volet pratique concernant la rédaction de lettres, l'envoi de fax, la communication téléphonique, les noms de pays, etc.

Since a bilingual secretary can work in a great variety of environments, this glossary contains a wide-ranging and very varied selection of French and English vocabulary, including specialist terms from fields such as finance, book-keeping, international commerce and more. But it also sets out to identify what is common to many of these environments - office equipment, computers, dealing with customers etc - and lists relevant words and expressions for these. This glossary also contains practical sections on letter writing, faxing, telephoning, names of countries etc.

*abréviations/*abbreviations

adj	*adjectif/*adjective
Am	American English/*anglais américain*
Br	British English/*anglais britannique*
f	*féminin/*feminine
qch	*quelque chose*/something
qn	*quelqu'un*/somebody
m	*masculin/*masculine
pl	*pluriel/*plural
sb	somebody/*quelqu'un*
sth	something/*quelque chose*
vi	*verbe intransitif/*intransitive verb
vt	*verbe transitif/*transitive verb

A

A3 *m* A3
A4 *m* A4
A5 *m* A5
abaisser [*prix etc*] to lower
abonné *m* subscriber; *être abonné à* to subscribe to
abonnement *m* subscription
*s'***abonner à** to take out a subscription to, to subscribe to
aboutir à un accord to lead to an agreement
absence *f* absence
absence non rémunérée *f* unpaid leave
absence rémunérée *f* paid leave
absent absent
absentéisme *m* absenteeism
accéder à [*fichier, menu*] to access
accéder à une demande to comply with a request
accent *m* accent
accent aigu *m* acute (accent)
accent circonflexe *m* circumflex
accent grave *m* grave (accent)
acceptable acceptable
acceptation *f* acceptance
accepter to accept
accident du travail *m* industrial accident
accidenté *m* [*du travail*] victim of an accident
accolade *f* curly bracket
accompagné accompanied
accord *m* agreement; *être d'accord*

avec to agree with; *se mettre d'accord sur* to come to an agreement on; *tomber d'accord sur* to come to an agreement on
accorder to grant
accorder un escompte to give a discount
accrédité [*représentant*] authorized
accréditif *m* letter of credit
accroissement *m* increase
accroître to increase
accueil *m* welcome; [*bureau*] reception
accueillir to welcome
accumulation *f* accumulation
accumuler to accumulate
accusé de bonne réception *m* [*de télécopie*] acknowledgement of receipt
accusé de réception *m* acknowledgement (of receipt)
accuser réception de to acknowledge receipt of
achat *m* purchase
achat à crédit *m* purchase on credit, credit purchase
achat au comptant *m* cash purchase
acheter to buy, to purchase
acheter à crédit to buy on credit
acheter à tempérament to buy by instalments
acheter au comptant to buy for cash
acheteur *m* buyer, purchaser
achèvement *m* completion

achever to complete

acompte *m* down payment, payment on account; [*versement*] instalment; **donner un acompte** to make a down payment, to make a payment on account

acompte mensuel *m* monthly payment, monthly instalment

acquéreur *m* purchaser

acquisition *f* acquisition

acquit *m* receipt; **pour acquit** payment received, received with thanks

acquitté [*facture*] paid

acquittement *m* [*de facture*] payment

acquitter [*un impôt*] to pay; [*considérer pour acquit*] to receipt

acte notarié *m* notarized deed

acte de vente *m* deed of sale

actif *m* [*bancaire*] credit balance; [*de société*] assets

actif circulant *m* floating assets, current assets

action *f* share; [*juridique*] legal action

actionnaire *mf* shareholder

actionnariat *m* share ownership

actions *fpl* shares, stock *Am*; **avoir des actions dans** to have a shareholding in; **détenir des actions d'une société** to have shares in a company

activité *f* business; [*d'entreprise*] activity

actualisation *f* [*mise à jour*] update

actualiser [*mettre à jour*] to update

actuel current

adaptateur (secteur) *m* adaptor

adapter to adapt

s'adapter à to adjust to

addition *f* addition

additionner to add

adhérent *m* member

adhérer à to join

adhésion *f* membership

adjoindre [*inclure*] to enclose

adjoint *m* deputy

adjoint [*directeur etc*] associate; [*document*] enclosed

adjudicataire *mf* successful tenderer

adjudicateur *m* contract-awarding party

adjudication *f* [*de contrat*] award

administrateur *m* director; **avoir des talents d'administrateur** to be a good administrator

administrateur délégué *m* managing director

administratif administrative

administration *f* administration

administration fiscale *f* tax authorities

administration du personnel *f* personnel management

admission *f* admission

adopter une résolution to adopt a resolution

adressage *m* addressing

adresse *f* address

adresse personnelle *f* home address

adresse au bureau *f* office address

adresse de facturation *f* address for invoicing

adresse de livraison *f* delivery address; [*d'objets volumineux*] shipping address

adresse du siège social *f* head office address, registered office address

adresser to address

s'adresser à [*à un service etc*] to apply to

adresser une lettre à to address a letter to

affaire *f* matter; [*marché*] deal; [*entreprise*] business; **avoir affaire**

à [*à qn*] to deal with
affaires *fpl* business
affectation *f* [*de personnel*] assignment
affecter [*personnel*] to assign
affichage *m* display
afficher to display
afficher les prix to display prices
afficheur *m* VDU, visual display unit
affilié affiliated
affilié *m* affiliated member
*s'***affilier à** to join
affirmation *f* statement
affirmer to state
affranchi: insuffisamment affranchi insufficient postage
affranchir une lettre to stamp a letter; [*tamponner*] to frank a letter
affranchissement *m* stamping; [*avec tampon*] franking; [*valeur*] postage
affranchisseuse *f* franking machine
AG (=Assemblée générale) *f* AGM
agence *f* agency; [*de banque*] branch
Agence nationale pour l'emploi *f* Jobcentre®
agence de placement *f* employment agency
agence de publicité *f* advertising agency
agence de voyages *f* travel agency
agencement *m* layout
agencements *mpl* fixtures and fittings
agenda *m* [*carnet*] notebook; [*calendrier*] diary; [*organisateur*] personal organizer; [*de bureau*] desk diary
agent *m* agent
agent commercial *m* sales representative
agent exclusif *m* sole agent
agent technico-commercial *m* sales engineer

agent de contact *m* contact
agent de fret *m* freight forwarder
agrafage *m* stapling
agrafe *f* staple
agrafer to staple
agrafeuse *f* stapler
agrandir to enlarge
agréé [*attitré*] approved, authorized
agréer [*demande*] to approve
agrément *m* approval
aide *f* aid
aide-comptable *mf* assistant accountant, accounts clerk
aide sociale *f* social security
aide au logement *f* accommodation allowance
ajournement *m* postponement
ajourner to postpone
ajouter to add, to append
ajustement *m* adjustment
ajustement des salaires *m* wage adjustment
ajuster to adjust
aligner to align
alimenter un compte to pay money into an account
alinéa *m* [*retrait*] indent; [*paragraphe*] paragraph; *créer un alinéa* to indent; *mettre à l'alinéa* to indent
allègement des impôts *m* reduction of taxes
alléger [*impôts, charges*] to reduce
allocataire *mf* recipient, beneficiary
allocation *f* benefit; [*bourse*] grant
allocation de maternité *f* maternity allowance
allocations familiales *fpl* family allowance
allocations de chômage *fpl* unemployment benefit
allocution *f* speech
allouer to allocate

alphabétique alphabetical
alphabétiquement alphabetically
ambassade *f* embassy
ambassadeur *m* ambassador
amélioration *f* improvement
améliorer to improve
aménagement *m* [*disposition*] layout
aménagement paysager *m* open plan
amende *f* fine
amendement *m* amendment
amiable: à l'amiable out of court
an *m* year; *par an* per year, annually
analyse *f* analysis
analyser to analyse
analyste *mf* analyst
ancienneté *f* seniority
animation des ventes *f* sales
  promotion
animer [*conférence*] to lead
année *f* year
année budgétaire *f* financial year,
  fiscal year *Am*
année civile *f* calendar year
année comptable *f* financial year
année fiscale *f* financial year, fiscal
  year *Am*
annexe *f* appendix
annexe related
annexé à attached to
annonce *f* advertisement; *insérer une
  annonce* to put an advertisement
  in; *répondre à une annonce* to
  reply to an advertisement
annotation *f* annotation
annoter to annotate
annuaire *m* directory
annuaire papier *m* printed directory
annuaire téléphonique *m* telephone
  directory
annuaire du commerce *m* trade
  directory
annuaire du téléphone *m* telephone
  directory

annuel annual
annuité *f* [*rente*] annuity
annulation *f* cancellation
annuler to cancel
annuler un chèque to cancel a
  cheque
annuler un ordre to cancel an order
ANPE (=Agence nationale pour
  l'emploi) *f* Jobcentre®
antenne *f* [*de société*] branch
antérieur prior
anticipé [*remboursement de dette*]
  early
anticiper un paiement to pay in
  advance
antidater to backdate
APEC (=Association pour l'emploi
  des cadres) *f* executive
  recruitment agency
appareil de lecture *m* [*de microfilm*]
  reader
appauvrissement *m* [*d'une
  entreprise*] decline in the financial
  position
appel *m* call
appel téléphonique *m* telephone call
appelant *m* caller
appeler [*au téléphone*] to ring, to call
appeler qn au téléphone to ring sb,
  to call sb
appendice *m* appendix
application: en application de [*loi*]
  in enforcement of; [*contrat*]
  pursuant to
appliquer to apply
appointements *mpl* salary
apposer sa signature à to put one's
  signature to
apprentissage *m* [*formation*] training
approbation *f* approval
approuver to approve
approvisionnement *m* supply
approvisionner to supply

approvisionner qn en qch to supply sb with sth

approvisionner un compte to pay money into an account

approximatif approximate

après imposition after tax

après impôt *m* after tax

apurement *m* [*de comptes*] auditing

apurer [*comptes*] to audit

arbitrage *m* [*de conflit*] arbitration

arbitrer to arbitrate

archivage *m* filing

archiver to file

archives *fpl* files; [*gros volume*] archives

archiviste *mf* archivist

argent *m* money

argent comptant *m* cash

argent liquide *m* cash

argent en caisse *m* cash in hand; [*recettes*] takings

argumentation *f* argument

armoire ignifugée *f* fireproof cabinet

armoire à fournitures *f* stationery supplies cupboard

arrache-agrafes *m* staple remover

arrangement *m* arrangement

arrangement à l'amiable *m* out of court settlement

arrérages *mpl* arrears

arrêt de paiement *m* stopping of payment(s)

arrêt de travail *m* stoppage

arrêté *m* decree

arrêter un marché to close a deal

arrhes *fpl* deposit

arriéré *m* arrears

arriéré in arrears

arriver à échéance to fall due; [*bail*] to expire

arrondir to round off; [*vers le haut*] to round up; [*vers le bas*] to round down

article *m* [*clause*] article; [*de compte*] entry

article de journal *m* newspaper article

articles de bureau *mpl* office supplies

ASBL (=Association sans but lucratif) *f* non-profit-making organization

ASSEDIC (=Association pour l'emploi dans l'industrie et le commerce) *f* French unemployment benefits department

assemblée *f* meeting

assemblée annuelle *f* annual (general) meeting

assemblée générale *f* annual general meeting

assemblée générale extraordinaire *f* extraordinary general meeting

assemblée générale ordinaire *f* annual general meeting, AGM

assemblée des actionnaires *f* shareholders' meeting

assembler to assemble

s'assembler to meet

assistant *m* assistant

assisté par ordinateur computer-aided, computer-assisted

assister à to attend

assister à une assemblée to attend a meeting

association *f* society, association; [*entreprise*] partnership

assujetti *m* person liable for tax

assurance *f* insurance

assurance incendie *f* fire insurance

assurance maintenance étendue *f* extended maintenance insurance

assurance maintenance visite *f* callout maintenance insurance

assurance maladie *f* health insurance

assurance multirisque *f* comprehensive insurance

5

assurance tous risques *f* comprehensive insurance, all-risks insurance

assurance-vie *f* life insurance, life assurance *Br*

assurance vieillesse *f* old-age insurance

assurance vol *f* theft insurance

assurance aux tiers *f* third party insurance

assurances *fpl* insurance

assuré *m* insured (party), assured

*s'***assurer** to take out insurance

assureur *m* insurer

astérisque *m* asterisk

attache de bureau *f* clip

attendre to wait for; *faire attendre qn* to keep sb waiting

attente *f* wait

attention *f* attention; *à l'attention de* for the attention of

attestation *f* certificate

attestation de rejet *f* [*de chèque*] notification of refusal to pay

attitré [*agent*] appointed; [*fournisseur*] regular

audioconférence *f* audioconference

audioconférence multipoint *f* multipoint audioconference

audioconférence point à point *f* point-to-point audioconference

audiotypie *f* audiotyping

audiotypiste *mf* audiotypist

audit *m* audit

augmentation *f* increase

augmentation de prix *f* price increase

augmentation de salaire *f* pay rise, raise *Am*

augmenter to increase

authenticité *f* [*de documents*] authenticity

authentifier to authenticate

authentique [*copie*] certified

autocollant [*étiquette*] self-adhesive; [*enveloppe*] self-sealing

automatisable computerizable, automatable

autorisé authorized

autoriser to authorize

aval: pour aval guaranteed by

avance *f* advance

avance de fonds *f* advance

avancement *m* [*d'employé*] promotion

avant imposition before tax

avant impôt before tax

avantage en nature *m* benefit in kind

avantages sociaux *mpl* fringe benefits

avion: par avion *m* by air; [*lettre*] by air, by airmail

avis *m* notification; [*document*] notice, note, advice

avis d'expédition *m* dispatch note

avis d'imposition *m* tax assessment

avis de crédit *m* credit advice

avis de débit *m* debit advice

avis de paiement *m* payment advice

avis de prélèvement *m* direct debit advice

avis de réception *m* acknowledgement (of receipt)

avis de rejet *m* [*de chèque*] notice of returned cheque

avis de virement *m* (bank) transfer advice

avis de la banque *m* bank notification, bank advice note

aviser to inform, to advise

avocat *m* lawyer

avoir *m* [*biens*] possessions; [*capital*] capital; [*sur compte*] credit

avoir de compte *m* account credit

B

bac *m* tray
bac roulant *m* file trolley
bac à correspondance *m* correspondence tray
badge *m* badge
bail *m* lease; *renouveler un bail* to renew a lease
bail emphytéotique *m* long lease
bailleur *m* lessor
bailleur de fonds *m* backer
baisse des prix *f* drop in prices
baisser [*prix*] to lower
balance *f* balance; [*pour peser*] scales
bancaire banking, bank
bande *f* tape
banque *f* bank
banque centrale *f* central bank
banque commerciale *f* commercial bank
banque compensatrice *f* clearing bank
banque confirmatrice *f* confirming bank
banque notificatrice *f* advising bank
banque d'affaires *f* merchant bank
banqueroute *f* bankruptcy
banquier *m* banker
barème des prix *m* price scale
barème des salaires *m* salary scale
barre *f* oblique, slash
barre oblique inversée *f* backslash
barre d'espacement *f* space bar
barrer to cross out

barrer un chèque to cross a cheque
bas: en bas de page at the bottom of the page
bas de gamme down-market
base *f* [*fondement*] basis
base de calcul *f* basis of calculations
base de données *f* database
base hors taxe *f* [*de TVA*] amount exclusive of VAT
bénéfice *m* profit
bénéfice imposable *m* taxable profit
bénéficiaire *mf* beneficiary, payee
bible de paragraphes *f* library of standard paragraphs
bibliothèque de paragraphes *f* library of standard paragraphs
BICS (adresse BIC) bank indicator code
bien-fondé *m* validity
bilan *m* balance sheet
bilan comptable *m* balance sheet
bilan financier *m* financial statement
billet de banque *m* banknote, note
bloc *m* [*de texte*] block
bloc adresse *m* address block
bloc-notes *m* memo pad, note pad
bloc de texte *m* block of text
boîte postale *f* PO Box
boîte à disques *f* diskette box
boîte à fiches *f* card index box
boîte aux lettres *f* letter box
boîte aux lettres électronique *f* electronic mailbox
bon *m* voucher, slip, coupon

bon d'entrée *m* stock received docket/form
bon d'expédition *m* dispatch note
bon de commande *m* purchase order
bon de garantie *m* guarantee slip
bon de livraison *m* delivery note
bon de réception des marchandises *m* receipt note
bon de sortie *m* stock issued docket/form
boni *m* [*supplément*] bonus
bonification *f* rebate; [*supplément*] bonus
bonus *m* bonus
bordereau *m* [*formulaire*] form; [*liste*] list
bordereau d'achat *m* inventory of purchases
bordereau d'opération *m* paying-in slip
bordereau de compte *m* statement of account
bordereau de crédit *m* credit note
bordereau de remise *m* pay-in slip
bordereau de remise d'espèces *m* pay-in slip
bordereau de saisie *m* record form; [*comptabilité*] accounting entry sheet/form
bordereau de salaires *m* wages sheet
bordereau de versement *m* paying-in slip
bordereau de versement d'espèces *m* paying-in slip
bottin *m* telephone directory
boule de commande *f* trackball
Bourse *f* Stock Exchange
bourse des valeurs *f* Stock Exchange
boursier *adj* stock market
BP (=boîte postale) *f* PO Box
BPF (=bon pour francs) good for ... francs

branche *f* line of business
branche d'activité *f* area of operations
bras porte-copies *m* copy-holder
bref: en bref in brief; *dans les plus brefs délais* as soon as possible
brevet *m* patent
brevet d'invention *m* patent
breveté patented
breveter to patent
briefer [*qn sur qch*] to brief
briefing *m* briefing
briseur de grève *m* strike breaker
bristol *m* thin cardboard
brochure *f* brochure
brouillard *m* day book, cash book
brouillard de caisse *m* cash book
brouillon *m* [*de lettre*] draft
brouillon annoté *m* annotated draft
broyer to shred
broyeur *m* shredder
brut [*salaire*] gross
budget *m* budget
budget mensuel *m* monthly budget
budget de trésorerie *m* cash budget
budget des ventes *m* sales budget
budgétaire budget, budgetary
budgétisation *f* budgeting
bulletin *m* bulletin; [*revue*] report
bulletin-réponse *m* reply coupon
bulletin d'inscription *m* registration form
bulletin de commande *m* order slip, order form
bulletin de paie *m* payslip
bulletin de salaire *m* payslip
bulletin de versement *m* receipt
bureau *m* office; [*meuble*] desk
bureau distributeur *m* [*des Postes*] main sorting post office
bureau paysager *m* open-plan office
bureau-satellite *m* branch office
bureau d'achat *m* purchase office

bureau d'études *m* design department; [*de recherche*] R&D department
bureau de placement *m* employment agency
bureau de poste *m* post office

bureau de publicité *m* advertising agency
bureau de traduction *m* translation agency
bureautique *f* office automation
buvard *m* blotter

C

CA (=chiffre d'affaires) *m* sales, turnover
cabinet conseil *m* consultancy
cabinet juridique *m* law firm
cabinet d'audit *m* firm of auditors
cabinet d'expertise comptable *m* accounting firm
câble *m* cable
câble d'imprimante *m* printer cable
cachet *m* seal
cachet d'arrivée *m* received stamp
cachet de la poste *m* postmark
cacheter [*une enveloppe*] to seal
cadre *m* executive
cadre-adresse *m* address space
cadre moyen *m* middle manager
cadre réservé à l'organisation *m* for official use only
cadre supérieur *m* senior executive
cadres moyens *mpl* middle management
cadres supérieurs *mpl* senior management

CAF (=coût assurance fret) CIF
cahier d'enregistrement *m* [*de courrier*] mail book; [*d'appels reçus*] telephone log
cahier des charges *m* [*de contrat*] technical specifications
caisse *f* [*liquide*] cash
caisse d'épargne *f* savings bank
caisse de garantie *f* credit guarantee institution
caisse de maladie *f* health insurance scheme
caisse de retraite *f* pension fund
calcul *m* calculation
calculateur *m* calculator, desktop calculator
calculatrice *f* calculator, desktop calculator
calculer [*prix etc*] calculate
calculette *f* calculator, pocket calculator
calepin *m* notebook
calquer to trace

9

camion *m* lorry

camionnage *m* road haulage

camionnette de livraison *f* delivery van

camionneur *m* lorry driver

campagne publicitaire *f* advertising campaign

campagne de publicité *f* advertising campaign

campagne de vente *f* sales campaign

candidat *m* applicant

candidature *f* [*pour poste*] application; ***poser sa candidature pour un poste*** to apply for a job

canevas *m* [*de lettre etc*] outline

caoutchouc *m* [*ruban*] rubber band

capital *m* capital

capot antibruit *m* soundproof hood, acoustic hood

caractère *m* character

caractère gras *m* bold character

caractères d'imprimerie *mpl* block capitals; ***en caractères d'imprimerie*** please print

carbone *m* carbon

cargaison *f* cargo

carnet *m* notebook

carnet à souches *m* counterfoil book

carnet d'adresses *m* address book

carnet de chèques *m* cheque book

carnet de commandes *m* order book

carnet de route *m* logbook

carrière *f* career

carte *f* card

carte accréditive *f* credit card; [*de magasin*] charge card

carte-guide *f* file separator, file divider

carte-lettre *f* letter-card

carte Pastel *f* phone card [*use of which is debited to one's own phone number*]

carte perforée *f* punch card

carte postale *f* postcard

carte professionnelle *f* practising certificate

carte-réponse *f* reply coupon

carte téléphone *f* phone card

carte à prépaiement *f* phone card

carte à puce *f* smartcard

carte d'identité *f* identity card

carte de crédit *f* credit card

carte de fidélité *f* valued customer card, frequent user card

carte de visite *f* card, business card

carton *m* cardboard; ***un carton*** a cardboard box; ***en carton*** cardboard

carton de classement *m* file box

cartonnage *m* [*mise en carton*] packing

cartouche *f* cartridge

cartouche de toner *f* toner cartridge

case *f* box

case postale *f* post office box

casier *m* [*à tiroirs*] filing cabinet, file cabinet *Am*

cassette d'alimentation *f* [*de copieuse*] paper tray

catalogue *m* catalogue

cataloguer to catalogue

catégorie *f* category

catégorie de produit *f* product category

caution *f* guarantee

cautionnement *m* guarantee

cautionner to stand surety for

cavalier *m* tab

C/C (=compte de chèque) *m* C/A

CCB (=compte de chèque bancaire) *m* C/A

CCI (=Chambre de commerce et de l'industrie) *f* Chamber of Commerce and Industry

CCP (=compte courant postal) *m* post office cheque account, giro account

CDI (=Centre des impôts) *m* tax centre

cedex (=courrier d'entreprise à distribution exceptionnelle) *m* central sorting office for business mail

cédille *f* cedilla

CEE (=Communauté économique européenne) *f* EEC; **de la CEE** EEC

cellule *f* [*de tableur*] cell

centrage *m* [*de texte*] centring

centrage automatique *m* [*de texte*] automatic centring

central central

central téléphonique *m* telephone exchange

centrale d'achat *f* central buying group

centralisation *f* centralization

centraliser to centralize

centre d'analyse *m* cost centre

centre de chèques postaux *m* PO cheque account centre

centre des impôts *m* tax centre

centré [*texte*] centred

centrer [*texte*] to centre

certificat *m* certificate

certificat médical *m* medical certificate

certificat d'arrêt de travail *m* [*pour cause de maladie*] medical certificate

certificat d'assurance *m* insurance certificate

certificat de capacité *m* [*d'employé*] certificate of proficiency

certificat de garantie *m* guarantee certificate, warranty certificate

certificat de non-paiement *m* [*de chèque*] notification of unpaid cheque

certificat de travail *m* reference, testimonial

certification *f* certification

certifier to certify

cesser [*le travail*] to stop

C et F (=coût et fret) C&F

CFDT (=Confédération française du travail) *f* socialist trade union

CGI (=Code général des impôts) *m* general tax code

CGT (=Confédération générale du travail) *f* Communist trade union

CH No (=chèque numéro) cheque number

Chambre de commerce *f* Chamber of Commerce

champ *m* [*rubrique*] field

charge: être à la charge de [*appel etc*] to be chargeable to

chargé: être chargé de to be in charge of

charges locatives *fpl* [*de locaux*] rental expenses; [*de matériel*] lease charges; [*de téléphone, d'électricité*] standing charges

charges nettes *fpl* net costs

charges patronales *fpl* employer contributions

charges sociales *fpl* social security charges

charges sociales patronales *fpl* employer contributions

charges sociales salariales *fpl* employee contributions

charges d'exploitation *fpl* operating costs, running costs

chasseur de têtes *m* head hunter

chef *m* [*dans hiérarchie*] superior; [*de service*] manager, head; [*d'entreprise*] head; [*d'employé*] boss

chef comptable *m* chief accountant

chef d'atelier *m* shop foreman

11

chef d'équipe *m* foreman
chef de bureau *m* office manager
chef de produit *m* product manager
chef de service *m* head of department, departmental manager
chef de zone *m* area manager
chef des études *m* research manager
chef des informations *m* PR manager
chef des traitements *m* DP manager
chef des ventes *m* sales manager
chemin de fer *m* railway
chemise *f* [*cartonnée*] folder
chèque *m* cheque, check *Am*
chèque barré *m* crossed cheque
chèque postal *m* post office cheque
chèque-restaurant *m* luncheon voucher
chèque au porteur *m* cheque made out to bearer, bearer cheque
chèque de salaire *m* pay cheque
chèque de virement *m* transfer cheque
chèque de voyage *m* traveller's cheque
chèque en blanc *m* blank cheque
chèque en bois *m* rubber cheque
chèque sans provision *m* rubber cheque, cheque that bounces
chéquier *m* cheque book
cher [*coûteux*] expensive
chercheur *m* researcher
chevron *m* angle bracket
chevronné experienced
chiffrage *m* adding up, totalling
chiffre *m* figure; *en chiffres* [*montant*] in figures
chiffre d'affaires *m* sales, turnover
chiffre d'affaires annuel *m* annual sales figures, annual turnover
chiffre d'affaires global *m* total sales
chiffre de vente *m* sales figures

chiffré [*codé*] coded
chiffrer to quantify; [*pages*] to number
se **chiffrer à** to add up to, to total
chiffreur *m* payments coding clerk
chômage *m* unemployment; *être au chômage* to be unemployed
chômage chronique *m* chronic unemployment
chômage conjoncturel *m* cyclical unemployment
chômage partiel *m* short time, short-time working
chômage saisonnier *m* seasonal unemployment
chômage structurel *m* long-term unemployment
chômé: jour chômé public holiday, bank holiday *Br*
chômeur *m* unemployed worker; *les chômeurs mpl* the unemployed
chrono *m* day file
chronogramme *m* planner
chronologique chronological
chronologiquement chronologically
ci-après below
ci-contre opposite
ci-dessous below
ci-dessus above
ci-inclus enclosed
ci-joint enclosed; *ci-joint les documents demandés* please find enclosed the requested documents
cible *f* target
circonflexe [*accent*] circumflex
circonscription téléphonique *f* telephone code area
circonstances *fpl* circumstances
circonstances exceptionnelles *fpl* exceptional circumstances
circonstances indépendantes de notre volonté *fpl* circumstances beyond our control

circuit de commercialisation *m* marketing network

circuit de distribution *m* distribution network

circulaire *f* circular

ciseaux *mpl* scissors

citation *f* summons

cité administrative *f* government buildings

citer [*un prix*] to quote

classe *f* class; [*comptabilité*] group of accounts

classement *m* classification; [*rangement*] filing

classement alphanumérique *m* alphanumerical filing

classement décimal *m* decimal filing

classement géographique *m* filing by geographical area

classement horizontal *m* horizontal filing

classement idéologique *m* filing by subject

classement latéral *m* lateral filing

classement numérique *m* numerical filing

classement vertical *m* vertical filing

classement par ordre alphabétique *m* alphabetical filing

classement par ordre chronologique *m* chronological filing

classement par ordre numérique *m* numerical filing

classer to classify; [*ranger*] to file

classeur *m* [*meuble*] filing cabinet

classeur distributeur *m* index card box

classeur à anneaux *m* ring binder

classeur à levier *m* lever-arch file

classeur à tiroirs *m* filing cabinet

classification *f* classification

classification décimale *f* decimal classification

classifier to classify

clause contractuelle *f* clause of a/the contract

clause d'arbitrage *f* arbitration clause

clavier *m* [*d'une machine*] keyboard

clavier AZERTY *m* AZERTY keyboard

clavier numérique *m* numeric keypad

clavier QWERTY *m* QWERTY keyboard

claviste *mf* keyboarder

clé RIB (=relevé d'identité bancaire) *f* bank details

clerc *m* clerk

client *m* customer, client

client douteux *m* doubtful debt

clientèle *f* clientele, customers

cliquer (sur) to click (on)

cliquer deux fois to double-click

clore un compte to close an account

clôture de compte *f* closing of account

clôture de l'exercice *f* end of the financial year

clôturer un compte to close an account

coadministrateur *m* co-director

coassocié *m* co-partner

cocher la case appropriée tick the appropriate box, check the appropriate box *Am*

code assujetti TVA *m* VAT reference number

code banque *m* bank sort code

code (à) barre *m* bar code

code barres *m* bar code

code fournisseur *m* supplier's code

code général des impôts *m* general tax code

code guichet *m* bank branch code

code postal *m* post code, postal code, zip code *Am*

code taxe *m* tax code

code du travail *m* employment code, employment law, labour code *Am*, labor laws *Am*

codification *f* coding

codification décimale *f* decimal coding

codification significative *f* coding by means of symbols

codifier to code

codirecteur *m* co-director

coefficient *m* coefficient

coéquipier *m* team mate

coffre *m* safe

coffre bancaire *m* safe deposit (box)

coffre-fort *m* safe

cogérance *f* co-management

cogérer to manage jointly

cogestion *f* joint management

colis *m* package, parcel

colis chargé *m* registered and insured parcel

colis postal *m* parcel post

collaborateur *m* [*dans entreprise*] colleague; *des collaborateurs participant à un projet* the people working together on a project

collaboration *f* collaboration

collaborer to collaborate

colle de bureau *f* glue

collectif collective

collection *f* collection

collectivité *f* community

collègue *mf* colleague

colloque *m* seminar

colonnage *m* putting into columns

colonne *f* column

colonne de chiffres *f* column of figures

cols blancs *mpl* white-collar workers

combiné téléphonique *m* handset

combler [*déficit, perte*] to make good

combler un retard to make up for lost time

comité consultatif *m* advisory board

comité d'entreprise *m* employee association

comité de direction *m* management committee, executive committee

commande *f* order; [*ordinateur*] command

commandement *m* order

commander to order

commencer en retrait to indent

commerçant *m* merchant

commerce *m* trade; [*achat et vente*] commerce; [*fonds de commerce*] business

commerce extérieur *m* foreign trade

commerce intérieur *m* domestic trade

commerce d'exportation *m* export trade

commerce d'importation *m* import trade

commerce de détail *m* retail trade

commerce de gros *m* wholesale trade

commercer to trade

commercial business; [*droit*] commercial; [*embargo, tribunal*] trade

commercialisation *f* marketing

commercialiser to market

commis *m* clerk

commis principal *m* senior clerk

commis voyageur *m* commercial traveller

commis de banque *m* bank clerk

commission *f* commission

commission bancaire *f* bank commission, bank charge

Commission européenne *f* European Commission

commission paritaire *f* joint committee

commission de change *f* commission

commission de paiement *f* collection charge, collection fee

communautaire Community

communication *f* message; *mettre qn en communication avec qn* [*au téléphone*] to put sb through to sb; *prendre la communication* to take the call

communication intra-circonscription *f* local call

communication téléphonique *f* phone call

communication en PCV *f* reverse charge call

communication hors circonscription *f* long-distance call

communiqué de presse *m* press release

communiquer des renseignements to convey information

compagnie *f* company

compagnie d'assurances *f* insurance company

compagnie d'aviation *f* airline

compagnie de navigation *f* shipping company

compagnie des chemins de fer *f* railway company

comparatif comparative

compatible *m* compatible

compenser [*chèque*] to clear

compétences de claviste *fpl* keyboard skills

compétitif [*marché*] competitive

compétitivité *f* competitiveness

complémentaire [*somme*] additional

compléter un formulaire to complete a form

compliment: avec les compliments de with the compliments of

composer [*un numéro*] to dial

composeur de numéros *m* dialler

compositeur *m* typesetter

composition automatique de numéros *f* automatic dialling

compression de personnel *f* reduction in staff

compromis *m* compromise

compromis de vente *m* sale agreement

compta *f* accounting

comptabiliser to record in the accounts, to enter in the accounts

comptabilité *f* accounts; [*discipline*] accountancy; [*système*] accounting; *qui est-ce qui fait votre comptabilité ?* who does your accounts?

comptable *mf* accountant

comptage *m* counting

comptant: au comptant cash

compte *m* account; *avoir un compte en banque* to have a bank account

compte bancaire *m* bank account

compte bloqué *m* frozen account, blocked account

compte chèque *m* current account, check account, checking account *Am*

compte chèque postal *m* Post Office cheque account

compte client *m* account receivable

compte courant *m* current account, check account, checking account *Am*

compte courant bancaire *m* current account with a bank

compte courant postal *m* current account with the post office, post office current account

compte créditeur [*à la banque*] account in credit

15

compte individuel *m* personal account

compte joint *m* joint account

compte livret *m* deposit account

compte postal *m* post office account

compte rendu *m* [*rapport*] report; [*procès-verbal*] minutes

compte à découvert *m* overdrawn account

compte de charges *m* expense account

compte de dépôt *m* savings account, deposit account

compter to count

comptes annuels *mpl* annual accounts

concerner: en ce qui concerne with regard to

concession *f* concession; [*d'automobiles*] dealership; [*contrat de franchisage*] franchise

concession de franchise *f* grant of franchise

concessionnaire *mf* agent, licensee; [*d'automobiles*] dealer; [*de contrat de franchisage*] franchisee

conclure [*accord, contrat*] to enter into

conclure un marché to strike a deal

conclusion d'un contrat *f* signing of a contract

concurrence *f* competition

concurrence acharnée *f* cut-throat competition

concurrence déloyale *f* unfair competition

concurrencer to compete with

concurrent *m* competitor

concurrentiel competitive

conditionnement *m* packaging

conditionner to package

conditions avantageuses *fpl* favourable conditions

conditions générales de vente *fpl* general terms and conditions of sale

conditions d'un contrat *fpl* terms and conditions of a contract

conditions de paiement *fpl* terms of payment

conditions de travail *fpl* working conditions

conditions de vente *fpl* conditions of sale

conférence *f* meeting; [*à grande échelle*] conference

conférence de presse *f* press conference

conférencier *m* speaker

confidentialité *f* confidentiality

confidentiel confidential

confirmation *f* confirmation; *en confirmation de* in confirmation of

confirmation de commande *f* confirmation of an order

confirmer to confirm

conforme à in accordance with

conformément à in accordance with

se **conformer à** to comply with

conformité *f*: **en conformité avec** in accordance with

congé *m* leave; [*vacances*] holiday, vacation *Am*; *être en congé* to be on leave

congé sabbatique *m* sabbatical

congé d'adoption *m* adoption leave

congé de maladie *m* sick leave

congé de maternité *m* maternity leave

congé de naissance *m* maternity leave

congé pour convenance personnelle *m* leave for personal reasons

congédiement m dismissal
congédier to dismiss
congés payés mpl paid leave
congrès m convention
congressiste mf participant at a/the convention
conjoint m spouse
conjointement jointly
conjoncture économique f economic situation
connaissement m bill of lading, waybill
connaissement aérien m air waybill
connaissement maritime m bill of lading
connecteur m plug
conscience professionnelle f professional integrity
consciencieux conscientious
conseil juridique m legal adviser
conseil syndical m trade union council
conseil d'administration m board
conseil d'entreprise m board of directors; [assemblée] board meeting
conseil de prud'hommes m industrial tribunal
conseil de surveillance m supervisory board
conseiller to advise
conseiller m consultant
conseiller juridique m legal adviser
conseiller du travail m personnel consultant
consentement m consent
consentir un prêt to grant a loan
conséquence: agir en conséquence to take appropriate action
consignataire m consignee
consignation f consignment
consigne f [mot d'ordre] instruction
consigner des marchandises to consign goods
consigner une somme to deposit a sum of money
consommateur m consumer
constatation de stock f stock taking
constater to note; [par écrit] to record
constructeur m manufacturer
consultant m consultant
consulter [avocat etc] to consult
contact m contact; **prendre contact avec qn** to contact sb
contacter to contact
container m container
conteneur m container
contenir to contain
contentieux m litigation; [service] legal department
contestation f dispute
contractant m contracting party
contracter [emprunt, assurance, bail] to take out
contracter une assurance to take out insurance
contraire au contrat contrary to the terms of the contract
contrat m contract
contrat collectif m collective agreement
contrat exclusif m sole contract
contrat à durée déterminée m fixed term contract
contrat à durée indéterminée à temps plein m permanent full-time contract
contrat à temps partiel m part-time contract
contrat à temps plein m full-time contract
contrat d'achat m purchase contract, bill of sale
contrat d'agence m agency agreement, agency contract

contrat d'apprentissage *m* training contract

contrat d'assurance *m* insurance contract

contrat de distribution *m* distribution contract

contrat de location *m* rental contract

contrat de mission d'intérim *m* temporary contract

contrat de prêt *m* loan agreement

contrat de représentation exclusive *m* sole agency contract

contrat de service *m* service contract

contrat de travail *m* contract of employment

contrat de travail à durée déterminée *m* fixed term contract

contrat de vente *m* sales contract

contravention *f* [*de loi*] violation

contrefaçon *f* [*d'argent*] forgery

contremaître *m* foreman

contre-offre *f* counter-offer

contresigner to countersign

contribuable *mf* taxpayer

contribuer à to contribute to

contribution *f* contribution

contribution sociale généralisée *f* general social security contributions

contributions directes *fpl* direct taxation

contributions indirectes *fpl* indirect taxation

contrôle *m* [*de document*] check

contrôle de comptes *m* audit

contrôler to check; [*surveiller*] to monitor; [*maîtriser*] to control

contrôleur financier *m* financial controller

contrôleur de gestion *m* controller

contrôleur des contributions *m* inspector of taxes

convenance: à votre convenance at your own convenience

convenir de to agree on

convention *f* agreement

convention collective *f* collective agreement

convention écrite *f* written agreement

convention verbale *f* verbal agreement

convenu: comme convenu as agreed

conversation "mains libres" *f* hands-free conversation

conversion de monnaies *f* currency conversion

convertibilité *f* convertibility

convertible convertible

convertir to convert

convertir des francs en dollars to convert francs into dollars

convivial user-friendly

convocation *f* [*message*] notice of a/ the meeting

convocation à une réunion *f* summons to a meeting

convocation d'une assemblée *f* calling of a meeting

convoquer les actionnaires to call the shareholders to a meeting

convoquer une assemblée générale to call a general meeting

convoyer [*des fonds*] to transport by armed guard

convoyeur de fonds *m* security guard

coopératif co-operative

coopération *f* co-operation

coopérer to co-operate

coordinateur *m* co-ordinator

coordination *f* co-ordination

coordonnées *fpl* [*de personne*] address and phone number; [*ponctuelles*] whereabouts

copie *f* copy

copie authentique *f* certified copy
copie certifiée conforme *f* certified true copy
copie conforme *f* true copy
copie papier *f* paper copy
copie (sur) papier *f* hard copy
copie de lettre *f* duplicate
copie de secours *f* back-up (copy)
copie pour les archives *f* file copy
copieur *m* copier
copieuse *f* copier
coposséder to have joint ownership of, to own jointly
copossession *f* joint ownership, co-ownership
copropriétaire *mf* joint owner, co-owner
copropriété *f* joint ownership, co-ownership
corbeille à papier *f* wastepaper basket
corporatif corporate
corps de métier *m* guild, trade association
correcteur orthographique *m* spell-checker
correction *f* correction
correspondance *f* correspondence
correspondance commerciale *f* business correspondence
correspondant *m* correspondent; [*au téléphone*] caller
correspondre avec to correspond with
corrigé en fonction des variations saisonnières seasonally adjusted
corriger to correct
cosignataire *mf* co-signatory
coter [*prix*] to quote
cotisation *f* contribution
cotisation annuelle *f* annual contribution
cotisation chômage *f* unemployment

contribution
cotisation patronale *f* employer's contribution
cotisation vieillesse *f* pension contribution
cotisation de sécurité sociale *f* social security contribution
cotisations ouvrières *fpl* employee contributions
cotisations salariales *fpl* employee contributions
cotiser to contribute
coupe-papier *m* paper knife, letter opener
couper/coller *m* cut and paste
coupon *m* coupon
coupon-réponse *m* reply coupon
coupure *f*: **en coupures de** in denominations of
coupure de mot *f* word split
coupure de page *f* page break
Cour d'Appel *f* court of Appeal
Cour de Cassation *f* Supreme Court of Appeal
Cour de Justice *f* Court of Justice
courrier *m* mail, post *Br*; [*messager*] courier; *un courrier* a letter
courrier électronique *m* electronic mail, e-mail
courrier interne *m* internal mail
courrier reçu *m* [*bac*] in-tray
courrier à expédier *m* [*bac*] out-tray
cours *m* [*boursier*] price
cours des changes *m* exchange rates
cours du change *m* rate of exchange
coursier *m* courier, biker
court: à court terme short-term
courtage *m* brokerage
courtier *m* broker
courtier d'assurances *m* insurance broker
coût préétabli *m* standard cost
coût standard *m* standard cost

coût d'achat *m* purchase cost; [*comptabilité*] cost of goods purchased

coût de fonctionnement *m* running cost

coût de revient *m* cost price

coût et fret *m* cost and freight

coûter to cost

coûter cher to be expensive

coûteux expensive

coûts administratifs *mpl* administrative costs

couvert covered

couverture *f* cover

couverture suffisante *f* adequate cover

couvrir to cover

cps (=caractères par seconde) cps

crayon *m* pencil

crayon feutre *m* felt tip (pen)

crayon à bille *m* ballpoint (pen)

créance *f* debt

créance douteuse *f* doubtful debt

créance impayée *f* unpaid debt, unrecovered debt

créances *fpl* accounts receivable

créances clients *fpl* accounts receivable

créancier *m* creditor

création d'entreprise *f* setting up of a business

crédit *m* credit; *à crédit* credit; [*acheter*] on credit

crédit-acheteur *m* buyer credit

crédit-bail *m* lease

crédit bancaire *m* bank credit; *un crédit bancaire* a bank loan

crédit documentaire *m* letter of credit

crédit documentaire irrévocable *m* irrevocable letter of credit

crédit (à) long terme *m* long-term credit

crédit (à) moyen terme *m* medium-term credit

crédit personnel *m* personal loan

crédit à la consommation *m* consumer credit

crédit à reporter *m* credit to be carried forward

crédit au consommateur *m* consumer credit

crédit de TVA *m* VAT credit

crédité de credited with

créditer to credit

créditer un compte to credit an account

créditeur [*solde etc*] credit; *être créditeur* to be in credit

créer un chèque to write a cheque

creuser un écart to widen a gap

crise de main d'œuvre *f* manpower crisis

crochet *m* hook

croissant growing, increasing

CSG (=contribution sociale généralisée) *f* general social security contributions

curriculum vitae *m* curriculum vitae, resumé *Am*

curseur *m* cursor

CV *m* CV

D

dactylo *mf* typist
dactylographe *mf* typist
dactylographie *f* typing
dactylographié typed
dactylographier to type
date *f* date; *à date fixe* on a fixed
date; *en date de ce jour* dated this
day; *votre lettre en date du* your
letter of, your letter dated
date limite *f* deadline
date d'achèvement *f* completion
date, date of completion
date d'échéance *f* [*de dû*] maturity
date; [*de terme*] expiry date
date d'envoi *f* date of dispatch
date d'expiration *f* expiry date
date de départ *f* departure date
date de naissance *f* date of birth
date de parution *f* publication date
date de la poste *f* posting date
daté: lettre datée du letter dated
the
dater to date; *à dater de ce jour* from
today
dateur automatique *m* automatic
time and date stamping machine
débarquement *m* [*de marchandises*]
unloading
débarquer des marchandises to
unload goods
débauchage *m* laying off
débaucher to lay off
débit *m* debit; *au débit de* to the
debit of

débit de caisse *m* cash debit
débiter to debit
débiter un compte to debit an
account
débiter un compte d'une somme to
debit a sum to an account
débiteur *m* debtor
débiteur [*solde*] debit
déboursement *m* disbursement
débourser to pay
débrayage *m* stoppage
débrayer to down tools
débuter une réunion to start a
meeting
décacheter une lettre to unseal a
letter
décaissable payable
décaissement *m* cash withdrawal
décaisser to pay
décalage horaire *m* time difference
décalage latéral *m* indent
décentralisation *f* decentralization
décentraliser to decentralize
déchargement *m* unloading
décharger to unload
déchéance *f*: tomber en déchéance
to lapse
décider un programme to decide on
a programme
décimal decimal
décision *f* decision
décision arbitrale *f* arbitration
ruling, decision by arbitration
décision de justice *f* court ruling

déclarant de TVA *m* VAT-registered person
déclaration *f* [*écrite*] return
déclaration fiscale *f* tax return
déclaration de revenus *f* income tax return
déclaration de TVA *f* VAT return
déclaration en douane *f* customs declaration
déclaré declared
décoder to decode
décommander to cancel
décompte *m* count; [*calcul*] calculation
décompte d'une somme *m* deduction of a sum
décompter [*somme*] to deduct
décote de TVA *f* VAT rebate
découvert: à découvert overdrawn
découvert de compte *m* overdraft
décroché off the hook
décrocher to lift the receiver
dédommagement *m* compensation
dédommager [*client*] to compensate; *être dédommagé de* to be compensated for
déductibilité *f* deductibility
déductible deductible
déductible des impôts tax deductible
déduction *f* deduction
déduire to deduct
défaillance *f* fault
défalcation *f* deduction
défalquer une somme to deduct a sum of money
défaut *m* defect; [*ordinateur*] default; *le lecteur par défaut* the default drive
défauts de fabrication *mpl* manufacturing defects
défavorable unfavourable
défectueux defective

déficit *m* deficit
déficitaire [*entreprise*] showing a deficit
défiler [*sur ordinateur*] to scroll
définition de poste *f* job description
déflation *f* deflation
déflationniste deflationary
degré *m* degree
dégrèvement *m* [*d'impôts*] tax relief
dégrèvement fiscal *m* tax relief
déjeuner d'affaires *m* business lunch
déjeuner de travail *m* working lunch
délai *m* period; [*date limite*] deadline; *dans un délai de* within; *dans les plus brefs délais* as soon as possible, asap
délai-congé *m* period of notice
délai d'exécution *m* deadline
délai de crédit *m* credit period
délai de livraison *m* delivery time
délai de paiement *m* credit period
délai de réclamation *m* deadline for submitting claims
délai de rigueur *m* absolute deadline
délais légaux *mpl* legal time limit
délais de paiement *mpl* payment schedule
délégation *f* delegation
délégué *m* delegate
délégué syndical *m* shop steward, union representative
délégué du personnel *m* employee representative, personnel representative
déléguer to delegate
délibération *f* [*d'une assemblée*] vote, resolution
délivrance *f* issue
délivrance d'un certificat *f* issue of a certificate
délivrer [*marchandises*] to deliver
déloyal [*concurrence*] unfair

demande f request; [offre et demande] demand; [d'emploi, de congé] application; **sur demande** on request; **à la demande de** at the request of

demande d'emploi f job wanted advertisement

demande d'ouverture de crédit documentaire f [document] documentary credit application

demande de délai de paiement f request for further time to pay

demande de paiement f request for payment

demande de règlement f request for payment

demande de renseignements f enquiry, request for information

demander to request, to ask for; **on vous demande au téléphone** there is a call for you

demandeur d'emploi m job seeker

démarche de sélection f selection procedure

démarrer un travail to start a job

démettre qn de ses fonctions to remove sb from his/her post

demi-journée f half-day

demi-tarif m half-price

démission f resignation; **donner sa démission** to hand in one's resignation

démissionner to resign

démonstrateur m demonstrator

démonstration f demonstration

deniers mpl money

dénomination f name

dénomination commerciale f [de produit] trade name

dénomination sociale f company name

dénommer: ci-après dénommé hereinafter referred to as

dénoncer un contrat to terminate a contract, to cancel a contract

dépanner [ordinateur etc] to repair

département m department

dépasser [chiffre etc] to exceed

dépenser to spend

dépenses fpl [déboursés] expenditure

dépenses courantes fpl current expenditure(s)

dépenses diverses fpl sundry expenses

dépenses extraordinaires fpl extraordinary expenses

déplacement m moving

déplacer to move

dépliant m folder

déposant m depositor

déposer to deposit

déposer son bilan to file a petition in bankruptcy

déposer une plainte to lodge a complaint

déposer une réclamation to make a claim

dépôt d'espèces m cash deposit

dépôt de bilan m petition in bankruptcy

dépôt de brevet m patent application

dépôt de marque m trade mark registration

dépouillement du courrier m going through the mail, sorting through the mail

dépouiller le courrier to go through the mail, to sort through the mail

se déprécier to depreciate

dépression f depression

dépt (=département) dept

dérangement: en dérangement out of order

dérogation f exception

dérogation à f departure from, exception to

descriptif des travaux *m* specification

description de poste *f* job description

désignation *f* description

désignation du contenu *f* description of contents

désigner qn à la position de to appoint sb to the position of

dessous-de-table *m* backhander

destinataire *mf* [*de document*] addressee; [*sur fiche téléphonique etc*] to

destination *f* destination

destiné à [*lettre*] addressed to; [*marchandises*] being sent to

détail *m* [*vente*] retail

détaillant *m* retailer

détaillé [*facture*] itemized

détailler to itemize

détaxe *f* tax refund

détenteur *m* holder

détention *f* holding

dette *f* debt

deux-points *m* colon

développement *m* development

développer to develop

devis *m* estimate

devis estimatif *m* estimate

devise *f* currency

devises étrangères *fpl* foreign currency

devoir to owe

devoir de l'argent to owe money

diagramme *m* diagram

diagramme circulaire *m* pie chart

diagramme à barres *m* bar chart

dictaphone *m* dictaphone®

dictée *f* dictation

dicter to dictate

dictionnaire *m* dictionary

différer le paiement to defer payment

diffuser [*brochures*] to distribute

diffusion *f* distribution

dimension *f* size

dimensions *fpl* [*de machine etc*] dimensions

diminution *f* decrease

diplôme *m* degree, diploma

diplômé qualified

directeur *m* manager; [*plus haut dans hiérarchie*] director

directeur adjoint *m* deputy manager; [*plus haut dans hiérarchie*] deputy director

directeur administratif *m* executive director

directeur commercial *m* commercial manager; [*en chef*] commercial director

directeur export *m* export manager; [*en chef*] export director

directeur financier *m* financial manager; [*en chef*] financial director

directeur général *m* [*d'entreprise*] managing director, chief executive officer

directeur général adjoint *m* deputy managing director

directeur gérant *m* executive director

directeur intérimaire *m* temporary manager, acting manager; [*en chef*] temporary director

directeur régional *m* regional manager, area manager; [*en chef*] regional director, area director

directeur technique *m* technical manager; [*en chef*] technical director

directeur d'agence *m* branch manager

directeur de banque *m* bank manager

directeur de marketing *m* marketing manager; [*en chef*] marketing director

directeur de production *m* production manager; [*en chef*] production director

directeur de produit *m* brand manager, product manager

directeur de succursale *m* branch manager

directeur de l'exploitation *m* operations manager

directeur de la clientèle *m* customer relations manager

directeur de la communication *m* communications manager; [*en chef*] communications director

directeur de la publicité *m* publicity manager; [*en chef*] publicity director

directeur des ventes *m* sales manager; [*en chef*] sales director

directeur du personnel *m* personnel manager; [*en chef*] personnel director

direction *f* management; [*service*] department

direction financière *f* [*service*] financial department

direction générale *f* general management, senior management

direction mercatique *f* marketing department

direction de la production *f* production control, production management

direction du personnel *f* personnel management

directive *f* instruction; [*de gouvernement, CEE*] directive

directive européenne *f* EC directive

directoire *m* executive board

dirigeant *m* manager

diriger [*entreprise*] to run, to manage

discours *m* speech

discours d'ouverture *m* opening speech

discret discreet

disponibilité *f* availability

disponible available

disposer d'une somme to have a sum of money at one's disposal

disposer un chèque sur to draw a cheque on

disposition *f* [*de lettre, clavier*] layout; [*légal*] provision

disposition fiscale *f* tax provision

disque *m* disk

disque dur *m* hard disk

disquette *f* disk, diskette, floppy (disk)

disquette système *f* system disk

disquette de copie *f* copy disk

distance tarifaire *f* chargeable distance

distribuer to distribute

distributeur *m* distributor

distributeur agréé *m* authorized distributor

distributeur automatique *m* cash dispenser

distribution *f* distribution

distribution de courrier *f* [*par facteur*] mail delivery

diviser to divide

division *f* division

document *m* document

document canevas *m* form document

document commercial *m* commercial document

document interne à l'entreprise *m* internal company document

document légal *m* legal document

document maître *m* master document

document source *m* source
document

document type *m* standard
document

document d'assurance *m* insurance
document

document d'expédition *m* shipping
document

document de synthèse *m* summary

document de transport *m* transport
document

document de travail *m* working
document

documentaliste *mf* archivist

documentation *f* documentation

documents *mpl* documents

documents commerciaux *mpl*
commercial documents, business
documents

documents d'expédition *mpl*
shipping documents

doit et avoir *m* debits and credits

donner son congé to give notice

donneur d'ordre *m* principal

dossier *m* file; [*ordinateur*] folder

dossier "divers" *m* miscellaneous
file

dossier suspendu *m* suspension file

dossier de lancement *m* product
launch file

douane *f* customs

douanier *m* customs officer

douanier *adj* customs

double *m* duplicate

double interligne *m* double spacing

doubler to double

dresser [*la balance, le compte*] to
draw up

droit *m* law; [*imposition*] duty;
[*prérogative*] right; [*taxe*] tax

droit bancaire *m* banking law

droit commercial *m* commercial law

droit communautaire *m*
Community law

droit coutumier *m* common law

droit fiscal *m* tax law

droit de souscription *m* subscription
fee

droit de timbre *m* stamp duty

droit des sociétés *m* company law

droit du travail *m* labour laws

droits de douane *mpl* customs
duties, duty

dû due, owing; *en due forme* in due
form

dûment duly

dûment signé duly signed

duplicata *m* duplicate

duplicateur *m* duplicator,
duplicating machine

duplicatum *m* duplicate

dupliquer [*document*] to copy

durée *f* duration; [*de contrat*] term

durée du travail *f* working hours

E

ébauche *f* draft
échange *m* exchange
échange d'informations *m* exchange of information
échange de lettres *m* exchange of letters
échange de marchandises *m* exchange of goods
échange intra-communautaire *m* intra-Community trade
échangeable exchangeable
échanger des lettres to exchange letters
échanges commerciaux *mpl* trade
échanges internationaux *mpl* international trade
échantillon *m* sample
échantillon gratuit *m* free sample
échantillonner to sample
échapper à l'impôt to avoid tax
échéance *f* [*de lettre de change*] maturity
échéance de contrat *f* expiry date of a contract
échéance de police *f* maturity of a policy
échéancier *m* planner, flow chart
échéancier de paiement *m* payment schedule
échelle des salaires *f* salary scale
échelonner des livraisons to spread out deliveries
échelonner des paiements to stagger payments, to spread out payments

échu [*abonnement*] expired
économie *f* economy
économie d'entreprise *f* business management, business studies
économies *fpl* savings
économique economic
économiser to save
économiser son temps to save time
économiste *mf* economist
écouler [*marchandise*] to sell
écouler à perte to sell at a loss
écouler des marchandises to sell off goods
écouteur du téléphone *m* receiver
écouteurs *mpl* headphones
écran *m* screen
écran d'aide *m* help screen
écrire to write
écrire à la machine to type
écrit *m* written document; *par écrit* in writing
écrit à la machine typed
écrit à la main longhand, handwritten
écriture *f* writing; [*comptabilité*] entry, item
écriture abrégée *f* speedwriting
écriture grasse *f* bold typeface, boldface
écu *m* ecu
éditer to edit
effacement *m* deletion
effacement *m* [*de message*] erasing
effacer [*texte*] to erase, to delete

effectif *m* number of employees, employees, staff

effectuer des démarches to take steps

effet *m* bill of exchange

effet de commerce *m* commercial bill, bill

effondrement *m* [*de cours, marché*] collapse

*s'***effondrer** [*cours, marché*] to collapse

élaborer [*projet*] to draw up

élection des délégués du personnel *f* election of employee representatives

élection du bureau *f* election of officers

électronique electronic

élever to raise

émargement du courrier *m* signing for the post

émarger to sign for; [*parapher*] to initial

emballage *m* [*de marchandise*] packing

emballage consigné *m* returnable packaging

emballage perdu *m* non-refundable packaging

emballage perdu *m* throwaway packaging, disposable packaging

emballage récupérable *m* recoverable packaging

emballages consignés *mpl* refundable packaging

emballer to pack, to package

embarquement *m* loading

embarquer to load

embauche *f* recruitment, hiring

embaucher to recruit, to hire

émettre [*actions, chèque etc*] to issue

émettre des avis to express opinions

émission *f* [*de chèque, billets de banque*] issue

émission d'actions *f* share issue

emmagasinage *m* storage, warehousing

emmagasiner to store, to warehouse

émoluments *mpl* emoluments

empaquetage *m* packing

empaqueter to package

emplacement *m* location, site; [*d'ordinateur*] slot

emploi *m* employment; [*poste*] job

emploi vacant *m* vacancy

employé *m* employee

employé aux écritures *m* book-keeper

employé de banque *m* bank clerk, bank employee

employé de bureau *m* office worker

employer to use

employer des ouvriers to employ workers

employeur *m* employer

emprunt *m* loan

emprunt à court terme *m* short-term loan

emprunt à long terme *m* long-term loan

emprunter to borrow

emprunter qch à qn to borrow sth from sb

emprunteur *m* borrower

emprunts à court terme *mpl* short-term borrowings

emprunts à long terme *mpl* long-term borrowings

encadré *m* [*dans un texte*] box

encadrement *m* [*cadres*] executives

encadrement du crédit *m* credit restriction, credit squeeze

encaisse *f* cash in till

encaissement *m* [*de chèque*] paying in, encashment *Br*; *présenter un chèque à l'encaissement* to present a cheque for payment

encaisser [*chèque*] to cash, to encash *Br*

encaisser de l'argent to pay in cash

encart *m* insert

encoder to encode

encre *f* ink

encre en poudre *f* toner

endetté in debt

endettement *m* indebtedness

*s'***endetter** to get into debt

endommagé damaged

endommagement *m* damage

endommager to damage

endos *m* [*endossement*] endorsement

endossable [*chèque*] endorsable

endossataire *mf* endorsee

endossement *m* endorsement

endosser [*chèque*] to endorse

endosseur *m* endorser

engagement *m* commitment; [*de personnel*] hiring; *sans engagement de notre part* without commitment on our part; *sans aucun engagement de votre part* without any commitment on your part

engagement antérieur *m* prior engagement

engagement écrit *m* written undertaking

enlèvement et livraison *m* collection and delivery

énoncé d'une clause *m* wording of a clause

enquête *f* [*pour déterminer les faits*] investigation; [*pour recueillir les avis*] survey

enquête de prix *f* price survey

enregistrement *m* recording; [*de données*] logging; [*de base de données*] record

enregistrement d'une commande *m* logging of an order, recording of an order

enregistrer to record, to log

enregistrer le courrier to log the mail

ensemble de données *m* set of data

entamer un travail to begin a piece of work

entente *f* agreement

entériner [*accord*] to ratify

en-tête *m* header; [*de lettre*] letterhead; *à en-tête* headed

en-tête d'entreprise *m* company letterhead

en-tête de lettre *m* letterhead

entier: en entier in full

entorse au règlement *f* stretching of the rules

entrée: l'entrée en fonction du nouveau directeur est prévue pour ... the new director is scheduled to take up his post on ...

entrée d'argent *f* cash received

entreposage *m* storage, warehousing

entreposer des marchandises to warehouse goods, to put goods in a warehouse

entrepositaire *m* warehouseman

entrepôt *m* warehouse

entreprise *f* business

entreprise commerciale *f* business enterprise

entreprise commune *f* joint venture

entreprise exportatrice *f* export company

entreprise familiale *f* family business

entreprise en participation *f* joint venture

entrer [*caractère, commande etc*] to enter; [*texte, données*] to input

entrer en fonction to take up one's duties

entretenir [*comptes*] to keep in order; [*machine*] to service

entretenir une correspondance to keep up a correspondence

entretien m [*entrevue*] interview; [*de machine*] maintenance

entretien téléphonique m telephone conversation

entrevue f interview

enveloppe f envelope

enveloppe autocollante f self-sealing envelope

enveloppe budgétaire f budget, allotted budget, budget allocation

enveloppe timbrée f stamped envelope

enveloppe à fenêtre f window envelope

envelopper to wrap up

envoi m dispatch; [*action*] sending

envoi exprès m express delivery

envoi postal m postal delivery

envoi recommandé m recorded delivery

envoi contre paiement m cash with order

envoyer to send

envoyer par fax to fax

envoyer sa démission to hand in one's resignation

envoyer un télex à qn to telex sb

envoyeur m sender

épargne f saving

épargner to save

épeler [*mot*] to spell

épingle de signalisation f marker tag

épreuves d'imprimerie fpl printer's proofs

épuisé [*article*] out of stock

épuisement des réserves m depletion of reserves

équilibrer to balance

équipe f team

équipe commerciale f marketing team

équipe de dactylos f typing pool

équipe de vente f sales team, sales force

équipement m equipment

équipements mpl equipment

équiper un bureau to fit out an office

erreur typographique f printing error

erreur de calcul f miscalculation

escompte m discount

escompter to discount

espace m space

espace disque m disk space

espace publicitaire m advertising space

espacement m spacing

espacement des caractères m character spacing

espacement des lignes m line spacing

espacer des lignes to space out lines

espèces fpl cash

esperluette f ampersand

essai m test, trial; *à l'essai* on approval

essayer un nouveau produit to test a new product

estimation approximative f rough estimate

estimation des frais f estimation of costs

"et" commercial (&) m ampersand

établir un chèque to make out a cheque, to write a cheque

établir un chèque à l'ordre de to make a cheque payable to

établir un prix to set a price

établir une facture to draw up an

invoice
établissement *m* institution
établissement bancaire *m* bank
établissement financier *m* financial
  institution
établissement payeur *m* paying bank
établissement d'un compte *m*
  opening an account
état *m* [*statistique etc*] report
état de compte *m* statement of
  account
état de situation *m* status report,
  state-of-play report
étiquetage *m* labelling
étiqueter [*colis*] to label
étiquette *f* label
étiquette autocollante *f* sticky label
étiquette gommée *f* sticky label
étiquette d'adresse *f* address label
étoile *f* star, asterisk
étranger foreign; *à l'étranger* abroad
Ets (=établissements) *mpl*
  establishment
étude *f* study
étude comparative *f* comparative
  study
étude de communication *f*
  communications study
étude de faisabilité *f* feasibility study
étude de marché *f* market research;
  une étude de marché a market
  study
étude des besoins *f* needs study
études de marché *f* market research
  studies
évaluation *f* valuation
évasion fiscale *f* tax evasion
éventail de produits *m* range of
  products
examiner to examine
excédent *m* surplus
excéder to exceed
exclusion *f* exclusion

excuse *f* apology
*s'***excuser** to apologize
exécuter to carry out
exécuter un contrat to execute a
  contract, to perform a contract
exécuter une commande to fulfil an
  order
exécution d'ordre *f* carrying out an
  order
exécution de contrat *f* performance
  of a contract
exemplaire *m* copy; *en deux*
  exemplaires in duplicate
exempt d'impôts tax exempt
exempter d'impôts to exempt from
  tax
exemption d'impôts *f* tax exemption
exercer des fonctions to carry out
  duties
exercice *m* financial year, fiscal year
  Am
exercice *m* [*d'un droit*] exercise
exercice comptable *m* financial year,
  fiscal year *Am*
exercice écoulé *m* last financial year
exercice fiscal *m* tax year
exiger to demand
exonération de TVA *f* exemption
  from VAT, VAT exemption
exonéré de exempt from
exonérer to exempt
exonérer d'impôt to exempt from
  tax
expansion *f* expansion
expédier to dispatch, to send; [*gros*
  colis] to ship
expédier le courrier to send off the
  mail
expédier un télégramme to send a
  telegram
expéditeur *m* sender; [*de gros colis*
  etc] sender, shipper; *expéditeur*
  [*sur formulaire*] from:

expédition f shipment
expédition par bateau f shipping
expédition par chemin de fer f sending by rail
expédition par la poste f mailing
expéditions fpl [service] dispatch (department)
expérimenté [collaborateur] experienced
expert m expert
expert-comptable m chartered accountant, certified public accountant Am
expertise f valuation
expiration f expiry
expirer [délai] to expire
exportateur m exporter

exportation f export
exporter to export
exposant m [dans une foire commerciale] exhibitor; **3 en exposant** superscript 3
exposition f exhibition
exposition commerciale f trade fair
exprès [lettre] express
extension f [d'un contrat] extension
externe [ressource] outside
extincteur d'incendie m fire extinguisher
extrait de compte m statement of account
extrait de naissance m birth certificate

F

FAB (=franco à bord) FOB
fabricant m manufacturer
fabrication f manufacture
fabrication en série f mass production
fabriquer [produit] to manufacture
face: faire face à la demande to meet demand
facilités de paiement fpl payment facilities
fac-similé m facsimile
facturation f invoicing, billing

facture f invoice, bill
facture commerciale f commercial invoice
facture pro-forma f pro forma invoice
facture rectificative f amended invoice
facture d'avoir f credit note
facture de vente f sales invoice
facturer to invoice for
facturer qch à qn to invoice sb for sth

faillite *f* bankruptcy; *être en faillite* to be bankrupt; *faire faillite* to go bankrupt
faire attendre qn to keep sb waiting
faire crédit to give credit
faire glisser [*avec souris*] to drag
faire des affaires to do business
faire des frais to run up expenses
faire du commerce to trade
faire un prix to quote a price
fait en double exemplaire duplicate
fascicule *m* brochure, leaflet
fatigue oculaire *f* eye strain
fausse facture *f* false invoice
faute lourde *f* grave error
faute professionnelle *f* professional misconduct
faute d'impression *f* misprint
faute d'orthographe *f* spelling mistake
faute de frappe *f* typing error, typo, keying error
faute de paiement because of non-payment
faute de provision for lack of funds
faux chèque *m* forged cheque
faux frais *mpl* incidental expenses
faveur *f:* **en faveur de** in favour of
favorable [*cours*] favourable
fax *m* fax (machine); *envoyer par fax* to fax, to send by fax; *envoyer un fax à* to fax, to send a fax to
faxer to fax
femme cadre *f* female executive
femme d'affaires *f* businesswoman
ferme firm
fermer [*lettre, compte*] to close
fermeture d'un compte *f* closing of an account
ferroviaire [*transport*] railway
feuille *f* sheet (of paper)
feuille d'accompagnement *f* covering document

feuille d'impôts *f* tax return
feuille de calcul *f* spreadsheet
feuille de maladie *f* sick note
feuille de paie *f* payroll; [*de l'employé*] pay slip
feuille de présence *f* [*à signer lors d'une réunion*] attendance sheet
feuille de style *f* style sheet
feuille de versement *f* paying-in slip
feuillet *m* [*de relevé, facture*] sheet; *à feuillets rechargeables* loose-leaf
ficeler [*paquet*] to tie up
ficelle *f* string
fiche *f* form; [*avec informations*] record, file; [*cartonnée*] card
fiche cartonnée *f* index card
fiche client *f* customer record
fiche courrier *f* mail checklist
fiche fournisseur *f* supplier file
fiche signalétique *f* personnel file card
fiche signalétique *f* descriptive report
fiche téléphonique *f* [*pour message*] telephone memo; [*broche*] telephone jack
fiche verticale suspendue *f* vertical suspension file
fiche à perforations marginales *f* edge punched card
fiche à visibilité *f* visible card record
fiche d'état *f* report form
fiche de courrier *f* mail file
fiche de paie *f* pay slip
fiche de présence *f* [*de salarié*] attendance sheet
fiche de stock *f* stock sheet
fiche en T *f* T-card
fichier *m* [*fiches*] card-index system; [*boîte*] card-index box; [*à tiroirs*] card-index filing cabinet; [*sur disquette*] file
fichier ASCII *m* ASCII file

fichier rotatif *m* rotating card index

fichier des salariés *m* personnel files

figurer [*sur une liste*] to appear

filiale *f* subsidiary

filiale de vente *f* sales subsidiary

filière *f* transfer form

filière électronique *f* electronic transfer

fin: de fin d'exercice year-end; *de fin de mois* end-of-month

finance *f* finance

financement *m* financing, funding

financer to finance, to fund

financier *m* financier

financier financial

financièrement financially

firme *f* firm, business

fisc *m* tax man, Inland Revenue, Internal Revenue *Am*

fiscal tax

fiscaliste *mf* tax consultant

fiscalité *f* tax system

fixation de l'impôt *f* tax assessment

fixation des prix *f* price setting

fixe [*prix, salaire*] fixed

fixer les conditions d'un contrat to stipulate the terms of a contract

fixer un prix to set a price

fixer une date de réunion to fix a date for a meeting

flèche *f* [*sur clavier*] arrow

flexibilité *f* flexibility

flexible flexible

FMI (=Fonds monétaire international) *m* IMF

FNGS (=Fonds de garantie des salaires) *m* national guarantee fund for the payment of salaries

foire commerciale *f* trade fair

foire-exposition *f* trade exhibition

foire internationale *f* international (trade) fair

foire professionnelle *f* trade fair

fonctionnaire *mf* official, civil servant

fonctions *fpl* [*d'employé*] duties, responsibilities

fonds commercial *m* goodwill

Fonds monétaire international *m* International Monetary Fund

fonds publics *mpl* government funds

fonds de commerce *m* good will; [*magasin etc*] business

Fonds de garantie des salaires *m* national guarantee fund for the payment of salaries

fonte *f* font

forfait *m* lump sum

forfaitaire lump sum, in one amount

forfaitairement in a lump sum, in one amount

formalité *f* formality

format *m* format

format paysage *m* landscape format

format portrait *m* portrait format

formater to format

formateur *m* trainer

formation *f* [*d'employé*] training

formation continue *f* continuous training

formation permanente *f* continuous training

formation professionnelle *f* vocational training

former to train

formulaire *m* form

formule finale *f* closure

formule de calcul *f* mathematical formula

formule de début *f* opening

formule de politesse *f* [*au début*] standard opening; [*à la fin*] standard closure

formule de réponse *f* reply form

formule de télégramme *f* telegram form

fourchette de prix *f* price range
fournir des fonds to provide funds
fournir des renseignements to supply information
fournisseur *m* supplier
fournisseur attitré *m* regular supplier
fourniture *f* supply(ing)
fournitures *fpl* supplies
fournitures de bureau *fpl* office supplies
fraction *f* fraction
frais *mpl* expenses, costs
frais accessoires *mpl* incidental expenses
frais généraux *mpl* overheads, overhead *Am*
frais inclus inclusive of costs
frais postaux *mpl* postage costs
frais d'accès *mpl* [*au réseau*] connection charge
frais d'administration générale *mpl* general overheads, general overhead *Am*, general administration costs
frais d'emballage *mpl* packing costs
frais d'entreposage *mpl* storage costs
frais d'expédition *mpl* delivery charges
frais de banque *mpl* bank charges
frais de communication *mpl* call charges
frais de déplacement *mpl* travel expenses
frais de douane *mpl* customs duties
frais de gestion *mpl* administration costs
frais de port *mpl* carriage
frais de tenue de compte *mpl* account charges, bank charges

frais de transport *mpl* transport charges
frais de voyage *mpl* travel expenses
franc d'impôts tax free, free of tax
franc de port carriage free
française: à la française [*imprimer*] portrait
franchisage *m* [*contrat*] franchising
franchise *f* franchise
franchise douanière *f* exemption from customs duty
franchise postale: en franchise postale postage paid
franchise de TVA *f* VAT exemption; *en franchise de TVA* free of VAT
franchisé *m* franchisee, franchise holder
franchisé franchised
franchiseur *m* franchisor
franco à bord free on board
franco d'emballage free of packing charges
franco de douane free of customs duty
franco de port carriage free, carriage paid
frappe *f* typing; [*ordinateur*] keying; *vitesse de frappe à la minute* keystrokes per minute
frappe d'une lettre *f* typing of a letter; [*ordinateur*] keying of a letter
frapper to type; [*ordinateur*] to key
freiner [*l'économie, la production*] to slow down
fréter [*navire, avion*] to charter
frontière *f* border
fusion *f* [*d'entreprises*] merger
fusionner to merge

G

gagner de l'argent to earn money
gamme de prix f price range
gamme de produits f product range
garant m guarantor
garantie f guarantee, warranty; *sous garantie* under guarantee, under warranty
garantie bancaire f bank guarantee
garantie pièces et main d'œuvre f parts and labour warranty
garantie d'origine f original guarantee
garantir to guarantee
garçon de bureau m office boy
garçon de courses m message boy
gaspillage d'argent m waste of money
gaspiller son argent to waste one's money
geler les prix to freeze prices
gens d'affaires mpl business people
gérant m manager
gérant d'affaires m business manager
gérer to manage
gérer un compte to manage an account
gérer une affaire to handle a matter
gestion f management
gestion administrative f administration, admin
gestion financière f financial management
gestion d'entreprise f business management
gestion de portefeuille f portfolio management
gestion de stocks f stock control, inventory management
gestionnaire mf manager
gomme à crayon f eraser, rubber *Br*
gomme pour machine à écrire f typewriter rubber *Br*
gommer to rub out, to erase
gommette f sticker
gonflement m increase
grand livre m ledger
grand livre général m nominal ledger
graphe m graph
graphique m chart; [*mathématique*] graph
graphique à secteurs m pie chart
graphique à tuyaux d'orgue m bar chart
graphiques mpl graphics
gras m bold
gratification de fin d'année f end of year bonus
gratter un mot to scribble a note
gratuit free (of charge)
gré: nous vous saurions gré de bien vouloir ... we would be grateful if you would ...
grébiche f loose-leaf binder
grève f strike; *faire (la) grève* to go on strike
grève générale f general strike

grève sauvage *f* wildcat strike
grève surprise *f* lightning strike
grève tournante *f* staggered strike
grève de solidarité *f* sympathy strike
grève des cheminots *f* rail workers' strike
grève des dockers *f* dockers' strike
grève des transports *f* transport (workers') strike
grève du zèle *f* work to rule
grevé de dettes saddled with debts
grever un budget to put a strain on a budget
gréviste *mf* striker
gribiche *f* loose-leaf binder
griffe *f* signature stamp
griffe de réception *f* received stamp
grille des salaires *f* salary scale
gros: acheter en gros to buy wholesale

gros caractères *mpl* large print
grosse somme *f* large sum
grosses coupures *fpl* [*billets*] large denominations
grossiste *mf* wholesaler
groupe de pression *m* pressure group
groupement *m* group
groupement d'achat *m* purchasing co-operative, purchasing group
guichet *m* [*de banque*] counter
guichet automatique *m* cash dispenser
guichetier *m* [*de banque*] counter clerk, teller
guide-classement *m* file divider
guide-papier *m* paper feed
guide-sortie *m* file extraction marker
guillemets *mpl* inverted commas, quotation marks, quotes; *entre guillemets* in quotation marks

H

H. TVA net of VAT
habilité à signer [*employé de banque*] authorized to sign
habituel usual
hall d'exposition *m* exhibition hall
hamac *m* suspension file
haut de gamme up-market; [*d'une série*] top of the range
haute direction *f* senior management

haute finance *f* high finance
hauteur: à hauteur de [*s'engager*] up to
hebdomadaire weekly
heure d'ouverture *f* opening time
heure de fermeture *f* closing time
heures creuses *fpl* offpeak time
heures supplémentaires *fpl* overtime

heures d'ouverture *fpl* opening
  hours
heures de bureau *fpl* office hours
heures de pointe *fpl* peak time
hiérarchie *f* hierarchy
hiérarchie administrative *f*
  administrative hierarchy
**hiérarchique: par la voie
  hiérarchique** through official
  channels
homme d'affaires *m* businessman
homologation d'un brevet *f* grant of
  a patent
homologue *mf* counterpart
**honneur: j'ai l'honneur d'accuser
  réception de votre lettre** I
  acknowledge receipt of your letter
honoraire [*membre de société*]
  honorary
honoraires *mpl* fees
honorer to honour
honorifique [*titre*] honorary
horaire *m* [*de train, d'avion*]
  timetable

horaire flexible *m* flexible hours,
  flexitime
horaire variable *m* flexible hours,
  flexitime
horloge contrôleuse *f* time clock
horloge pointeuse *f* time clock
horodatage *m* time and date
  stamping
horodateur *m* time and date stamp
hors service out of order
hors taxe [*exempt de taxe*] tax free;
  [*avant d'ajouter une taxe*] net of
  tax
hors TVA net of VAT
hors d'état out of order
hors d'usage out of use
hôtesse d'accueil *f* receptionist
hôtesse d'accueil téléphonique *f*
  switchboard operator
HT (=hors taxe) before tax,
  exclusive of tax; *le montant HT de
  la facture* the invoice value net of
  tax
huissier *m* bailiff

I

icône *f* icon
illégal illegal
illégalité *f* illegality
illicite [*gain*] illicit
illustré illustrated

illustrer to illustrate
image de marque *f* brand image
immatriculation *f* registration
immatriculer des marchandises to
  register goods

immeuble de bureaux *m* office block
immobilier *m* property
immobilisation de capitaux *f* freezing of capital
immobilisations *fpl* fixed assets
immobiliser des actifs to freeze assets
impayé *m* unpaid bill
impayé unpaid
implicite implicit, implied
importateur *m* importer
importateur [*pays*] importing
importations *fpl* imports
importer to import
importer des marchandises to import goods
import-export *m* import-export
imposable taxable
imposé [*prix*] fixed
imposition *f* taxation
impôt *m* tax
impôt direct *m* direct tax
impôt foncier *m* property tax
impôt indirect *m* indirect tax
impôt progressif *m* graduated income tax
impôt sur le revenu *m* income tax
impôt sur les sociétés *m* corporation tax
impression *f* printing; [*copie*] printout
imprimante *f* printer
imprimante matricielle *f* dot matrix (printer)
imprimante (à) jet d'encre *f* ink-jet (printer)
imprimante (à) laser *f* laser (printer)
imprimante à marguerite *f* daisywheel (printer)
imprimé *m* [*formulaire*] form
imprimé fiscal *m* tax return
imprimer to print (out)

imprimés *mpl* [*de la poste*] printed matter
imprimeur *m* printer
inacquitté [*dette*] unpaid
incapacité de travail *f* disability
inchangé unchanged
incitation fiscale *f* tax incentive
inclusivement inclusive
inconnu à l'adresse indiquée not known at this address
indemnisable [*dommage*] compensable
indemnisation *f* compensation
indemniser to compensate
indemniser qn de qch to compensate sb for sth
indemnité *f* compensation
indemnité journalière *f* daily allowance
indemnité de chômage *f* unemployment benefit
indemnité de déplacement *f* travel allowance
indemnité de licenciement *f* severance pay
indemnité de logement *f* accommodation allowance
indemnité de maladie *f* sickness benefit
indemnité de transport *f* travel allowance
indemnité de vie chère *f* cost-of-living allowance
indexage *m* indexing
indexation *f* [*de prix, salaires*] index-linking
indexé index-linked
indexer to index
indicatif *m* [*ordinateur*] prompt
indicatif d'appel *m* [*téléphonique*] dialling code
indicatif (du) DOS *m* DOS prompt
indice: 3 en indice subscript 3

indice hiérarchique *m* salary scale code

indisponible unavailable

indûment [*payé*] incorrectly

industrie *f* industry

industriel *m* industrialist

industriel [*produit*] industrial

inescomptable undiscountable

inflation *f* inflation

inflation des prix *f* price inflation

inflation rampante *f* rampant inflation

inflation des salaires *f* wage inflation

inflationniste inflationary

information *f* information; *pour votre information* for your information; *une information* a piece of information; *à titre d'information* for (your) information

informations *fpl* information

informatique *f* information technology

informatiser to computerize

informer qn de qch to inform sb of sth

ingénieur technico-commercial *m* sales technician

ingénieur des ventes *m* sales engineer

initial initial

initialiser to initialize

innovation *f* innovation

INPI (=Institut national de la propriété industrielle) *m* *equivalent to* Patent Office

inscription *f* registration

s'inscrire à [*cours, conférence*] to register for

inscrire une adresse sur to address

insérer to insert

insertion *f* insertion

insertion publicitaire *f* advertisement

insertion de caractère *f* character insert

insertion de ligne *f* line insert

insolvabilité *f* insolvency

insolvable insolvent

inspecteur des contributions *m* tax inspector

inspecteur du travail *m* factory inspector

Inspection du Travail *f* factory inspectorate

installer to install

Institut national de la propriété industrielle *m* *equivalent to* Patent Office

institut de crédit *m* credit institution

institution de crédit *f* credit institution

instruction *f* instruction; *conformément à vos instructions* in accordance with your instructions

insuffisamment: être insuffisamment affranchi to have insufficient postage

insuffisance de provision *f* insufficient funds

intégrer une somme dans une facture to include a sum in an invoice

intention *f* intention; *à l'intention de* for the attention of

intercalaire *m* [*dans classeur*] divider

intercaler un mot dans un texte to insert a word in a text

interdit: frapper d'interdit to impose a ban on

intéressement aux résultats *m* employee profit-sharing scheme

intéresser les employés aux bénéfices to provide an employee profit-sharing scheme

intérêt *m* interest

intérêt bancaire *m* bank interest

intérêt composé *m* compound interest

intérêt couru *m* accrued interest

intérêt fixe *m* fixed interest

intérêt simple *m* simple interest

intérêt variable *m* variable-rate interest

intérêt de retard *m* interest on arrears

intérêts dus *mpl* interest due

intérêts échus *mpl* interest due

intérêts moratoires *mpl* penalty interest

intérêts à échoir *mpl* accruing interest

interface *f* interface

interface parallèle *f* parallel interface

interface série *f* serial interface

intérim *m* temping, temporary work; *par intérim* [*président*] acting

intérimaire *mf* temp; *travailler comme intérimaire* to temp

intérimaire temporary, acting

interligne *m* line spacing

interligne double *m* double spacing; *à interligne double* double-spaced

interligne simple *m* single spacing; *à interligne simple* single-spaced

international international

interne internal; [*de la société*] in-house

interphone *m* intercom

interprétation d'un contrat *f* interpretation of a contract

interprète *mf* interpreter

introduire sur le marché to launch, to bring onto the market

invendable [*produit*] unsaleable

invendus *mpl* unsold goods

inventaire *m* inventory

inventaire de stock *m* physical inventory

inventorier to list

inversion de chiffres *f* inversion of figures

invertir [*chifffres*] to invert

investir to invest

investissement *m* investment

investissement à l'étranger *m* foreign investment

investisseur *m* investor

invite *f* [*ordinateur*] prompt

irrécouvrable [*créance*] unrecoverable

italienne: à l'italienne landscape

italique *m* italics; *en italique* in italics

italique italic

J

jaquette *f* jacket
jetons de présence *mpl* director's fees
jeu complet de connaissements *m* full set of bills of lading
jeu de lettres de change *m* set of bills of exchange
joindre [*à lettre*] to enclose; [*qn*] to contact
jour: à jour up to date; *mettre à jour* to update; *à 30 jours fin de mois* 30 days from the end of the month
jour chômé *m* bank holiday *Br*, public holiday
jour férié *m* bank holiday *Br*, public holiday
jour ouvrable *m* working day
jour ouvré *m* working day
journal *m* ledger
journal factures-clients *m* sales invoice ledger

journal factures-fournisseurs *m* purchase invoice ledger
journal d'entreprise *m* company magazine
journal des achats *m* purchase ledger
journal des ventes *m* sales ledger
journée de huit heures *f* eight-hour day
journée de travail *f* working day
jugement *m* judgement
jumelage d'entreprises *m* twinning of companies
juridique legal
juriste *mf* lawyer
justificatif de paiement *m* proof of payment
justification *f* [*de texte*] justification
justifié à droite right justified
justifié à gauche left justified
justifier [*texte*] to justify

K

kilo-octet *m* kilobyte
Ko (=kilo-octet) K

kraft *m* brown wrapping paper

L

label *m* label; [*marque*] trademark
laissé-pour-compte *m* reject
laisser des arrhes to make a deposit
lampe de bureau *f* desk lamp
lancement *m* launch
lancer une nouvelle entreprise to launch a new company
l/c (=lettre de crédit) L/C
LCR (=lettre de change relevé) *f* bills of exchange statement
lecteur *m* drive
lecteur de disquettes *m* disk drive
légal legal
légalisation *f* legalization; [*de documents d'importation*] authentication
légaliser des documents to certify documents
légaliser une signature to authenticate a signature
législation *f* legislation
législation commerciale *f* commercial law
législation fiscale *f* tax law
législation du travail *f* employment law
lettrage *m* lettering
lettre *f* letter; *en lettres* in words
lettre circulaire *f* circular
lettre commerciale *f* business letter
lettre recommandée *f* registered letter
lettre recommandée avec accusé de réception *f* registered letter with confirmation of receipt
lettre type *f* form letter
lettre d'accompagnement *f* covering letter
lettre d'avis *f* advice note
lettre d'excuse *f* letter of apology
lettre de change *f* bill of exchange
lettre de change relevé *f* bills of exchange statement
lettre de confirmation *f* letter of confirmation
lettre de convocation *f* notice of meeting
lettre de crédit *f* letter of credit
lettre de crédit irrévocable *f* irrevocable letter of credit
lettre de garantie *f* letter of guarantee
lettre de garantie bancaire *f* bank guarantee
lettre de licenciement *f* letter of dismissal
lettre de poursuite *f* letter threatening legal action, chasing letter
lettre de rappel *f* reminder
lettre de réclamation *f* letter of complaint
lettre de recommandation *f* reference
lettre de relance *f* follow-up letter
lettre de vente *f* sales letter
levée des impôts *f* collection of taxes
lever des impôts to collect taxes

lever une séance to close a meeting
levier de dégagement du chariot *m* [*machine à écrire*] carriage release arm
levier de dégagement du papier *m* [*machine à écrire*] paper release arm
lexique financier *m* financial glossary
liasse *f* bundle
liasse de billets de banque *f* wad of bank notes
libellé *m* description
libellé au porteur [*chèque*] made out to bearer
libellé en [*chèque*] made out in; [*cours*] quoted in, given in
libeller à l'ordre de to make out to the order of
libeller un chèque to make out a cheque, to write a cheque
libeller une facture to make out an invoice
libre circulation *f* free movement
libre-échange *m* free trade
licence *f* licence
licence d'exportation *f* export licence
licence d'importation *f* import licence
licence de brevet *f* patent licence
licence de fabrication *f* manufacturing licence
licence de vente *f* sales licence
licencié *m* licence holder
licenciement *m* dismissal
licenciement avec préavis *m* dismissal with notice
licenciement sans préavis *m* dismissal without notice
licencier un travailleur to dismiss a worker
lieu de naissance *m* place of birth

ligne *f* line; **être en ligne** [*téléphonique*] to be on the line; [*ordinateur*] to be on line
ligne extérieure *f* outside line
ligne principale *f* [*de téléphone*] switchboard line, main line
ligne privée *f* [*de téléphone*] private line
ligne de crédit *f* line of credit, credit line
ligne de produits *f* line of products, product line
limitatif [*clause*] restrictive
limite de crédit *f* credit limit
liquidateur *m* liquidator
liquidation *f* [*d'entreprise*] liquidation; [*de dette, compte*] settlement
liquidation de biens *f* liquidation of assets
liquide [*actif*] liquid
liquide correcteur *m* correction fluid
liquider [*affaire, société*] to wind up
liquider une dette to pay off a debt
liquidités *fpl* liquid assets
lisibilité *f* legibility
lisible legible
liste d'adresses *f* mailing list
liste de clients *f* customer list, client list
liste de présence *f* attendance list
liste des correspondants *f* list of correspondents
liste des prestataires *f* services supplier list
liste des signatures autorisées *f* authorized signatory list
litige *m* legal dispute
livrable [*marchandise*] ready for delivery
livraison *f* delivery
livraison à domicile *f* home delivery
livre d'achats *m* purchase ledger

livre d'inventaire *m* annual accounts ledger

livre de caisse *m* cash book

livre de commandes *m* order book

livre de comptes *m* book of accounts, ledger

livre de dépenses *m* cash book

livre des créanciers *m* accounts payable book, accounts payable ledger

livre des débiteurs *m* accounts receivable book, accounts receivable ledger

livre des réclamations *m* claims book

livre des ventes *m* sales ledger

livrer to deliver

livret d'accueil *m* visitors book

livret de compte *m* bank book

livret de dépôts *m* deposit book, pass book

livreur *m* delivery man

locataire *mf* [*de locaux commerciaux*] tenant

location *f* [*de matériel*] rental; [*de locaux*] lease

location *f* leasing

location-bail *f* leasing, lease purchase

location-vente *f* hire purchase, installment plan *Am*

locaux *mpl* premises

locaux commerciaux *mpl* business premises

logiciel *m* software; *un logiciel* a software package

logiciel de communication *m* communications software

logiciel de comptabilité *m* accounts software

logiciel de traitement de texte *m* word-processing package

loi de l'offre et de la demande *f* law of supply and demand

long: à long terme long-term

lot *m* batch

louer to rent, to lease

lourd heavy

loyer commercial *m* commercial rent

lu et approuvé [*contrat*] read and approved

lucratif lucrative

M

machine agrafeuse *f* stapling
  machine, stapler
machine interprète de cartes
  perforées *f* punch card reader
machine poinçonneuse *f* [*de cartes
  perforées*] punch
machine trieuse *f* sorter
machine à adresser *f* addressing
  machine
machine à affranchir *f* franking
  machine
machine à copier *f* photocopier
machine à dicter *f* dictating machine
machine à écrire *f* typewriter
machine à écrire électrique *f*
  electric typewriter
machine à écrire électronique *f*
  electronic typewriter
machine à écrire à mémoire *f*
  memory typewriter
machine à écrire portative *f*
  portable typewriter
machine à plier les documents *f*
  paper folding machine
machine à polycopier *f* duplicating
  machine
magasinage *m* storage, warehousing
magasinier *m* storesman,
  warehouseman
mailing *m* mailshot
main courante *f* day book
main-d'œuvre *f* work force,
  manpower
main-d'œuvre qualifiée *f* skilled
  labour
main-d'œuvre temporaire *f*
  temporary labour
maintenance *f* [*des équipements*]
  maintenance
maison mère *f* parent company
maison de commerce *f* company
majoration *f* markup
majoration de prix *f* price markup
majorer [*prix*] to mark up; [*salaires*]
  to increase
majuscule *f* capital letter, capital; *en
  majuscules* in capitals
majuscule upper-case
malfaçon *f* defect
mali *m* losses
malus *m* [*assurance*] loss of no-
  claims bonus
malversation *f* embezzlement
mandat-carte *m* postal order
mandat international *m*
  international money order
mandat-lettre *m* postal order
mandat postal *m* postal order
mandat télégraphique *m*
  telegraphic money order
mandater to pay by money order
manque à gagner *m* loss of earnings
manquer à ses engagements
  financiers to fail to meet one's
  financial liabilities
manuel manual
manufacturé manufactured
manutention *f* handling

manutentionnaire *mf* storesman
manutentionner to handle
marc: au marc le franc pro rata
marchand *m* dealer
marchand market
marchandage *m* bargaining, haggling
marchander to bargain, to haggle
marchandisage *m* merchandizing
marchandise *f* merchandise, goods; *une marchandise* a piece of merchandise
marchandises *fpl* goods, merchandise
marchandiseur *m* merchandizer
marché *m* market; [*affaire, transaction*] deal
marché-cible *m* target market
Marché Commun *m* Common Market
marché extérieur *m* foreign market
marché grand publique *m* consumer market
marché unique *m* single market
marché à l'export *m* export market
marché au comptant *m* cash transaction
marché des changes *m* foreign exchange market
marché du travail *m* labour market
marge *f* margin
marge bénéficiaire *f* profit margin
marge inférieure *f* bottom margin
marge de crédit *f* credit margin
marge du haut *f* top margin
marger une page to set the page margins
marginer to set the margins on
marketing *m* marketing
marque *f* trademark
marque déposée *f* registered trademark
marque protégée *f* registered

trademark
marque d'origine *f* origin of goods label
marque de commerce *f* trademark
marque de fabrique *f* trademark
marqueur *m* marker pen
marqueur surligneur *m* highlighter
mass media *mpl* mass media
masse salariale *f* staff costs
massicot *m* guillotine
massicoter [*des papiers*] to guillotine
matériel d'emballage *m* packaging
matériel de bureau *m* office equipment
matières premières *fpl* raw material
matricule *m* [*numéro d'inscription*] number
matriculer to register
maturité: arriver à maturité to mature
maximum maximum
mécanographe *mf* punch card operator
média *m* media
médiateur d'entreprises *m* mediator
médiation *f* mediation
mégaoctet *m* megabyte
membre *m* member
membre fondateur *m* founding member
membre honoraire *m* honorary member
membre du comité *m* committee member
membre du conseil d'administration *m* member of the board
mémo *m* memo
mémoire *m* report; *pour mémoire* for your information
mémoire *f* memory
mémoire vive *f* RAM, random access memory

mémorandum *m* memo

mensualiser to make payable by the month

mensualités *fpl* monthly instalments

mensuel monthly

mensuellement monthly

mention écrite *f* written indication

mentionné ci-dessus above-mentioned

mentions *fpl* information

mentions obligatoires *fpl* essential information

mentions de service *fpl* positions held

menu *m* menu

menus frais *mpl* petty expenses, incidental expenses

mercatique *f* marketing

message *m* message; ***prendre un message*** to take a message

message téléphoné *m* telephone message

message téléphonique *m* telephone message

message télex *m* telex (message)

messagerie *f* parcels service; [*électronique*] electronic mail

méthode de travail *f* work method

mettre à jour to update

mettre au point [*plan d'action*] to finalize

mettre en forme [*texte*] to format

meuble classeur *m* filing cabinet

MGP (=marché grand public) *m* consumer market

microfiche *f* microfiche

microfilm *m* microfilm

micrographique micrographic

minimum minimum

ministère *m* department

Ministère de l'Economie et des Finances *m* Treasury

Ministère des Affaires étrangères *m* Foreign Office

Ministère des Finances *m* Exchequer

Ministère du Commerce extérieur *m* foreign trade department

Ministère du Commerce et de l'Industrie *m* Department of Trade and Industry

minuscule *f* lower case letter; ***en minuscules*** lower case

mise à jour *f* update

mise à pied *f* [*d'un ouvrier*] dismissal

mise en attente d'appels *f* call holding

mise en demeure *f* formal notice

mise en page *f* page layout

mission *f* [*d'employé*] assignment

mission commerciale *f* business assignment

mi-temps: à mi-temps part-time

mobile *m* mobile

mobilier de bureau *m* office furniture

mobilité *f* mobility

modalités de paiement *fpl* methods of payment

mode brouillon *m* draft mode

mode d'emploi *m* directions for use

mode d'expédition *m* method of delivery

mode de classement *m* filing system

mode de codification *m* coding method

mode de paiement *m* method of payment

mode de règlement *m* method of payment

mode de transport *m* method of transport

modèle déposé *m* registered model

modem *m* modem
modification *f* change, amendment
modification d'un contrat *f* amendment of a contract
mois: au mois by the month
monétaire monetary
monétique *f* electronic money
moniteur *m* monitor
monnaie électronique *f* electronic methods of payment
monnaie étrangère *f* foreign currency
monnaie de papier *f* paper money
monopole de vente *m* sales monopoly
monoposte *m* standalone
montant *m* amount
montant brut *m* gross (amount)
montant net *m* net (total)
moratoire *m* moratorium
mot de passe *m* password
motif de réclamation *m* reason for claim

moyennant paiement in exchange for payment, subject to payment
moyenne *f* average; [*en statistique*] mean
moyenne annuelle *f* yearly average
moyenne mensuelle *f* monthly average
moyens disponibles *mpl* available means
moyens de paiement *mpl* means of payment
moyens de production *mpl* means of production
moyens de transport *mpl* means of transport
multilatéral multilateral
multinationale *f* multinational
multiplier to multiply
multisectoriel multisector
mutuel [*accord, assurance*] mutual
mutuelle *f* mutual insurance company

N

nantir un prêt to secure a loan
nantissement *m* pledge, guarantee, security
nationalisation *f* nationalization
nationalisé nationalized
nationaliser to nationalize
navigation maritime *f* maritime navigation
navire marchand *m* merchant ship
navire de commerce *m* merchant ship
NCM (=négociations commerciales multilatérales) multilateral trade negotiations

nécessités du service *fpl* operational requirements

négoce *m* trade

négociable negotiable

négociant *m* merchant

négociation *f* negotiation

négociation collective *f* collective bargaining

négociations commerciales multilatérales *fpl* multilateral trade negotiations

négocier to negotiate

net net; *au net* clean; *mettre au net* to make a clean copy of

net commercial *m* net profit

net à payer *m* net payable

net d'impôt net of tax

nolisé [*avion*] charter

nolisement *m* chartering

noliser to charter

nom commercial *m* trade name

nom de fichier *m* file name

nombre index *m* index number

nomenclature douanière *f* customs nomenclature

nomenclature générale des produits *f* customs nomenclature

nominal *m* [*des créances*] face value; [*de titres*] par value

nomination à un poste *f* appointment to a post

nommer des experts to appoint experts

nommer qn directeur to appoint sb manager

non-conformité d'un produit *f* non-conformity of a product

non-paiement *m* non-payment

non-salarié unsalaried

normal [*caractères*] roman

normalisation *f* standardization

normalisé standard

normaliser to standardize

norme technique *f* technical standard

norme de production *f* production norm

norme de productivité *f* productivity norm

nota bene *m* NB

notaire *m* notary

notarié [*frais*] certified by a notary, notarized

notation *f* noting down

note *f* note; *prendre des notes* to take notes

note marginale *f* note in the margin

note de couverture *f* cover note

note de crédit *f* credit note

note de débit *f* debit note

note de frais *f* expense account; [*présenté après coup*] expenses

note de rappel *f* reminder

note de service *f* memo

noter to note

noter une commande to log an order, to note an order

notice explicative *f* explanatory leaflet, directions for use

notice technique *f* technical specification

notice du constructeur *f* manufacturer's instructions

notification *f* notification

notifier qn de qch to notify sb of sth

nul et non avenu null and void

nullité d'un contrat *f* invalidity of a contract

numéraire *m* cash

numéraire [*valeur*] cash

numéro azur *m* type of 0800 number in which costs are shared between caller and company

numéro vert *m* 0800 number, toll-free number *Am*

numéro d'identité bancaire *m* bank

sort code
numéro d'ordre *m* order number
numéro de code postal *m* post code, ZIP code *Am*
numéro de compte *m* account number
numéro de poste *m* extension · number
numéro de référence *m* reference

number
numéro de téléphone *m* telephone number
numérotation *f* numbering; [*téléphone*] dialling
numérotation abrégée *f* short code dialling
numéroter [*pages*] to number; [*téléphone*] to dial

objectif de vente *m* sales objective
objet *m* [*de lettre etc*] subject
objet d'un contrat *m* object of a contract
obligation *f* obligation; [*Bourse*] bond, debenture
obligation cautionnée *f* secured bond
obligation garantie *f* guaranteed bond
obligation nominative *f* registered bond
obligation au porteur *f* bearer bond
obligatoire compulsory
oblitérateur *m* franker
oblitérer to postmark
observer un contrat to comply with a contract
obtenir to obtain
obtention d'un prêt *f* obtaining of a loan

occuper un emploi to hold a job
OCDE (=Organisation de coopération et de développement économique) *f* OECD
octroi *m* granting
œil *m* typeface
office de publicité *m* advertising agency
Office du commerce extérieur *m* foreign trade office
offre *f* offer; [*dans appel d'offres*] bid, tender
offre commerciale *f* bid
offre export *f* export bid
offre publique d'achat *f* takeover bid
offre d'emploi *f* job offer, offer of employment
offre de service *f* offer of services
offre de vente *f* offer for sale

offres d'emploi *fpl* offers of employment; [*rubrique*] situations vacant

offrir un prix to offer a price

OIT (=Organisation internationale du travail) *f* ILO

onéreux costly

onglet *m* tab

onglet à fenêtre *m* window tab

ONU (=Organisation des Nations Unies) *f* UN

OPA (=offre publique d'achat) *f* takeover bid

opération *f* operation; [*bancaire*] transaction

opérer un virement to make a transfer

opposition: faire opposition à un chèque to stop a cheque

option d'achat *f* option to buy

ordinateur *m* computer

ordonnance *f* order

ordonnance de paiement *f* order to pay

ordonnancement *m* [*de paiement*] order to pay; [*mise en ordre*] scheduling

ordonnancer un paiement to order a payment

ordre: à l'ordre de payable to the order of

ordre alphabétique *m* alphabetic(al) order

ordre chronologique *m* chronological order

ordre permanent *m* standing order

ordre de classement *m* filing method

ordre de paiement *m* payment order

ordre de prélèvement permanent *m* direct debit

ordre de virement *m* transfer order

ordre du jour *m* [*de réunion*] agenda

organigramme *m* organization chart

organigramme de production *m* production flowchart

organisateur *m* organizer

organisation *f* organization

Organisation internationale de normalisation *f* International Standards Organization

Organisation internationale du travail *f* International Labour Organization

Organisation de coopération et de développement économique *f* Organization for Economic Co-operation and Development

Organisation des Nations Unies *f* United Nations

organisation syndicale *f* trade union organization

organiser to organize

organisme *m* body

organisme international *m* international organization

organisme professionnel *m* professional body

organisme de crédit *m* credit institution

original *m* original

origine: d'origine française of French origin

orthographe *f* spelling

orthographier to spell

outil de travail *m* work instrument

ouverture d'un compte *f* opening of an account

ouverture de crédit *f* granting of a loan

ouvrage de référence *m* reference book

ouvrier *m* manual worker

ouvrier qualifié *m* skilled worker

ouvrir [*compte, séance, succursale*] to open

ouvrir un crédit to grant a loan

P

page blanche *f* blank page
page de garde *f* [*de fax*] cover sheet
paie *f* pay
paiement anticipatif *m* advance payment
paiement anticipé *m* advance payment, payment in advance
paiement arriéré *m* payment in arrears
paiement comptant *m* cash payment, payment in cash
paiement différé *m* deferred payment
paiement échelonné *m* staged payments
paiement électronique *m* electronic payment, payment by electronic transfer
paiement intégral *m* payment in full
paiement mensuel *m* monthly payment
paiement partiel *m* partial payments
paiement progressif *m* graduated payments
paiement à échéance *m* payment at maturity
paiement à vue *m* payment at sight
paiement à la livraison *m* cash on delivery
paiement au comptant *m* cash payment
paiement contre documents *m* payment against documents
paiement d'avance *m* payment in advance, advance payment
paiement du solde *m* payment of the balance
paiement en espèces *m* cash payment
paiement en nature *m* payment in kind
paiement en souffrance *m* overdue payment, outstanding payment
paiement par acomptes *m* payment by instalments
paiement par anticipation *m* payment in advance
paiement par chèque *m* payment by cheque
Palais de Justice *m* Law Courts
panneau d'affichage *m* noticeboard
PAO (=publication assistée par ordinateur) *f* DTP
papeterie *f* stationery
papier *m* paper
papier avion *m* airmail paper
papier bancable *m* bankable paper
papier commercial *m* commercial paper
papier continu *m* continuous paper
papier listing *m* listing paper
papier-monnaie *m* paper money
papier thermique *m* thermal paper
papier à en-tête *m* headed notepaper
papier d'emballage *m* packing paper
papillon *m* [*sur document*] flag
paquet postal *m* parcel
paradis fiscal *m* tax haven

parafiscal [*taxe*] exceptional
parafiscalité *f* special taxation
paragraphe *m* paragraph
paraphe *m* initials
parapher to initial
parapheur *m* signature book
parcourir to scroll through
parenthèse *f* bracket; *entre parenthèses* in brackets
Parlement européen *m* European Parliament
parrainage *m* sponsorship
parrainer to sponsor
part: de la part de on behalf of
part aux bénéfices *f* share of profits
part de marché *f* market share
partager le bénéfice to share the profits
partenaires commerciaux *mpl* trading partners
partenaires sociaux *mpl* workers and management
partenariat *m* partnership
participant *m* participant
participation *f* holding
participation aux bénéfices *f* profit sharing
participer à to take part in
participer aux bénéfices to have a share in the profits
pas d'écriture *m* pitch
passation de commande *f* placing of an order
passer commande à qn to place an order with sb
passer commande de qch to place an order for sth
passer un contrat to sign a contract
passer un marché to sign a deal
passer une commande to place an order
passible d'impôts liable to tax
passible de taxe liable to tax

passif *m* liabilities
patente *f* licence
patenté [*commerçant*] licensed
patron *m* boss
patronage *m:* **sous le patronage de** under the sponsorship of
patronal employer's
patronat *m* employers
payable comptant payable in cash
payable à l'arrivée payable on arrival
payable à l'échéance payable at maturity
payable à la banque payable at the bank
payable à la livraison payable on delivery
payé d'avance prepaid
payer à tempérament to pay by instalments
payer à vue to pay at sight
payer au comptant to pay cash
payer en espèces to pay in cash
payer par chèque to pay by cheque
payeur *m* payer
pays hors communauté *m* non-EC country
PC (=pièce de caisse) *f* cash voucher
PCG (=plan comptable général) *m* chart of accounts
PDG (=président-directeur général) *m* chairman and managing director, CEO, president *Am*
pénalité *f* penalty
pension de retraite *f* retirement pension
PER (=plan d'épargne-retraite) *m* retirement savings plan
percepteur *m* tax collector
perception *f* collection
perception douanière *f* collection of customs duties
percevoir [*impôts*] to collect

perforatrice *f* (hole) punch
performance *f* performance
performant [*entreprise*] efficient
période d'essai *f* trial period
périodique periodic(al)
permis d'embarquement *m* shipping note, shipping permit
permis d'exportation *m* export licence
permis d'importation *m* import licence
permis de débarquement *m* unloading note, unloading permit
permis de travail *m* work permit
personnaliser to personalize
personne morale *f* legal entity, body corporate
personne physique *f* natural person
personnel *m* staff, personnel
personnel administratif *m* administrative staff
personnel de bureau *m* office staff
perte *f* loss
pertes et profits *mpl* profit and loss
pèse-lettre *m* letter scales
peser to weigh
petite annonce *f* classified ad, small ad
petite caisse *f* petty cash
petites et moyennes entreprises *fpl* small (and medium-sized) businesses
phoning *m* telesales
photocopie *f* photocopy
photocopier to photocopy
photocopieuse *f* photocopier
PIB (=produit intérieur brut) *m* GDP
pièce détachée *f* spare part
pièce jointe *f* enclosure
pièce justificative *f* voucher
pièce à joindre *f* enclosure
pièce de caisse *f* cash voucher

pièce de rechange *f* spare part
pièces justificatives *fpl* documentary evidence
pied de page *m* footer
piloté par menu menu-driven
piloter [*projet*] to be in charge of
pique-notes *m* spike
PJ (=pièce jointe) encl
place commerciale *f* trade centre
place financière *f* financial centre
place marchande *f* market place
placement *m* investment
placer [*argent*] to invest
plafond de crédit *m* credit ceiling
plafonnement des prix *m* levelling off of prices
plafonner to level out, to level off
plage horaire *f* time slot
plainte *f* complaint
plan comptable général *m* chart of accounts
plan d'épargne-retraite *m* retirement savings plan
plan de classement *m* filing method
plan de financement *m* funding plan, financing plan
planning *m* schedule
planning à gouttières *m* slot-in planner
plaque d'identification *f* sign
plaquette publicitaire *f* advertising brochure
plastifier to laminate
plein emploi *m* full employment
plein tarif *m* full price
plein temps: à plein temps full-time
pli cacheté *m* sealed envelope
pli chargé *m* registered and insured letter
pli recommandé *m* registered letter; *par pli recommandé* by registered mail
plus-value *f* capital gain

**PME (=petites et moyennes
entreprises)** *fpl* small (and
medium-sized) businesses; **une
PME** a small business
**PMI (=petites et moyennes
industries)** *fpl* small (and
medium-sized) industries
PNB (=produit national brut) *m*
GNP
pochette *f* [*pour protéger document*]
document cover
pochette matelassée *f* Jiffy bag®
point *m* [*ponctuation*] full stop; *"i"
surmonté de deux points* i with
two dots; *faire le point* to take
stock
point-virgule *m* semi-colon
point d'exclamation *m* exclamation
mark
point d'interrogation *m* question
mark
pointage *m* [*d'employé*] clocking on
pointage des salariés *m* signing-in
of employees
pointer to sign in; [*ouvrier*] to clock
in; [*au départ*] to sign out; to clock
out
pointeuse *f* time clock
pointillé *m* dotted line
points de tabulation *mpl* tab sets
police *f* [*assurance*] policy;
[*impression*] font
police tous risques *f* comprehensive
policy, all-risks policy
police au voyage *f* travel insurance
policy
police d'assurance *f* insurance
policy
polycopie *f* duplicate
polycopier to duplicate
ponctualité *f* punctuality
ponctuation *f* punctuation
pont: faire le pont to make a long

weekend of it
pool de secrétaires *m* secretarial
pool
population active *f* labour force
port *m* port
port avancé carriage forward
port dû carriage forward
port franc [*de marchandise*]
carriage free
port payé [*revue, journal*] postage
paid; [*marchandise*] carriage paid
port payé, assurance comprise
carriage insurance paid
port de lettres *m* postage
port et emballage *m* postage and
packing, p&p
portable *m* portable, laptop
porte-copies *m* copy holder
porte-parole du personnel *m* staff
spokesperson
portefeuille *m* portfolio
porter plainte to make a complaint
**porter un montant au crédit d'un
compte** to credit an amount to an
account
**porter un montant au débit d'un
compte** to debit an amount to an
account
porter une signature to bear a
signature
porteur *m* bearer
porteur d'actions *m* bearer of shares
porteur d'une procuration *m*
holder of a power of attorney,
holder of a proxy
pose de tabulations *f* tabbing
poser des tabulations dans to tab
position créditrice *f* credit balance
position débitrice *f* debit balance
position de compte *m* account
balance
post scriptum *m* post script
postal postal

postdater to postdate
poste *m* [*téléphonique*] extension; [*au bilan*] entry, item
poste *f* post, mail; *aller à la poste* to go to the post office
poste aérienne *f* airmail
poste restante *f* poste restante, general delivery *Am*
poste à pourvoir *m* vacancy
poste de travail *m* workstation
poster le courrier to post the mail
postulant *m* applicant
postuler un travail to apply for a job
pot-de-vin *m* backhander; bribe
pourcentage *m* percentage
poursuivre qn en justice to sue sb, to take legal action against sb
pouvoir d'achat *m* purchasing power
pouvoirs publics *mpl* public authorities
pp (=par procuration) pp
préalables d'un accord *mpl* pre-contract conditions
préavis *m* notice
préavis de grève *m* strike notice
préavis de paiement *m* payment advice
précédent *m* precedent
précision de frappe *f* keying accuracy
précompte *m* advance deduction
précompter to withhold
préfacturation *f* prebilling
préférentiel [*tarif*] preferential
prélèvement *m* withholding, deduction
prélèvement automatique *m* direct debit
prélèvement bancaire *m* direct debit
prélèvement fiscal *m* tax deduction
prélèvement salarial *m* deduction from wages, stoppage
prélever to withhold, to deduct

prélever une commission to deduct a commission
prendre une commande to take an order
prendre une police d'assurance to take out an insurance policy
preneur de lettre de change *m* payee of a bill of exchange
préposé *m* clerk
préretraite *f* early retirement
présentation *f* presentation
président *m* chairman, president
Président-directeur général *m* chairman and managing director
Président du conseil *m* chairman of the board
présider une assemblée to chair a meeting
presse: la presse the press
prestataire de services *m* service provider, service supplier
prestations *fpl* services
prestation de services *f* provision of services
prêt bancaire *m* bank loan
prêt personnalisé *m* personal loan
prête-nom *m* figurehead
prêter à intérêt to lend at interest
prêter sur titres to lend against securities
prêteur *m* lender
prévention des accidents du travail *f* prevention of industrial accidents
prévision *f* forecast
prévision des ventes *f* sales forecast
prévisionnel estimated
prévoyance sociale *f* social security provisions
prime *f* premium
prime annuelle *f* annual premium
prime familiale *f* family allowance

prime d'ancienneté *f* long service award

prime d'assurance *f* insurance premium

prime d'éloignement *f* isolated post allowance

prime d'intéressement *f* reversionary bonus

prime de transport *f* transport allowance

principal et intérêts *m* principal and interest

prise *f* plug

prise de décision *f* decision-making

prise de notes *f* note-taking

prise en charge *f* charge

privatisation *f* privatization

privatiser to privatize

privé private

privilégié [*créancier*] preferred

prix contractuel *m* contractual price

prix coûtant *m* cost price

prix départ usine *m* price ex-works

prix facturé *m* invoice price

prix taxe comprise *m* price inclusive of tax

prix unitaire *m* unit price

prix d'achat *m* purchase price

prix d'offre *m* supply price

prix de détail *m* retail price

prix de gros *m* wholesale price

prix de revient *m* cost price

prix de transport *m* freight price

prix de vente *m* selling price

prix hors taxe *m* price before tax

procédure douanière *f* customs procedure

procédure de faillite *f* bankruptcy proceedings

procès-verbal *m* report; [*de réunion*] minutes

procuration *f* proxy

procureur général *m* public prosecutor

producteur *m* producer

production *f* production

production à la chaîne *f* mass production

production en masse *f* mass production

production en série *f* mass production

productivité *f* productivity

produire to produce

produit *m* product

produit fini *m* finished product

produit intérieur brut *m* gross domestic product

produit manufacturé *m* manufactured product

produit national brut *m* gross national product

produits finis *mpl* finished products

produits semi-finis *mpl* semi-finished goods

produits de grande consommation *mpl* consumer goods

profession *f* profession

professionnel [*formation*] vocational

profil de poste *m* job description

profit *m* profit

pro forma [*facture*] pro forma

programme *m* program

programme de formation *m* training programme

programmer to program

projecteur *m* overhead projector

projet *m* project

projet de contrat *m* draft agreement

projet de loi *m* bill

prolongation *f* extension

prolonger to extend

promesse écrite *f* written promise

promotion *f* promotion

promotion interne *f* internal

promotion, promotion from within the company
promotion des ventes *f* sales promotion
promotionnel [*article*] promotional
promouvoir to promote
se **prononcer** to give a decision
proposition *f* proposal
proposition de prix *f* price proposal
propriétaire *mf* owner
propriété immobilière *f* property
proroger une échéance to extend payment terms
prospecter la clientèle to canvass for new business
prospecter le marché to explore the market
prospecteur *m* canvasser
prospection téléphonique *f* telephone marketing
prospectus *m* leaflet
protégé par mot de passe password protected

protocole d'accord *m* [*contrat*] outline agreement
provenance *f* [*de produit*] origin
provision *f* provision
provisionnel provisional
provisoire provisional, interim
prud'homme *m* industrial arbitrator
PTT (=Postes, Télécommunications et Télédiffusion) *fpl* Post Office and Telecommunications Department
PU (=prix unitaire) UP
publication assistée par ordinateur *f* desktop publishing
publicitaire advertising
publicité *f* advertising, publicity
publicité par correspondance *f* direct mail advertising
publipostage *m* mailshot; [*logiciel*] mailmerge
punaise *f* drawing pin, thumb tack *Am*

Q

qualité *f* [*emploi*] occupation; [*fonction*] position; *en sa qualité de* in one's capacity as
qualité courrier *f* letter quality
quittance *f* receipt; [*facture*] bill

quittance finale *f* final payment
quittancer to receipt
quota *m* quota
quote-part *f* share
quotidien daily

R

rabais *m* reduction
rabaissement *m* [*de prix*] lowering
rabaisser [*prix*] to lower
rabat *m* [*d'enveloppe*] flap
rabattre [*prix*] to reduce
raccrocher to hang up
radiotéléphone *m* cellular telephone, mobile phone
raison sociale *f* company name
rappel *m* reminder
rappel de compte *m* reminder of account outstanding
rappel de salaire *m* back pay
rapport *m* report
rapport de gestion *m* management report; [*de rapport annuel*] report of the board of directors
rapporter des intérêts to yield interest
rationalisation *f* rationalization
rationaliser [*fabrication*] to rationalize
rature *f* deletion; *sans ratures ni surcharges* without deletions or additions
raturer [*un texte*] to delete
rayer to delete
rayez les mentions inutiles delete as appropriate
réaliser un profit to make a profit
réamorcer to reboot
réapprovisionnement des stocks *m* restocking
réapprovisionner [*un magasin*] to restock

récépissé *m* receipt
récépissé de dépôt *m* deposit receipt
récépissé de versement *m* receipt of payment
réception *f* [*de marchandises*] receipt; *la réception* [*accueil*] reception
réceptionnaire *mf* consignee
réceptionniste *mf* receptionist
recette annuelle *f* annual income, annual receipts
recette brute *f* gross income, gross receipts
recette journalière *f* daily takings
recette nette *f* net income, net receipts
recettes *fpl* receipts
recettes fiscales *fpl* tax revenue
recettes publiques *fpl* government revenue
recettes et dépenses *fpl* revenue and expenditure
recherche et remplacement *f* search and replace
recherche et remplacement global *f* global search and replace
rechercher et remplacer to search and replace
réclamant *m* claimant; [*en droit civil*] plaintiff
réclamation *f* claim; [*plainte*] complaint
réclamer to complain

réclamer auprès de to make a claim against; [*se plaindre*] to lodge a complaint with

réclamer le paiement to demand payment

reclassement professionnel *m* redeployment

recommandation *f* [*de lettre*] registration

recommandé registered

recommander une lettre to register a letter

reconductible renewable

reconduction *f* renewal

reconnaissance de dette *f* promissory note, IOU

se **reconvertir** [*employé*] to retrain

recours contentieux *m* legal recourse

recouvrable [*dette*] recoverable

recouvrement d'impôts *m* tax collection

recouvrement de créances *m* debt collection

recouvrer to recover

recrutement *m* recruitment

recruter to recruit

rectificatif *m* correction

rectification *f* correction

rectifier to correct

reçu *m* receipt

recyclage *m* [*de personnel*] retraining

se **recycler** to retrain

rédacteur *m* [*de document, de lettre*] writer

rédaction *f* [*de document, de lettre*] writing

redevable *mf* person liable for tax

rédiger [*bon de commande*] to make out; [*contrat*] to draw up

redû *m* balance due

réduction de personnel *f* staff cutback

réduction des impôts *f* tax cut

réduction des prix *f* price reduction

réduction des salaires *f* wage cut

réduire to reduce

réduire le personnel to cut staff

réduit [*tarif*] reduced

réembaucher to rehire

réentraînement *m* retraining

réexpédier [*lettre*] to forward

réexpédition *f* [*de lettre*] forwarding

référence *f* reference

référence à rappeler *f* please quote reference

références bancaires *fpl* bank references

références commerciales *fpl* trade references

se **référer à** to refer to

régime d'imposition *m* tax system

régime de retraite *m* pension plan

registre de présence *m* attendance register

registre des procès-verbaux *m* minutes book

Registre du Commerce *m* trade register

règle *f* rule; [*objet*] ruler

règle à calculer *f* slide rule

règlement *m* [*de facture*] payment; [*statut*] regulation

règlement au comptant *m* payment in cash

règlement par chèque *m* payment by cheque

réglementation *f* regulations

réglementation douanière *f* customs regulations

réglementation du change *f* exchange control regulations

réglementation du travail *f* labour legislation

règlements douaniers *mpl* customs regulations

régler [*fournisseur*] to pay; [*compte*] to settle

régler à l'amiable to settle out of court

régler au comptant to pay in cash

relancer la production to boost production

relancer un débiteur to chase up a debtor

relations commerciales *fpl* business relations

relations publiques *fpl* public relations, PR

relations d'affaires *fpl* business relations

relations de travail *fpl* labour relations

relevé d'identité bancaire *m* bank details

relevé de compte *m* bank statement

relevé de factures *m* statement of invoices

relief: mettre en relief to highlight

relieur *m* binder

reliquat *m* balance

reliquat de caisse *m* cash balance

reliquat de compte *m* account balance

remanier une lettre to rework a letter

remboursable repayable, refundable

remboursement *m* repayment, refund; [*de prêt*] redemption

remboursement anticipé *m* early repayment

rembourser to repay, to refund, to pay back; [*prêt*] to redeem

remerciements anticipés *mpl* with thanks in advance

remise *f* discount

remise de caisse *f* cash discount

remplir un questionnaire to fill in a questionnaire

rémunération *f* remuneration; [*salaire*] pay

rémunérer to pay

rendez-vous *m* appointment

rendez-vous d'affaires *m* business meeting

rendu, droits acquittés delivery duty paid

rendu, droits non acquittés delivery duty unpaid

rendu franco bord delivered free on board

rengager [*personnel*] to rehire

renouveler une commande to repeat an order

renouveler une traite to renew a bill of exchange

renouvellement *m* [*d'effet*] renewal

renseignements *mpl* directory enquiries, information *Am*

renseignements complémentaires *mpl* further information

renseignements de crédit *mpl* status enquiry

renseigner qn sur qch to give sb information on sth

se **renseigner sur qch** to get information about sth

rentabilité *f* profitability

rentable profitable

renvoi *m* [*de marchandises*] return; [*de projet*] postponement, deferral; [*d'employé*] dismissal; [*dans un texte*] cross-reference

renvoyer [*à plus tard*] to postpone, to defer; [*employé*] to dismiss

renvoyer à l'expéditeur to return to sender

réouverture *f* re-opening

répartition du bénéfice *f* distribution of profits

repas d'affaires *m* business lunch

répertoire *m* directory
répertoire racine *m* root directory
répertoire d'adresses *m* list of adresses
répertorier to list
répondeur *m* answering machine
répondre à une lettre to answer a letter
répondre au courrier to reply to the mail
réponse *f* answer
réponse d'attente *f* holding reply
report *m* postponement; [*de somme*] carrying forward; *"report"* carried forward
reporté deferred
repos compensateur *m* time off in lieu
reprendre le travail to return to work
représentant *m* representative, agent
représentant syndical *m* union representative
reprise économique *f* economic recovery
reproduire [*texte*] to reproduce
reprographie *f* reprography
reprographier to duplicate
réseau *m* network
réseau local local area network, LAN
réseau de commercialisation *m* marketing network
réseau de distribution *m* distribution network
réseau de vente *m* sales network
résiliable [*contrat*] rescindable
résiliation *f* [*de contrat*] termination
résilier un contrat to terminate a contract
résoluble [*contrat*] rescindable
respecter les délais de livraison to meet delivery schedules

respectueuses salutations *fpl* yours faithfully
responsabilité patronale *f* employer's liability
responsabilité du fabricant *f* manufacturer's liability
responsable *mf* person in charge
responsable syndical *m* union leader
responsable des ventes *mf* sales manager
restant *m* remainder, balance
restructuration *f* [*d'entreprise*] restructuring
restructurer to restructure
résultat *m* profit or loss
résumé *m* abstract, summary
retard *m* delay
retard à la livraison *m* delay in delivery
retardataire [*contribuable*] late
retarder le paiement to delay payment
retenu à la source deducted at source
retenue *f* deduction, withholding
retenue sur salaire *f* wage deduction
retenues patronales *fpl* employer's contributions
retenues salariales *fpl* wage deductions, stoppages, employee's contributions
retirer [*somme d'argent*] to withdraw
retour *m* return; *par retour du courrier* by return (of mail)
retour arrière *m* backspace
retour chariot *m* carriage return
retour net *m* net return
retour à l'envoyeur *m* return to sender
retour sur l'investissement *m* return on investment

retourner à l'expéditeur to return to sender

retrait *m* withdrawal; ***mettre en retrait*** to indent

retraite *f* retirement

rétribuer to pay

rétribution *f* payment

rétroactif back-dated

réunion *f* meeting; ***être en réunion*** to be in a meeting

réunion de comité *f* committee meeting

réunion du conseil *f* board meeting

réunion du conseil d'administration *f* board meeting

revendications syndicales *fpl* union demands

revenu annuel *m* annual income

revenu disponible *m* disposable income

revenu imposable *m* taxable income

revenu net *m* net income

revenu d'entreprise *m* company earnings

réviser to revise

révocable [*crédit*] revocable, callable

révoquer to dismiss

revue professionnelle *f* trade journal

revue d'entreprise *f* company magazine, in-house magazine

RIB (=relevé d'identité bancaire) *m* bank details

ristourne *f* rebate

rond en affaires businesslike

rouge: en rouge in the red; ***dans le rouge*** in the red

roulant [*capital*] working

rouleau *m* [*de machine à écrire*] platen

roulement de capitaux *m* turnover of capital

roulement du personnel *m* staff turnover

RRR (=remise, rabais, ristourne) discounts and allowances

ruban *m* ribbon

ruban de machine à écrire *m* typewriter ribbon

rubrique *f* heading

rupture *f* [*de contrat*] breach

rupture abusive *f* [*de contrat*] breach

rupture de stock *f* stock outage; ***être en rupture de stock*** to be out of stock

S

SA (=société anonyme) *f* plc

sacoche à courrier *f* mail bag

saisie *f* [*de biens*] seizure; [*de texte, de données*] capture

saisir to key

salaire *m* wage; [*mensuel*] salary

salaire annuel garanti *m* annual guaranteed salary

salaire brut *m* gross wage; [*mensuel*] gross salary

salaire indirect *m* benefits in kind

salaire plafond *m* maximum salary

salaire plafonné *m* wage ceiling

salaire réel *m* real salary

salaire de base *m* basic wage; [*mensuel*] basic salary

salarial salary

salarié *m* wage earner; [*payé mensuellement*] salaried employee

salariés *mpl* [*de société*] employees

salle d'attente *f* waiting room

salle d'exposition *f* exhibition hall

salle de conférence *f* conference room

salle du conseil *f* board room

salutations distinguées *fpl* yours truly

SARL (=société à responsabilité limitée) *f* Ltd

sauf avis contraire unless otherwise advised

sauf bonne fin under usual reserve

sauf erreur ou omission errors and omissions excepted

sauvegarder to save, to back up

SAV (=service après-vente) after-sales service

savoir-faire *m* expertise, know-how

scanneur *m* scanner

sceau privé *m* private seal

sceller [*lettre, acte*] to seal

schéma *m* diagram

schématiser to make a diagram of

SCI (=société de commerce international) *f* international trading corporation

scotch *m*® sellotape®, scotch tape® *Am*

secours: de secours backup

secrétaire *mf* secretary

secrétaire bilingue *mf* bilingual secretary

secrétaire général *m* company secretary

secrétaire de direction *mf* executive secretary

secrétaire de séance *mf* meetings secretary

secrétariat *m* secretariat

secteur privé *m* private sector

secteur public *m* public sector

sécurité sociale *f* social security, welfare *Am*

seing: sous seing privé under private seal

selon facture as per invoice

selon vos instructions in accordance with your instructions

semaine de cinq jours *f* five-day week

semainier *m* diary

semestre *m* six months, half year

séminaire *m* seminar

série complète de connaissements *f* full set of bills of lading

série de prix *f* contract price list

série de produits *f* product line

serveur de fichiers *m* file server

service *m* [*direction*] department; [*rendu*] service

service administratif *m* administration (department)

service après-vente *m* [*direction*] after-sales (department); [*service rendu*] after-sales service

service clientèle *m* [*direction*] customer service (department); [*service rendu*] customer service

service commercial export *m* export department

service comptable *m* accounts (department)

service contrôle qualité *m* quality control (department)

service financier *m* finance (department)

service de recouvrement *m* collection (department)

service de renseignements *m* information department

service de la prospection *m* marketing (department)

service des achats *m* purchasing (department), buying (department); [*plus grand*] procurement (department)

service du courrier *m* mail room

service du personnel *m* personnel (department)

services extérieurs *mpl* external services

seuil de rentabilité *m* breakeven point

SICAV (=Société d'investissement

à capital variable) *f* unit trust, mutual fund *Am*

siège administratif *m* administrative headquarters

siège principal *m* head office

siège social *m* registered office, head office

siéger au conseil d'administration to have a seat on the board

sigle *m* [*d'entreprise*] logo

signataire *mf* signatory

signature légalisée *f* authenticated signature

signature sociale *f* company signature (and stamp)

signature d'un contrat *f* signing of a contract

signature par procuration *f* per pro signature, pp

signe dollar *m* dollar sign

signe de classification *m* number of section or paragraph

signer to sign

signer par procuration to sign per pro, to pp

signer un chèque en blanc to sign a blank cheque

signes de ponctuation *mpl* punctuation marks

simulation *f* [*prévision*] forecast

sinistre *m* damage

sinistré damaged

SIRET: No SIRET company registration number

situation de banque *f* bank balance

situation de caisse *f* cash balance

situation de compte *f* account balance, account position

SME (=Système monétaire européen) *m* EMS

SMIC (=salaire minimum interprofessionnel de croissance) *m* minimum wage

smicard *m* minimum wage earner
SNC (=société en nom collectif) *f*
  commercial/industrial partnership
société *f* company
société affiliée *f* affiliated company
société anonyme *f* public limited
  company
société commerciale *f* company
société commune *f* joint venture
société fiduciaire *f* trust company
société mère *f* parent company
société à responsabilité limitée *f*
  limited liability company
société d'affacturage *f* factoring
  company
société de gestion *f* holding company
société en commandite *f* form of
  partnership limited by shares
solde bénéficiaire *m* credit balance
solde créditeur *m* credit balance
solde débiteur *m* debit balance
solde de tout compte *m* final
  settlement
solvabilité *f* solvency
solvable solvent
sommaire *m* summary
sommation *f* summons
somme due *f* amount due
somme nette *f* net (amount)
sommer qn de payer to require sb to
  pay
sortir [*de programme*] to exit
souche de chéquier *f* chequebook
  stub
souffrance: en souffrance [*colis,
  marchandises*] awaiting collection;
  [*courrier, paiement*] outstanding
soulignement *m* underlining
souligner to underline
soumettre une lettre à la signature
  to present a letter for signature
soumissionner pour qch to tender
  for sth

souris *f* mouse
sous-directeur *m* assistant manager;
  [*supérieur*] assistant director
sous-dossier *m* subfolder
sous-produit *m* by-product
sous-répertoire *m* subdirectory
sous-titre *m* subheading
sous-total *m* subtotal
sous-traitance *f* subcontracting
sous-traitant *m* sub-contractor
sous-traiter to subcontract
souscripteur *m* [*d'effet de
  commerce*] drawer; [*d'emprunt*]
  subscriber
souscription *f* [*de société*]
  subscribed capital
souscrire [*police d'assurance*] to
  take out
soussigner: je, soussigné ..., I the
  undersigned ...
soustraire to subtract
spécification *f* [*normalisation*]
  specification
spécimen de signature *m* specimen
  signature
spéculation *f* speculation
spéculer to speculate
staff de direction *m* managerial staff
stage *m* training period
stage de formation *m* training period
stagiaire *mf* trainee
standard standard
standard (téléphonique) *m*
  switchboard
standardisation *f* standardization
standardiser to standardize
standardiste *mf* operator,
  switchboard operator
statuts de société *mpl* memorandum
  and articles of association, bylaws
  Am
stencil *m* stencil
sténodactylo *mf* shorthand typist

sténodactylographie *f* shorthand-typing
sténographe *mf* shorthand writer, stenographer *Am*
sténographie *f* shorthand
sténographier to take down in shorthand
sténographique [*dictée*] shorthand
sténotype *m* stenotype®
sténotypie *f* stenotypy
sténotypiste *mf* stenotypist
stipuler des conditions to stipulate conditions
stipuler par contrat to stipulate in a contract
stock *m* stock
stocker des marchandises to stock goods
streamer *m* tape streamer
strictement confidentiel strictly confidential
stylo *m* pen
stylo-bille *m* ballpoint (pen), biro®
stylo-feutre *m* felt-tip (pen)
stylo-surligneur *m* highlighter
subside *m* subsidy, grant
subvention *f* subsidy
succursale *f* branch
suite: donner suite à to follow up; *suite à votre demande* further to your request
suite de lettre *f* continuation of a letter
suivant avis as per advice
suivant connaissement as per bill of lading
suivant vos instructions as per your instructions
suivi des commandes *m* follow-up of orders
suivre: à faire suivre please forward
sujet à [*droits, impôt*] subject to
supérieur [*cadre*] senior

suppléance *f* temporary replacement
suppléant *m* temporary replacement
supplément de prix *m* additional charge
suppression des barrières douanières *f* removal of customs barriers
supprimer [*texte*] to delete
surligneur *m* highlighter
sursis de paiement *m* extra time to pay
surtaxe *f* [*postale*] surcharge
surveillant *m* supervisor
sus-dénommé aforementioned
suspendre les paiements to stop payments
suspension *f* [*de séance*] adjournment
suspension de paiement *f* stopping of payment
syndicalisme *m* trade unionism
syndicaliste *mf* trade unionist
syndicat *m* trade union
syndicat ouvrier *m* trade union
syndicat patronal *m* employers' organization
syndicat professionnel *m* trade association, professional association
syndiqué *m* trade union member; to be a member of a trade union
synopsis *f* synopsis
Système monétaire européen *m* European Monetary System
système d'exploitation *m* operating system
système de participation aux bénéfices *m* profit-sharing scheme
système de prévoyance *m* social benefits system
système de retraite *m* pension scheme, retirement plan

T

table *f* table
table ronde *f* round table
table d'intérêts *f* interest table
table des matières *f* table of contents
tableau *m* table
tableau synoptique *m* summary
tableau de conversion *m* conversion
  table
tableur *m* spreadsheet
tabulateur *m* tab key
tabulation *f* tab
tabulatrice *f* tabulator
taille-crayon *m* pencil sharpener
tampon *m* stamp, stamp pad
tampon de la poste *m* postmark
tamponner une lettre to frank a
  letter
taper to type
taper à la machine to type
taquet de tabulation *m* tab stop
tarif *m* [*prix*] rate; [*liste de prix*]
  pricelist; [*douanier*] tariff
tarif dégressif *m* tapering rate
tarif différentiel *m* differential rate
tarif douanier *m* customs tariff
tarif horaire *m* hourly rate
tarif postal *m* postage rate
tarif préférentiel *m* preferential rate
tarif réduit *m* reduced rate
tarif spécial *m* special rate
tarif de base *m* basic rate
tarifaire [*accord*] tariff
tarification *f* setting of rates
taux *m* rate

taux normal *m* standard rate
taux réduit *m* reduced rate
taux d'amortissement *m* rate of
  depreciation, depreciation rate
taux d'assurance *m* insurance rate
taux d'échange *m* rate of exchange
taux d'escompte *m* discount rate
taux d'intérêt *m* interest rate, rate of
  interest
taux de change *m* exchange rate
taux de TVA *m* rate of VAT, VAT
  rate
taxable taxable
taxation *f* taxation
taxe *f* tax
taxe locale *f* local tax
taxe à l'exportation *f* export tax
taxe de luxe *f* luxury tax
taxe sur la valeur ajoutée *f* value
  added tax
taxe sur le revenu *f* income tax
taxe sur les salaires *f* employment
  tax
taxer to tax
taxes comprises (toutes) *fpl*
  inclusive of tax
TCA (=taxe sur le chiffre
  d'affaires) *f* sales tax
technicien de maintenance *m*
  maintenance engineer, service
  engineer
technique de vente *f* sales technique
téléconférence *f* teleconference
téléconférences *fpl* teleconferencing

télécopie *f* fax

télécopieur *m* fax (machine)

télégramme *m* telegram

télégraphique [*adresse, style*] telegraphic

téléphone *m* telephone

téléphone portatif *m* mobile (phone)

téléphone sans fil *m* cordless phone

téléphoner à qn to telephone sb, to call sb, to phone sb

téléphonique telephone

téléphoniste *mf* telephonist

téléscripteur *m* teleprinter

télétex *m* teletex

télétravail *m* telecommuting

télétype *m* teletype®

télex *m* telex

télexer to telex

télexiste *mf* telex operator

temporaire *mf* temp

temporaire [*travail*] temporary

temps: à temps complet full-time; *à temps partiel* part-time

tendance de marché *f* market trend

teneur de contrat *f* contractual terms

tenir les livres à jour to keep the books up to date

tension *f* voltage

tenue de fichiers *f* file management

tenue des livres *f* bookkeeping

tenue des stocks *f* stock keeping

terme *m:* **à terme échu** on the due date; *à terme fixe* fixed-term

terme de liquidation *m* account period, settlement period

terme de livraison *m* delivery deadline

terme de préavis *m* notice period

terme de rigueur *m* deadline

termes commerciaux *mpl* incoterms

termes de contrat *mpl* contractual terms and conditions

termes de paiement *mpl* terms of payment

terminal monétique *m* cash point, cash dispenser

tête d'entreprise *f* company head

tête de lettre *f* letterhead

texte imprimé *m* printed text

thésaurisation *f* hoarding

thésauriser to hoard

ticket restaurant *m* luncheon voucher

ticket de caisse *m* receipt

tiers *m* third party

tiers possesseur *m* third party owner

timbrage *m* stamping

timbre dateur *m* date stamp

timbre fiscal *m* tax stamp

timbre-poste *m* postage stamp

timbre-quittance *m* receipt stamp

timbré [*document*] stamped

timbrer une lettre to stamp a letter

tirage *m* [*de chèque*] drawing; [*d'imprimés etc*] print run

tiré *m* drawee

tirer à découvert to overdraw

tirer à vue to draw at sight

tirer un chèque sur to draw a cheque on

tirer une traite sur to draw a bill on

tiret *m* dash

tireur *m* drawer

titre *m* security

titre: à titre d'information for information

titre d'action *m* share certificate

titre de civilité *m* salutation

titre de créance *m* loan note, debt instrument

titre de transport *m* [*connaissement etc*] transport document

titres *mpl* securities

titulaire *mf* [*de compte, police*] holder; [*de fonction*] incumbent

titulaire d'action *mf* shareholder

toner *m* toner
total *m* total
total à payer *m* total payable
total des recettes *m* total receipts
totaliser to total
touche *f* key
touche (d')entrée *f* enter key
touche majuscule *f* shift key
touche retour *f* return key
touche d'échappement *f* escape key
touche d'effacement *f* delete key
touche de contrôle *f* control key
touche de direction *f* arrow key
touche de fonction *f* function key
touche de verrouillage des majuscules *f* caps lock key
toucher qn par téléphone to reach sb by telephone
toucher ses appointements to draw one's salary
toucher un chèque to cash a cheque
toucher un intérêt to receive interest
tournez s'il vous plaît please turn over, PTO
tout compris [*prix*] all-in
traducteur *m* translator
traduction *f* translation
traductrice *f* translator
traduire to translate
trait d'union *m* hyphen
traite *f* draft, bill of exchange
traite bancaire *f* bank draft
traite documentaire *f* documentary bill
traite à courte échéance *f* short-dated bill
traite à date fixe *f* time bill
traite à longue échéance *f* long-dated bill
traite à vue *f* sight draft
traite contre acceptation *f* acceptance bill
traitement *m* salary

traitement fixe *m* fixed salary
traitement initial *m* starting salary
traitement de base *m* basic salary
traitement de texte *m* word processing; [*machine, logiciel*] word processor
traitement des données *m* data processing
tranche d'imposition *f* tax bracket
tranche de paiement *f* instalment
transcrire to transcribe
transférer to transfer
transfert de capitaux *m* transfer of capital
transitaire *m* forwarding agent
transiter to forward
transmettre to transmit
travail *m* work; [*poste*] job
travail administratif *m* administrative work
travail supplémentaire *m* overtime
travail à domicile *m* working at home
travail à mi-temps *m* part-time work
travail à plein temps *m* full-time work
travail à temps partiel *m* part-time work
travail à la chaîne *m* assembly line work
travail de bureau *m* office work
travail de nuit *m* night work
travailler to work
travailleur *m* worker
travailleur indépendant *m* self-employed person
travailleur manuel *m* manual worker
travailleur salarié *m* salaried worker
travailleur à temps réduit *m* person on short time

treizième mois *m* amount equal to one-thirteenth of annual salary paid at Christmas

tréma *m* diaeresis

trésorerie *f* cashflow; [*service d'entreprise*] accounts (department)

trésorier *m* financial manager

tri *m* [*ordinateur*] sort

tri postal *m* mail sorting

tribunal *m* court

tribunal de commerce *m* trade tribunal

tribunal des prud'hommes *m* industrial tribunal

trier to sort

trimestre *m* quarter

trimestriel quarterly

triple: en triple exemplaire in triplicate

trombone *m* paper clip

TSVP (=tournez s'il vous plaît) PTO

TTC (=toutes taxes comprises) inclusive of tax

TVA (=taxe sur la valeur ajoutée) *f* VAT

type de caractères *m* typeface

unité monétaire *f* monetary unit

urgent urgent

usine clés-en-main *f* turnkey plant

usine pilote *f* pilot plant

usufruit *m* usufruct, life interest

usure *f* wear

utilsateur final *m* end user

V

vacances *fpl:* **être en vacances** to be on holiday
vacataire *mf* holiday worker
vacations *fpl* holidays
valable valid
valeur comptable *f* book value
valeur marchande *f* market value
valeur d'achat *f* purchase value
valeur d'inventaire *f* balance sheet value
valeurs bancaires *fpl* bank shares
valeurs mobilières *fpl* shares
valeurs à revenu fixe *fpl* fixed income securities
valeurs à revenu variable *fpl* floating rate securities
valeurs de bourse *fpl* quoted securities
validation *f* [*d'un document*] authentication
valider to validate; [*document*] to authenticate; [*ordinateur*] to confirm
validité *f* validity
valoir to be worth
variation de stock *f* change in stock
vendre à crédit to sell on credit
vendre à perte to sell at a loss
vendre à terme to sell forward
vendre au comptant to sell for cash
vendre de gré à gré to sell privately
vente *f* sale
vente directe *f* direct selling
vente à crédit *f* credit sale

vente à domicile *f* door-to-door selling
vente à terme *f* forward sale
vente au détail *f* retailing
vente en gros *f* wholesaling
vente par correspondance *f* mail order (selling)
ventilation *f* [*de chiffres etc*] breakdown
ventiler [*chiffres etc*] to break down
vérificateur *m* auditor
vérification *f* audit
vérifier to audit
versement *m* payment, instalment
versement d'espèces *m* cash deposit
versements échelonnés *mpl* staggered payments
verser to pay; [*dans un compte*] to pay in, to deposit
verser qch au crédit de qn to credit sb with sth
verser un acompte to make a downpayment
VI (=valeur d'inventaire) *f* balance sheet value
vice apparent *m* obvious defect
vice-président *m* vice-chairman, vice-president *Am*
vice de fabrication *m* manufacturing defect
vice de forme *m* legal technicality
vidéoconférence *f* video-conference
vidéoconférences *fpl* videoconferencing

vigueur: en vigueur [*tarifs, règlements*] in force
virement *m* transfer
virement bancaire *m* bank transfer
virement postal *m* post office transfer
virement SWIFT *m* SWIFT transfer
virement télégraphique *m* cable transfer
virement par courrier *m* mail transfer
virement par télex *m* telex transfer
virer to transfer
virgule *f* comma
visé à l'article ... referred to in article ...
viser un effet to stamp a bill
vitesse de frappe à la minute/à l'heure *f* keystrokes per minute/hour
volume annuel de production *m* annual (volume of) production
volume des ventes *m* sales volume
voyage d'affaires *m* business trip; *être en voyage d'affaires* to be away on business
voyager pour affaires to travel on business
voyageur de commerce *m* commercial traveller, travelling salesman
VPC (=vente par correspondance) *f* mail order (selling)
vrac: en vrac [*marchandise*] in bulk
vu et approuvé seen and approved
vue: à vue at sight

Z

ZI (=zone industrielle) *f* industrial estate
zone postale *f* postal area

zone de libre-échange *f* free-trade area

A

A3 A3 *m*

A4 A4 *m*

A5 A5 *m*

above ci-dessus

above-mentioned mentionné ci-dessus

abroad à l'étranger

absence absence *f*

absent absent

absenteeism absentéisme *m*

abstract résumé *m*

accent accent *m*

to **accept** accepter

acceptable acceptable

acceptance acceptation *f*

acceptance bill traite contre acceptation *f*

to **access** accéder à

accommodation allowance aide au logement *f*, indemnité de logement *f*

accompanied accompagné

accordance: in accordance with conformément à, en conformité avec; *in accordance with your instructions* suivant vos instructions

account compte *m*; *to pay something on account* donner un acompte

account balance [*status*] situation de compte *f*; [*after audit*] reliquat de compte *m*

account charges frais de tenue de compte *mpl*

account credit avoir de compte *m*

account number numéro de compte *m*

account position situation de compte *f*

account receivable compte client *m*, créance (client) *f*

accountancy comptabilité *f*

accountant comptable *mf*

accounting comptabilité *f*, compta *f*

accounting entry sheet/form bordereau de saisie *m*

accounting firm cabinet d'expertise comptable *m*

accounts comptes *mpl*; *to enter in the accounts* comptabiliser; *who does your accounts?* qui est-ce qui fait votre comptabilité ?

accounts clerk aide-comptable *mf*

accounts (department) service comptable *m*

accounts payable book/ledger livre des créanciers *m*

accounts receivable book/ledger livre des débiteurs *m*

accounts software logiciel de comptabilité *m*

accrued interest intérêt(s) couru(s) *m(pl)*

accruing interest intérêt(s) à échoir *m(pl)*

to **accumulate** accumuler

accumulation accumulation *f*

to **acknowledge receipt of** accuser réception de

acknowledgement (of receipt) accusé de réception *m*, avis de réception *m*

acoustic hood capot antibruit *m*

acquisition acquisition *f*

acting par intérim, intérimaire

acting manager directeur intérimaire *m*

action action *f*; *legal action* action (en justice) *f*

activity activité *f*

acute (accent) accent aigu *m*

to **adapt** adapter

adaptor adaptateur *m*; [*mains*] adaptateur (secteur) *m*

to **add** additionner, ajouter

to **add up** additionner

to **add up to** se chiffrer à

adding up addition *f*

addition addition *f*

additional supplémentaire, complémentaire

additional charge supplément de prix *m*

address adresse *f*

to **address** adresser

to **address a letter to** adresser une lettre à

address and phone number coordonnées *fpl*

address book carnet d'adresses *m*

address for invoicing adresse de facturation *f*

address label étiquette d'adresse *f*

address space cadre-adresse *m*

addressed to destiné à

addressee destinataire *mf*

addressing adressage *m*

addressing machine machine à adresser *f*

adequate suffisant

adjournment suspension *f*

to **adjust** ajuster

to **adjust to** s'adapter à

adjustment ajustement *m*

admin gestion administrative *f*

administration administration *f*, gestion administrative *f*

administration costs frais de gestion *mpl*

administration (department) service administratif *m*

administrative administratif

administrative costs coûts administratifs *mpl*

administrative headquarters siège administratif *m*

administrative staff personnel administratif *m*

administrative work travail administratif *m*

administrator: to be a good administrator être un bon administrateur

admission admission *f*

to **adopt a resolution** adopter une résolution

adoption leave congé d'adoption *m*

advance avance *f*, avance de fonds *f*

advance payment paiement anticipé *m*, paiement d'avance *m*

advertisement annonce *f*; [*for product*] réclame *f*; *to reply to an advertisement* répondre à une annonce; *to put an advertisement in a paper* insérer une annonce dans un journal

advertising publicité *f*

advertising *adj* publicitaire

advertising agency agence de publicité *f*, bureau de publicité *m*

advertising brochure plaquette publicitaire *f*

advertising campaign campagne

publicitaire *f*, campagne de
publicité *f*

advertising space espace
publicitaire *m*

advice note avis *m*

to **advise** aviser; [*give consultancy*]
conseiller

advising bank banque notificatrice *f*

advisory board comité consultatif *m*

affiliated affilié

affiliated company société affiliée *f*

affiliated member affilié *m*

aforementioned sus-dénommé

after-sales (department) service
après-vente *m*

after-sales service service après-
vente *m*, SAV *m*

after tax après imposition, après
impôt

agency agence *f*

agency contract contrat d'agence *m*

agenda ordre du jour *m*

agent agent *m*, représentant *m*; [*for
product distribution*]
concessionnaire *mf*

AGM (=Annual General Meeting)
AG *f*

to **agree** être d'accord

to **agree on** convenir de

to **agree with** être d'accord avec

agreed: as agreed comme convenu

agreement accord *m*; [*formal*]
convention *f*

aid aide *f*

air: by air par avion

airline compagnie d'aviation *f*

airmail poste aérienne *f*; *by airmail*
par avion

airmail paper papier avion *m*

air waybill connaissement aérien *m*

to **align** aligner

all-in tout compris

all-risks insurance assurance tous

risques *f*, assurance multirisque *f*

to **allocate** allouer

allotted budget enveloppe
budgétaire *f*

alphabetical alphabétique

alphabetical filing classement par
ordre alphabétique *m*

alphabetical order ordre
alphabétique *m*

alphabetically alphabétiquement

alphanumerical filing classement
alphanumérique *m*

ambassador ambassadeur *m*

amended invoice facture
rectificative *f*

amendment modification *f*,
amendement *m*

amendment of a contract
modification d'un contrat *f*

amount montant *m*

amount due montant dû *m*

amount exclusive of VAT base hors
taxe *f*

ampersand "et" commercial (&) *m*

to **analyse** analyser

analysis analyse *f*

analyst analyste *mf*

angle bracket chevron *m*

to **annotate** annoter

annotated draft brouillon annoté *m*

annotation annotation *f*

annual annuel

annual accounts comptes
annuels *mpl*

annual contribution [*to pension
scheme etc*] cotisation annuelle *f*

annual earnings [*of company*]
recette(s) annuelle(s) *f(pl)*

annual general meeting assemblée
générale *f*, assemblée générale
ordinaire *f*

annual guaranteed salary salaire
annuel garanti *m*

annual income revenu annuel *m*

annual premium prime annuelle *f*

annual report rapport annuel *m*

annual sales figures chiffre d'affaires annuel *m*

annual turnover chiffre d'affaires annuel *m*

annual (volume of) production volume annuel de production *m*

annually par an

annuity annuité *f*

answer réponse *f*

to **answer a letter** répondre à une lettre

answering machine répondeur *m*

to **apologize** s'excuser

apology excuse *f*

to **appear** [*in accounts etc*] figurer

to **append** ajouter

appendix annexe *f*, appendice *m*

applicant candidat *m*, postulant *m*

application demande *f*; [*for job*] candidature *f*

to **apply** appliquer

to **apply for a job** poser sa candidature à un poste

to **apply to** s'adresser à

to **appoint sb manager** nommer qn directeur

to **appoint sb to the position of** nommer qn au poste de

appointment [*with sb*] rendez-vous *m*; *to make an appointment with* prendre rendez-vous avec

appointment to a post nomination à un poste *f*

appointments diary agenda *m*

appropriate approprié; *check the appropriate box* cocher la case appropriée; *to take appropriate action* agir en conséquence

approval agrément *m*, approbation *f*; *on approval* à l'essai

to **approve** approuver; [*dealer, distributor*] agréer

approximate approximatif

to **arbitrate** arbitrer

arbitration arbitrage *m*

arbitration clause clause d'arbitrage *f*

arbitration ruling décision arbitrale *f*

archives archives *fpl*

archivist archiviste *mf*

area director directeur régional *m*

area manager directeur régional *m*

area of operations branche d'activité *f*

argument [*for or against something*] argumentation *f*

arrangement arrangement *m*

arrears arrérages *mpl*, arriéré *m*; *in arrears* arriéré; *to pay in arrears* payer en arriéré

arrow key touche de direction *f*, touche fléchée *f*

article article *m*

as per advice suivant avis

as per bill of lading suivant connaissement

as per invoice selon facture

asap (=as soon as possible) dans les plus brefs délais

ASCII file fichier ASCII *m*

to **ask for** demander

to **assemble** assembler

assembly line chaîne *f*

assembly line work travail à la chaîne *m*

assets actif *m*

to **assign** affecter

assignment [*of resources*] affectation *f*; [*task*] tâche *f*

assistant assistant *m*

assistant *adj* adjoint

assistant accountant aide-

comptable *mf*
assistant director sous-directeur *m*
assistant manager sous-directeur *m*
associate *adj* adjoint
association association *f*
assured [*person insured*] assuré *m*
asterisk astérisque *m*
attached to annexé à
to **attend** assister à
to **attend a meeting** assister à une
assemblée
attendance list liste de présence *f*
attendance register registre de
présence *m*
attendance sheet fiche de présence *f*,
feuille de présence *f*
attention: for the attention of à
l'attention de
audioconference audioconférence *f*
audiotyping audiotypie *f*
audiotypist audiotypiste *mf*
audit audit *m*, contrôle de
comptes *m*
to **audit** apurer
auditing apurement *m*
auditor vérificateur *m*; *firm of
auditors* cabinet d'audit *m*
to **authenticate** authentifier, valider
to **authenticate a signature** légaliser
une signature
authenticated signature signature

légalisée *f*
authentication authentification *f*,
validation *f*; [*of signature*]
légalisation *f*
authenticity authenticité *f*
to **authorize** autoriser
to **authorize a payment** ordonnancer
un paiement
authorized autorisé
authorized distributor distributeur
agréé *m*
authorized signatory list liste des
signatures autorisées *f*
authorized to sign habilité à signer
automatable automatisable
automatic centring centrage
automatique *m*
automatic dialling composition
automatique de numéros *f*
**automatic time and date stamping
machine** dateur automatique *m*
availability disponibilité *f*
available disponible
available means moyens
disponibles *mpl*
average moyenne *f*
to **avoid tax** échapper à l'impôt
awaiting collection en souffrance
award [*of contract*] adjudication *f*
AZERTY keyboard clavier
AZERTY *m*

B

to **backdate** antidater
back-dated rétroactif
backhander pot-de-vin *m*, dessous-de-table *m*
back pay rappel de salaire *m*
backslash barre oblique inversée *f*
backspace retour arrière *m*
backup (copy) copie de secours *f*
backup *adj* [*disk, copy*] de secours
to **back up** [*disk*] sauvegarder
backer bailleur de fonds *m*
BACS (=bank automated credit service) mode bancaire de paiement automatisé *m*
bad debt créance non recouvrable *f*
badge badge *m*
bailiff huissier *m*
balance solde *m*; [*remainder*] restant *m*
to **balance** équilibrer
balance due redû *m*
balance of an account [*status*] situation d'un compte *f*; [*after audit*] reliquat d'un compte *m*
balance sheet bilan *m*, bilan comptable *m*
balance sheet value valeur d'inventaire *f*
ballpoint (pen) stylo-bille *m*
bank banque *f*
bank *adj* bancaire, de banque
to **bank with** avoir un compte à
bank account compte bancaire *m*; *to have a bank account* avoir un

compte en banque
bank advice note avis de la banque *m*
bank balance situation de compte *f*
bank book livret de compte *m*
bank branch code code guichet *m*
bank charges frais de tenue de compte *mpl*, frais de banque *mpl*
bank clerk employé de banque *m*, commis de banque *m*
bank commission commission bancaire *f*
bank credit crédit bancaire *m*
bank details relevé d'identité bancaire *m*, RIB *m*
bank draft traite bancaire *f*
bank employee employé de banque *m*
bank guarantee garantie bancaire *f*
bank holiday jour férié *m*, jour chômé *m*
bank interest intérêt bancaire *m*
bank loan prêt bancaire *m*
bank manager directeur de banque *m*
banknote billet de banque *m*
bank references références bancaires *fpl*
bank sort code code banque *m*, numéro d'identité bancaire *m*
bank statement relevé de compte *m*
bank transfer virement bancaire *m*
bank transfer advice avis de virement *m*
bankable paper papier bancable *m*

banker banquier *m*

banking *adj* bancaire

banking law droit bancaire *m*

bankrupt: to go bankrupt faire faillite; *to be bankrupt* être en faillite

bankruptcy faillite *f*

bankruptcy proceedings procédure de faillite *f*

bar chart diagramme à barres *m*, graphique à tuyaux d'orgue *m*

bar code code (à) barre *m*, code barres *m*

to **bargain** marchander

bargaining marchandage *m*

basic de base

basic rate tarif de base *m*

basic salary traitement de base *m*, salaire de base *m*

basic wage salaire de base *m*

basis base *f*

basis of calculations base de calcul *f*

batch lot *m*

B/E (=bill of exchange) lettre de change *f*

to **bear a signature** porter une signature

bearer porteur *m*; *made out to bearer* libellé au porteur

bearer bond obligation au porteur *f*

bearer cheque chèque au porteur *m*

bearer of shares porteur d'actions *m*

before tax hors taxe, HT; [*income*] avant impôt

to **begin a piece of work** entamer un travail

behalf: on behalf of sb de la part de qn

below ci-après, ci-dessous

beneficiary bénéficiaire *mf*; [*of family allowance etc*] allocataire *mf*

benefit [*paid by State*] allocation *f*

benefit in kind avantage en nature *m*

bid offre *f*, offre commerciale *f*

biker [*courier*] coursier *m*

bilingual secretary secrétaire bilingue *mf*

bill [*invoice*] facture *f*; [*commercial*] effet de commerce *m*

bill of exchange effet *m*, lettre de change *f*, traite *f*

bill of lading connaissement *m*, connaissement maritime *m*

bill of sale contrat d'achat *m*

billing facturation *f*

biro® stylo-bille *m*

birth certificate extrait de naissance *m*

black: to be in the black être en crédit

blank cheque chèque en blanc *m*

blank page page blanche *f*

block bloc *m*

block capitals caractères d'imprimerie *mpl*

block of text bloc de texte *m*

blocked account compte bloqué *m*

blotter buvard *m*

board conseil d'administration *m*, conseil d'entreprise *m*

board meeting réunion du conseil (d'administration) *f*

board of directors conseil d'administration *m*, conseil d'entreprise *m*

board room salle du conseil *f*

body organisme *m*

body corporate personne morale *f*

bold gras *m*

bold character caractère gras *m*

boldface écriture grasse *f*

bold typeface écriture grasse *f*

bond obligation *f*

bonus boni *m*, bonification *f*, bonus *m*

book-keeper employé aux
écritures *m*
bookkeeping tenue des livres *f*
book of accounts livre de comptes *m*
book value valeur comptable *f*
to **boost production** relancer la
production
border frontière *f*
to **borrow** emprunter
to **borrow sth from sb** emprunter
qch à qn
borrower emprunteur *m*
boss chef *m*, patron *m*
bottom: at the bottom of the page
en bas de page
bottom margin marge inférieure *f*
to **bounce: cheque that bounces**
chèque en bois *m*, chèque sans
provision *m*
box boîte *f*; [*on screen*] case *f*,
encadré *m*
box file boîte-archive *f*
bracket parenthèse *f*; *in brackets*
entre parenthèses
branch succursale *f*; [*of bank*]
agence *f*
branch manager directeur
d'agence *m*, directeur de
succursale *m*
branch office succursale *f*, bureau-
satellite *m*
brand image image de marque *f*
brand manager directeur de
produit *m*
breach rupture *f*, rupture abusive *f*
breakdown [*of figures*] ventilation *f*
to **break down** [*figures*] ventiler
breakeven point seuil de
rentabilité *m*
break-up value valeur d'inventaire *f*
bribe pot-de-vin *m*, dessous-de-
table *m*
brief: in brief en bref

to **brief** briefer
briefcase serviette *f*
briefing briefing *m*
brochure brochure *f*
broker courtier *m*
brokerage courtage *m*
brown wrapping paper (papier)
kraft *m*
budget budget *m*
budget *adj* budgétaire
budget allocation enveloppe
budgétaire *f*
budgetary budgétaire
budgeting budgétisation *f*
bulk: in bulk en gros
bulldog clip attache de bureau *m*
bulletin bulletin *m*
bundle liasse *f*
business: to do business faire des
affaires *fpl*
business [*company*] firme *f*,
entreprise *f*; [*line of business*]
activité *f*; [*activity*] affaires *fpl*;
business for sale fonds de
commerce à vendre; *to be away on
business* être en voyage d'affaires
business *adj* commercial, d'affaires
business assignment mission
commerciale *f*
business card carte de visite *f*
business correspondence
correspondance commerciale *f*
business documents documents
commerciaux *mpl*
business enterprise entreprise
commerciale *f*
business letter lettre commerciale *f*
business lunch déjeuner
d'affaires *m*
businessman homme d'affaires *m*
business management gestion
d'entreprise *f*; [*study*] économie
d'entreprise *f*

business manager gérant d'affaires *m*
business meeting rendez-vous d'affaires *m*
business people gens d'affaires *mpl*
business premises locaux commerciaux *mpl*
business relations relations d'affaires *fpl*, relations commerciales *fpl*
business studies économie d'entreprise *f*

business trip voyage d'affaires *m*
businesswoman femme d'affaires *f*
to **buy** acheter
buy-out rachat de société *m*
buyer acheteur *m*
buyer credit crédit-acheteur *m*
buying department service des achats *m*
bylaws [*Am: of company*] statuts de société *mpl*
by-product sous-produit *m*

C/A (=checking account) *Am* C/C *m*, CCB *m*
C/A (=cheque account) C/C *m*, CCB *m*
C/A (=current account) C/C *m*, CCB *m*
cable câble *m*
to **calculate** calculer
calculation calcul *m*, décompte *m*
calculator calculatrice *f*; [*pocket*] calculette *f*
calendar calendrier *m*
calendar year année civile *f*
call appel *m*; *there is a call for you* on vous demande au téléphone; *to take the call* prendre la communication
to **call** appeler

to **call a general meeting** convoquer une assemblée générale
to **call sb** appeler qn au téléphone, téléphoner à qn
to **call the shareholders to a meeting** convoquer les actionnaires
call charges frais de communication *mpl*
call holding mise en attente d'appels *f*
callout maintenance insurance assurance maintenance visite *f*
callable remboursable
caller correspondant *m*, appelant *m*
calling of a meeting convocation d'une assemblée *f*
to **cancel** annuler

to **cancel a cheque** annuler un chèque

to **cancel a contract** dénoncer un contrat

to **cancel an order** annuler une commande

cancellation annulation *f*

to **canvass** prospecter

canvasser prospecteur *m*

capacity: in one's capacity as en sa qualité de

capital [*assets*] capital *m*

capital [*letter*] majuscule *f*; *in capitals* en majuscules *fpl*

capital letter majuscule *f*

caps lock key touche de verrouillage des majuscules *f*

carbon carbone *m*

card carte *f*; [*business card*] carte (de visite) *f*; [*record card*] fiche *f*

cardboard carton *m*; [*thin*] bristol *m*

cardboard *adj* en carton

card index box boîte à fiches *f*, fichier *m*

card-index filing cabinet fichier *m*

card-index system fichier *m*

career carrière *f*

cargo cargaison *f*

carriage frais de port *mpl*

carriage forward port dû, port avancé

carriage free franco de port, franc de port

carriage insurance paid port payé, assurance comprise

carriage paid port payé

carriage release arm levier de dégagement du chariot *m*

carriage return retour chariot *m*

to **carry out** exécuter

to **carry out one's duties** exercer ses fonctions

carrying forward report *m*

carrying out an order exécution d'un ordre *f*

cartridge cartouche *f*

cash liquide *m*, argent liquide *m*, argent comptant *m*; *to buy for cash* acheter au comptant

cash *adv* au comptant

to **cash** encaisser

to **cash a cheque** encaisser un chèque

cash balance situation de caisse *f*

cash book brouillard *m*, livre de caisse *m*, livre de dépenses *m*

cash budget budget de trésorerie *m*

cash deposit versement d'espèces *m*, dépôt d'espèces *m*

cash discount remise sur paiement au comptant *f*

cash dispenser distributeur automatique *m*, guichet automatique *m*, terminal monétique *m*

cashflow trésorerie *f*

cash in hand argent en caisse *m*

cash in till encaisse *f*

cash on delivery paiement à la livraison *m*

cash payment paiement au comptant *m*, paiement comptant *m*, paiement en espèces *m*

cash point distributeur automatique *m*, guichet automatique *m*, terminal monétique *m*

cash purchase achat au comptant *m*

cash received entrée d'argent *f*

cash transaction marché au comptant *m*

cash voucher pièce de caisse *f*

cash with order envoi contre paiement *m*

catalogue catalogue *m*

to **catalogue** cataloguer

category catégorie *f*

cc: copie :
to **cc sb** envoyer une copie à qn
cedilla cédille *f*
ceiling plafond *m*
cell [*in spreadsheet*] cellule *f*
cellular telephone radio
  téléphone *m*
central central
central bank banque centrale *f*
central buying group centrale
  d'achat *f*
centralization centralisation *f*
to **centralize** centraliser
to **centre** centrer
centred centré
centring centrage *m*
CEO (=Chief Executive Officer)
  PDG *m*
certificate certificat *m*, attestation *f*
certification certification *f*
certified authentique
certified by a notary notarié
certified copy copie authentique *f*
certified public accountant *Am*
  expert-comptable *m*
certified true copy copie certifiée
  conforme *f*
to **certify** certifier
to **certify documents** légaliser des
  documents
C&F (=cost and freight) C et F
to **chair a meeting** présider une
  assemblée
chairman président *m*
chairman and managing director
  Président-directeur général *m*,
  PDG *m*
chairman of the board Président du
  conseil *m*
Chamber of Commerce Chambre de
  commerce *f*
**Chamber of Commerce and
  Industry** Chambre de commerce

et de l'industrie *f*
change modification *f*
change in stock variation de stock *f*
channels: to go through channels
  passer par la voie hiérarchique
character caractère *m*
character insert insertion de
  caractère *f*
character spacing espacement des
  caractères *m*
**charge: is there a charge for
  delivery?** est-ce qu'il faut payer la
  livraison ?
charge: to be in charge of être
  chargé de, piloter; *person in
  charge* responsable *mf*
charge card carte accréditive *f*
charge for calls frais de
  communication *mpl*
chargeable: to be chargeable to être
  à la charge de
chargeable distance distance
  tarifaire *f*
chart graphique *m*
charter *adj* nolisé
to **charter** fréter, noliser
chartered accountant expert-
  comptable *m*
chartering nolisement *m*
to **chase up a debtor** relancer un
  débiteur
check [*Am: financial*] chèque *m*
check contrôle *m*
to **check** contrôler
check the appropriate box *Am*
  cocher la case appropriée
checking account *Am* compte
  chèque *m*
cheque chèque *m*
cheque book carnet de chèques *m*,
  chéquier *m*
chequebook stub souche de
  chéquier *f*

cheque made out to bearer chèque
au porteur *m*

chief accountant chef comptable *m*

chief executive officer Président-
directeur général *m*

chronological chronologique; *in
chronological order* par ordre
chronologique

chronological filing classement par
ordre chronologique *m*

chronologically chronologiquement

CIF (=cost insurance freight) CAF

circular lettre circulaire *f*

circumflex accent circonflexe *m*

circumstances circonstances *fpl*

circumstances beyond our control
circonstances indépendantes de
notre volonté *fpl*

civil servant fonctionnaire *mf*

claim réclamation *f; to make a claim
against* faire une réclamation
auprès de

claimant réclamant *m*

claims book livre des réclamations *m*

classification classification *f*

classified ad petite annonce *f*

to **classify** classifier

clause of a/the contract clause
contractuelle *f*

clean: to make a clean copy of
mettre au net

to **clear** [*chèque*] compenser

clearing bank banque
compensatrice *f*

clerical error erreur *f*; [*in something
written*] faute d'écriture *f*

clerk commis *m*, clerc *m*

to **click (on)** [*with mouse*] cliquer
(sur)

client client *m*

client list liste de clients *f*

clientele clientèle *f*

to **clock on** pointer

clocking on pointage *m*

to **close** fermer

to **close a deal** arrêter un marché

to **close a meeting** mettre fin à une
réunion

to **close an account** clôturer un
compte, clore un compte

closing of an account clôture d'un
compte *f*, fermeture d'un compte *f*

closing time heure de fermeture *f*

closure [*to letter*] formule finale *f*

cod (=cash on delivery) paiement à
la livraison

to **code** codifier

coded [*encoded*] chiffré

coding codification *f*

coding method mode de
codification *m*

co-director codirecteur *m*

to **collaborate** collaborer

collaboration collaboration *f*

colleague collaborateur *m*,
collègue *mf*

to **collect** [*goods*] enlever; [*debt*]
recouvrer

to **collect taxes** lever des impôts

collection enlèvement *m*; [*of debt*]
recouvrement *m*

collection and delivery enlèvement
et livraison *m*

collection (department) service de
recouvrement *m*

collection of taxes levée des impôts *f*

collective collectif

collective agreement contrat
collectif *m*, convention collective *f*

collective bargaining négociation
collective *f*

colon deux-points *m*

column colonne *f; putting into
columns* colonnage *m*

column of figures colonne de
chiffres *f*

co-management cogérance *f*
to **come to an agreement on** se
  mettre d'accord sur, tomber
  d'accord sur
comma virgule *f*
command commande *f*
commerce commerce *m*
commercial commercial
commercial bank banque
  commerciale *f*
commercial bill effet de
  commerce *m*
commercial director directeur
  commercial *m*
commercial document document
  commercial *m*
commercial invoice facture
  commerciale *f*
commercial law législation
  commerciale *f*, droit commercial *m*
commercial manager directeur
  commercial *m*
commercial paper effets de
  commerce *mpl*
commercial rent loyer
  commercial *m*
commercial traveller commis
  voyageur *m*, voyageur de
  commerce *m*
commission commission *f*
commitment engagement *m*; *without
  any commitment on your part*
  sans aucun engagement de votre
  part
committee meeting réunion de
  comité *f*
committee member membre du
  comité *m*
Common Market Marché
  Commun *m*
communications director directeur
  de la communication *m*
communications manager directeur
de la communication *m*
communications software logiciel
  de communication *m*
Community law droit
  communautaire *m*
company société *f*, entreprise *f*
company earnings revenu
  d'entreprise *m*
company head tête d'entreprise *f*
company law droit des sociétés *m*
company letterhead en-tête de
  société *m*; *on company letterhead*
  sur papier à en-tête de société
company magazine revue
  d'entreprise *f*, journal
  d'entreprise *m*
company name dénomination
  sociale *f*, raison sociale *f*
company registration number
  numéro d'enregistrement de
  société *m*
company secretary secrétaire
  général *m*
company signature (and stamp)
  signature sociale *f*
comparative study étude
  comparative *f*
compatible compatible *m*
compensable indemnisable
to **compensate** indemniser,
  dédommager; *to be compensated
  for* être dédommagé de
to **compensate sb for sth** indemniser
  qn de qch
compensation indemnisation *f*,
  indemnité *f*, dédommagement *m*
to **compete with** concurrencer
competition concurrence *f*
competitive compétitif,
  concurrentiel
competitiveness compétitivité *f*
competitor concurrent *m*
to **complain** faire une réclamation

complaint réclamation *f*; *to make a complaint* faire une réclamation
to **complete** achever
to **complete a form** remplir un formulaire
completion achèvement *m*
completion date date d'achèvement *f*
compliment: with the compliments of avec les compliments de
compliments slip papillon présentant les compliments de la société *m*
to **comply with** se conformer à
to **comply with a contract** respecter un contrat
to **comply with a request** accéder à une demande
compound interest intérêt composé *m*
comprehensive insurance assurance tous risques *f*, assurance multirisque *f*
comprehensive policy police tous risques *f*
compromise compromis *m*
compulsory obligatoire
computer ordinateur *m*; *on computer* sur ordinateur
computer-aided assisté par ordinateur
computer-literate qui a des connaissances en informatique
computer manager directeur informatique *m*
computer network réseau informatique *m*, réseau d'ordinateurs *m*
computer operator opérateur (sur ordinateur) *m*, opératrice (sur ordinateur) *f*
computer printout impression *f*; [*continuous*] listing *m*, listage *m*
computerizable informatisable
to **computerize** informatiser

computerized informatisé
concession concession *f*
conditions of sale conditions de vente *fpl*
conference conférence *f*
conference room salle de conférence *f*
confidential confidentiel
confidentiality confidentialité *f*
to **confirm** confirmer
confirmation confirmation *f*; *in confirmation of* en confirmation de
confirmation of an order confirmation d'une commande *f*
confirmation of receipt accusé de réception *m*
confirming bank banque confirmatrice *f*
connection charge frais d'accès *mpl*
consent consentement *m*
to **consign goods** consigner des marchandises
consignee consignataire *m*, réceptionnaire *mf*
consignment consignation *f*, envoi *m*
to **consult** consulter
consultancy [*firm*] cabinet conseil *m*
consultant conseiller *m*, consultant *m*
consumer consommateur *m*
consumer credit crédit au consommateur *m*, crédit à la consommation *m*
consumer goods produits de grande consommation *mpl*
consumer market marché grand public *m*, MGP *m*
contact contact *m*; [*agent*] agent de contact *m*
to **contact: I'll contact you next week** je prendrai contact avec vous la semaine prochaine; *where can I contact you?* où puis-je vous

joindre ?

to **contain** contenir

container conteneur *m*

continuation of a letter suite de lettre *f*

continuous paper papier continu *m*

contract contrat *m*

contract of employment contrat de travail *m*

contract price list série de prix *f*

contracting party contractant *m*

contractual price prix contractuel *m*

contrary to the terms of the contract contraire au contrat

to **contribute to** contribuer à; [*to pension plan etc*] cotiser à

contribution contribution *f*; [*to pension plan etc*] cotisation *f*

to **control** contrôler

control key touche de contrôle *f*

controller contrôleur de gestion *m*

convenience: at your own convenience à votre convenance

convention congrès *m*

conversion table tableau de conversion *m*

to **convert** convertir

to **convert francs into dollars** convertir des francs en dollars

convertibility convertibilité *f*

convertible convertible

to **convey information** communiquer des renseignements

to **co-operate** coopérer

co-operation coopération *f*

co-operative coopératif

coordinator coordinateur *m*

coordination coordination *f*

co-owner copropriétaire *mf*

co-ownership copropriété *f*

co-partner coassocié *m*

copier copieur *m*, copieuse *f*

copy photocopie *f*; [*sample*]

exemplaire *m*

to **copy** [*photocopy*] photocopier

copy disk disquette de copie *f*

copy-holder porte-copies *m*

cordless phone téléphone sans fil *m*

corporate corporatif

corporate body personne morale *f*

corporate income revenu d'entreprise *m*

corporation tax impôt sur les sociétés *m*, IS *m*

to **correct** corriger, rectifier

correction correction *f*, rectificatif *m*, rectification *f*

correction fluid liquide correcteur *m*

to **correspond with** correspondre avec

correspondence correspondance *f*

correspondence tray bac à correspondance *m*

correspondent correspondant *m*

co-signatory cosignataire *mf*

cost: at cost à prix coûtant

cost and freight coût et fret *m*

cost centre centre d'analyse *m*

cost-of-living allowance indemnité de vie chère *f*

cost price prix coûtant *m*, prix de revient *m*, coût de revient *m*; *at cost price* à prix coûtant

costly onéreux

costs frais *mpl*

count décompte *m*

to **count** compter

counter guichet *m*

counter clerk guichetier *m*

counterfoil book carnet à souches *m*

counter-offer contre-offre *f*

counterpart homologue *mf*

to **countersign** contresigner

counting comptage *m*

coupon coupon *m*, bon *m*

courier [*international*] courrier *m*;
[*local*] coursier *m*
court tribunal *m*; *out of court* à
l'amiable
Court of Appeal Cour d'Appel *f*
Court of Justice Cour de Justice *f*
court ruling décision de justice *f*
cover couverture *f*
to **cover** couvrir
cover note note de couverture *f*
cover sheet page de garde *f*
covered couvert
covering document feuille
d'accompagnement *f*
covering letter lettre
d'accompagnement *f*
cps (=characters per second) cps
credit crédit *m*; [*in an account*]
avoir *m*; *on credit* à crédit; *to buy
on credit* acheter à crédit; *to be in
credit* être créditeur; *account in
credit* compte créditeur
credit *adj* à crédit
to **credit** créditer
to **credit an amount to an account**
porter un montant au crédit d'un
compte
to **credit sb with sth** verser qch au
crédit de qn
credit advice avis de crédit *m*
credit balance solde créditeur *m*
credit card carte de crédit *f*
credit ceiling plafond de crédit *m*
credit guarantee institution caisse
de garantie *f*
credit institution institut de
crédit *m*, institution de crédit *f*
credit limit limite de crédit *f*
credit line ligne de crédit *f*
credit margin marge de crédit *f*
credit note note de crédit *f*,
bordereau de crédit *m*, facture
d'avoir *f*

credit period délai de crédit *m*, délai
de paiement *m*
credit purchase achat à crédit *m*
credit restriction encadrement du
crédit *m*
credit sale vente à crédit *f*
credit squeeze encadrement du
crédit *m*
credit to be carried forward crédit à
reporter *m*
credit-worthiness solvabilité *f*
credit-worthy solvable
credited with crédité de
creditor créancier *m*
to **cross a cheque** barrer un chèque
to **cross out** barrer
cross-reference renvoi *m*
crossed cheque chèque barré *m*
curly bracket accolade *f*
currency devise *f*
currency conversion conversion de
monnaies *f*
current actuel
current account compte courant *m*,
compte chèque *m*
current account with a bank
compte courant bancaire *m*
current account with the post office
compte courant postal *m*
current assets actif circulant *m*
current expenditure(s) dépenses
courantes *fpl*
curriculum vitae curriculum vitae *m*
cursor curseur *m*
customer client *m*
customer file fichier client *m*
customer list liste de clients *f*
customer relations manager
directeur de la clientèle *m*
customer service service
clientèle *m*
customer service department
service clientèle *m*

customers clientèle *f*
customs douane *f*
customs *adj* douanier
customs declaration déclaration en
  douane *f*
customs duties droits de
  douane *mpl*, frais de douane *mpl*
customs officer douanier *m*
customs procedure procédure
  douanière *f*

customs regulations règlements
  douaniers *mpl*
customs tariff tarif douanier *m*
to **cut staff** réduire le personnel
cut and paste couper/coller *m*
cut-throat competition concurrence
  acharnée *f*
CV (=curriculum vitae) CV *m*
cwo (=cash with order) envoi contre
  paiement

D

daily quotidien
daily allowance indemnité
  journalière *f*
daily takings recette journalière *f*
daisywheel (printer) imprimante à
  marguerite *f*
damage dommages *mpl*, dégâts *mpl*
to **damage** endommager
damaged endommagé
dash tiret *m*
database base de données *f*
data processing traitement des
  données *m*
date date *f*; *to date* à ce jour
to **date** dater; *your letter dated* votre
  lettre en date du
date of birth date de naissance *f*
date of completion date
  d'achèvement *f*

date of dispatch date d'envoi *f*
date stamp timbre dateur *m*
day book brouillard *m*, main
  courante *f*
deadline date limite *f*
deadline for submitting claims délai
  de réclamation *m*
deal affaire *f*, marché *m*
to **deal with** avoir affaire à; [*look
  after*] s'occuper de
dealer marchand *m*; [*sole
  distributor*] concessionnaire *mf*
dealership concession *f*
dear cher
debenture obligation *f*
debit débit *m*; *to the debit of* au débit
  de
debit *adj* débiteur
to **debit** débiter

to **debit an account** débiter un compte

to **debit an amount to an account** porter un montant au débit d'un compte

debit advice avis de débit *m*

debit balance solde débiteur *m*

debit note note de débit *f*

debits and credits doit et avoir *m*

debt dette *f*; [*to be recovered*] créance *f*; *in debt* endetté; *to get into debt* s'endetter

debt collection recouvrement de créances *m*

debt instrument titre de créance *m*

debtor débiteur *m*

decentralization décentralisation *f*

to **decentralize** décentraliser

to **decide on sth** adopter une décision concernant qch

decimal décimal

decimal classification classification décimale *f*

decimal coding codification décimale *f*

decimal filing classement décimal *m*

decision décision *f*; *to give a decision* se prononcer; *to make a decision* prendre une décision

decision by arbitration décision arbitrale *f*

decision-making prise de décisions *f*

declared déclaré

decrease diminution *f*

decree arrêté *m*

to **deduct** déduire, décompter

to **deduct a commission** prélever une commission

to **deduct a sum of money** défalquer une somme

deducted at source retenu à la source

deductibility déductibilité *f*

deductible déductible

deduction déduction *f*; [*from salary*] retenue *f*

deduction from wages retenue salariale *f*, prélèvement salarial *m*

deduction of a sum décompte d'une somme *m*

deed of sale acte de vente *m*

deed under hand sous seing privé

default *adj* [*computers*] par défaut

default drive lecteur par défaut *m*

defect défaut *m*, malfaçon *f*

defective défectueux

to **defer** renvoyer

to **defer payment** différer le paiement

deferral renvoi *m*

deferred renvoyé

deferred payment paiement différé *m*

deficit déficit *m*; *showing a deficit* déficitaire

deflation déflation *f*

deflationary déflationniste

degree degré *m*; [*academic*] licence *f*

delay retard *m*

to **delay payment** retarder le paiement

delay in delivery retard à la livraison *m*

delegate délégué *m*

to **delegate** déléguer

delegation délégation *f*

to **delete** effacer, supprimer

delete as appropriate rayez les mentions inutiles

delete key touche d'effacement *f*

deletion effacement *m*; *without deletions or additions* sans ratures ni surcharges

to **deliver** livrer

to **deliver to domicile** livrer à domicile

delivered free on board rendu franco bord

delivery livraison *f*

delivery address adresse de livraison *f*

delivery charges frais d'expédition *mpl*

delivery deadline terme de livraison *m*

delivery man livreur *m*

delivery note bon de livraison *m*

delivery time délai de livraison *m*

delivery van camionnette de livraison *f*

demand demande *f*, exigence(s) *f(pl)*

to **demand** demander, exiger

to **demand payment** réclamer le paiement

to **demand payment from sb** sommer qn de payer

demonstration démonstration *f*

demonstrator démonstrateur *m*

denomination: in denominations of en coupures de *fpl*

department service *m*, direction *f*; [*government*] ministère *m*

Department of Trade and Industry Ministère du Commerce et de l'Industrie *m*

departmental manager chef de service *m*

departure date date de départ *f*

departure from écart par rapport à *m*

deposit [*down payment*] arrhes *fpl*; *to make a deposit* laisser des arrhes

to **deposit** [*in bank*] déposer

to **deposit a sum of money** consigner une somme

deposit account compte livret *m*, compte de dépôt *m*

deposit book livret de dépôts *m*

deposit receipt récépissé de dépôt *m*

depositor déposant *m*

to **depreciate** se déprécier

depreciation rate taux d'amortissement *m*

depression dépression *f*

dept (=department) dépt

deputy adjoint *m*

deputy director directeur adjoint *m*

deputy manager directeur adjoint *m*

deputy managing director directeur général adjoint *m*

description of contents désignation du contenu *f*

design department bureau d'études *m*

desk diary agenda *m*

desktop calculator calculatrice *f*

desktop publishing publication assistée par ordinateur *f*

destination destination *f*

to **develop** développer

development développement *m*

diaeresis tréma *m*

diagram diagramme *m*, graphique *m*, schéma *m*; *to make a diagram of* schématiser

to **dial** *vi* numéroter

to **dial** *vt* composer

dialler composeur de numéros *m*

dialling numérotation *f*

dialling code indicatif d'appel *m*

diary agenda *m*

dictaphone® dictaphone *m*®

to **dictate** dicter

dictating machine machine à dicter *f*

dictation dictée *f*

dictionary dictionnaire *m*

differential rate tarif différentiel *m*

dimensions dimensions *fpl*

diploma diplôme *m*

direct direct

direct debit prélèvement automatique *m*

direct debit advice avis de prélèvement *m*

direct mail advertising publicité par correspondance *f*

direct selling vente directe *f*

direct tax impôt direct *m*

direct taxation contributions directes *fpl*

directions for use mode d'emploi *m*, notice explicative *f*

directive directive *f*

director directeur *m*

director's fees jetons de présence *mpl*

directory annuaire *m*; [*computers*] répertoire *m*

directory enquiries renseignements *mpl*

disability incapacité de travail *f*

discount remise *f*; [*bank*] escompte *m*

discount rate taux d'escompte *m*

disk disque *m*; [*floppy*] disquette *f*

disk drive lecteur de disques *m*; [*floppy*] lecteur de disquettes *m*

disk space espace disque *m*

diskette disquette *f*

diskette box boîte à disquettes *f*

to **dismiss** licencier, congédier, renvoyer

dismissal licenciement *m*, congédiement *m*, renvoi *m*

dismissal with notice licenciement avec préavis *m*

dismissal without notice licenciement sans préavis *m*

dispatch envoi *m*

to **dispatch** expédier

dispatch (department) expéditions *fpl*

dispatch note avis d'expédition *m*, bon d'expédition *m*

display affichage *m*

to **display** afficher

to **display prices** afficher les prix

disposable income revenu disponible *m*

disposable packaging emballage perdu *m*

dispute contestation *f*

to **distribute** distribuer, diffuser

distribution distribution *f*, diffusion *f*

distribution contract contrat de distribution *m*

distribution network réseau de distribution *m*, circuit de distribution *m*

distribution of profits répartition du bénéfice *f*

distributor distributeur *m*

to **divide** diviser

divider [*for files*] intercalaire *m*

division division *f*

dockers' strike grève des dockers *f*

docket bordereau *m*

document document *m*

document cover pochette *f*

documentary bill traite documentaire *f*

documentary credit crédit documentaire *m*

documentary credit application demande d'ouverture de crédit documentaire *f*

documentary evidence pièces justificatives *fpl*

documentation documentation *f*

documents documents *mpl*

dollar sign signe dollar *m*

domestic trade commerce intérieur *m*

door-to-door selling vente à domicile *f*

DOS prompt indicatif (du) DOS *m*

dot: "i" with two dots "i" surmonté de deux points

dot matrix printer imprimante matricielle *f*
dotted line pointillé *m*
to **double** doubler
to **double-click** cliquer deux fois
double-spaced à l'interligne double, à double interligne
double spacing interligne double *m*, double interligne *m*
doubtful debt créance douteuse *f*, client douteux *m*
to **down tools** débrayer
down-market bas de gamme
down payment acompte *m*; *to make a down payment* donner un acompte
draft ébauche *f*, brouillon *m*; [*financial*] traite *f*
draft agreement projet de contrat *m*
draft mode mode brouillon *m*
to **drag** [*with mouse*] faire glisser
to **draw a bill on** tirer une traite sur
to **draw a cheque on** tirer un chèque sur, disposer un chèque sur
to **draw at sight** tirer à vue
to **draw one's salary** toucher ses appointements
to **draw up** rédiger, élaborer

to **draw up an invoice** établir une facture
drawee tiré *m*
drawer tireur *m*; [*of bill*] souscripteur *m*
drive [*computers*] lecteur *m*
drop in prices baisse des prix *f*
DTI (=Department of Trade and Industry) Ministère du Commerce et de l'Industrie *m*
DTP (=desktop publishing) PAO *f*
due dû; *on the due date* à terme échu; *in due form* en due forme
duly dûment; *duly signed* dûment signé
dunning letter lettre de poursuite *f*
duplicate double *m*, duplicata *m*; *in duplicate* en deux exemplaires
duplicate *adj* fait en double exemplaire
to **duplicate** reprographier, polycopier
duplicating machine duplicateur *m*, machine à polycopier *f*
duplicator duplicateur *m*
duration durée *f*
duties fonctions *fpl*
duty [*excise*] droits de douane *mpl*

E

early: at your earliest convenience
dès que possible
early repayment remboursement
anticipé *m*
early retirement préretraite *f*
to **earn money** gagner de l'argent
EC (=European Community) CEE *f*
EC *adj* de la CEE
economic économique
economic recovery reprise
économique *f*
economic situation situation
économique *f*
economist économiste *mf*
economy économie *f*
ecu écu *m*
edge punched card fiche à
perforations marginales *f*
to **edit** éditer
efficient performant
eight-hour day journée de huit
heures *f*
election of employee
representatives élection des
délégués du personnel *f*
election of officers élection du
bureau *f*
electric typewriter machine à écrire
électrique *f*
electronic électronique
electronic mail courrier
électronique *m*
electronic mailbox boîte aux lettres
électronique *f*

electronic methods of payment
monnaie électronique *f*
electronic money monétique *f*
electronic payment paiement
électronique *m*
electronic transfer transfert
électronique *m*
electronic typewriter machine à
écrire électronique *f*
e-mail (=electronic mail) courrier
électronique *m*
embassy ambassade *f*
embezzlement malversation *f*
emoluments émoluments *mpl*
to **employ workers** employer des
ouvriers
employee employé *m*
employee association comité
d'entreprise *m*
employee contributions cotisations
salariales *fpl*, charges sociales
salariales *fpl*, retenues salariales *fpl*
employee profit-sharing scheme
intéressement aux résultats *m*; *to*
provide an employee profit-
sharing scheme intéresser les
employés aux bénéfices
employee representative délégué du
personnel *m*
employee's contributions
cotisations salariales *fpl*, charges
sociales salariales *fpl*, retenues
salariales *fpl*
employer employeur *m*

employer's contributions retenues patronales *fpl*, cotisations patronales *fpl*

employer's liability responsabilité patronale *f*

employers patronat *m*

employers' organization syndicat patronal *m*

employment emploi *m*

employment agency agence de placement *f*, bureau de placement *m*

employment code code du travail *m*

employment law code du travail *m*, législation du travail *f*

employment tax taxe sur les salaires *f*

EMS (=European Monetary System) SME *m*

to **encash** *Br* encaisser

encashment *Br* encaissement *m*

encl (=enclosure) PJ

to **enclose** joindre

enclosed ci-joint, ci-inclus; *please find enclosed the requested documents* veuillez trouver ci-joint les documents demandés

enclosure pièce jointe *f*

end-of-month de fin de mois

end of the financial year clôture de l'exercice *f*

end-of-year bonus gratification de fin d'année *f*

end user utilisateur final *m*

endorsable endossable

to **endorse** endosser

endorsee endossataire *mf*

endorsement endos *m*, endossement *m*

endorser endosseur *m*

to **enlarge** agrandir

enquiry demande de renseignements *f*

to **enter** enregistrer; [*data into a computer*] entrer

to **enter into** conclure

enter key touche (d')entrée *f*

entering enregistrement *m*

entering of an order enregistrement d'une commande *m*

entry [*accounts*] poste *m*, écriture *f*

envelope enveloppe *f*

equipment équipement *m*, équipements *mpl*

to **erase** [*with rubber*] gommer; [*on disk*] effacer

eraser gomme à crayon *f*

errors and omissions excepted sauf erreur ou omission

escape key touche d'échappement *f*

essential information mentions obligatoires *fpl*

establishment établissement *m*

estimate devis *m*, devis estimatif *m*

estimation of costs estimation des frais *f*

European Commission Commission européenne *f*

European Monetary System Système monétaire européen *m*

European Parliament Parlement européen *m*

to **examine** examiner

to **exceed** excéder, dépasser

exceptional circumstances circonstances exceptionnelles *fpl*

exchange échange *m*; *in exchange for payment* moyennant paiement

to **exchange letters** échanger des lettres

exchange control regulations réglementation du change *f*

exchange of goods échange de marchandises *m*

exchange of information échange d'informations *m*

exchange of letters échange de lettres *m*

exchange rate taux de change *m*

exchange rates cours des changes *m*

exchangeable échangeable

Exchequer Ministère des Finances *m*

exclusion exclusion *f*

exclusive of tax hors taxe

to **execute a contract** exécuter un contrat

executive cadre *m*

executive board directoire *m*

executive committee comité de direction *m*

executive director directeur administratif *m*, directeur gérant *m*

executive recruitment agency association pour l'emploi des cadres *f*

executive secretary secrétaire de direction *mf*

to **exempt** exonérer

to **exempt from tax** exonérer d'impôt

exempt from exonéré de

exemption from customs duty franchise douanière *f*

exemption from VAT exonération de TVA *f*

exhibition exposition *f*

exhibition hall salle d'exposition *f*, hall d'exposition *m*

exhibitor exposant *m*

to **exit** [*from a computer file*] sortir

expansion expansion *f*

expenditure dépenses *fpl*

expense account note de frais *f*

expenses frais *mpl*, note de frais *f*

expensive cher; *to be expensive* coûter cher

experienced expérimenté, chevronné

expert expert *m*

expertise savoir-faire *m*

to **expire** expirer, arriver à échéance

expired échu

expiry expiration *f*

expiry date date d'échéance *f*, date d'expiration *f*

expiry date of a contract échéance d'un contrat *f*

explanatory leaflet notice explicative *f*

to **explore the market** prospecter le marché

export exportation *f*

to **export** exporter

export bid offre export *f*

export company entreprise exportatrice *f*

export department service commercial export *m*

export director directeur export *m*

export licence licence d'exportation *f*, permis d'exportation *m*

export manager directeur export *m*

export market marché à l'export *m*

export tax taxe à l'exportation *f*

export trade commerce d'exportation *m*

exporter exportateur *m*

express exprès

to **express opinions** émettre des avis

express delivery envoi exprès *m*; *to send sth express delivery* envoyer qch par voie expresse

to **extend** prolonger

to **extend payment terms** proroger une échéance

extended maintenance insurance assurance maintenance étendue *f*

extension extension *f*, prolongation *f*; [*telephone*] poste *m*

extension number numéro de poste *m*

extra time to pay sursis de

paiement *m*
extraordinary expenses dépenses
extraordinaires *fpl*

extraordinary general meeting
assemblée générale extraordinaire *f*
eye strain fatigue oculaire *f*

facsimile fac-similé *m*
factoring company société
d'affacturage *f*
factory inspector inspecteur du
travail *m*
factory inspectorate Inspection du
Travail *f*
to **fall due** arriver à échéance
false invoice fausse facture *f*
family allowance allocations
familiales *fpl*
family business entreprise familiale *f*
FAS (=free alongside ship) FAS,
franco quai
fault défaillance *f*
favour: in favour of en faveur de
favourable favorable
favourable conditions conditions
avantageuses *fpl*
fax télécopie *f*, fax *m*
to **fax** [*a person*] envoyer un fax à;
[*a document*] faxer, envoyer par
fax
fax (machine) télécopieur *m*, fax *m*
faxable: are you faxable? est-ce
qu'on peut vous joindre par fax ?

feasibility study étude de faisabilité *f*
fees honoraires *mpl*
felt tip (pen) stylo-feutre *m*
female executive femme cadre *f*
field [*in database*] champ *m*
figure chiffre *m*; *in figures* en
chiffres
figurehead prête-nom *m*
file dossier *m*; [*computers*] fichier *m*
to **file** classer, archiver
to **file a petition in bankruptcy**
déposer son bilan
file cabinet *Am* classeur *m*
file copy copie à ranger dans les
archives *f*
file divider carte-guide *f*, guide-
classement *m*
file management [*computers*] tenue
de fichiers *f*
file name [*computers*] nom de
fichier *m*
file separator carte-guide *f*
file server serveur de fichiers *m*
file trolley bac roulant *m*
files archives *fpl*
filing classement *m*, archivage *m*

filing by geographical area classement géographique *m*

filing by subject classement idéologique *m*

filing cabinet classeur *m*, classeur à tiroirs *m*

filing clerk employé chargé du classement *m*

filing method plan de classement *m*, ordre de classement *m*

filing system mode de classement *m*

to **fill in a questionnaire** remplir un questionnaire

final payment quittance finale *f*

final settlement solde de tout compte *m*

to **finalize** mettre au point

finance finance *f*

to **finance** financer

finance (department) service financier *m*, direction financière *f*

finance director directeur financier *m*

financial financier

financial centre place financière *f*

financial controller contrôleur financier *m*

financial director directeur financier *m*

financial glossary lexique financier *m*

financial institution établissement financier *m*

financial management gestion financière *f*

financial manager directeur financier *m*

financial statement bilan financier *m*

financial year exercice *m*, exercice comptable *m*

financially financièrement

financier financier *m*

financing financement *m*

financing plan plan de financement *m*

fine [*punishment*] amende *f*

finished product produit fini *m*

fire extinguisher extincteur d'incendie *m*

fire insurance assurance incendie *f*

fireproof cabinet armoire ignifugée *f*

firm [*company*] firme *f*

firm ferme

first class mail courrier première classe *m*

fiscal year *Am* exercice *m*, exercice comptable *m*

to **fit out an office** équiper un bureau

five-day week semaine de cinq jours *f*

to **fix a date for a meeting** fixer une date de réunion

fixed fixe; *on a fixed date* à date fixe

fixed assets immobilisations *fpl*

fixed income securities valeurs à revenu fixe *fpl*

fixed interest intérêt fixe *m*

fixed salary traitement fixe *m*

fixed-term à terme fixe

fixed term contract contrat à durée déterminée *m*

fixtures and fittings agencements *mpl*, installations fixes *fpl*

flag [*for file*] papillon *m*

flap [*on envelope etc*] rabat *m*

flexibility flexibilité *f*

flexible flexible

flexible hours horaire flexible *m*, horaire variable *m*

flexitime horaire flexible *m*, horaire variable *m*

floating assets actif circulant *m*

floating rate securities valeurs à revenu variable *fpl*

floppy (disk) disquette *f*

flowchart organigramme *m*

FOB (=free on board) FOB, FAB, franco à bord

folder chemise *f*; [*computers*] dossier *m*

to **follow up** donner suite à

follow-up letter lettre de relance *f*

follow-up of orders suivi des commandes *m*

font police *f*, fonte *f*

footer pied de page *m*

force: in force en vigueur

forecast prévision *f*

foreign étranger

foreign currency monnaie étrangère *f*, devises étrangères *fpl*

foreign exchange market marché des changes *m*

foreign market marché extérieur *m*

Foreign Office Ministère des Affaires étrangères *m*

foreign trade commerce extérieur *m*

foreman contremaître *m*, chef d'équipe *m*

forged cheque faux chèque *m*

forgery contrefaçon *f*

form formulaire *m*, imprimé *m*, fiche *f*

form document document canevas *m*

form letter lettre type *f*

formal notice mise en demeure *f*

formality formalité *f*

format format *m*

to **format** mettre en forme; [*disk*] formater

to **forward** transiter; [*letter, package*] réexpédier; *please forward* à faire suivre

forward sale vente à terme *f*

forwarding réexpédition *f*

forwarding address adresse où faire suivre le courrier *f*

forwarding agent transitaire *m*

founding member membre fondateur *m*

fraction fraction *f*

franchise franchise *f*

franchise holder franchisé *m*

franchised franchisé

franchisee franchisé *m*

franchising franchisage *m*

franchisor franchiseur *m*

to **frank a letter** affranchir une lettre; [*post office*] oblitérer une lettre

franker oblitérateur *m*

franking affranchissement *m*

franking machine affranchisseuse *f*, machine à affranchir *f*

free (of charge) gratuit

free of customs duty franco de douane

free of packing charges franco d'emballage

free of tax franc d'impôts

free of VAT en franchise de TVA

free sample échantillon gratuit *m*

free trade libre-échange *m*

free-trade area zone de libre-échange *f*

to **freeze assets** immobiliser des actifs

to **freeze prices** geler les prix

freezing of capital immobilisation de capitaux *f*

freight forwarder agent de fret *m*, transitaire *m*

freight price prix de transport *m*

frequent user card carte de fidélité *f*

fringe benefits avantages sociaux *mpl*

from: expéditeur :

frozen account compte bloqué *m*

to **fulfil an order** exécuter une commande

full: in full [*written out*] en entier; [*to pay*] intégralement

full employment plein emploi *m*
full price plein tarif *m*
full set of bills of lading jeu complet de connaissements *m*
full stop point *m*
full-time à plein temps, à temps complet
full-time contract contrat à temps plein *m*
full-time work travail à plein temps *m*
function key touche de fonction *f*
to **fund** financer
funding financement *m*
funding plan plan de financement *m*
further information renseignements complémentaires *mpl*
further to your request suite à votre demande

G

GDP (=gross domestic product) PIB *m*
general administration costs frais d'administration générale *mpl*
general delivery *Am* poste restante *f*
general management direction générale *f*
general overhead *Am* frais d'administration générale *mpl*
general overheads frais d'administration générale *mpl*
general strike grève générale *f*
general terms and conditions of sale conditions générales de vente *fpl*
giro account compte courant postal *m*
to **give a discount** faire une remise; [*bank*] accorder un escompte
to **give credit** faire crédit
given in [*quoted*] libellé en
global search and replace recherche et remplacement global *f*
glue colle de bureau *f*
GNP (=gross national product) PNB *m*
to **go through the mail** dépouiller le courrier
good will fonds de commerce *m*, fonds commercial *m*
goods marchandise *f*, marchandises *fpl*
government decree ordonnance *f*
government funds fonds publics *mpl*
government revenue recettes publiques *fpl*
government stocks bons du Trésor *mpl*

graduated income tax impôt progressif *m*

grant allocation *f*; [*to company*] subvention *f*

to **grant** accorder

to **grant a loan** ouvrir un crédit, consentir un prêt

grant of a patent homologation de brevet *f*

grant of franchise concession de franchise *f*

granting of a loan ouverture de crédit *f*

graph graphe *m*, graphique *m*

graphics graphiques *mpl*

grateful: we would be grateful if you would ... nous vous saurions gré de bien vouloir ...

gratuity gratification *f*

grave (accent) accent grave *m*

gross brut

gross (amount) montant brut *m*

gross domestic product produit intérieur brut *m*

gross income recette brute *f*

gross national product produit national brut *m*

gross salary salaire brut *m*

gross wage salaire brut *m*

group groupe *m*

growing croissant

guarantee garantie *f*; [*financial deposit*] caution *f*, cautionnement *m*; ***under guarantee*** sous garantie

to **guarantee** garantir

guarantee certificate certificat de garantie *m*

guarantee slip bon de garantie *m*

guaranteed bond obligation garantie *f*

guarantor garant *m*

guidelines directives *fpl*

guild corps de métier *m*

guillotine massicot *m*

to **guillotine** massicoter

to **haggle** marchander

haggling marchandage *m*

half-day demi-journée *f*

half-price demi-tarif *m*

half year semestre *m*

to **hand in one's resignation** remettre sa démission

to **handle** [*goods*] manutentionner

to **handle a matter** gérer une affaire

handling [*of goods*] manutention *f*

hands-free conversation conversation "mains libres" *f*

handset combiné téléphonique *m*

handwritten écrit à la main

to **hang up** raccrocher

hard copy copie (sur) papier *f*

hard disk disque dur *m*

head chef *m*

head hunter chasseur de têtes *m*

head of department chef de service *m*

head office siège principal *m*, siège social *m*

head office address adresse du siège social *f*

headphones écouteurs *mpl*

headed à en-tête

headed notepaper papier à en-tête *m*

header en-tête *m*

heading rubrique *f*

health insurance assurance maladie *f*

health insurance scheme caisse de maladie *f*

help screen écran d'aide *m*

hierarchy hiérarchie *f*

high finance haute finance *f*

high value added à haute valeur ajoutée

to **highlight** mettre en relief, surligner

highlighter stylo surligneur *m*, marqueur souligneur *m*

to **hire** louer; [*staff*] embaucher

hire purchase location-vente *f*

hiring location *f*; [*of staff*] embauche *f*

to **hoard** thésauriser

hoarding thésaurisation *f*

to **hold a job** occuper un emploi

hold the line ne coupez pas !

holder titulaire *mf*, détenteur *m*

holder in due course tiers porteur *m*

holder of a power of attorney porteur d'une procuration *m*

holder of a proxy porteur d'une procuration *m*

holding [*in company*] participation *f*

holding company société de gestion *f*

holding letter réponse d'attente *f*

holding reply réponse d'attente *f*

hole punch perforatrice *f*

holiday congé *m*

holiday worker vacataire *mf*

holidays vacations *fpl*

home address adresse personnelle *f*

home delivery livraison à domicile *f*

honorary honoraire

honorary member membre honoraire *m*

to **honour** honorer

hook crochet *m*; ***off the hook*** décroché

horizontal filing classement horizontal *m*

hourly rate tarif horaire *m*

hyphen trait d'union *m*

I

icon icône *f*
identity card carte d'identité *f*
illegal illégal
illegality illégalité *f*
illicit illicite
to **illustrate** illustrer
illustrated illustré
ILO (= International Labour Organization) OIT *f*
IMF (=International Monetary Fund) FMI *m*
implied implicite
to **import** importer
to **import goods** importer des marchandises
import bonus prime d'importation *f*
import-export import-export *m*
import licence licence d'importation *f*, permis d'importation *m*
import trade commerce d'importation *m*
importer importateur *m*
importing importateur
imports importations *fpl*
to **impose a ban on** frapper d'interdit
to **improve** améliorer
improvement amélioration *f*
Inc (=incorporated) SARL
incidental costs frais accessoires *mpl*
incidental expenses faux frais *mpl*, frais accessoires *mpl*, menus frais *mpl*

to **include** inclure; [*with letter*] joindre
to **include a sum in an invoice** intégrer une somme dans une facture
included inclus
inclusive inclusivement
inclusive of costs frais inclus
inclusive of tax toutes taxes comprises
income revenu *m*
income tax impôt sur le revenu *m*
income tax return déclaration de revenus *f*
incorrectly [*invoiced*] indûment
incoterms termes commerciaux *mpl*
increase augmentation *f*
to **increase** augmenter
increasing croissant
incumbent titulaire *mf*
indebtedness endettement *m*
indent [*for paragraph*] alinéa *m*
to **indent** commencer en retrait, mettre à l'alinéa
to **indent for sth** commander qch
to **index** indexer
index card fiche *f*
index card box boîte à fiches *f*, fichier *m*
index-linked indexé
index-linking indexation *f*
index number nombre index *m*
indexing indexage *m*
indirect tax impôt indirect *m*

indirect taxation contributions indirectes *fpl*

industrial industriel

industrial accident accident du travail *m*

industrial arbitrator prud'homme *m*

industrial estate zone industrielle *f*

industrial tribunal conseil de prud'hommes *m*

industrialist industriel *m*

industry industrie *f*

inflation inflation *f*

inflationary inflationniste

to **inform** informer

to **inform sb of sth** informer qn de qch

information informations *fpl*; *a piece of information* une information, un renseignement; *to give sb information on sth* renseigner qn sur qch; *for (your) information* à titre d'information

information department service de renseignements *m*

information technology informatique *f*

in-house interne

in-house magazine revue d'entreprise *f*

initial initial

to **initial** parapher

to **initialize** initialiser

initials paraphe *m*

ink encre *f*

ink-jet (printer) imprimante (à) jet d'encre *f*

Inland Revenue fisc *m*

innovation innovation *f*

to **input** entrer

insert encart *m*

to **insert** insérer

to **insert a word in a text** intercaler un mot dans un texte

insertion insertion *f*

insolvency insolvabilité *f*

insolvent insolvable

inspector of taxes contrôleur des contributions *m*

to **install** installer

instalment acompte *m*, tranche de paiement *f*, versement *m*; *to buy by instalments* acheter à tempérament

institution établissement *m*

instruction instruction *f*, directive *f*

insufficient: insufficient funds insuffisance de provision *f*; *to have insufficient postage* être insuffisamment affranchi

insurance assurance *f*; *to take out insurance* s'assurer

insurance broker courtier d'assurances *m*

insurance certificate certificat d'assurance *m*

insurance company compagnie d'assurances *f*

insurance contract contrat d'assurance *m*

insurance document document d'assurance *m*

insurance policy police d'assurance *f*; *to take out an insurance policy* souscrire une police d'assurance

insurance portfolio portefeuille d'assurances *m*

insurance premium prime d'assurance *f*

insurance rate taux d'assurance *m*

insured (party) assuré *m*

insurer assureur *m*

intercom interphone *m*

interest intérêt *m*

interest due intérêts dus *mpl*, intérêts échus *mpl*

interest on arrears intérêt de

retard *m*
interest rate taux d'intérêt *m*
interface interface *f*
interim provisoire
interim manager directeur
   intérimaire *m*
internal interne
internal company document
   document interne à l'entreprise *m*
internal mail courrier interne *m*
internal promotion promotion
   interne *f*
Internal Revenue *Am* fisc *m*
international international
international fair foire
   internationale *f*
International Labour Organization
   Organisation internationale du
   travail *f*
International Monetary Fund
   Fonds monétaire international *m*
international money order mandat
   international *m*
international organization
   organisme international *m*
International Standards
   Organization Organisation
   internationale de normalisation *f*
international trade échanges
   internationaux *mpl*
international trade fair foire
   internationale *f*
international trading corporation
   société de commerce
   international *f*, SCI *f*
to **interpret** interpréter
interpretation of a contract
   interprétation d'un contrat *f*
interpreter interprète *mf*
interview entretien *m*, entrevue *f*
intra-Community trade échange
   intra-communautaire *m*

in-tray courrier reçu *m*
invalidity of a contract nullité d'un
   contrat *f*
inventory inventaire *m*
inventory management gestion des
   stocks *f*
inventory of purchases bordereau
   d'achat *m*
inversion of figures inversion de
   chiffres *f*
to **invert** invertir
inverted commas guillemets *mpl*; *in*
   inverted commas entre guillemets
to **invest** investir, placer
investigation enquête *f*
investment investissement *m*,
   placement *m*
investor investisseur *m*
invoice facture *f*
to **invoice for** facturer
to **invoice sb for sth** facturer qch à
   qn
invoice price prix facturé *m*
invoicing facturation *f*
IOU reconnaissance de dette *f*
irrevocable letter of credit lettre de
   crédit irrévocable *f*, crédit
   documentaire irrévocable *m*
isolated post allowance prime
   d'éloignement *f*
issue délivrance *f*; [*of banknote,*
   share] émission *f*
to **issue** émettre
issue of a certificate délivrance d'un
   certificat *f*
italic italique
to **italicize** mettre en italiques
italics italique *m*; *in italics* en
   italique
item article *m*
to **itemize** détailler
itemized détaillé

J

jacket jaquette *f*
jiffy bag® pochette matelassée *f*
job emploi *m*, travail *m*
Jobcentre® Agence nationale pour l'emploi *f*, ANPE *f*
job description profil de poste *m*, description de poste *f*, définition de poste *f*
job offer offre d'emploi *f*
job seeker demandeur d'emploi *m*
job wanted advertisement demande d'emploi *f*
to **join** adhérer à, s'affilier à
joint account compte joint *m*
joint committee commission paritaire *f*

joint management cogestion *f*
joint owner copropriétaire *mf*
joint ownership copropriété *f*; *to have joint ownership of* coposséder
joint venture entreprise commune *f*, entreprise en participation *f*, société commune *f*
jointly conjointement; *to own jointly* coposséder
journal livre de comptes *m*
judgement jugement *m*
justification justification *f*
to **justify** justifier; *left justified* justifié à gauche; *right justified* justifié à droite

K

k (=kilobyte) Ko
to **keep in order** tenir en ordre
to **keep sb waiting** faire attendre qn
to **keep the books up to date** tenir

les livres à jour
to **keep up a correspondence** entretenir une correspondance
key [*computer*] touche *f*

to **key** frapper, saisir
keyboard clavier *m*
keyboard skills compétences de
  claviste *fpl*
keyboarder claviste *mf*
keystrokes per minute/hour vitesse
de frappe à la minute/à l'heure *f*
keying accuracy précision de
  frappe *f*
keying error faute de frappe *f*
kilobyte kilo-octet *m*
know-how savoir-faire *m*

L

label label *m*, étiquette *f*
to **label** étiqueter
labelling étiquetage *m*
labor code *Am* code du travail *m*
labour main-d'œuvre *f*
labour force population active *f*
labour laws code du travail *m*, droit
  du travail *m*
labour legislation réglementation du
  travail *f*
labour market marché du travail *m*
labour relations relations de
  travail *fpl*
lack: for lack of funds faute de
  provision
LAN (=local area network) réseau
  local *m*
landlord propriétaire *m*
landscape [*to print*] à l'italienne
landscape format format
  paysage *m*
to **lapse** tomber en déchéance
laptop portable *m*

large denominations grosses
  coupures *fpl*
large print gros caractères *mpl*
large sum grosse somme *f*
laser (printer) imprimante (à) laser *f*
last financial year exercice
  écoulé *m*
late en retard
lateral filing classement latéral *m*
latest: at the latest au plus tard
launch lancement *m*
to **launch** [*product*] lancer, introduire
  sur le marché
to **launch a new company** lancer une
  nouvelle entreprise
Law Courts Palais de Justice *m*
law firm cabinet juridique *m*
law of supply and demand loi de
  l'offre et de la demande *f*
lawsuit action *f*
lawyer juriste *mf*, avocat *m*
layoff licenciement *m*
to **lay off** débaucher, licencier

111

laying off débauchage *m*, licenciement *m*
layout [*of page*] disposition *f*; [*of offices*] agencement *m*
L/C (=letter of credit) l/c
to **lead to an agreement** aboutir à un accord
leaflet dépliant *m*
lease bail *m*; [*lease purchase*] crédit-bail *m*
to **lease** louer
lease charges charges locatives *fpl*
leasing location *f*; [*lease purchase*] crédit-bail *f*
leave congé *m*; *to be on leave* être en congé
leave for personal reasons congé pour convenance personnelle *m*
ledger grand livre *m*, journal *m*
legal juridique, légal
legal action: to take legal action against sb poursuivre qn en justice
legal adviser conseil juridique *m*, conseiller juridique *m*
legal department contentieux *m*
legal dispute litige *m*
legal document document légal *m*
legal entity personne morale *f*
legal recourse recours contentieux *m*
legal technicality vice de forme *m*
legibility lisibilité *f*
legible lisible
legislation législation *f*
to **lend against securities** prêter sur titres
to **lend at interest** prêter à intérêt
lender prêteur *m*
to **let by the month** louer au mois
letter lettre *f*; *your letter of* votre lettre en date du
letter box boîte à lettres *f*
letter-card carte-lettre *f*
letterhead en-tête *m*, en-tête de

lettre *m*; [*paper*] papier à en-tête *m*
letter of apology lettre d'excuse *f*
letter of complaint lettre de réclamation *f*
letter of confirmation lettre de confirmation *f*
letter of credit lettre de crédit *f*
letter of dismissal lettre de licenciement *f*
letter of guarantee lettre de garantie *f*
letter quality qualité courrier *f*
letter scales pèse-lettre *m*
letter threatening legal action lettre de poursuite *f*
to **level off** plafonner
to **level out** plafonner
levelling off of prices plafonnement des prix *m*
lever-arch file classeur à levier *m*
liabilities passif *m*
liable to tax passible de taxe, passible d'impôts; *person liable for tax* assujetti *m*
licence licence *f*, patente *f*
licence holder licencié *m*
licensed patenté
licensee concessionnaire *mf*
life assurance *Br* assurance-vie *f*
life insurance assurance-vie *f*
life interest usufruit *m*
to **lift the receiver** décrocher
ligatured ligaturé
lightning strike grève surprise *f*
limited liability company société à responsabilité limitée *f*, SARL *f*
line ligne *f*
line insert insertion de ligne *f*
line of business branche *f*
line of credit ligne de crédit *f*
line of products ligne de produits *f*
line spacing interligne *m*, espacement de lignes *m*

liquid liquide
liquid assets liquidités *fpl*
liquidation liquidation *f*; *to go into liquidation* entrer en liquidation
liquidation of assets liquidation de biens *f*
liquidator liquidateur *m*
list liste *f*
to **list** inventorier, répertorier
list of addresses liste d'adresses *f*
list of correspondents liste des correspondants *f*
listing paper papier listing *m*
litigation contentieux *m*
to **load** embarquer
loading embarquement *m*
loan emprunt *m*
loan agreement contrat de prêt *m*
loan note titre de créance *m*
local area network réseau local *m*
local call communication locale *f*
local tax taxe locale *f*
location emplacement *m*
to **lodge a complaint** faire une réclamation
to **lodge a complaint with** faire une réclamation auprès de
to **log** enregistrer
to **log an order** enregistrer une commande
to **log the mail** enregistrer le courrier
logbook carnet de route *m*
logging enregistrement *m*
logging of an order enregistrement d'une commande *m*
logo sigle *m*

long-dated bill traite à longue échéance *f*
long-distance call communication hors circonscription *f*
longhand écrit à la main; *in longhand* écrit à la main
long lease bail emphytéotique *m*
long service award prime d'ancienneté *f*
long-term à long terme
long-term borrowings emprunts à long terme *mpl*
long-term credit crédit (à) long terme *m*
long-term loan emprunt à long terme *m*
long-term unemployment chômage de longue durée *m*
loose-leaf à feuillets rechargeables
loose-leaf binder grébiche *f*
lorry camion *m*
lorry driver camionneur *m*
loss perte *f*
loss of earnings manque à gagner *m*
loss of no-claims bonus malus *m*
to **lower** baisser
lower case en minuscules
lower case letter minuscule *f*
lowering baisse *f*
Ltd (=limited) SARL
lucrative lucratif
lump sum forfait *m*; *in a lump sum* forfaitairement
lump sum *adj* forfaitaire
luncheon voucher chèque-restaurant *m*, ticket restaurant *m*
luxury tax taxe de luxe *f*

M

made out in libellé en

mail courrier *m*, poste *f*

to **mail** poster, mettre à la poste

mail bag sacoche à courrier *f*

mail book cahier d'enregistrement du courrier *m*

mail checklist fiche courrier *f*

mail delivery distribution de courrier *f*

mailmerge publipostage *m*

mail order (selling) vente par correspondance *f*, VPC

mail room service du courrier *m*

mailshot publipostage *m*, mailing *m*

mail sorting tri postal *m*

mail transfer virement par courrier *m*

mailing expédition par la poste *f*; [*mailshot*] publipostage *m*, mailing *m*

mailing list liste d'adresses *f*

maintenance maintenance *f*, entretien *m*

maintenance engineer technicien de maintenance *m*

to **make a cheque payable to** établir un chèque à l'ordre de

to **make a claim** déposer une réclamation

to **make a downpayment** verser un acompte

to **make a profit** réaliser un profit

to **make a transfer** effectuer un virement

to **make good a deficit** combler un déficit

to **make out a cheque** libeller un chèque, établir un chèque

to **make out an invoice** libeller une facture

to **make out to the order of** libeller à l'ordre de

to **make up for lost time** combler un retard

to **manage** diriger, gérer

to **manage an account** gérer un compte

to **manage jointly** cogérer

management direction *f*, gestion *f*; [*managers*] direction *f*

management committee comité de direction *m*

management report rapport de gestion *m*

manager directeur *m*; [*of department*] chef *m*; [*of shop*] gérant *m*; **as a manager** en tant que gestionnaire

managerial staff staff de direction *m*

managing director directeur général *m*

manpower main-d'œuvre *f*

manpower crisis crise de main d'œuvre *f*

manual manuel

manual worker ouvrier *m*, travailleur manuel *m*

manufacture fabrication *f*

to **manufacture** fabriquer
manufactured manufacturé
manufactured product produit
manufacturé *m*
manufacturer fabricant *m*,
constructeur *m*
manufacturer's instructions notice
du constructeur *f*
manufacturer's liability
responsabilité du fabricant *f*
manufacturing defect vice de
fabrication *m*
manufacturing faults défauts de
fabrication *mpl*
manufacturing licence licence de
fabrication *f*
margin marge *f*
marginal marginal
marker pen marqueur *m*
marker tag épingle de signalisation *f*
market marché *m*
market *adj* marchand
to **market** commercialiser
market place marché *m*
market research étude de marché *fpl*
market research studies études de
marché *fpl*
market share part de marché *f*
market study étude de marché *f*
market trend tendance du marché *f*
market value valeur marchande *f*
marketing commercialisation *f*;
[*discipline*] marketing *m*,
mercatique *f*
marketing department direction
mercatique *f*
marketing director directeur de
marketing *m*
marketing manager directeur de
marketing *m*
marketing network réseau de
commercialisation *m*, circuit de
commercialisation *m*

marketing team équipe
commerciale *f*
markup majoration *f*
to **mark up** majorer
mass media mass media *mpl*
mass production production en
série *f*, fabrication en série *f*
master document document
maître *m*
maternity allowance allocation de
maternité *f*
maternity leave congé de
maternité *m*
mathematical formula formule de
calcul *f*
matter affaire *f*
to **mature** arriver à échéance
maturity échéance *f*
maturity date date d'échéance *f*
maturity of a policy échéance de
police *f*
maximum maximum
maximum salary salaire plafond *m*
MD (=managing director) directeur
général *m*
mean [*average*] moyenne *f*
means of payment moyens de
paiement *mpl*
means of production moyens de
production *mpl*
means of transport moyens de
transport *mpl*
media média *m*
mediation médiation *f*
mediator médiateur
d'entreprises *m*
medical certificate certificat
médical *m*
medium-term credit crédit (à)
moyen terme *m*
to **meet** se réunir
to **meet delivery schedules** respecter
les délais de livraison

to **meet demand** faire face à la demande

meeting réunion *f*; [*larger*] assemblée *f*, conférence *f*; *to be in a meeting* être en réunion

meetings secretary secrétaire de séance *mf*

megabyte mégaoctet *m*

member membre *m*, adhérent *m*

member of the board membre du conseil d'administration *m*

membership adhésion *f*; [*members*] membres *mpl*

memo mémorandum *m*, note de service *f*

memo pad bloc-notes *m*

memorandum and articles of association statuts de société *mpl*

memory mémoire *f*

memory typewriter machine à écrire à mémoire *f*

menu menu *m*

menu-driven piloté par menu

merchandise marchandise *f*, marchandises *fpl*

merchandiser marchandiseur *m*

merchandizing marchandisage *m*

merchant négociant *m*, commerçant *m*

merchant bank banque d'affaires *f*

merchant ship navire de commerce *m*, navire marchand *m*

to **merge** fusionner

merger fusion *f*, fusionnement *m*

message message *m*, communication *f*; *to take a message* prendre un message

message boy garçon de courses *m*

messenger coursier *m*

method of delivery mode d'expédition *m*

method of payment mode de règlement *m*, mode de paiement *m*

method of transport mode de transport *m*

microfiche microfiche *f*

microfilm microfilm *m*

micrographic micrographique

middle management cadres moyens *mpl*

middle manager cadre moyen *m*

minimum minimum

minimum charge charge minimale *f*

minimum wage salaire minimum *m*

minimum wage earner smicard *m*

minutes procès-verbal *m*

minutes book registre des procès-verbaux *m*

miscalculation erreur de calcul *f*

miscellaneous file dossier "divers" *m*

misprint faute d'impression *f*

mobile (phone) radio-téléphone *m*

mobility mobilité *f*

modem modem *m*

monetary monétaire

monetary unit unité monétaire *f*

money argent *m*

monitor moniteur *m*

to **monitor** contrôler

monthly mensuel

monthly *adv* mensuellement

monthly average moyenne mensuelle *f*

monthly budget budget mensuel *m*

monthly instalment acompte mensuel *m*, versement mensuel *m*

monthly instalments mensualités *fpl*

monthly payment paiement mensuel *m*

moratorium moratoire *m*

moratorium on payment suspension des paiements *f*

motorcycle courier coursier *m*, porteur *m*

mouse [*computers*] souris *f*

to **move** *vt* déplacer
moving déplacement *m*
multilateral multilatéral
multinational multinationale *f*
to **multiply** multiplier
multipoint audioconference
  audioconférence multipoint *f*

multisector multisectoriel
mutual mutuel
mutual fund société
  d'investissement à capital
  variable *f*, SICAV *f*
mutual insurance company
  mutuelle *f*

name nom *m*; [*of company*] raison
  sociale *f*, dénomination sociale *f*
nationalization nationalisation *f*
to **nationalize** nationaliser
nationalized nationalisé
NB NB
needs study étude des besoins *f*
négotiable négociable
to **negotiate** négocier
negotiation négociation *f*
net net
net (amount) somme nette *f*
net costs charges nettes *fpl*
net income revenu net *m*
net of tax hors taxe, net d'impôt; *the
  invoice value net of tax* le montant
  HT de la facture
net of VAT hors TVA
net payable net à payer *m*
net profit net commercial *m*
net receipts recette nette *f*
net return retour net *m*

net (total) montant net *m*
network réseau *m*
new paragraph alinéa *m*
newspaper article article de
  journal *m*
**NIC (=National Insurance
  contribution)** cotisation à la
  Sécurité sociale *f*
night work travail de nuit *m*
nominal ledger grand livre général *m*
non-conformity of a product non-
  conformité d'un produit *f*
non-EC country pays hors
  communauté *m*
non-fulfilment non-exécution *f*
non-payment non-paiement *m*
non-profit-making organization
  association à but non lucratif *f*
non-refundable packaging
  emballage perdu *m*
not known at this address inconnu à
  l'adresse indiquée

117

notarized deed acte notarié *m*

notary notaire *m*

note note *f*; [*banknote*] billet de banque *m*; *to take notes* prendre des notes

to **note** noter

to **note an order** noter une commande

notebook calepin *m*, carnet *m*, agenda *m*; [*computer*] notebook *m*

note in the margin note marginale *f*

note pad bloc-notes *m*

note-taking prise de notes *f*

notice avis *m*; [*warning*] préavis *m*; *to give notice* donner son préavis; *to give an employee notice* signifier à un employé son licenciement; *to give an employee four weeks notice* donner à un employé un préavis de quatre semaines

notice board panneau d'affichage *m*

notice of a/the meeting convocation *f*, lettre de convocation *f*

notice of receipt accusé de réception *m*

notice period terme de préavis *m*

notification avis *m*, notification *f*

notification of unpaid cheque certificat de non-paiement *m*

to **notify sb of sth** notifier qn de qch

noting down notation *f*

null and void nul et non avenu

number chiffre *m*; [*telephone, fax etc*] numéro *m*; [*of company*] matricule *m*; *0800 number* numéro vert

to **number** numéroter

number of employees effectif *m*

numbering numérotation *f*

numeric keypad clavier numérique *m*

numerical filing classement numérique *m*, classement par ordre numérique *m*

O

object of a contract objet d'un contrat *m*

obligation obligation *f*

oblique barre *f*

to **obtain** obtenir

obtaining of a loan obtention d'un prêt *f*

obvious defect vice apparent *m*

occupation profession *f*

OECD (=Organization for Economic Co-operation and Development) OCDE *f*

offer offre *f*
to **offer a price** offrir un prix
offer of employment offre d'emploi *f*
offer of services offre de service *f*
office bureau *m*
office address adresse au bureau *f*
office automation bureautique *f*
office block immeuble de bureaux *m*
office boy garçon de bureau *m*
office equipment matériel de
   bureau *m*
office furniture mobilier de
   bureau *m*
office hours heures de bureau *fpl*
office manager chef de bureau *m*
office staff personnel de bureau *m*
office supplies articles de
   bureau *mpl*, fournitures de
   bureau *fpl*
office work travail de bureau *m*
office worker employé de bureau *m*
official fonctionnaire *mf*
official officiel; *for official use only*
   cadre réservé à l'administration; *to
   go through official channels*
   passer par la voie hiérarchique
offpeak time heures creuses *fpl*;
   [*telephone*] heures de tarif
   blanc *fpl*
ono (=or nearest offer) ou l'offre la
   plus proche
to **open** ouvrir
to **open a meeting** ouvrir une réunion
open plan aménagement paysager *m*
open-plan office bureau paysager *m*
opening [*start of letter*] formule de
   début *f*
opening hours heures d'ouverture *fpl*
opening of an account établissement
   d'un compte *m*, ouverture d'un
   compte *f*
opening speech discours
   d'ouverture *m*

opening time heure d'ouverture *f*
operating costs charges
   d'exploitation *fpl*
operating system [*computers*]
   système d'exploitation *m*
operations manager directeur de
   l'exploitation *m*
operator opérateur *m*, opératrice *f*;
   [*telephone*] standardiste *mf*
opposite en face; [*on opposite page*]
   ci-contre
opposite number homologue *mf*
option to buy option d'achat *f*
order commande *f*; *to take an order*
   prendre une commande
to **order** commander
to **order a payment** ordonnancer un
   paiement
order book carnet de commandes *m*,
   livre de commandes *m*
order form bulletin de commande *m*
order number numéro d'ordre *m*
order slip bulletin de commande *m*
order to pay ordonnance de
   paiement *f*
organization organisation *f*
organization chart organigramme *m*
**Organization for Economic Co-
   operation and Development**
   Organisation de coopération et de
   développement économique *f*
to **organize** organiser
organizer organisateur *m*;
   [*electronic*] organiseur *m*
origin origine *f*, provenance *f*; *of
   French origin* d'origine française
origin of goods label marque
   d'origine *f*
original original *m*
out of court settlement arrangement
   à l'amiable *m*
out of order en dérangement, hors
   service

out of stock épuisé
out of use hors d'usage
outline canevas *m*
outline agreement protocole
   d'accord *m*
outside externe
outside line ligne extérieure *f*
out-tray courrier à expédier *m*
overdraft découvert *m*; *to have an
   overdraft* avoir un découvert, être
   à découvert
to **overdraw** tirer à découvert
overdrawn à découvert
overdrawn account compte à
   découvert *m*

overdue payment paiement en
   souffrance *m*
overheads frais généraux *mpl*
overseas outre-mer
overseas trade department
   Ministère du Commerce
   extérieur *m*
overtime heures supplémentaires *fpl*;
   to work overtime faire des heures
   supplémentaires
to **owe** devoir
to **owe money** devoir de l'argent
owing dû
owner propriétaire *mf*

P

to **pack** emballer
package colis *m*
to **package** emballer, empaqueter,
   conditionner
packaging matériel d'emballage *m*;
   [*action*] conditionnement *m*
packing emballage *m*,
   empaquetage *m*
packing costs frais d'emballage *mpl*
packing paper papier d'emballage *m*
page break coupure de page *f*
page layout mise en page *f*
paid payé; [*bill*] acquitté
paid leave absence rémunérée *f*,

   congés payés *mpl*
paper papier *m*; [*newspaper*]
   journal *m*
paper clip trombone *m*
paper feed guide-papier *m*
paper folding machine machine à
   plier les documents *f*
paper knife coupe-papier *m*
paper money monnaie de papier *f*,
   papier-monnaie *m*
paper release arm levier de
   dégagement du papier *m*
paper tray bac à papier *m*
par nominal

par value nominal *m*
paragraph paragraphe *m*, alinéa *m*
parallel interface interface parallèle *f*
parcel paquet *m*, colis *m*
parcel post colis postal *m*
parcels service messagerie *f*
parent company maison mère *f*, société mère *f*
part payment paiement partiel *m*
part-time à mi-temps, à temps partiel
part-time contract contrat à temps partiel *m*
part-time work travail à mi-temps *m*, travail à temps partiel *m*
partial payment paiement partiel *m*
participant participant *m*
partnership partenariat *m*
parts and labour warranty garantie pièces et main d'œuvre *f*
pass book livret de dépôts *m*
password mot de passe *m*
password-protected protégé par mot de passe
patent brevet *m*, brevet d'invention *m*
to **patent** breveter
patent application dépôt de brevet *m*
patent licence licence de brevet *f*
Patent Office *equivalent to* Institut national de la propriété industrielle *m*
patented breveté
paternity leave congé de paternité *m*
pay paie *f*, rémunération *f*
to **pay** payer; [*employee*] payer, rémunérer; [*invoice*] régler; [*taxes*] acquitter
to **pay at sight** payer à vue
to **pay back** rembourser
to **pay by cheque** payer par chèque
to **pay by instalments** payer à tempérament
to **pay cash** payer (au) comptant
to **pay for** payer
to **pay in** verser
to **pay in advance** payer à l'avance
to **pay in cash** payer (au) comptant
to **pay in cash** [*into the bank*] encaisser de l'argent
to **pay money into an account** alimenter un compte, approvisionner un compte
to **pay off a debt** liquider une dette
pay cheque chèque de salaire *m*
pay deductions retenues salariales *fpl*
pay-in slip bordereau de remise *m*
pay rise augmentation de salaire *f*
payroll feuille de paie *f*
payslip feuille de paie *f*, bulletin de salaire *m*
payable payable; *to make payable by the month* mensualiser; *to make a cheque payable to sb* faire un chèque au nom de qn
payable at maturity payable à l'échéance
payable at the bank payable à la banque
payable in cash payable comptant
payable on arrival payable à l'arrivée
payable on delivery payable à la livraison
payable to the order of à l'ordre de
PAYE (=pay as you earn) impôt sur le revenu *m*
payee bénéficiaire *mf*
payee of a bill of exchange preneur de lettre de change *m*
payer payeur *m*
paying bank établissement payeur *m*
paying in encaissement *m*

paying-in slip bordereau
d'opération *m*, bordereau de
versement *m*, feuille de
versement *f*

payment paiement *m*; [*of employee*]
rétribution *f*; [*of invoice*]
règlement *m*; [*of taxes*]
acquittement *m*; [*instalment*]
versement *m*; ***monthly payment***
versement mensuel *m*, acompte
mensuel *m*

payment advice préavis de
paiement *m*

payment at maturity paiement à
échéance *m*

payment at sight paiement à vue *m*

payment by cheque paiement par
chèque *m*, règlement par chèque *m*

payment by electronic transfer
paiement électronique *m*

payment by instalments paiement
par acomptes *m*

payment facilities facilités de
paiement *fpl*

payment in advance paiement
anticipé *m*, paiement par
anticipation *m*, paiement
d'avance *m*

payment in arrears paiement
arriéré *m*

payment in cash paiement
comptant *m*, règlement au
comptant *m*

payment in full paiement intégral *m*

payment in kind paiement en
nature *m*

payment of the balance paiement du
solde *m*

payment on account acompte *m*

payment order ordre de paiement *m*

payment received pour acquit

payment schedule échéancier de
paiement *m*, délais de

paiement *mpl*

payments coding clerk chiffreur *m*

peak time heures de pointe *fpl*;
[*telephone*] heures de tarif
rouge *fpl*

pen stylo *m*

penalty pénalité *f*

penalty interest intérêts
moratoires *mpl*

pencil crayon *m*

pencil sharpener taille-crayon *m*

pension contribution cotisation
vieillesse *f*

pension fund caisse de retraite *f*

pension plan régime de retraite *m*

pension scheme système de
retraite *m*

per pro signature signature par
procuration *f*

percentage pourcentage *m*

to **perform a contract** exécuter un
contrat

performance performance *f*

period période *f*; ***within a period of
seven days*** dans un délai de sept
jours

period of notice délai-congé *m*

periodic(al) périodique

permanent full-time contract
contrat à durée indéterminée à
temps plein *m*

person liable for tax redevable *mf*

person on short time travailleur à
temps réduit *m*

personal personnel

personal account compte
individuel *m*

personal loan prêt personnalisé *m*,
crédit personnel *m*

personal organizer [*electronic*]
organiseur *m*; [*book form*]
agenda *m*

to **personalize** personnaliser

personnel personnel *m*

personnel consultant conseiller du travail *m*

personnel (department) service du personnel *m*

personnel director directeur du personnel *m*

personnel file card fiche signalétique *f*

personnel files fichiers des salariés *mpl*

personnel management direction du personnel *f*, administration du personnel *f*

personnel manager directeur du personnel *m*

personnel representative délégué du personnel *m*

petition in bankruptcy dépôt de bilan *m*

petty cash petite caisse *f*

petty expenses menus frais *mpl*

to **phone sb** téléphoner à qn

phone call communication téléphonique *f*

phonecard carte téléphone *f*

photocopier photocopieuse *f*, photocopieur *m*

photocopy photocopie *f*

to **photocopy** photocopier

physical inventory inventaire de stock *m*

pie chart graphique à secteurs *m*, camembert *m*

piece: a piece of information une information, un renseignement; *a piece of merchandise* une marchandise

pilot plant usine pilote *f*

pitch [*of print*] pas d'écriture *m*

to **place an order** passer une commande

to **place an order for sth** passer

commande de qch

to **place an order with sb** passer commande à qn

place of birth lieu de naissance *m*

placing of an order passation de commande *f*

plaintiff réclamant *m*

planner chronogramme *m*

platen rouleau *m*

plc (=public limited company) SA *f*

pledge nantissement *m*

PO Box boîte postale *f*, BP *f*

pocket calculator calculette *f*

point-to-point audioconference audioconférence point à point *f*

port [*ships, computers*] port *m*

portable portable *m*

portable typewriter machine à écrire portative *f*

portfolio portefeuille *m*

portfolio management gestion de portefeuille *f*

portrait [*to print*] à la française

portrait format format portrait *m*

position [*job*] poste *m*; [*in company*] position *f*; [*title*] qualité *f*

possessions avoir *m*

post *Br* courrier *m*, poste *f*; *by post* par la poste

to **post the mail** poster le courrier, mettre le courrier à la poste

postcard carte postale *f*

post code code postal *m*

to **postdate** postdater

Post-it® Post-it *m*

postmark cachet de la poste *m*, tampon de la poste *m*

to **postmark** oblitérer

post office bureau de poste *m*; *to go to the post office* aller à la poste

post office account compte postal *m*

post office cheque chèque postal *m*

post office cheque account compte chèque postal *m*

post office current account compte courant postal *m*

post office transfer virement postal *m*

post script post scriptum *m*

postage port de lettres *m*, affranchissement *m*; *insufficient postage* insuffisamment affranchi

postage and packing port et emballage *m*

postage costs frais postaux *mpl*

postage paid port payé *m*

postage rate tarif postal *m*

postage stamp timbre-poste *m*

postal postal

postal area zone postale *f*

postal code code postal *m*

postal delivery envoi postal *m*

postal order mandat postal *m*

poste restante poste restante *f*

posting date date de la poste *f*

to **postpone** renvoyer, ajourner

postponement renvoi *m*, ajournement *m*

pp (=per procurationem) pp; *shall I pp it?* est-ce que je signe à votre/sa place ?

p&p (=postage and packing) port et emballage *m*

PR (=public relations) relations publiques *fpl*

prebilling préfacturation *f*

precedent précédent *m*

preferential préférentiel

preferential rate tarif préférentiel *m*

preferred privilégié

premises locaux *mpl*

premium prime *f*

prepaid payé d'avance

to **present a cheque for payment** présenter un chèque à

l'encaissement

to **present a letter for signature** soumettre une lettre à la signature

presentation présentation *f*

president président *m*

press: the press la presse

press conference conférence de presse *f*

press release communiqué de presse *m*

pressure group groupe de pression *m*

prevention of industrial accidents prévention des accidents du travail *f*

price prix *m*

price before tax prix hors taxe *m*

price ex-works prix départ usine *m*

price inclusive of tax prix taxe comprise *m*

price increase augmentation de prix *f*

price inflation inflation des prix *f*

price list tarif *m*

price markup majoration de prix *f*

price proposal proposition de prix *f*

price range fourchette de prix *f*, gamme de prix *f*

price reduction réduction des prix *f*

price scale barème des prix *m*

price setting fixation des prix *f*

price survey enquête de prix *f*

principal [*in transaction*] donneur d'ordre *m*

principal and interest principal et intérêts *m*

to **print** imprimer; *please print* prière d'utiliser des caractères d'imprimerie

to **print out** imprimer

printout impression *f*

printed directory annuaire papier *m*

printed matter imprimés *mpl*

printed text texte imprimé *m*

printer imprimante *f*; [*person*] imprimeur *m*

printer cable câble d'imprimante *m*

printer's proofs épreuves d'imprimerie *fpl*

printing error erreur typographique *f*

prior antérieur

prior engagement engagement antérieur *m*

priority priorité *f*

private privé

private line ligne privée *f*

private seal sceau privé *m*; *under private seal* sous seing privé

private sector secteur privé *m*

privatization privatisation *f*

to **privatize** privatiser

PR manager responsable des relations publiques *mf*

procurement (department) service des achats *m*

to **produce** produire

producer producteur *m*

product produit *m*

product category catégorie de produit *f*

product line ligne de produits *f*, série de produits *f*

product manager directeur de produit *m*, chef de produit *m*

product range gamme de produits *f*

production production *f*

production control direction de la production *f*

production director directeur de production *m*

production flowchart organigramme de production *m*

production management direction de la production *f*

production manager directeur de production *m*

production norm norme de production *f*

productivity productivité *f*

productivity norm norme de productivité *f*

profession profession *f*

professional association syndicat professionnel *m*

professional body organisme professionnel *m*

professional integrity conscience professionnelle *f*

professional misconduct faute professionnelle *f*

profit bénéfice *m*, profit *m*

profit and loss pertes et profits *mpl*

profit and loss account compte de pertes et profits *m*

profit margin marge bénéficiaire *f*

profit sharing participation aux bénéfices *f*

profit-sharing scheme système de participation aux bénéfices *m*

profitability rentabilité *f*

profitable rentable

pro forma pro forma

pro forma document document type *m*

pro forma invoice facture pro-forma *f*

program programme *m*

to **program** programmer

project projet *m*

promissory note reconnaissance de dette *f*

to **promote** promouvoir

promotion promotion *f*

promotion from within the company promotion interne *f*

promotional promotionnel

prompt [*computers*] indicatif *m*, invite *f*

prompt *adj* prompt, rapide

proof of payment justificatif de paiement *m*
property propriété *f*
property tax impôt foncier *m*
proposal proposition *f*
pro rata proportionnel
to **provide funds** fournir des fonds
provisional provisoire
proxy procuration *f*; *by proxy* par procuration
PTO (=please turn over) TSVP
public authorities pouvoirs publics *mpl*
public holiday jour chômé *m*
public limited company société anonyme *f*
public prosecutor procureur général *m*
public relations relations publiques *fpl*
public sector secteur public *m*
publication date date de parution *f*
publicity publicité *f*
publicity director directeur de la publicité *m*
punch perforatrice *f*
punch card carte perforée *f*
punch card operator mécanographe *mf*
punch card reader machine interprète de cartes perforées *f*
punching machine machine poinçonneuse *f*
punctuality ponctualité *f*
punctuation ponctuation *f*
punctuation marks signes de ponctuation *mpl*
purchase achat *m*
to **purchase** acheter
purchase contract contrat d'achat *m*
purchase invoice ledger journal factures-fournisseurs *m*
purchase ledger livre d'achats *m*, journal des achats *m*
purchase on credit achat à crédit *m*
purchase order bon de commande *m*
purchase price prix d'achat *m*
purchase value valeur d'achat *f*
purchaser acheteur *m*
purchasing co-operative groupement d'achat *m*
purchasing (department) service des achats *m*
purchasing group groupement d'achat *m*
purchasing power pouvoir d'achat *m*
pursuant to conformément à
to **put sb through to sb** mettre qn en communication avec qn

Q

qualified diplômé
quality control (department)
  service contrôle qualité *m*
to **quantify** chiffrer
quarter trimestre *m*
quarterly trimestriel; *to pay*
  quarterly payer par trimestre
question mark point
  d'interrogation *m*
quota quota *m*

quotation marks guillemets *mpl*; *in*
  quotation marks entre guillemets
to **quote** citer; [*on Stock Exchange*]
  coter
to **quote a price** indiquer un prix
quote marks guillemets *mpl*
quoted securities valeurs de
  bourse *fpl*
QWERTY keyboard clavier
  QWERTY *m*

R

railway chemin de fer *m*
railway *adj* ferroviaire
railway company compagnie des
  chemins de fer *f*
rail workers' strike grève des
  cheminots *f*
raise *Am* augmentation de salaire *f*
to **raise** élever
RAM (=random access memory)
  mémoire vive *f*

rampant inflation inflation
  rampante *f*
range of products éventail de
  produits *m*
rate taux *m*; [*price*] tarif *m*
rate of depreciation taux
  d'amortissement *m*
rate of exchange taux de change *m*,
  cours du change *m*
rate of interest taux d'intérêt *m*

rate of VAT taux de TVA *m*

to **ratify** entériner

rationalization rationalisation *f*

to **rationalize** rationaliser

raw material matières premières *fpl*

R&D (=research and development) department bureau d'études *m*

to **reach sb by telephone** toucher qn par téléphone

reader appareil de lecture *m*

ready for delivery livrable

real salary salaire réel *m*

reason for claim motif de réclamation *m*

rebate remise *f*, rabais *m*

to **reboot** réamorcer

receipt reçu *m*; [*for rent, electricity bill*] quittance *f*; [*in shop*] ticket de caisse *m*; [*of goods*] réception *f*

to **receipt** acquitter

receipt stamp timbre-quittance *m*

receipts recettes *fpl*

to **receive interest** toucher un intérêt

received stamp cachet d'arrivée *m*, griffe de réception *f*

received with thanks pour acquit

receiver [*telephone*] écouteur *m*; [*in bankruptcy cases*] syndic de faillite *m*

reception accueil *m*; [*in hotel*] réception *f*

receptionist réceptionniste *mf*; [*at trade fair*] hôtesse d'accueil *f*

recipient allocataire *mf*; [*of letter, parcel*] destinataire *mf*

recognized agréé

record [*in database*] enregistrement *m*

to **record** enregistrer

record form bordereau de saisie *m*

recorded delivery envoi recommandé *m*; **to send sth recorded delivery** envoyer qch en recommandé

recording enregistrement *m*

recording of an order enregistrement d'une commande *m*

recoverable recouvrable

recoverable packaging emballage récupérable *m*

recovery reprise *f*

to **recruit** recruter, embaucher

recruitment recrutement *m*, embauche *f*

red: in the red dans le rouge

to **redeem** rembourser *m*

redemption remboursement *m*

redeployment reclassement professionnel *m*

to **reduce** réduire

reduced réduit

reduced rate tarif réduit *m*, taux réduit *m*

reduction rabais *m*

reduction in staff compression de personnel *f*

reduction of taxes allègement des impôts *m*

to **refer to** [*to consult*] se référer à; **hereinafter referred to as** ci-après dénommé

reference référence *f*; [*from employer*] certificat de travail *m*, lettre de recommandation *f*; **please quote reference** référence à rappeler

reference book ouvrage de référence *m*

reference number numéro de référence *m*

refund remboursement *m*

to **refund** rembourser

refundable remboursable

refundable packaging emballages consignés *mpl*

regard: with regard to en ce qui

concerne

regional director directeur régional *m*

regional manager directeur régional *m*

to **register** inscrire

to **register a letter** recommander une lettre

to **register for** s'inscrire à

to **register goods** immatriculer des marchandises

registered recommandé (*avec assurance*); *by registered mail* par pli recommandé; *to send sth registered* envoyer qch en recommandé

registered letter pli recommandé *m*, lettre recommandée *f*

registered model modèle déposé *m*

registered office siège social *m*

registered office address adresse du siège social *f*

registered trademark marque déposée *f*, marque protégée *f*

registration inscription *f*; [*of goods*] immatriculation *f*; [*of letter*] recommandation *f*

registration form bulletin d'inscription *m*

regular régulier

regular supplier fournisseur habituel *m*

regulation règlement *m*

regulations réglementation *f*

to **rehire** réembaucher, rengager

related annexe

remainder restant *m*

reminder rappel *m*, note de rappel *f*

reminder letter lettre de rappel *f*

reminder of account outstanding rappel de compte *m*

removal of customs barriers suppression des barrières douanières *f*

to **remove sb from his/her post** démettre qn de ses fonctions

remuneration rémunération *f*

to **renew a bill of exchange** renouveler une traite

renewal renouvellement *m*

rent loyer *m*

to **rent** louer

to **rent by the month** louer au mois

rental location *f*

rental contract contrat de location *m*

rental expenses charges locatives *fpl*

re-opening réouverture *f*

to **repair** dépanner

to **repay** rembourser

repayable remboursable

repayment remboursement *m*

to **repeat an order** renouveler une commande

repeat order commande renouvelée *f*

replacement [*person*] suppléant *m*

reply réponse *f*

to **reply to a letter** répondre à une lettre

reply coupon coupon-réponse *m*, bulletin-réponse *m*

reply form formule de réponse *f*

report rapport *m*, compte rendu *m*

report form fiche d'état *f*

report of the board of directors rapport de gestion *m*

representative représentant *m*

to **reproduce** reproduire

request demande *f*; *at the request of* à la demande de; *on request* sur demande

to **request** demander

request for further time to pay demande de délai de paiement *f*

request for information demande de renseignements *f*

request for payment demande de paiement *f*, demande de règlement *f*

rescindable résiliable

research manager chef des études *m*

researcher chercheur *m*

to **resign** démissionner

resignation démission *f*; *to hand in one's resignation* donner sa démission

resolution résolution *f*

response: in response to your ... suite à votre ...

responsibilities fonctions *fpl*

responsible responsable

to **restock** réapprovisionner

restocking réapprovisionnement des stocks *m*

restrictive limitatif

to **restructure** restructurer

restructuring restructuration *f*

resumé *Am* curriculum vitae *m*

retail détail *m*

retail price prix de détail *m*

retail trade commerce de détail *m*

retailer détaillant *m*

retailing vente au détail *f*

retirement retraite *f*

retirement pension pension de retraite *f*, retraite *f*

retirement plan système de retraite *m*

retirement savings plan plan d'épargne-retraite *m*

to **retrain** *vi* se reconvertir, se recycler

retraining recyclage *m*

return renvoi *m*, retour *m*; [*tax etc*] déclaration *f*; *by return of post* par retour de courrier

to **return to work** reprendre le travail

return key touche retour *f*

return on investment retour sur l'investissement *m*

return to sender (à) renvoyer à l'expéditeur, renvoi à l'expéditeur

returnable packaging emballage consigné *m*

revenue and expenditure recettes et dépenses *fpl*

reversionary bonus prime d'intéressement *f*

to **revise** réviser

revocable révocable

to **rework a letter** remanier une lettre

ribbon ruban *m*

ribbon cartridge ruban encreur *m*

right droit *m*

to **ring** appeler

to **ring sb** téléphoner à qn, appeler qn au téléphone

ring binder classeur à anneaux *m*

road haulage camionnage *m*

roman [*print*] normal

root directory répertoire racine *m*

rotating card index fichier rotatif *m*

rough book brouillard *m*

rough estimate estimation approximative *f*

to **round down** arrondir

to **round off** arrondir

to **round up** arrondir

round table table ronde *f*

to **rub out** gommer

rubber *Br* [*eraser*] gomme à crayon *f*

rubber band caoutchouc *m*

rubber cheque chèque en bois *m*, chèque sans provision *m*

ruler règle *f*

to **run** [*company*] diriger; [*work: machine*] fonctionner

to **run up expenses** faire des frais

running cost [*of equipment*] coût de fonctionnement *m*

running costs charges d'exploitation *fpl*

S

sabbatical congé sabbatique *m*
sae (=stamped addressed envelope) enveloppe timbrée *f*
safe coffre *m*, coffre-fort *m*
safe deposit (box) coffre bancaire *m*
salaried employee salarié *m*
salaried worker travailleur salarié *m*
salary salaire *m*
salary *adj* salarial
salary scale barème des salaires *m*, échelle des salaires *f*
sale vente *f*
sale agreement compromis de vente *m*
sales ventes *fpl*; [*turnover*] chiffre d'affaires *m*
sales budget budget des ventes *m*
sales campaign campagne de vente *f*
sales contract contrat de vente *m*
sales department service des ventes *m*
sales director directeur des ventes *m*
sales engineer ingénieur des ventes *m*
sales figures chiffre de vente *m*
sales force équipe de vente *f*
sales forecast prévision des ventes *f*

sales invoice facture de vente *f*
sales invoice ledger journal factures-clients *m*
sales ledger journal des ventes *m*, livre des ventes *m*
sales letter lettre de vente *f*
sales licence licence de vente *f*
salesman vendeur *m*
sales manager chef des ventes *m*, responsable des ventes *m*
sales monopoly monopole de vente *m*
sales network réseau de vente *m*
sales objective objectif de vente *m*
sales promotion promotion des ventes *f*, animation des ventes *f*
sales representative agent commercial *m*
sales subsidiary filiale de vente *f*
sales tax taxe sur le chiffre d'affaires *f*, TCA *f*
sales team équipe de vente *f*
sales technician ingénieur technico-commercial *m*
sales technique technique de vente *f*
sales volume volume des ventes *m*
salutation titre de civilité *m*

131

sample échantillon *m*

to **sample** essayer

to **save** économiser, épargner; [*file on disk*] sauvegarder

to **save time** économiser son temps

saving épargne *f*

savings économies *fpl*

savings account compte de dépôt *m*

savings bank caisse d'épargne *f*

scales balance *f*

scanner scanneur *m*

scheduling ordonnancement *m*

scissors ciseaux *mpl*

Scotch tape® *Am* scotch *m*®

screen écran *m*

to **scribble a note** griffonner un mot

to **scroll through** parcourir

seal cachet *m*

to **seal** cacheter

sealed envelope pli cacheté *m*

search and replace recherche et remplacement *f*

to **search and replace** rechercher et remplacer

seasonal saisonnier

seasonally adjusted corrigé en fonction des variations saisonnières

seat: to have a seat on the board siéger au conseil d'administration

secretarial post poste de secrétaire *m*

secretariat secrétariat *m*

secretary secrétaire *mf*

to **secure a loan** nantir un prêt

secured bond obligation cautionnée *f*

securities titres *mpl*

security [*safety*] sécurité *f*; [*collateral*] nantissement *m*

security guard [*for premises*] garde *m*; [*carrying money*] convoyeur de fonds *m*

seizure saisie *f*

selection procedure démarche de sélection *f*

self-adhesive label étiquette autocollante *f*

self-employed person travailleur indépendant *m*

self-sealing envelope enveloppe autocollante *f*

to **sell** vendre

to **sell at a loss** vendre à perte

to **sell for cash** vendre au comptant

to **sell forward** vendre à terme

to **sell on credit** vendre à crédit

to **sell off goods** écouler des marchandises

to **sell privately** vendre de gré à gré

selling price prix de vente *m*

sellotape® scotch *m*®

semi-colon point-virgule *m*

semi-finished goods produits semi-finis *mpl*

seminar séminaire *m*, colloque *m*

to **send** envoyer, expédier; *I'll have them sent to you* je vous les ferai parvenir; *being sent to* destiné à

to **send a telegram** envoyer un télégramme, expédier un télégramme

to **send off the mail** expédier le courrier

sender envoyeur *m*, expéditeur *m*

sending envoi *m*

sending by rail expédition par chemin de fer *f*

senior supérieur

senior clerk commis principal *m*, chef de bureau *m*

senior executive cadre supérieur *m*

senior management haute direction *f*, direction générale *f*

seniority ancienneté *f*

serial interface interface série *f*

service service *m*

to **service** entretenir

service contract contrat
d'entretien *m*
service engineer technicien de
maintenance *m*
service provider prestataire de
services *m*
service supplier prestataire de
services *m*
services prestations *fpl*
set *adj* [*fixed*] fixe
to **set a date for a meeting** fixer une
date de réunion
to **set a price** fixer un prix, établir un
prix
to **set the page margins** marger une
page
set of bills of exchange jeu de lettres
de change *m*
set of data ensemble de données *m*
setting of rates tarification *f*
setting up of a business création
d'entreprise *f*
to **settle** régler
to **settle out of court** régler à
l'amiable
settlement [*payment*] liquidation *f*
settlement period terme de
liquidation *m*
severance pay indemnité de
licenciement *f*
share action *f*; *to have shares in a*
company détenir des actions dans
une société; *to have a share in the*
profits participer aux bénéfices
share certificate titre d'action *m*
shareholder actionnaire *mf*, titulaire
d'action *mf*
shareholders' meeting assemblée
des actionnaires *f*
shareholding: to have a
shareholding in avoir des actions
dans
share issue émission d'actions *f*

share of the profits part des
bénéfices *f*
share ownership actionnariat *m*
sheet (of paper) feuille *f*
shift key touche majuscule *f*
to **ship** [*send*] envoyer, expédier;
[*load*] embarquer
shipment envoi *m*, expédition *f*
shipper expéditeur *m*
shipping expédition *f*; [*loading*]
embarquement *m*
shipping address adresse de
livraison *f*
shipping company compagnie de
navigation *f*
shipping (department)
expéditions *fpl*
shipping document document
d'expédition *m*
shipping office agence maritime *f*
shop foreman chef d'atelier *m*
shop steward délégué syndical *m*
short code dialling numérotation
abrégée *f*
short-dated bill traite à courte
échéance *f*
shorthand sténographie *f*, sténo *f*; *to*
take down in shorthand prendre
en sténo
shorthand *adj* sténographique
shorthand-typing
sténodactylographie *f*
shorthand typist sténodactylo *mf*
shorthand writer sténographe *mf*
short-term à court terme
short-term borrowings emprunts à
court terme *mpl*
short-term loan emprunt à court
terme *m*
short time chômage partiel *m*
short-time working chômage
partiel *m*
to **shred** broyer

shredder broyeur *m*
sick leave congé de maladie *m*
sick note certificat médical *m*
sickness benefit indemnité de maladie *f*
sight: at sight à vue
sight draft traite à vue *f*
sign plaque d'identification *f*
to **sign** signer
to **sign a bill** viser un effet
to **sign a blank cheque** signer un chèque en blanc
to **sign a contract** signer un contrat
to **sign a deal** passer un marché
to **sign by proxy** signer par procuration
to **sign for** émarger
to **sign in** pointer
to **sign per pro** signer par procuration
signatory signataire *mf*
signature signature *f*; *to put one's signature to* apposer sa signature à
signature book parapheur *m*
signature by proxy signature par procuration *f*
signature stamp griffe *f*
signing for the post émargement du courrier *m*
signing-in of employees pointage des salariés *m*
signing of a contract signature d'un contrat *f*, conclusion d'un contrat *f*
simple interest intérêt simple *m*
single market marché unique *m*
single-spaced à interligne simple
single spacing interlignage simple *m*
site emplacement *m*
situations vacant offres d'emploi *fpl*
size dimension *f*
skilled labour main-d'œuvre qualifiée *f*
skilled worker ouvrier qualifié *m*

slide rule règle à calculer *f*
slip [*paper*] bon *m*
to **slow down** ralentir
slump effondrement *m*
to **slump** s'effondrer
small ad petite annonce *f*
small business PME *f*
smartcard carte à puce *f*
social benefits system système de prévoyance *m*
social security sécurité sociale *f*, aide sociale *f*
social security charges charges sociales *fpl*
social security contribution cotisation de sécurité sociale *f*
social security provisions prévoyance sociale *f*
society association *f*
software logiciel *m*
sole agency contract contrat de représentation exclusive *m*
sole agent agent exclusif *m*
sole contract contrat exclusif *m*
solvency solvabilité *f*
solvent solvable
soon: as soon as possible dans les plus brefs délais
sort [*computers*] tri *m*
to **sort** trier
to **sort through the mail** dépouiller le courrier
sorter machine trieuse *f*
soundproof hood capot antibruit *m*
source document document source *m*
space espace *m*
to **space out lines** espacer des lignes
spacebar barre d'espacement *f*
spacing espacement *m*
spare part pièce de rechange *f*, pièce détachée *f*
speaker [*at conference etc*]

conférencier *m*

special delivery express

special rate tarif spécial *m*

specification spécification *f*

specifications [*in tender*] cahier des charges *m*

specimen signature spécimen de signature *m*

to **speculate** spéculer

speculation spéculation *f*

speech allocution *f*, discours *m*

speedwriting écriture abrégée *f*

to **spell** orthographier, épeler

spell-checker correcteur orthographique *m*

spelling orthographe *f*

spelling mistake faute d'orthographe *f*

to **spend** dépenser

spike pique-notes *m*

to **sponsor** parrainer

sponsorship parrainage *m*; *under the sponsorship of* sous le patronage de

spouse conjoint *m*

to **spread out deliveries** échelonner les livraisons

to **spread out payments** échelonner les paiements

spreadsheet feuille de calcul *f*; [*software*] tableur *m*

staff personnel *m*, effectif *m*

staff costs masse salariale *f*

staff cutback réduction de personnel *f*

staff spokesperson porte-parole du personnel *m*

staff turnover roulement du personnel *m*

staged payments paiements échelonnés *mpl*

to **stagger payments** échelonner les paiements

staggered payments paiements échelonnés *mpl*

stamp [*for letter*] timbre *m*; [*for marking*] tampon *m*; [*for signature*] griffe *f*; *to put one's stamp on* apposer sa griffe sur

to **stamp a bill** viser un effet

to **stamp a letter** timbrer une lettre; [*frank*] affranchir une lettre

stamp duty timbre fiscal *m*, droit de timbre *m*

stamp pad tampon *m*

stamped timbré

stamped addressed envelope enveloppe timbrée *f*

stamped envelope enveloppe timbrée *f*

stamping affranchissement *m*, timbrage *m*

to **stand surety for** cautionner

standalone monoposte *m*

standard standard, normalisé

standard closure formule de politesse pour terminer une lettre *f*

standard cost coût préétabli *m*, coût standard *m*

standard document document type *m*

standard opening formule de politesse pour commencer une lettre *f*

standard rate taux normal *m*

standardization standardisation *f*, normalisation *f*

to **standardize** standardiser, normaliser

standing charges charges locatives *fpl*

standing order ordre permanent *m*, ordre de virement permanent *m*

staple agrafe *f*

to **staple** agrafer

staple remover arrache-agrafes *m*

stapler agrafeuse *f*
stapling agrafage *m*
stapling machine machine
  agrafeuse *f*
to **start a job** démarrer un travail
to **start a meeting** débuter une
  séance
starting salary traitement initial *m*
to **state** affirmer
state-of-play report état de
  situation *m*
statement affirmation *f*
statement of account état de
  compte *m*, relevé bancaire *m*
statement of invoices relevé de
  factures *m*
stationery papeterie *f*
stationery supplies cupboard
  armoire à fournitures *f*
status enquiry [*about credit*]
  renseignements de crédit *mpl*
status report état de situation *m*
stencil stencil *m*
stenographer Am sténographe *mf*
stenotype® sténotype *m*
stenotypist sténotypiste *mf*
stenotypy sténotypie *f*
sticky label étiquette autocollante *f*,
  étiquette gommée *f*
to **stipulate conditions** stipuler des
  conditions
to **stipulate in a contract** stipuler par
  contrat
to **stipulate the terms of a contract**
  fixer les conditions d'un contrat
stock stock *m*; *to be out of stock* être
  en rupture de stock
stock Am [*shares*] actions *fpl*
to **stock goods** stocker des
  marchandises
stock control gestion de stocks *f*
Stock Exchange Bourse *f*
stock issued docket bon de sortie *m*

stock keeping tenue des stocks *f*
Stock Market Bourse *f*
stock market *adj* boursier
stock outage rupture de stock *f*
stock received docket bon
  d'entrée *m*
stock sheet fiche de stock *f*
stock take constatation de stock *f*
to **stop** cesser
to **stop a cheque** faire opposition à
  un chèque
to **stop payments** suspendre les
  paiements
stoppage débrayage *m*, arrêt de
  travail *m*; [*on salary*] retenue *f*
stoppage of payment(s) arrêt de
  paiement *m*
stopping of payment suspension de
  paiement *f*
storage magasinage *m*,
  emmagasinage *m*, entreposage *m*;
  [*on disk*] stockage *m*
storage costs frais d'entreposage *mpl*
to **store** emmagasiner
storesman magasinier *m*
strain: to put a strain on a budget
  grever un budget
stretching of the rules entorse au
  règlement *f*
strict deadline délai de rigueur *m*
strictly confidential strictement
  confidentiel
strike grève *f*; *to go on strike* faire
  (la) grève
to **strike a deal** conclure un marché
strike breaker briseur de grève *m*
strike notice préavis de grève *m*
striker gréviste *mf*
string ficelle *f*
study étude *f*
style sheet feuille de style *f*
to **subcontract** sous-traiter
subcontracting sous-traitance *f*

sub-contractor sous-traitant *m*
subdirectory [*computers*] sous-répertoire *m*
subfolder [*computers*] sous-dossier *m*
subheading sous-titre *m*
subject sujet *m*, objet *m*
subject to sujet à
subject to payment moyennant paiement
to **subscribe to** être abonné à, s'abonner à
subscribed capital souscription *f*
subscriber [*to magazine etc*] abonné *m*; [*of loan, shares*] souscripteur *m*
subscript 3 3 en indice
subscription abonnement *m*; *to take out a subscription to* s'abonner à
subscription fee [*for share purchase*] droit de souscription *m*
subsidiary filiale *f*
subsidy subside *m*, subvention *f*
subtotal sous-total *m*
to **subtract** soustraire
to **sue sb** poursuivre qn en justice
summary résumé *m*, sommaire *m*
summons citation *f*, sommation *f*
summons to a meeting convocation à une réunion *f*
sums due from customers créances clients *fpl*
sundry expenses dépenses diverses *fpl*
superior chef *m*
superscript 3 3 en exposant
supervisor surveillant *m*
supervisory board conseil de surveillance *m*
supplier fournisseur *m*
supplier file fichier fournisseur *m*
supplier's code code fournisseur *m*
supplies fournitures *fpl*
supply(ing) approvisionnement *m*
to **supply** approvisionner
to **supply information** fournir des renseignements
to **supply sb with sth** approvisionner qn en qch
supply price prix d'offre *m*
surcharge surtaxe *f*
surplus excédent *m*
survey enquête *f*
suspension file hamac *m*, dossier suspendu *m*
suspension points points de suspension *mpl*
SWIFT transfer virement SWIFT *m*
switchboard standard (téléphonique) *m*
switchboard line ligne principale *f*
switchboard operator standardiste *mf*
sympathy strike grève de solidarité *f*
synopsis synopsis *f*
system disk disquette système *f*

T

tab onglet *m*; [*for file, removable*]
cavalier *m*; [*in text, figures*]
tabulation *f*
to **tab** [*text, figures*] poser des
tabulations dans
tab key tabulateur *m*
tab points points de tabulation *mpl*
tab stop taquet de tabulation *m*
table [*of figures etc*] table *f*,
tableau *m*
table of contents table des matières *f*
tabulator tabulatrice *f*
to **take out insurance** contracter une
assurance
to **take part in** participer à
to **take steps** effectuer des démarches
to **take stock** faire le point
to **take up one's duties** entrer en
fonction
takeover bid offre publique
d'achat *f*, OPA *f*
takings recettes *fpl*
tape bande *f*; [*sticky, for wrapping*]
papier collant *m*
tape streamer dévideur *m*,
streamer *m*
tapering rate tarif dégressif *m*
target cible *f*
target market marché-cible *m*
tariff tarif *m*
tariff *adj* tarifaire
tax impôt *m*, taxe *f*
to **tax** taxer
tax assessment avis d'imposition *m*,

fixation de l'impôt *f*
tax authorities administration
fiscale *f*
tax bracket tranche d'imposition *f*
tax centre centre des impôts *m*
tax code code taxe *m*
tax collection recouvrement
d'impôts *m*
tax collector percepteur *m*
tax consultant fiscaliste *mf*
tax cut réduction des impôts *f*
tax deductible déductible des impôts
tax deduction prélèvement fiscal *m*
tax evasion évasion fiscale *f*
tax exempt exempt d'impôts
tax exemption exemption d'impôts *f*
tax free franc d'impôts, hors taxe;
[*salary*] franc d'impôts
tax haven paradis fiscal *m*
tax incentive incitation fiscale *f*
tax inspector inspecteur des
contributions *m*
tax law législation fiscale *f*, droit
fiscal *m*
tax man fisc *m*
taxpayer contribuable *mf*
tax provision disposition fiscale *f*
tax refund [*on goods*] détaxe *f*; [*on
salary*] remboursement d'impôts
tax relief dégrèvement *m*,
dégrèvement fiscal *m*
tax return déclaration fiscale *f*
tax revenue recettes fiscales *fpl*
tax stamp timbre fiscal *m*

tax system fiscalité *f*, régime d'imposition *m*
tax year exercice fiscal *m*
taxable imposable, taxable
taxable income revenu imposable *m*
taxable profit bénéfice imposable *m*
taxation imposition *f*, taxation *f*
T-card fiche en T *f*
team équipe *f*
team mate coéquipier *m*
technical director directeur technique *m*
technical manager directeur technique *m*
technical specification notice technique *f*
technical specifications [*in tender*] cahier des charges *m*
technical standard norme technique *f*
telecommuting télétravail *m*
teleconference téléconférence *f*
teleconferencing téléconférences *fpl*
telegram télégramme *m*
telegram form formule de télégramme *f*
telegraphic télégraphique
telegraphic money order mandat télégraphique *m*
telephone téléphone *m*
telephone *adj* téléphonique
to **telephone sb** téléphoner à qn
telephone call appel téléphonique *m*
telephone code area circonscription téléphonique *f*
telephone conversation entretien téléphonique *m*
telephone directory annuaire téléphonique *m*, bottin *m*
telephone exchange central téléphonique *m*
telephone jack fiche téléphonique *f*
telephone log cahier d'enregistrement *m*
telephone marketing prospection téléphonique *f*
telephone memo fiche téléphonique *f*
telephone message message téléphoné *m*, message téléphonique *m*
telephone message pad bloc télé-mémo *m*
telephone number numéro de téléphone *m*
telephonist téléphoniste *mf*
teleprinter téléscripteur *m*
telesales phoning *m*
teletex télétex *m*
teletype® télétype *m*
telex télex *m*
to **telex** télexer
to **telex sb** envoyer un télex à qn
telex (message) message télex *m*
telex operator télexiste *mf*
telex transfer virement par télex *m*
teller guichetier *m*
temp intérimaire *mf*, temporaire *mf*
to **temp** travailler comme intérimaire
temping intérim *m*
temporary temporaire, intérimaire
temporary contract contrat de mission d'intérim *m*
temporary director directeur intérimaire *m*
temporary labour main-d'œuvre temporaire *f*
temporary manager directeur intérimaire *m*
temporary replacement suppléance *f*
temporary work intérim *m*
temporary worker intérimaire *mf*
tenant locataire *mf*
tender soumission *f*, offre *f*
to **tender for sth** soumissionner pour qch

tenderer: successful tenderer
adjudicataire *mf*
term durée *f*
to **terminate a contract** résilier un
contrat, dénoncer un contrat
termination [*of contract*] résiliation *f*
terms and conditions of a contract
termes d'un contrat *mpl*,
conditions d'un contrat *fpl*
terms of payment conditions de
paiement *fpl*, termes de
paiement *mpl*
test essai *m*
to **test a new product** essayer un
nouveau produit
testimonial certificat de travail *m*
thanks: with thanks in advance
remerciements anticipés
theft policy police vol *f*
thermal paper papier thermique *m*
third party tiers *m*
third party insurance assurance aux
tiers *f*
30 days: to pay at 30 days payer
dans les 30 jours
throwaway packaging emballage
perdu *m*
thumb tack *Am* punaise *f*
tick the appropriate box cocher la
case appropriée
to **tie up** [*parcel*] ficeler; **he's tied up**
il est occupé
time and date stamp horodateur *m*
time and date stamping
horodatage *m*
time bill traite à date fixe *f*
time clock (horloge) pointeuse *f*,
horloge contrôleuse *f*
time difference décalage horaire *m*
time off in lieu repos
compensateur *m*
time slot plage horaire *f*
timetable horaire *m*

to: destinataire :
today: from today à dater de ce jour
toll-free number *Am* numéro vert *m*
toner toner *m*, encre en poudre *f*
toner cartridge cartouche de toner *f*
top copy copie originale *f*
top margin marge du haut *f*
top of the range haut de gamme
total total *m*
to **total** [*amount to*] se chiffrer à;
[*add up*] totaliser
total payable total à payer *m*
total receipts total des recettes *m*
total sales chiffre d'affaires global *m*
totalling chiffrage *m*
to **trace** calquer
trackball boule de commande *f*
trade commerce *m*, échanges
commerciaux *mpl*
trade *adj* commercial
to **trade** commercer, faire du
commerce
trade association corps de métier *m*,
syndicat professionnel *m*
trade centre place commerciale *f*
trade debtors créances clients *fpl*
trade directory annuaire de
commerce *m*
trade exhibition foire-exposition *f*
trade fair foire commerciale *f*, foire
professionnelle *f*, exposition
commerciale *f*
trade journal revue
professionnelle *f*
trademark marque *f*
trademark registration dépôt de
marque *m*
trade name dénomination
commerciale *f*, nom commercial *m*
trade references références
commerciales *fpl*
trade register Registre du
Commerce *m*

trade tribunal tribunal de commerce *m*

trade union syndicat *m*, syndicat ouvrier *m*; *to be a member of a trade union* être syndiqué

trade union council conseil syndical *m*

trade union member syndiqué *m*

trade union organization organisation syndicale *f*

trade unionism syndicalisme *m*

trade unionist syndicaliste *mf*

trading partners partenaires commerciaux *mpl*

to **train** former

trainee stagiaire *mf*

trainer formateur *m*

training formation *f*, apprentissage *m*

training contract contrat d'apprentissage *m*

training period stage *m*, stage de formation *m*

training programme programme de formation *m*

transaction opération *f*

to **transcribe** transcrire

transfer transfert *m*; [*of money*] virement *m*

to **transfer** transférer; [*funds*] virer

to **transfer a call** transférer un appel

transfer cheque chèque de virement *m*

transfer of capital transfert de capitaux *m*

transfer order ordre de virement *m*

to **translate** traduire

translation traduction *f*

translation agency bureau de traduction *m*

translator traducteur *m*, traductrice *f*

to **transmit** transmettre

to **transport by armed guard** convoyer

transport allowance prime de transport *f*

transport charges frais de transport *mpl*

transport document document de transport *m*, titre de transport *m*

transport (workers') strike grève des transports *f*

to **travel on business** voyager pour affaires

travel agency agence de voyages *f*

travel allowance indemnité de déplacement *f*

travel expenses frais de déplacement *mpl*, frais de voyage *mpl*

travel insurance policy police au voyage *f*

traveller's cheque chèque de voyage *m*

travelling salesman voyageur de commerce *m*

tray [*for printer etc*] bac *m*

Treasury Ministère de l'Economie et des Finances *m*

trial essai *m*

trial period période d'essai *f*

triplicate: in triplicate en triple exemplaire

true copy copie conforme *f*

trust company société fiduciaire *f*

turnkey plant usine clés-en-main *f*

turnover chiffre d'affaires *m*, CA *m*

turnover of capital roulement de capitaux *m*

twinning of companies jumelage d'entreprises *m*

to **type** dactylographier, écrire à la machine, taper

typed dactylographié, écrit à la machine

typeface œil *m*, type de caractères *m*

typesetter compositeur *m*

typewriter machine à écrire *f*
typewriter ribbon ruban de machine à écrire *m*
typewriter rubber *Br* gomme pour machine à écrire *f*
typing frappe *f*, dactylographie *f*;

typing of a letter frappe d'une lettre *f*
typing error faute de frappe *f*
typist dactylo *mf*, dactylographe *mf*
typo faute de frappe *f*, coquille *f*

U

UN (=United Nations) ONU *f*
unavailable indisponible
under usual reserve sauf bonne fin
to **underline** souligner
underlining soulignement *m*
undersigned: I, the undersigned ... je, soussigné ...,
undiscountable inescomptable
unemployed: to be unemployed être au chômage; *the unemployed* les chômeurs *mpl*
unemployed worker chômeur *m*
unemployment chômage *m*
unemployment benefit allocations de chômage *fpl*, indemnité de chômage *f*
unemployment contribution cotisation chômage *f*
unfair competition concurrence déloyale *f*
unfavourable défavorable
union demands revendications syndicales *fpl*
union leader responsable syndical *m*

union representative représentant syndical *m*, délégué syndical *m*
unit price prix unitaire *m*
unit trust société d'investissement à capital variable *f*, SICAV *f*
United Nations Organisation des Nations Unies *f*
unless otherwise advised sauf avis contraire
to **unload** décharger
unloading déchargement *m*
unloading note/permit [*from ship*] permis de débarquement *m*
unpaid impayé
unpaid bill impayé *m*
unpaid debt créance impayée *f*
unpaid leave absence non rémunérée *f*
unrecoverable irrécouvrable
unrecovered debt créance impayée *f*
unsalaried non-salarié
unsaleable invendable
to **unseal a letter** décacheter une lettre

unsold goods invendus *mpl*
UP (=unit price) PU
up to: up to 500 jusqu'à 500
up to date à jour
update mise à jour *f*, actualisation *f*
to **update** mettre à jour, actualiser
updating mise à jour *f*, actualisation *f*

up-market haut de gamme
upper-case *adj* majuscule
urgent urgent
to **use** employer
user-friendly convivial
usual habituel
usufruct usufruit *m*

vacancy poste à pourvoir *m*, poste
    vacant *m*
vacation *Am* vacances *fpl*
valid valable
validity validité *f*, bien-fondé *m*
valuation évaluation *f*, expertise *f*
value added tax taxe sur la valeur
    ajoutée *f*
valued customer card carte de
    fidélité *f*
variable-rate interest intérêt
    variable *m*
VAT (=value added tax) TVA *f*
VAT credit crédit de TVA *m*
VAT exemption franchise de TVA *f*,
    exonération de TVA *f*
VAT rate taux de TVA *m*
VAT rebate décote de TVA *f*
VAT reference number code
    assujetti TVA *m*
VAT-registered person déclarant de
    TVA *m*
VAT return déclaration de TVA *f*

VDU (=visual display unit)
    afficheur *m*
verbal agreement convention
    verbale *f*
vertical filing classement vertical *m*
vertical suspension file fiche
    verticale suspendue *f*
vice-chairman vice-président *m*
vice-president vice-président *m*
**victim of an accident at the
    workplace** accidenté du travail *m*
video-conference vidéoconférence *f*
videoconferencing
    vidéoconférences *fpl*
violation of infraction à
visible card record fiche à visibilité *f*
visitors book livret d'accueil *m*
vocational professionnel
vocational training formation
    professionnelle *f*
voltage tension *f*
voucher bon *m*; [*accounting*] pièce
    justificative *f*

W

wad of bank notes liasse de billets de banque *f*

wage salaire *m*

wage adjustment ajustement des salaires *m*

wage ceiling salaire plafonné *m*

wage cut réduction des salaires *f*

wage deductions retenues salariales *fpl*

wage earner salarié *m*

wage inflation inflation des salaires *f*

wages sheet bordereau de salaires *m*

wait attente *f*

to **wait for** attendre

waiting room salle d'attente *f*

warehouse entrepôt *m*; *to put goods in a warehouse* entreposer des marchandises

to **warehouse** entreposer, emmagasiner

warehouseman entrepositaire *m*, magasinier *m*

warehousing entreposage *m*, magasinage *m*, emmagasinage *m*

warranty garantie *f*; *under warranty* sous garantie

warranty certificate certificat de garantie *m*

waste of money gaspillage d'argent *m*

to **waste one's money** gaspiller son argent

wastepaper basket corbeille à papier *f*

waybill connaissement *m*

wear usure *f*

weekly hebdomadaire

to **weigh** peser

welcome accueil *m*

to **welcome** accueillir

welfare *Am* sécurité sociale *f*

whereabouts coordonnées *fpl*

white-collar workers cols blancs *mpl*

wholesale: to buy wholesale acheter en gros

wholesale price prix de gros *m*

wholesale trade commerce de gros *m*

wholesaler grossiste *mf*

wholesaling vente en gros *f*

wildcat strike grève sauvage *f*

to **wind up a business** liquider une entreprise

window envelope enveloppe à fenêtre *f*

window tab onglet à fenêtre *m*

to **withdraw** retirer

withdrawal retrait *m*; *cash withdrawal* décaissement *m*

to **withhold** [*from amount of money*] prélever, retenir

withholding [*from amount of money*] prélèvement *m*, retenue *f*

within [*timescale*] dans un délai de; *within the legal time limit* dans les délais légaux

word: in words en lettres

word-processing traitement de

texte *m*
word-processing package logiciel de traitement de texte *m*
word processor traitement de texte *m*
word split coupure *f*
wording of a clause énoncé d'une clause *m*
work travail *m*
to **work** travailler; [*machine etc*] fonctionner
work force main-d'œuvre *f*
work method méthode de travail *f*
work permit permis de travail *m*
work station poste de travail *m*
work to rule grève du zèle *f*
working at home travail à domicile *m*
working capital fonds de roulement *m*
working conditions conditions de travail *fpl*

working day jour ouvrable *m*, journée de travail *f*, jour ouvré *m*
working document document de travail *m*
working hours heures de travail *fpl*
working lunch déjeuner de travail *m*
worker travailleur *m*
worth: to be worth valoir
to **wrap up** envelopper
to **write** écrire
to **write a cheque** libeller un chèque, établir un chèque
writer rédacteur *m*
writing rédaction *f*; [*handwriting*] écriture *f*; *in writing* par écrit
written agreement convention écrite *f*
written document écrit *m*
written indication mention écrite *f*
written promise promesse écrite *f*
written undertaking engagement écrit *m*

YZ

year an *m*, année *f*; *per year* par an
year-end *adj* de fin d'exercice
yearly annuel
yearly average moyenne annuelle *f*

to **yield interest** rapporter des intérêts
zip code *Am* code postal *m*

Annexes
Appendices

PASSER UNE COMMANDE

13 mai 1993

Société HENRARD
179 rue des Peupliers
75010 PARIS – CEDEX 903
FRANCE

A l'attention de M. Lucas DUMONCEAU

Monsieur,

Nous vous remercions de votre lettre en date du 26 avril à laquelle vous aviez joint votre dernier catalogue et des échantillons.

Je suis heureux de vous informer que, après étude du catalogue, nous aimerions passer une première commande, libellée comme suit :

100 nappes en dentelle (réf. 23906) de couleur blanche;
150 serviettes en dentelle (réf. 45097) de couleur blanche;
50 cols en dentelle (réf. 34067) de couleur crème.

Nous attirons votre attention sur le fait que ces articles doivent nous être livrés avant le 15 juin au plus tard.

Veuillez agréer, Monsieur, nos salutations distinguées.

La Responsable des ventes,

Carla McDONNELL

PLACING AN ORDER

13 May 1993

Société Henrard
179 rue des Peupliers
75010 Paris – CEDEX 903
FRANCE

For the attention of Mr Lucas Dumonceau

Dear Sir,

Thank you for your letter of 26 April in which you enclosed a copy of your latest catalogue and samples.

I am happy to inform you that we have studied your catalogue, and would like to place an initial order as follows:

100 lace tablecloths (ref. 23906) in white
150 lace napkins (ref. 45097) in white
50 lace collars (ref. 34067) in cream

Please note that we require delivery of these articles by 15 June at the latest.

Yours faithfully,

Carla McDonnell
(Sales Representative)

DEMANDER DES INFORMATIONS

17 mars 1993

Quality Fabrics Ltd
13/16 Oxford Place
LIVERPOOL
L13 5WQ
ANGLETERRE

Messieurs,

Je vous écris à propos de votre gamme de tissus d'ameublement, tissus que j'ai récemment découverts à la Foire commerciale de Londres. Je représente McMANUS BROS, un important fabricant de meubles écossais.

Nous aimerions recevoir de plus amples informations concernant vos produits. Nous vous saurions gré de bien vouloir nous faire parvenir une liste de prix actuelle ainsi que tout échantillon disponible.

Si les échantillons nous satisfont, nous serions très heureux de passer sous peu une commande importante à votre société.

Dans l'attente de vous lire, nous vous prions d'agréer, Messieurs, l'expression de nos sentiments distingués.

Claude WILLIAMS
Directeur des ventes

MAKING AN ENQUIRY

17 March 1993

Quality Fabrics Ltd
13/16 Oxford Place
Liverpool
L13 5WQ
ENGLAND

Dear Sir/ Madam,

I am writing with reference to your range of upholstery fabrics which I
recently saw on display at the London trade fair. I represent McManus Bros, a
large Scottish furniture manufacturer, and we would be very interested in
receiving further information about your products.

We would be grateful if you could send us a copy of your current price list
together with any available samples.

If these prove to be satisfactory we would be very interested in placing a
substantial order with your company in the near future.

We look forward to hearing from you,

Yours faithfully,

Claude Williams
(Sales Manager)

DONNER DES INFORMATIONS

27 janvier 1993

Mademoiselle Gloria DUCKWORTH
542 Ashford Avenue
MANCHESTER
M20 9SW
ANGLETERRE

Mademoiselle,

Nous vous remercions de votre lettre en date du 21 janvier et de votre intérêt pour nos articles de papeterie en papier recyclé.

Veuillez trouver ci-joint un exemplaire de notre dernier catalogue offrant une illustration de notre gamme complète de papier à lettres, enveloppes, cartes de vœux et carnets, tous produits écologiques de grande qualité. Je suis sûr que vous trouverez cette gamme à la fois très intéressante et originale, et nos prix compétitifs.

Vous trouverez également ci-joint des échantillons de nos produits qui vous permettront de juger de leur qualité. Si vous souhaitez de plus amples informations, n'hésitez pas à nous contacter.

Dans l'attente d'une réponse, nous vous prions d'agréer, Madame, l'expression de nos sentiments respectueux.

La Directrice des ventes,

Isabelle MOUTARD

REPLYING TO AN ENQUIRY

27 January 1993

Miss Gloria Duckworth
542 Ashford Avenue
Manchester
M20 9SW
ENGLAND

Dear Miss Duckworth,

Thank you for your letter of 21 January in which you expressed an interest in our recycled paper products.

Please find enclosed a copy of our latest catalogue illustrating our full range of high quality, environmentally friendly note paper, envelopes, greeting cards and notebooks. I am sure you will find our range both exciting and original, and our prices competitive.

I am also enclosing samples of our products to allow you to judge the quality for yourself. If you should require any further information, please do not hesitate to contact us.

We look forward to hearing from you soon.

Yours sincerely,

Isabelle Moutard
(Sales Manager)

LETTRE DE REMERCIEMENTS

Louvain-la Neuve, le 2 juin 1993

Professeur Quentin RAMEAU
34 allée des Glycines
67000 STRASBOURG
FRANCE

Cher Collègue,

Nous vous remercions d'avoir honoré de votre présence ce premier congrès européen consacré aux derniers développements en matière de conception de systèmes optiques pour robots.

L'exposé détaillé et original que vous avez fait sur l'état d'avancement des recherches dans votre département n'a pas manqué de nous intéresser au plus haut point.

En attendant de vous revoir très prochainement, recevez, cher Collègue, mes meilleures amitiés.

Le Directeur de la Recherche en Sciences appliquées,

M. CORIN

A THANK YOU LETTER

Louvain-la Neuve, 2 June 1993

Professor Quentin Rameau
34 allée des Glycines
67000 Strasbourg
FRANCE

Dear Colleague,

We would like to thank you for attending the first European convention on the latest developments in the design of optical systems for robots.

The detailed and original talk you gave on the research advances in your department was of great interest.

I look forward to seeing you again very soon.

Best wishes,

M. Corin
(Director of Research in Applied Science)

FAIRE UNE RECLAMATION

10 novembre 1992

Société BOUGARD
134 rue H. Barbusse
30000 NIMES
FRANCE

A l'attention de Mme PUISERVERT

Madame,

Nous venons de prendre livraison de la commande de 500 chemises en soie, commande passée avec vous le 30 septembre. Je suis au regret de vous faire savoir que tant les articles livrés que le service rendu ne nous satisfont pas.

Nous avions spécifié au moment de passer commande que c'était urgent et que les articles devaient nous parvenir avant le 30 octobre au plus tard. La commande, toutefois, ne nous a été livrée qu'aujourd'hui et ce délai nous a causé de sérieux ennuis. De plus, 2 caisses ont été endommagées et leur contenu a été sali.

Au regard de ces circonstances, nous demandons une réduction de prix sur cette commande et exigeons une explication immédiate.

Veuillez agréer, Madame, nos salutations distinguées.

La Directrice des Ventes,

Mavis EVANS
Copie : Harold Holdsworth

MAKING A COMPLAINT

10 November 1992

Société Bougard
134 rue H. Barbusse
30000 Nîmes
FRANCE

For the attention of Madame Puiservert

Dear Madam,

We have just taken delivery of the order for 500 silk shirts placed with you on the 30 September, and I am sorry to say that we are extremely dissatisfied with both the merchandise and the service we have received.

We specified when placing the order that it was urgent, and that the goods should reach us no later than 30 October. However, the order did not arrive until today, and this delay has caused us serious inconvenience. Furthermore, 2 boxes were damaged and the contents soiled.

Under the circumstances we are requesting a price reduction on this order, and an immediate explanation.

Yours sincerely,

Mavis Evans
(Sales Director)

cc: Harold Holdsworth

REPONDRE A UNE RECLAMATION

2 janvier 1993

Monsieur G. LARDINOIS
34 rue Salengro
59540 CAUDRY
FRANCE

Monsieur,

Je vous écris suite à votre lettre du 31 décembre concernant le non-règlement de la commande n° 34907.

Nous déplorons très vivement cet incident et nous tenons à vous assurer qu'il s'agit là d'un oubli de notre part. Comme vous le savez, nous avons récemment changé de bureaux et dans l'agitation suscitée par le déménagement, votre facture s'est momentanément égarée.

Nous nous acquitterons naturellement du paiement dans un bref délai et nous vous prions d'accepter nos sincères excuses.

Veuillez agréer, Monsieur, l'assurance de nos sentiments distingués.

La Directrice,

Béatrice PARADIS

REPLYING TO A COMPLAINT

2 January 1993

Mr G. Lardinois
34 rue Salengro
59540 Caudry
FRANCE

Dear Mr Lardinois,

I am writing with regard to your letter dated 31 December concerning an outstanding payment on order no. 34907.

I am very sorry that this situation has arisen, due to an oversight on our part. As you know, we have recently moved offices, and in the turmoil your invoice was temporarily mislaid.

Payment will be made immediately of course, and we hope you will accept our sincere apologies.

Yours sincerely,

Béatrice Paradis
(Director)

FAIRE UNE RESERVATION

14 février 1993

MadameVera PLUNKETT
Grand Central Hotel
121 Cedar Crescent
GUILDFORD
GU5 8HD
ANGLETERRE

Madame,

Notre directeur général, M. Jean-Luc Delatte, sera en visite à Guildford le mois prochain pour trois jours. Aussi aimerais-je réserver en son nom une chambre pour une personne avec salle de bain pour les 15, 16 et 17 mars inclus.

Je vous saurais gré de bien vouloir confirmer cette réservation dès que possible.

Mathieu SOREL
Directeur du Personnel

MAKING A RESERVATION

14th February 1993

Mrs Vera Plunkett,
Grand Central Hotel
121 Cedar Crescent
Guildford
GU5 8HD
ENGLAND

Dear Mrs Plunkett,

Our Managing Director, Mr Jean-Luc Delatte, will be visiting Guildford next month for three days. Consequently, I would like to reserve a single room with private facilities in his name for the 15th to the 17th of March inclusive.

I would be grateful if you could confirm this booking as soon as possible.

Yours sincerely,

Mathieu Sorel
(Personnel Manager)

ENVOI DE FAX

DATE : 27/6/93   REF. : 3405Z

A L'ATTENTION DE : M. George STOKES

EXPEDITEUR : June RIVERS, Blackheath Ltd

OBJET : Facture en souffrance

NOMBRE TOTAL DE PAGES : 1

Monsieur,

Le règlement de la facture n° 89500, exigible au 07/06/93 ne nous est toujours pas parvenu. Je vous serais donc reconnaissant de régulariser au plus vite cette situation.

Bien à vous,

June RIVERS

SENDING A FAX

DATE: 27/6/93   REF: 3405Z

ATT.: Mr George Stokes

FROM: June Rivers, Blackheath Ltd

RE.: Outstanding invoice

TOTAL NO. OF PAGES: 1

Dear Mr Stokes,

It has come to my attention that payment of invoice no.89500 due on 7/6/93 is still outstanding. I would be grateful if you could give this matter your immediate attention.

Regards,

June Rivers

BEGINNING/ENDING A LETTER	COMMENCER/TERMINER UNE LETTRE
Dear Sir	Monsieur
Dear Sirs	Messieurs
Dear Madam	Madame
Dear Sir or Madam	Messieurs
Dear Mr Williams	Cher M. Williams
Dear Ms Rigsby	Chère Mme Rigsby
Dear Mrs Thomas	Chère Mme Thomas
Dear Christine	Chère Christine
For the attention of	A l'attention de
To whom it may concern	A qui de droit
Yours sincerely, Yours truly *Am*	Veuillez agréer, Monsieur (Madame, Mademoiselle, Messieurs, Mesdames), l'expression de mes (nos) sentiments les meilleurs.
Yours faithfully, Yours truly *Am*	Veuillez agréer, Monsieur (Madame, Mademoiselle, Messieurs, Mesdames), mes (nos) salutations distinguées.
	Veuillez croire, Monsieur (Madame, Mademoiselle, Messieurs, Mesdames), à l'assurance de mes (nos) sentiments respectueux.
Best wishes	Mes amitiés

'Yours faithfully' s'emploie quand on ne fait pas référence à un nom particulier dans la formule de salutation.

'Yours faithfully' is used when no reference is made to a personal name in the salutation.

USEFUL PHRASES FOR FAXES	*EXPRESSIONS UTILES POUR FAXER*
To:	A:
For the attention of:	A l'attention de:
Firm:	Société:
From:	De la part de:
Best Wishes,	Salutations,
Thanks,	Merci d'avance,
If the transmission is not clear, please call us.	Nous contacter SVP si la transmission est mauvaise.
If any page is illegible telephone:	En cas d'illisibilité, prière d'appeler le:
If you do not receive all the pages of this transmission, please call us.	Prière de nous contacter si vous ne recevez pas la totalité des pages.
Number of pages including this one:	Nombre de pages celle-ci incluse:

TELEPHONING	*COMMUNICATION TELEPHONIQUE*
Answering a call	*Répondre à un appel*
Good morning/ Good afternoon/ Hello, Lexus Ltd, how may I help you?	Lexus Ltd, bonjour, en quoi puis-je vous être utile ?
I'll see if he is available.	Je vais voir s'il est là.
Please hold the line.	Ne quittez pas.
Mr Chevalier isn't here at the moment. Could you call back later?	Monsieur Chevalier n'est pas ici en ce moment. Pourriez-vous rappeler plus tard?
Who's speaking?	Qui est à l'appareil ?
I'll put you through to him.	Je vous le passe.
Mrs Mackintosh is in a meeting. Can I take a message?	Madame Mackintosh est en réunion. Puis-je prendre un message ?
Sorry to keep you waiting.	Désolé(e) de vous faire attendre.
There's no answer.	Ça ne répond pas.
One moment, please.	Un moment, s'il vous plaît.
It's a very bad line.	La ligne est très mauvaise.
You have the wrong number.	Vous vous êtes trompé(e) de numéro.
You can get through to me direct by dialling 450678.	Vous pouvez me joindre directement en composant le 450678.
(En anglais, 45-06-78 s'énonce : "four, five, o, six, seven, eight")	(In French, 450678 becomes "quarante-cinq, zéro six, soixante-dix-huit")
His line is engaged/ busy.	Sa ligne est occupée.
She's on another line.	Elle est sur une autre ligne.
May I tell her who's calling?	Puis-je lui dire qui appelle?
I'm sorry, I didn't catch that.	Je regrette, je n'ai pas compris.
There is a call for you.	On vous demande au téléphone.

Answering machines

This is Glasgow 64016.
Sorry there's no one here
to take your call at the
moment. Please leave your
name and number after the tone.

Répondeurs

Glasgow 64016. Il n'y a
malheureusement personne en ce
moment pour vous répondre. Veuillez
laisser votre nom et votre numéro de
téléphone après le signal sonore.

Making a call

Hello, can I speak to Mrs
Meunier please?

Hello, can you put me through
to extension 139 please?

Hello, can you help me?
I'm looking for some
information about your
office supplies.

Hello, I'm ringing about
your advertisement for a
temporary secretary.

Hello, I'm calling on
behalf of O'Donnell and
Sons, your paper suppliers.

Can I leave a message?

I'll hold.

I'll ring back later.

When will she be back?

Can you ask him/her to call
me?

Téléphoner

Allô, pourrais-je parler à
madame Meunier, s'il vous plaît ?

Allô, pourriez-vous me passer le
poste 139, s'il vous plaît ?

Allô, pouvez-vous m'aider ?
J'aimerais obtenir des informations
concernant vos fournitures de
bureau.

Allô, je téléphone au
sujet de l'annonce concernant
le poste de secrétaire intérimaire.

Allô, je téléphone de la
part de O'Donnell and Sons,
vos fournisseurs en papier.

Puis-je laisser un message ?

J'attends.

Je rappellerai plus tard.

Quand sera-t-elle de retour ?

Pouvez-vous lui demander de
me rappeler ?

Directory enquiries

Can you give me the number
of The Clothing Company,
Manchester, please?

Can you tell me the code
for Croydon, please?

Renseignements

Pourriez-vous me communiquer le
numéro de "The Clothing Company",
Manchester, s'il vous plaît ?

Pourriez-vous me donner
l'indicatif de Croydon, s'il vous plaît ?

COMMUNICATIONS TELEPHONIQUES VERS L'ETRANGER DEPUIS LA FRANCE
MAKING INTERNATIONAL CALLS FROM FRANCE

a) *Composez le préfixe international 19.*
Dial the international code 19.

b) *Attendez la tonalité.*
Wait for the dialling tone.

c) *Composez l'indicatif du pays.*
Dial the country code.

d) *Composez l'indicatif de la région/ ville suivi du numéro de l'abonné.*
Dial the area code, followed by the number.

Exemple pour un abonné à Londres/ for example, when dialling a London number:

19 →   *tonalité*   → 44 → 71/81 →   *numéro de l'abonné*
      dialling tone   telephone number

N.B. : *vous ne devez pas composer le (0). Par ex. 071/081 = 71/81.*
Omit the (0) when making an international call eg 071/081 = 71/81.

COMMUNICATIONS INTERNES
MAKING CALLS INSIDE FRANCE

Pour appeler la province de Paris, composez le 16 avant le numéro de l'abonné.
When calling a non-Paris number from Paris, dial 16 before the number.

Pour appeler Paris de la province, composez le 16-1 avant le numéro de l'abonné.
When calling Paris from outside Paris, dial 16-1 before the number.

LES INDICATIFS DES ETATS-UNIS
UNITED STATES DIALLING CODES

Indicatif du pays depuis la France/country code from France: 1

Indicative du pays depuis la Grande-Bretagne/country code from Britain: 0101

Alaska	907	Minneapolis		612
Atlanta	404	Nashville		615
Atlantic City	609	New Haven		203
Austin	512	New Orleans		504
Baltimore	301	New York City:		
Birmingham	205	Bronx		212
Boston	617	Brooklyn		718
Chicago	312	Manhattan		212
Cincinnati	513	Queens		718
Cleveland	216	Staten Island		718
Columbia	803	Yonkers		914
Corpus Christi	512	Oklahoma City		405
Dallas	214	Omaha		402
Denver	303	Palm Springs		619
Detroit	313	Philadelphia		215
Hawaii	808	Phoenix		602
Hollywood	213	Pittsburgh		412
Houston	713	Portland		503
Indianapolis	317	Richmond		804
Jackson	601	Sacramento		916
Jersey City	201	St. Louis		314
Kansas City	816	Salt Lake City		801
Las Vegas	702	San Diego		61
Los Angeles	213	San Francisco		415
Memphis	901	Seattle		206
Miami	305	Washington		202

169

LES INDICATIFS DE LA GRANDE-BRETAGNE
BRITISH DIALLING CODES

Depuis la France, on ne compose pas le zéro.
Do not use the 0 when calling from France.

Aberdeen	0224	Hull	0482
Bath	0225	Ipswich	0473
Belfast	0232	Leeds	0532
Birmingham	021	Leicester	0533
Bournemouth	0202	Liverpool	051
Bradford	0274	London	071/081
Bristol	0272	(London)derry	0504
Cambridge	0223	Manchester	061
Cardiff	0222	Newcastle	091
Chester	0244	Norwich	0603
Colchester	0206	Nottingham	0602
Derby	0332	Plymouth	0752
Edinburgh	031	Portsmouth	0705
Exeter	0392	Reading	0734
Glasgow	041	Southampton	0703
Gloucester	0452	Southend	0702
Guildford	0483	Sunderland	091
Huddersfield	0484	Swansea	0792

COMMUNICATIONS TELEPHONIQUES VERS L'ETRANGER DEPUIS LA GRANDE-BRETAGNE
MAKING AN INTERNATIONAL CALL FROM BRITAIN

a)   *Composez le préfixe international 010.*
     Dial the international code 010.

b)   *Composez l'indicatif du pays.*
     Dial the country code.

c)   *Composez l'indicatif de la région/ville suivi du numéro de l'abonné.*
     Dial the area code followed by the number.

N.B. : *en France, l'indicatif de la région est compris dans le numéro de l'abonné.*
       Pour appeler Paris, composez le 1 avant le numéro de l'abonné.
       French area codes are incorporated in the telephone number.
       For Paris, add 1 before the number.

       For example, when dialling Paris/*exemple pour un abonné à Paris:*
       010 → 33 → 1 → telephone number/*numéro de l'abonné*

INTERNAL/EXTERNAL RELATIONS

RELATIONS INTERNES/ EXTERNES

Hello, I'm here to see Mr Dumézier.

Bonjour, je suis venu voir monsieur Dumézier.

I have an appointment with your managing director at 3 pm.

J'ai rendez-vous avec votre directeur général à 15 heures.

I'd like to make an appointment to see Miss Kershaw, please.

J'aimerais prendre rendez-vous avec mademoiselle Kershaw, s'il vous plaît.

Is Mrs Harrison free at the moment?

Est-ce que madame Harrison est libre en ce moment ?

Would you like to take a seat?

Voulez-vous vous asseoir ?

Mr Carpentier will be with you in one minute.

Monsieur Carpentier sera avec vous dans un instant.

Would you like to come through?

Entrez, je vous prie.

Miss McTavish is in a meeting at the moment. Would you mind waiting?

Mademoiselle McTavish est en réunion pour le moment. Ça ne vous fait rien d'attendre ?

Mr von Trapp won't be long.

Monsieur von Trapp ne sera pas long.

Would you like to wait?

Voulez-vous attendre ?

Would you like a cup of tea/coffee while you're waiting?

Puis-je vous offrir une tasse de thé/café pendant que vous attendez ?

Mrs Hautier isn't available at the moment. Can I be of any help?

Madame Hautier n'est pas libre en ce moment. Puis-je vous être utile ?

I'm afraid he may be some time.

Je crains qu'il ne soit occupé encore pour quelque temps.

Mr. Hersan isn't here today. Would you like to see the assistant manager?

Monsieur Hersan n'est pas là aujourd'hui. Voulez-vous voir le sous-directeur ?

His office is on the third floor.

Son bureau se trouve au troisième étage.

171

I'll just see if he's free.	Je vais voir s'il est libre.
Would Monday 21 May suit you?	Est-ce que le lundi 21 mai vous arrange ?
Mr Molloy will see you now.	Monsieur Molloy va vous recevoir maintenant.
Mr Souriant is here to see you.	Monsieur Souriant est ici et veut vous voir.
Shall I ask him to wait?	Dois-je le faire attendre ?
Shall I send him up?	Dois-je le faire monter ?
He is here in connection with the MacDougall contract.	Il vient vous voir au sujet du contrat MacDougall.

TABLES DE CONVERSION/
CONVERSION TABLES

Longueur
Length

centimètres	cm/inches	inches
2,54	1	0.39
5,08	2	0.79
7,62	3	1.18
10,16	4	1.58
12,70	5	1.97
15,24	6	2.36
17,78	7	2.76
20,32	8	3.15
22,86	9	3.54
25,40	10	3.94
50,80	20	7.87
76,20	30	11.81
101,60	40	15.75
127,00	50	19.69

kilomètres	km/miles	miles
1,61	1	0.62
3,22	2	1.24
4,83	3	1.86
6,44	4	2.49
8,05	5	3.11
9,66	6	3.73
11,27	7	4.35
12,88	8	4.97
14,48	9	5.59
16,09	10	6.21
32,19	20	12.43
48,28	30	18.64
64,37	40	24.86
80,47	50	31.07

Surface
Area

hectares	hectares acres	acres
0,41	1	2.47
0,81	2	4.94
1,21	3	7.41
1,62	4	9.88
2,02	5	12.36
2,43	6	14.83
2,83	7	17.30
3,24	8	19.77
3,64	9	22.24
4,05	10	24.71
8,09	20	49.42
12,14	30	74.13
16,19	40	98.84
20,23	50	123.56

Poids
Weight

kilogrammes	kg/lb	pounds
0,45	1	2.20
0,91	2	4.41
1,36	3	6.61
1,81	4	8.82
2,27	5	11.02
2,72	6	13.23
3,18	7	15.43
3,63	8	17.64
4,08	9	19.84
4,54	10	22.05
9,07	20	44.09
13,61	30	66.14
18,14	40	88.19
22,68	50	110.23

tonnes	tonnes tons	tons
1,02	1	0.98
2,03	2	1.97
3,05	3	2.95
4,06	4	3.94
5,08	5	4.92
6,10	6	5.91
7,11	7	6.89
8,13	8	7.87
9,14	9	8.86
10,16	10	9.84
20,32	20	19.68
30,48	30	29.53
40,64	40	39.37
50,80	50	49.21

Volume
Volume

litres	litres gallons	gallon
4,55	1	0.22
9,09	2	0.44
13,64	3	0.66
18,18	4	0.88
22,73	5	1.10
27,28	6	1.32
31,82	7	1.54
36,37	8	1.76
40,91	9	1.98
45,46	10	2.20
90,92	20	4.40
136,38	30	6.60
181,84	40	8.80
227,30	50	11.00

N.B. : *les anglophones indiquent la décimale en utilisant un point.*
    In France the decimal point is indicated by a comma.

POIDS ET MESURES
WEIGHTS AND MEASURES

Mesures
Metric Measures

Longueur/ Length

1 millimètre (mm)		=0.0394 inch (in)
1 centimètre (cm)	= 10 mm	=0.3937 in
1 mètre (m)	= 100 cm	=1.0936 yards (yds)
1 kilomètre (km)	= 1000 m	=0.6214 mile

*Poids/*weight

1 milligramme (mg)		=0.0154 grain
1 gramme (g)	= 1000 mg	=0.0353 ounce (oz)
1 kilogramme (kg)	= 1000 g	=2.2046 pounds (lbs)
1 tonne (t)	= 1000 kg	=0.984 ton

*Surface/*Area

1 cm^2	= 100 mm^2	=0.1550 square (sq.) in
1 m^2	= 10000 cm^2	=1.1960 sq. yds
1 are (a)	= 100 m^2	=119.60 sq. yds
1 hectare (ha)	= 100 ares	=2.4711 acres

*Capacité/*capacity

1 cm^3		=0.0610 cubic (cu.) in
1 dm^3	= 1000 cm^3	=0.0353 cu. ft
1 m^3	= 1000 dm^3	=1.3080 cu. yds
1 litre	= 1 dm^3	=0.2200 gallon

Mesures britanniques
Imperial Measures

*Longueur/*Length

1 inch		= 2,54 cm
1 foot	=12 inches	= 0,3048 m
1 yard	=3 feet	= 0,9144 m
1 mile	=1760 yards	= 1,6093 km

Poids/Weight

1 ounce	=16 drams	= 28,35 g
1 pound	=16 ounces	= 0,4536 kg
1 stone	=14 pounds	= 6,3503 kg
1 hundredweight (cwt)	=112 pounds	= 50,802 kg
1 ton	=20 cwt	= 1,0161 tonnes

Surface/Area

1 sq. inch		= 6,4516 cm²
1 sq. foot	=144 sq. ins	= 0,0929 m²
1 sq. yard	=9 sq. ft.	= 0,8361 m²
1 acre	=4840 sq. yds	= 4046,9 m²
1 sq. mile	=640 acres	= 259 hectares

Capacité/Capacity

1 cu. inch		= 16,387 cm³
1 cu. foot	=1728 cu. inches	= 0,0283 m³
1 cu. yard	=27 cu. ft.	= 0,7646 m³
1 pint	=4 gills	= 0,5683 litre
1 quart	=2 pints	= 1,1365 litres
1 gallon	=8 pints	= 4,5461 litres

Mesures US: matières sèches
US: dry measures

1 pint	=0.9689 UK pint	= 0,5506 litre

Mesures US: liquides
US: liquid measures

1 fluid ounce	=1.0408 UK fl oz	= 0,0296 litre
1 pint (16 oz)	=0.8327 UK pint	= 0,4732 litre
1 gallon	=0.8327 UK gal	= 3,7853 litres

LES JOURS FERIES/
PUBLIC HOLIDAYS

Grande-Bretagne
Great Britain

1 January/*janvier*: New Year's Day/*Nouvel An*

2 January/*janvier* (Scotland/*Ecosse*)

17 March/*mars*: St Patrick's Day/*la Saint-Patrick* (Ireland/*Irlande*)

Easter Monday/*Lundi de Pâques*

May Day (first Monday in May/*1ᵉʳ lundi de mai*)

Spring holiday (last Monday in May/*dernier lundi de mai*)

Late Summer Holiday (last Monday in August/*dernier lundi d'août*)

25 December/*décembre*: Christmas Day/*Noël*

26 December: Boxing Day/*Lendemain de Noël*

France

1 janvier/January: *Nouvel An*/New Year's Day

Ascension/Ascension Thursday (*40 jours après Pâques*/40 days after Easter)

Vendredi Saint/Good Friday

Lundi de Pâques/Easter Monday

Lundi de Pentecôte/Whit Monday

1 mai/May: *Fête du Travail*/May Day

8 mai/May: *Armistice*/Armistice Day (1945)

14 juillet/July: *Fête nationale*/Bastille Day

15 août/August: *Assomption*/the Assumption

1 novembre/November: *Toussaint*/All Saints Day

11 novembre/November: *Armistice*/Armistice Day (1918)

25 décembre/December: *Noël*/Christmas Day

USA

1 January/*janvier*: New Year's Day/*Nouvel An*

Martin Luther King's Birthday/*Anniversaire de M.L. King*

(3rd Monday in January/*3ème lundi de janvier*)

Washington's birthday/*Anniversaire de Washington*

(3rd Monday in February/*3ème lundi de février*)

Memorial Day (last Monday in May/*le dernier lundi de mai*)

4 July/*juillet*: Independence Day/*Jour de l'Indépendance*

Labour Day/*Fête du Travail* (first Monday in September/*le premier lundi de septembre*)

Columbus day (2nd Monday in October/*2ème lundi d'octobre*)

11 November/*novembre*: Veteran's Day/*Armistice*

Thanksgiving (last Thursday in November/*dernier jeudi de novembre*)

25 December/*décembre*: Christmas Day/*Noël*

NOMS GEOGRAPHIQUES

Afghanistan *m* Afghanistan
Afrique *f* Africa
Afrique du Sud *f* South Africa
Algérie *f* Algeria
Allemagne *f* Germany
Amérique *f* America
Amérique du Nord *f* North America
Amérique du Sud *f* South America
Andorre *f* Andorra
Angleterre *f* England
Angola *m* Angola
Antilles *fpl* West Indies
Arabie Saoudite *f* Saudi Arabia
Argentine *f* Argentina
Arménie *f* Armenia
Asie *f* Asia
Australie *f* Australia
Autriche *f* Austria
Azerbaïdjan *m* Azerbaijan
Bahreïn *m* Bahrain
Bangladesh *m* Bangladesh
Barbade *f* Barbados
Belgique *f* Belgium
Bélize *m* Belize
Bhoutan *m* Bhutan
Biélorussie *f* Byelorussia
Bolivie *f* Bolivia
Botswana *m* Botswana
Brésil *m* Brazil
Brunei *m* Brunei
Bulgarie *f* Bulgaria
Cambodge *m* Cambodia
Cameroun *m* Cameroon
Canada *m* Canada
CEI (Communauté d'Etats Indépendants) *f* CIS (Commonwealth of Independent States)
Chili *m* Chili
Chine *f* China
Colombie *f* Colombia
Congo *m* Congo
Corée du Nord *f* North Korea

Corée du Sud *f* South Korea
Corse *f* Corsica
Costa Rica *m* Costa Rica
Côte d'Ivoire *f* Ivory Coast
Danemark *m* Denmark
Ecosse *f* Scotland
Egypte *f* Egypt
Eire *f* Eire
Emirats arabes unis *mpl* United Arab Emirates
Espagne *f* Spain
Estonie *f* Estonia
Etats-Unis *mpl* United States
Europe *f* Europe
Finlande *f* Finland
France *f* France
Gabon *m* Gabon
Gambie *f* Gambia
Géorgie *f* Georgia
Ghana *m* Ghana
Grande-Bretagne *f* Great Britain
Grèce *f* Greece
Groenland *m* Greenland
Guadeloupe *f* Guadeloupe
Guatemala *m* Guatemala
Guinée *f* Guinea
Guyana *f* Guyana
Guyane française *f* French Guiana
Hollande *f* Holland
Honduras *m* Honduras
Hong Kong Hong Kong
Hongrie *f* Hungary
îles de la Manche *fpl* Channel Islands
Inde *f* India
Indonésie *f* Indonesia
Irak *m* Iraq
Iran *m* Iran
Irlande *f* Ireland
Irlande du Nord *f* Northern Ireland
Islande *f* Iceland
Israël *m* Israel
Italie *f* Italy

Jamaïque *f* Jamaica
Japon *m* Japan
Jordanie *f* Jordan
Kenya *m* Kenya
Koweït *m* Kuwait
Laos *m* Laos
Lettonie *f* Latvia
Liban *m* Lebanon
Liberia *m* Liberia
Libye *f* Libya
Liechtenstein *m* Liechtenstein
Lituanie *f* Lithuania
Luxembourg *m* Luxemburg
Madagascar *m* Madagascar
Maghreb *m* countries of North Africa
Malawi *m* Malawi
Malaysia *f* Malaysia
Mali *m* Mali
Maroc *m* Morocco
Mauritanie *f* Mauritania
Mexique *m* Mexico
Moldavie *f* Moldavia
Moyen-Orient *m* Middle East
Mozambique *m* Mozambique
Namibie *f* Namibia
Népal *m* Nepal
Nicaragua *m* Nicaragua
Niger *m* Niger
Nigeria *m* Nigeria
Norvège *f* Norway
Nouvelle-Zélande *f* New Zealand
Oman *m* Oman
Ouganda *m* Uganda
Pakistan *m* Pakistan
Palestine *f* Palestine
Papouasie-Nouvelle-Guinée *f* Papua New Guinea
Paraguay *m* Paraguay
Pays-Bas *mpl* Netherlands
Pays de Galles *m* Wales
Pérou *m* Peru

Philippines *fpl* Philippines
Pologne *f* Poland
Portugal *m* Portugal
République dominicaine *f* Dominican Republic
République tchèque *f* Czech Republic
Roumanie *f* Romania
Royaume-Uni *m* United Kingdom
Russie *f* Russia
Scandinavie *f* Scandinavia
Sénégal *m* Senegal
Sierra Leone *f* Sierra Leone
Singapour *m* Singapore
Slovaquie *f* Slovakia
Somalie *f* Somalia
Soudan *m* Sudan
Sri Lanka *m* Sri Lanka
Suède *f* Sweden
Suisse *f* Switzerland
Syrie *f* Syria
Taiwan Taiwan
Tanzanie *f* Tanzania
Tasmanie *f* Tasmania
Tchad *m* Chad
Thaïlande *f* Thailand
Tiers Monde *m* Third World
Tobago Tobago
Togo *m* Togo
Trinidad *f* Trinidad
Tunisie *f* Tunisia
Turquie *f* Turkey
Ukraine *f* Ukraine
Uruguay *m* Uruguay
Venezuela *m* Venezuela
Viêt-nam *m* Vietnam
Yémen du Nord *m* North Yemen
Yémen du Sud *m* South Yemen
Zaïre *m* Zaire
Zambie *f* Zambia
Zimbabwe *m* Zimbabwe

GEOGRAPHICAL NAMES

* *employé sans article*　　　　　　　　* used without any article

Afghanistan Afghanistan *m*
Africa Afrique *f*
Algeria Algérie *f*
America Amérique *f*
Andorra Andorre *f* *
Angola Angola *m*
Argentina Argentine *f*
Armenia Arménie *f*
Asia Asie *f*
Australia Australie *f*
Austria Autriche *f*
Azerbaijan Azerbaïdjan *m*
Bahrain Bahreïn *m*
Bangladesh Bangladesh *m*
Barbados Barbade *f*
Belgium Belgique *f*
Belize Bélize *m*
Bhutan Bhoutan *m*
Bolivia Bolivie *f*
Botswana Botswana *m*
Brazil Brésil *m*
Brunei Brunei *m*
Bulgaria Bulgarie *f*
Byelorussia Biélorussie *f*
Cambodia Cambodge *m*
Cameroon Cameroun *m*
Canada Canada *m*
Chad Tchad *m*
Channel Islands îles de la
　　Manche *fpl*
Chili Chili *m*
China Chine *f*
**CIS (Commonwealth of Independent
　　States)** CEI (Communauté d'Etats
　　Indépendants) *f*
Colombia Colombie *f*
Congo Congo *m*
Corsica Corse *f*
Costa Rica Costa Rica *m*
Czech Republic République tchèque *f*
Denmark Danemark *m*

Dominican Republic République
　　dominicaine *f*
Egypt Egypte *f*
Eire Eire *f*
England Angleterre *f*
Estonia Estonie *f*
Ethiopia Ethiopie *f*
Europe Europe *f*
Finland Finlande *f*
France France *f*
French Guiana Guyane française *f*
Gabon Gabon *m*
Gambia Gambie *f*
Georgia Géorgie *f*
Germany Allemagne *f*
Ghana Ghana *m*
Great Britain Grande-Bretagne *f*
Greece Grèce *f*
Greenland Groenland *m*
Guadeloupe Guadeloupe *f*
Guatemala Guatemala *m*
Guinea Guinée *f*
Guyana Guyana *f*
Holland Hollande *f*
Honduras Honduras *m*
Hong Kong * Hong Kong
Hungary Hongrie *f*
Iceland Islande *f*
India Inde *f*
Indonesia Indonésie *f*
Iran Iran *m*
Iraq Irak *m*
Ireland Irlande *f*
Israel Israël *m* *
Italy Italie *f*
Ivory Coast Côte d'Ivoire *f*
Jamaica Jamaïque *f*
Japan Japon *m*
Jordan Jordanie *f*
Kenya Kenya *m*
Kuwait Koweït *m*

Laos Laos *m*
Latvia Lettonie *f*
Lebanon Liban *m*
Liberia Liberia *m*
Libya Libye *f*
Liechtenstein Liechtenstein *m*
Lithuania Lituanie *f*
Luxemburg Luxembourg *m*
Madagascar Madagascar *m* *
Malawi Malawi *m*
Malaysia Malaysia *f*
Mali Mali *m*
Mauritania Mauritanie *f*
Mexico Mexique *m*
Middle East Moyen-Orient *m*
Moldavia Moldavie *f*
Morocco Maroc *m*
Mozambique Mozambique *m*
Namibia Namibie *f*
Nepal Népal *m*
Netherlands Pays-Bas *mpl*
New Zealand Nouvelle-Zélande *f*
Nicaragua Nicaragua *m*
Niger Niger *m*
Nigeria Nigeria *m*
North America Amérique du Nord *f*
North Korea Corée du Nord *f*
North Yemen Yémen du Nord *m*
Northern Ireland Irlande du Nord *f*
Norway Norvège *f*
Oman Oman *m* *
Pakistan Pakistan *m*
Palestine Palestine *f*
Papua New Guinea Papouasie-Nouvelle-Guinée *f*
Paraguay Paraguay *m*
Peru Pérou *m*
Philippines Philippines *fpl*
Poland Pologne *f*
Portugal Portugal *m*
Romania Roumanie *f*
Russia Russie *f*
Saudi Arabia Arabie Saoudite *f*

Scandinavia Scandinavie *f*
Scotland Ecosse *f*
Senegal Sénégal *m*
Sierra Leone Sierra Leone *f*
Singapore Singapour *m* *
Slovakia Slovaquie *f*
Somalia Somalie *f*
South Africa Afrique du Sud *f*
South America Amérique du Sud *f*
South Korea Corée du Sud *f*
South Yemen Yémen du Sud *m*
Spain Espagne *f*
Sri Lanka Sri Lanka *m*
Sudan Soudan *m*
Sweden Suède *f*
Switzerland Suisse *f*
Syria Syrie *f*
Taiwan Taiwan *
Tanzania Tanzanie *f*
Tasmania Tasmanie *f*
Thailand Thaïlande *f*
Third World Tiers Monde *m*
Tobago Tobago *
Togo Togo *m*
Trinidad Trinidad *f*
Tunisia Tunisie *f*
Turkey Turquie *f*
Uganda Ouganda *m*
Ukraine Ukraine *f*
United Arab Emirates Emirats arabes unis *mpl*
United Kingdom Royaume-Uni *m*
United States Etats-Unis *mpl*
Uruguay Uruguay *m*
USA Etats-Unis *mpl*
Venezuela Venezuela *m*
Vietnam Viêt-nam *m*
Wales Pays de Galles *m*
West Indies Antilles *fpl*
Zaire Zaïre *m*
Zambia Zambie *f*
Zimbabwe Zimbabwe *m*

VILLES

Alger Algiers
Athènes Athens
Barcelone Barcelona
Bruxelles Brussels
Le Caire Cairo
Copenhague Copenhagen
Douvres Dover
Edimbourg Edinburgh
Francfort Frankfurt
Gênes Genoa
Genève Geneva
Hambourg Hamburg
La Haye The Hague
Lisbonne Lisbon
Londres London
Lyon Lyons
Marseille Marseilles
Montréal Montreal
Moscou Moscow
Québec Quebec City
Téhéran Tehran
Varsovie Warsaw
Venise Venice
Vienne Vienna

CITIES

Algiers Alger
Athens Athènes
Barcelona Barcelone
Brussels Bruxelles
Cairo Le Caire
Copenhagen Copenhague
Dover Douvres
Edinburgh Edimbourg
Frankfurt Francfort
Geneva Genève
Genoa Gênes
The Hague La Haye
Hamburg Hambourg
Lisbon Lisbonne
London Londres
Lyons Lyon
Marseilles Marseille
Montreal Montréal
Moscow Moscou
Quebec City Québec
Tehran Téhéran
Venice Venise
Vienna Vienne
Warsaw Varsovie

MONNAIES

couronne *f* crown
dinar *m* dinar
dollar *m* dollar
dollar australien *m* Australian dollar
dollar canadien *m* Canadian dollar
dollar de Hong Kong *m* Hong Kong dollar
drachme *f* drachma
escudo *m* escudo
florin *m* florin
franc *m* franc
franc belge *m* Belgian franc.
franc français *m* French franc
franc suisse *m* Swiss franc
lire *f* lira
livre *f* pound
livre irlandaise *f* punt
livre sterling *f* pound sterling
mark *m* mark
peseta *f* peseta
peso *m* peso
rand *m* rand
rial *m* rial
rouble *m* rouble
roupie *f* rupee
schilling *m* schilling
shilling *m* shilling
yen *m* yen

CURRENCIES

Australian dollar dollar australien *m*
Belgian franc franc belge *m*
Canadian dollar dollar canadien *m*
crown couronne *f*
dinar dinar *m*
dollar dollar *m*
drachma drachme *f*
escudo escudo *m*
florin florin *m*
franc franc *m*
French franc franc français *m*
Hong Kong dollar dollar de Hong-Kong *m*
lira lire *f*
mark mark *m*
peseta peseta *f*
peso peso *m*
pound livre sterling *f*
pound livre *f*
punt livre irlandaise *f*
rand rand *m*
rial rial *m*
rouble rouble *m*
rupee roupie *f*
schilling schilling *m*
shilling shilling *m*
Swiss franc franc suisse *f*
yen yen *m*

CLAVIERS QWERTY ET AZERTY
QWERTY AND AZERTY KEYBOARDS

DEDICATION

For everyone who told me not to give up on this book,
even when I thought it was deader than most of the
characters.

PROLOGUE

The White Lady: immediately before

When Jen thinks about that day, what she remembers is the heat. How it settles on her skin from the moment she wakes up, the lightest of pressures that starts to feel like a tightening vice, making her head throb and her pores prickle. London suffers in the humidity, the Central Line a direct route to hell, every conversation about how unbearable—yet wonderful—the summer is.

Jen knows she's been hotter than this before, but it is difficult to remember when. It feels like living on the surface of the sun. Until Ethan Sullivan walks into the public bar of the White Lady Inn, and she realises that all the heat in the city radiates from him. When you look at Ethan, you understand why planets revolve around the sun.

"He is so lush," moans Abby, batting her eyelashes whenever Ethan happens to glance their way. He flashes her a lazy grin, and Jen has to reach out to steady the drink Abby is pouring.

"Do remind him we don't do table service," she says, trying not to drip sweat into anybody's drink and wondering if she can fit herself inside the wine fridge.

"For Ethan Sullivan I'd do any sort of service," Abby breathes, and sets off across the bar, swinging her hips and flipping her hair. Abby has long blonde hair, straightened and highlighted to within an inch of its life. Jen is fascinated by the way it moves as one solid mass, with no give in it.

Movement catches her eye as the door opens and a young woman walks in, wild-eyed at the sight of the Amazing Ethan Sullivan, clutching a bulky parka around her.

Abby sets down Ethan's drink, completely ignoring the mirror image man sitting opposite him. Jen assumes this is his twin brother. He can't be anyone else. They have the same dark, unruly hair and dark, intense eyes, but while Ethan is all easy smiles and rockstar glamour, his brother is quiet, watchful, and obviously unhappy about something.

As the pub door swings shut, a hot breeze ripples over Jen's skin, and the pressure on her skull increases. Something is buzzing, a bee or a wasp, the drone maddening. She looks at her watch, trying to work out how long it'll be until she can go home.

The girl in the parka moves towards Ethan's table, her face drip white, perspiration beading her upper lip. The day is so hot, too hot for a coat like that. There is no wind outside, the July heat settling down over London like warm soup. Maybe that breeze heralds a storm. That might explain the headache and the scratchy feeling Jen's had all day.

Jen shakes herself and tries to banish her unease by making up scenarios in her head. Maybe the girl is knocked up and has come to demand child support from Ethan, and that's why she has the big coat on, to hide the baby bump. Or maybe she has proof the famous Irish charmer is putting the accent on, and—

The lights flicker.

"Ethan," the girl says, and the young god himself glances up, a ready smile on his lips. It dies a death when he sees her.

"Not you," he says, and his brother steps up, glowering. Ethan has a nice line in glowering but his brother could win a gold medal for it.

"I think you need to leave," he says, and she shakes her head, tears running down her face.

Jen chews her lip and turns to get the phone, her head pounding worse than ever. If there's going to be an incident maybe she should call the—

"Jenny?"

A little girl in a Victorian pinafore stands before the wine fridge, her face pale and serious and ever so slightly transparent.

"Get down," she says.

Jen ignores her, as she's been ignoring her for years now. But then an anguished wail comes from the girl in the parka, and suddenly the freezing mass of the child in the pinafore slams into her, knocking Jen off her feet and tripping over a box of crisps, to land sprawling on the floor, sprayed with lager from the drip tray she hits on the way down.

"I'm covered in—" she begins furiously, and then the girl in the parka detonates the bomb under her coat and plunges Jen into hell.

CHAPTER ONE

The trick was to focus on small things instead of the whole.

Take shaving, for instance. Quinn could put it off for as long as possible, but eventually he started looking like a hobo, and Tessa complained it was putting off clients. So he plugged in the electric razor and angled out the shaving mirror and focused solely on about two square inches of his face at a time. And when he was done he folded the mirror back where he didn't have to look at it any more, and avoided his reflection for another week or so.

He took one black sock from the drawer and put it on. Strange how he still kept them balled up in pairs. Force of habit, he supposed. The other one was already on his foot, inside his shoe, propped up neatly next to the bed where he'd left it last night.

Saved a fortune on socks, only having one leg.

Quinn rolled the latex liner up and over his knee, pulled on the prosthetic until it clicked into place, and finished dressing. His old flat used to have a big cheval

5

mirror, left behind by an ex-girlfriend, useful for checking his appearance before he left the house. Of course, she'd preferred it for altogether more kinky pastimes, including, Quinn suspected, fantasising that he was his twin brother.

He'd left it in Donnycarney when he moved. He saw Ethan enough in his nightmares. He didn't need to see him in the mirror too.

It was only a five minute drive to work, but Quinn walked, mostly because he damn well could. The breeze blew in off the sea, bringing with it a fine mist and the scent of gently rotting seaweed. Wirpness-on-Sea had a handful of charms, chief among them its wide sandy beach and abundance of pleasant seaside pubs, but that wasn't why Quinn had moved here.

Sullivan Investigations occupied a series of rooms above a flower shop on the High Street. There was a discreet door in the side of the building, bearing a discreet sign in a discreet font. If his business was anything, it was discreet.

Tessa was already at her desk when he went in, talking on the phone to someone who seemed to need a lot of reassurance. Tessa usually worked the infidelity cases, of which they had a staggering amount. She was much better at being sympathetic than he was.

The phone rang, and since they didn't have a receptionist, Quinn picked it up. "Sullivan Investigations."

"Hi," said the voice, "it's Beth from downstairs. The flower shop?"

Since said shop was called Flowers By Beth, he didn't really think this needed clarifying, but he said, "Hi, howareya, Beth?" as politely as he could.

"We have a delivery for you. Um. A wreath."

He closed his eyes. "Who from?"

"Couple of ladies. Think they're here on holiday."

"Cancel it."

"They've already paid. They want me to send them a picture of it when it's finished."

"Then give it to the church or something. I don't want it."

"It, er, has Ethan's name on it."

Quinn counted to ten.

"Tessa usually tells me to make a bouquet instead since she can use that in Reception," Beth admitted.

"Usually? How many of these have we had?" There were often flowers in the shabby reception area, but he'd just assumed it was something Tessa brought in.

"Er, I'll check." He heard computer keys being clicked. "This would be the twentieth."

"What? Jaysus. Really? In five years?"

"No, since January. There used to be a lot more. They usually go to the church, or sometimes people take them home." She paused. "I used to try to dissuade them, but you know. Business is business. Funerals," her voice wobbled a bit, "are good business."

He sighed. Beth had rent to pay like everyone else. "Look, just… if they want the damn thing, send it back to them."

"They want you to have it."

"Then send them the picture and throw the fecking thing out. I don't want it. I get enough reminders of my brother, okay?"

There was another pause. "I understand," Beth said softly, and something in her tone told him she actually did. "I won't deliver it."

Quinn put the phone down, making a note to ask Tessa how many of their floral displays were actually tributes from Ethan's fans.

He sorted through the phone messages she'd left on his desk, the most prominent of which written entirely in capitals and said, "APPLICANT FOR

OFFICE MANAGER 11AM!!!" Quinn wasn't entirely sure they had enough work for an office manager, or receptionist or secretary or whatever the feck he was supposed to call her, but Tessa was adamant that she wasn't answering calls, typing up files, and 'updating that bastard website' any more.

He sent her a quick email: "You can interview her, then," and got another back, apparently typed at lightning speed with one hand, since she was still on the phone.

"Who says shes a she?"

He mentally inserted the appropriate apostrophe and replied, "Your fossilised old boss. Is she a she?"

A longer pause this time, then Tessa sent a single word, "Yes."

Quinn rolled his eyes. He turned from the computer and scanned the to-do list he'd made on Friday. He'd done several of these tasks over the weekend, and he congratulated himself on his efficiency, ignoring the little voice inside which said that working over the weekend when he didn't have to was a really tragic thing to do. There were a couple of security checks he needed to do, some corporate background work, and from Tessa's scribbled notes there were a few new jobs to look into. Another Scooby case. Some woman in Manchester being plagued by a ghost who Quinn could tell even from the briefest notes was probably a combination of deliberate drugging and suggestion.

Just once, Quinn thought, it'd be nice for some dame to bring trouble to his office and ask him to... ehm, to find a Maltese falcon or... something. Okay, he was fuzzy on the details. But infidelity and corporate background work, interspersed with the occasional fake ghost story, that was his lot.

You don't really want 'exciting', he told himself. *You've had enough of 'exciting' for a lifetime.*

He sighed, and got to work.

"Remind me again why we moved to Little Haunting-By-The-Sea?" said Alice, and Jen did her best to ignore her. Since she was sitting on the kitchen cupboard where Jen was trying to unpack her crockery, this wasn't easy, but she'd had a lifetime of denial to help her. "There is literally nothing here."

"Misuse of the word 'literally'," Jen said absently, and then cursed herself for engaging. "It's called Wirpness-on-Sea and it has a population of fifteen hundred, shops and services thereof, several churches, a primary school, revival cinema, and beach complete with ice cream stands, cafés, dinky little huts that cost a small fortune, and a pier. That's not nothing."

Alice sighed theatrically. "It's boring," she said, swinging her feet silently.

"Are you sure you died at nine? You sound more like a teenager every day."

"Oh, sure, bring up the fact that I'm dead. Thanks for reminding me."

Jen looked around the pocket-sized kitchen with its painted cupboards that weren't quite retro enough to be fashionable again. "Could you move your feet, please? Or I'll put these glasses straight through them."

Alice made a face, but she shifted her little leather clogs out of the way. She was as insubstantial as air, but Jen knew how she hated it when someone or something passed right through her.

"Sets a bad example," Alice had said, back when she was older than Jen. "Real children can't walk through plate glass windows. Trust me on this."

Jen finished the glasses and moved onto plates. Never particularly impressive in the first place, her mismatched collection of cheap or inherited crockery had been damaged in every successive house move, and there had been plenty of those.

For a long moment she stared at the plates wrapped neatly in newspaper. Her sister would have thrown them out and started fresh with something matching. Her mother would have put them at the back of the cupboard, out of sight. Jen had travelled with them, cracked and mismatched, all these years.

She shook herself. *They're just plates, Jennifer. Not everything is a metaphor.*

Why Wirpness? Well, it was somewhere she hadn't been before. Somewhere no one knew her, or even knew of her. Somewhere she hadn't had some kind of breakdown in the graveyard—the local churches didn't do burials any more and the nearest municipal site was twenty miles away. Somewhere she hadn't had a meltdown passing any terrible little roadside shrines to fatal crashes. She had checked that the sandy beach hadn't suffered any tragic accidents, that the wide bay wasn't home to any spectacular shipwrecks, and that no one had died in any other violent way in the environs.

All right, there had been a sea battle out in the bay a few hundred years ago, and any town trapped between the fens and the sea was probably going to have a few sad stories, but she'd walked all around town and no unhappy souls had leapt out at her.

Yet, anyway.

And it was quite hard to get to, what with Suffolk having no motorways and the nearest train station being twenty minutes away and not even having a direct line to London. Her family would find it inconvenient to turn up on the doorstep without notice.

"You're going to be late," Alice said helpfully, as Jen pushed her hair out of her sweaty face.

"It's a five minute walk."

"Have you timed it?"

"Nowhere in Wirpness is more than a five minute

walk."

"The harbour is. I went there the other day. Took me twenty minutes."

"Alice, your legs are only about a foot long. And you *float*. Your concept of walking-speed is not precisely normal."

Alice snorted. "What would you know about normal?"

Jen put the last of her ugly plates away and closed the cupboard. She had an hour to shower and find something suitable to wear for a job interview. There had been a time, once, when this comprised precisely one suit, bought cheaply on the high street, with some equally inexpensive heels to go with it. It used to sit at the Sensible End of her wardrobe, away from all the pinks and purples.

These days, the Sensible End of her wardrobe comprised, well, all of it. Jen told herself there was nothing wrong with growing up and wearing grey and navy, but the cowardly part of her brain knew it for the excuse it was.

Anyway, surely Sullivan Investigations would prefer a soberly dressed office manager. Someone who looked professional and discreet. Her previous wardrobe of neon purple and hot pink wouldn't precisely fit in.

She pushed back the hair that was as close to its natural blonde as it was ever going to get. "I'm going to get changed," she told Alice. "And you, you're going to disappear."

"You never take me anywhere any more," Alice complained.

Jen threw up her hands. It was like having a child. A dead, creepy, see-through child. "Don't mess up my interview."

"When have I ever messed up anything for you?" Alice asked, and Jen laughed hollowly as she climbed the stairs.

The wind whipped merrily along the seafront, blowing Quinn's hair into his eyes. He squinted at the numbers on the brightly-painted beach huts, shook his head at the more terrible puns being pressed into service as names, and spotted a man standing nervously by the steps down to the beach.

Thinning hair, suit jacket ineffective against the sea fret, nervous expression. "Mr Taggart?"

The man turned, eyes wide, nodded once, made some complicated gesture which Quinn was supposed to have memorised, and scurried down the steps onto the beach.

Quinn sighed. Fecking beach. "Can we do this up here?" he said, but Taggart had gone out of earshot. Quinn glanced down at the damp sand, paused to remember the last time he'd got grit in his prosthetic, and jammed his hands in his pockets to wait.

Taggart turned back, faltered to see Quinn simply waiting there, and peered at him.

Quinn gestured him closer. Taggart paused, and trotted back unwillingly.

The beach was several feet lower than the promenade. Quinn squatted on his haunches, which wasn't pleasant on his knee, and leaned down.

"Mr Taggart? From the Seaview Hotel?"

Taggart's eyes went wide, and Quinn repressed a sigh.

"Don't use my name!"

Quinn looked around. Nobody within earshot. Did the beach itself have ears? Was the lifebelt a listening device? Maybe there was a SWAT team hiding in a beach hut.

Or maybe he was just here to get proof of infidelity for a case Tessa was working on while she interviewed their new secretary.

"I'm Quinn, from Sullivan Investigations. We spoke on the phone? You had a list of guests for me?"

Taggart looked around as if expecting assassination. Quinn waited patiently.

"From the weekend of the 25th? I just need to know if this woman was staying with you."

Taggart fumbled a piece of paper out of his pocket. "I could get into trouble—"

"It's fine."

"Data protection—"

"Did you black out the other names like I asked?"

Taggart nodded. He still didn't want to hand over the paper.

"Then it's no one else's info." He snatched the sheet of printer paper, glanced at it and folded it into his own pocket before Taggart could regret anything. The poor fool had blacked out the other guest's names but not their phone numbers. No wonder he was nervous. He was an idiot.

"You won't tell anyone—"

"Of course not," Quinn said smoothly. After this, it was really the lawyer who'd be deciding what to do with the information. "You've been a great help. I'll let you get on now."

He stood, none too smoothly. Stupid knee. Taggart watched him, looking confused.

"That's it?"

Quinn shrugged. "That's it. We really could have done this over the phone."

"But—I thought—"

You thought it would be all codenames and pretending to talk to other people and maybe some kind of stylish hat. "Nope, all straightforward. You take care now," said Quinn, and strolled off along the promenade. He didn't look back to see if Taggart was still there.

Out at sea, several large ships waited on the horizon,

visible through patches of cloud. Containers bound for Lowestoft, Ipswich, Harwich. Passenger ferries on 'mini cruises' to Amsterdam or Bruges. The occasional fishing boat.

Quinn glanced at his watch, then back into town. Even if he walked slowly he still wouldn't give Tessa much time.

His hands patted his pockets, but they were empty of any cigarette packets. That was on purpose, of course, but it was also a shame. A ciggie was a great prop, an excuse to hang around outside and waste time.

He supposed a cup of overpriced, cardboard coffee would have to do instead.

There had been a Starbucks in Wirpness for about five minutes, a few years ago. The locals had not been kind, and the tourists preferred quirky cafés with sea views and room for buggies. The whole point of Wirpness was quirky individuality.

He bought a cup of something horribly sweet from Emma & Jo's self-consciously kooky teashop with the artisan vegan bakery attached, and sat at a pavement table painted pink. It was too cold to sit out, really, the sea mist lingering in the street, but the pink table had a view of the service alley that led to the office door.

Tessa's office was the one overlooking the High Street. He could see shadows moving inside, but no detail. Jennifer Hargrave's appointment had been for eleven o'clock, and Quinn had left at quarter to, not quite willing to reveal himself to her just yet. Better to get Tessa's impression of the applicant before she was exposed to Ethan Sullivan's twin.

Maybe we should change the name of the agency. Sullivan was his uncle's name, his mother's maiden name, and the stage name Ethan had chosen. Quinn had never thought it so unusual people would automatically make the connection, but maybe…?

His train of thought was stalled by movement inside Tessa's office, and then a minute or so later the door to the alley opened and he straightened in his seat.

The woman who exited Sullivan Investigations wore a plain grey suit and had fair hair. She was probably around thirty. That was about all he could tell from here. What did he expect?

At least she's not wearing a Devilborn *t-shirt.*

He wondered how long this one would last.

"Tessa Adams," said the smiling woman, holding out her hand for Jen to shake. She was petite, with dark curls and freckles and big brown eyes. Her glasses were smudged, her trousers had dog hair on them, and when she walked Jen could see her socks were mismatched. Her smile was easy, her demeanour friendly. Jen guessed this was probably a calculated move, to put nervous clients at ease. After all, no one came to a private detective for happy reasons.

"Jen Hargrave," she replied, shaking Tessa's hand and trying to look around without being obvious. The reception area contained a cheap-looking sofa, a table with some rather funereal-looking flowers on it, and a desk bearing an old computer. On the walls were a few tired-looking old photos of the town and behind the desk stood a row of filing cabinets and stacks of phone directories. The room was cold, but then Jen was always cold.

"Come on through." The office Tessa led her into was small, lined with bookshelves and filing cabinets, and contained a small, cheap desk with a laptop open on it. There was a frosted window to the reception area, and another small one looking over the High Street.

Leaning against the filing cabinets was a man in shirt and tie, a leather jacket over his shoulder. Tessa brushed past him to sit behind the desk, didn't introduce him, and after a moment spent wondering if she was supposed to say hello, Jen followed her cue.

This must be the other partner in the agency. Tessa Adams and James Quinn, according to the website, which didn't contain any photos. Jen presumed it was easier to stay incognito that way.

Maybe this was a test of some kind. Or maybe...

Tessa gestured her to a seat and began going through standard interview questions, asking Jen how much office experience she had, whether she'd ever worked on a reception desk, how she was at answering the phone. Jen breezed through them. She was good at getting jobs, just not at keeping them.

She tried not to let her gaze stray to the man with the leather jacket.

"Reason for leaving last job?"

"I moved away," Jen said easily.

"You have had a lot of jobs..." Tessa said doubtfully.

"Can't keep a position?" said the man, and Jen looked at him for the first time, a little startled by his confrontational technique.

"A lot of them were temporary," she said. "Temporary positions. I've moved a lot, you see, so I didn't take up long contracts."

"Can I ask why you've moved a lot?" asked Tessa. She didn't look round.

Because eventually either I freak people out too much or I can't handle the volume of ghosts who get to hear about me. "Just looking for the right place to settle, I guess."

The man snorted. "And Wirpness is it?"

"I like small towns. They're friendly, and the crime rate is low," said Jen, a suspicion beginning to form in her mind.

"You're not looking for excitement, then?" said Tessa.

"No. Exactly the opposite," Jen said firmly.

"Good, because I'm afraid excitement isn't really on the agenda here. PI work isn't like it is in film noir; there are very few mysteries to be solved and we tend to leave crimes to the police. We do a lot of background checks for corporate clients, infidelity cases, the occasional search for long-lost family members."

Jen nodded, and paid attention, and answered all the questions the right way. She was excellent at knowing what to say in interviews.

The man with the leather jacket leaned back against the filing cabinets, his head tipped to one side, and regarded her with an unreadable expression. When Tessa left the room to make a copy of Jen's ID, he said, "Oh, it's like that parlour game where you remove something from a tray and people have to guess what it is."

Jen blinked at him. "I'm sorry?"

"She's just checking you're not going to nick any—" he broke off abruptly, and stared at her. "You," he began, then stopped. He blinked hard. He smoothed back his hair. "You're not a thief," he said, his tone oddly accusatory.

"No, of course not. Clean record. I've even been DBS checked." And hadn't that been fun, with her background.

"What's that when—" he broke off again. Lowered his voice. "You can hear me?"

The cold in the room grew more intense. Jen looked at him, at his slicked back hair and retro leather bomber jacket, and she sighed.

Well, that was a whole two days without meeting a new dead person.

"You're surprised?" she asked heavily.

"Well—yes. I mean… no one else ever has. I mean… ever. Not since—"

"You died?" she said.

He stared. He opened his mouth a few times, then shut it again. "All right," he said. He cleared his throat. "How do you know that?"

Jen was debating how to reply when the door opened and Tessa came back in. Glancing easily around the room, her gaze didn't linger for a second on the man by the filing cabinets.

"There you go," she said, handing Jen her ID back. "Now, if you have any questions…?"

A shaft of weak sunlight penetrated the front window, and filtered right through the third person in the room.

Who is this dead guy? Can anyone else see him? Is he Mr Sullivan, the previous owner?

Is the previous owner any relation to Ethan Sullivan?

"Ask her," the ghost said slowly, "about the paranormal investigations."

"You do paranormal investigations?" Jen said, surprised. There hadn't been a lot about that on the website.

"Well, the odd one or two. Old Mr Sullivan—the previous owner, I trained under him—had quite an interest in them, and we still get a few. We get people coming to us with ghost stories, nearly all of which we can solve by exposing a fraud of some kind. I call them the Scooby cases." She laughed.

"What about the ones you can't solve?"

"Well, there are always cases you can't solve. That doesn't mean ghosts exist," Tessa added, as if by rote.

"No," Jen said, looking directly at the ghost. "It doesn't."

"My partner deals with them," Tessa said, and paused as if waiting for Jen to derive some meaning from that. For a dreadful moment Jen thought she was going to turn to the ghost, and he was her partner, and then Jen wouldn't just be plagued by bloody ghosts, she'd be working for one—but then Tessa said, "He's out at the moment. Now, is there anything else you'd like to ask me?"

Jen had these kinds of questions ready prepared too. She asked about the daily responsibilities that would be expected of her, client confidentiality, and why the last office manager had left.

"Ah. Personal issues. Quinn and I have been muddling along by ourselves for a while, but really there's too much admin for us."

"I see," said Jen. She didn't look at the ghost, but he gave her an answer anyway.

"It wasn't me! No one's seen me in years. She left because she was a fruitcake."

Jen felt her smile grow a little bit tight.

Tessa regarded her for a long moment, then she said, "All right. Now. We do quite often deal with sensitive cases, infidelity for one but also sometimes we're asked to look into a disappearance or death. Usually as a private matter. We do sometimes have quite recently bereaved clients coming to us looking for answers where quite often, I'm afraid, there are none. How do you think you'd deal with them?"

The ghost rolled his eyes in Jen's direction. "Yes, Miss Hargrave," he said with mock gravity. "How do you think you'd deal with dead people?"

"I think I'd manage pretty well," Jen said.

The rest of the interview went smoothly enough for Jen to think she might have got the job. She nearly slipped up when the ghost said, "Ask her about her dog, people love you asking about their pets," and she tried to ignore him only to blurt it out five minutes later.

"Oh, the dog hairs," Tessa said, brushing ineffectually at them. "Nothing really gets rid of them..."

They shook hands and Jen left, pausing on the cool damp street to get her bearings. The back of her neck prickled, but then the bomber jacket ghost zoomed through the wall, and she sighed.

"So you can see me?" He was practically dancing down the street, sunlight filtering through his body. Jen jammed her hands in her pockets.

"See you, hear you, if I got close enough I could probably smell you."

"Nah," Alice said, wrinkling her nose, "grave stink."

Through long habit, Jen did not jump as the little girl appeared in front of her. *Was she there all the time? Watching the interview? Christ Alice, can you leave me alone for five minutes!*

"I jolly well do not smell of the grave!" He sniffed his arm ostentatiously. "I smell pleasantly earthy and woodsy."

Jen rolled her eyes and kept walking. The morning sea fret was burning off, the day turning mild and pleasant, there were a handful of late holidaymakers around, and down the road someone was baking bread. It was all bright and autumnal and normal.

And beside her were two bickering ghosts. *So, normal then.*

"How long have you been dead?"

"Oh… seventy years? Maybe eighty. Give or take."

Jen glanced at him, then at the nearest shop window, where there was a poster advertising the RNLI open day. Generally it was better to look as if she had an excuse for talking to herself. Maybe she should get a dog. "World War Two?"

"Spitfire pilot," he replied proudly.

"Spitfire," Alice said primly, smoothing her pinafore. "What a ghastly name."

He gave her a withering look. "Don't bother," Jen advised. "It's water off a duck's back to her."

"Do you have a name, O Firespitter?" Alice asked.

"Flying Officer Daniel Jones." The ghost saluted

smartly. Jen tipped two fingers to her temple in response. *So not a Sullivan then. Not the previous owner of the detective agency. Just a random ghost kicking round the place.* "You," he added with a charming smile, "can call me Danny."

"Died in combat?" Alice asked.

"Returning home. Nearly made it, but they'd hit my fuel line and I ditched in Blighty. Only just made it to land, thought I was going to end up in the drink."

"You don't have to take me through it," Jen said quickly. She'd heard enough grisly 'how I died' stories to last her lifetime, Alice's lifetime, and probably Flight Officer Jones's too.

"No. Best not. Don't want you fainting now, do we?"

Jen nearly snorted at the irony. *You live with the memory of the White Lady, and tell me if the story of a leaky fuel line will make you faint.*

"Trust me, I've heard worse," she said, and when he opened his mouth to reply, she held up a hand. "No. Just… trust me."

CHAPTER TWO

"Christ, he's even left the phone numbers in."

Quinn watched Tessa scan Taggart's printout. "Man's an eejit. He wanted to talk in code."

"Some people. Still, it has what I need. One more divorce on the way."

"Doesn't it make you proud."

Tessa snorted. Divorced since her kids were small, she pretended to be tough about it all. She dropped a file on his desk and turned to go. "New girl."

The blonde. "You've offered her the job?"

"Yeah, I thought I'd go completely over your head on this one, Quinn."

He made a face at her sarcasm and picked up the file. "Jennifer Hargrave."

"To be honest, once I'd weeded out the crazies there weren't a lot of choices. I'm going to call her this afternoon, unless you've any objections?"

Yes, he did have objections. He didn't want an office manager, he didn't want to have to make friends or even be polite to anyone. He didn't want the pity and sympathy that inevitably followed on from making a new acquaintance. He didn't want another person staring at him, trying to work out why he'd survived and his brother was dead.

He didn't want someone else to try and be normal to.

But he picked up the file anyway and flicked through it. "The one who'd had lots of jobs?"

"Yes. Mostly temporary contracts. No one had anything bad to say about her. When pressed, a couple admitted she daydreamed a bit, but she always turns up for work, she's polite, learns fast, doesn't nick petty cash…"

He flicked past her CV to Tessa's report, which surmised that Jen Hargrave had done no more than a little light editing on her CV, which was more or less normal. She'd checked out with the Disclosure and Barring Service, and even her academic record was entirely unremarkable.

Under Hobbies and Interests she'd written, "Reading and television," which in Quinn's experience was what people put if they either had no interests whatsoever and were the most boring person alive, or occasionally if their actual hobbies were too weird to tell an employer about.

He thought about the girl with the pointed teeth, and had to make himself focus on Jennifer Hargrave's application again.

"Gaps in employment?" There were a few, and they seemed to coincide with a move from one area to another.

Tessa shrugged. "Nothing more than a few months. When I asked she said she had a small inheritance to live off if she found herself in between jobs. It checks out: her dad died when she was eleven and left a decent life insurance policy. She has one older sister, and her mother remarried a few years later. A banker. The family isn't short of a few quid."

"Then why's she after moving to a poky little seaside town to work for an even pokier detective agency?"

Tessa shrugged. "She said she was looking for the right place to settle."

Quinn flicked back through the pages, chewing his lip.

"I checked her out online as well," Tessa said quietly. "She's not with any of the fanclubs, doesn't have Twitter and hardly uses Facebook. Last mention of any celebrity she made was a teenage crush on Robbie Williams."

Quinn looked back at Tessa's report, his eyes automatically searching out the data from five years ago. Lived in London. Worked for a catering firm, for which she'd taken too many jobs for Tessa to bother noting down.

"You want me to check her out further, I can," Tessa said, and Quinn closed his eyes. What would she find? That this Jennifer girl had heard of his brother? So had everyone else.

Maybe she actually did like reading and television. And maybe in all the television she liked she wasn't an obsessive *Devilborn* fan. Maybe she was just... normal.

He glanced at his calendar. He'd got that job in Manchester that'd take him away for a day or two, so if this girl turned out to be a nightmare, Tessa could deal with her. If necessary, he could manufacture an excuse to stay away longer.

It wasn't cowardice, he told himself. It was self-preservation.

He sighed and looked up. "Unless she's one of the crazies, she'll do."

"I can offer her the job?"

"You can offer her the job." He tossed the file on the desk, and Tessa beamed at him and scurried out to make the call.

Quinn stared at her silhouette through the frosted glass until it disappeared, and then he stared at the glass a while longer.

The last receptionist they'd had was called Jeaniene and it had taken him most of the three months she'd lasted to remember how to spell that. She'd spent most of her time texting, tweeting and faffing about online, and whenever she saw him her eyes got all big and sad and she repeated, "Such a *shame*."

Technically, she didn't qualify as one of the crazies, but he was irritated by her nonetheless.

Jeaniene had left to 'find herself' at some retreat in… oh, he didn't care, he'd stopped listening. She'd followed Chloe, Leah, and Alison, who had lasted nine months between them and who, to be honest, blurred in his memory: a succession of nubile young moppets who'd tried everything from sympathy to Wonderbras to get his attention.

Before them there had been Janice, who was in her fifties and seemed so sensible that he and Tessa had been lulled into a false sense of security. Janice turned out to be called Mary, and she was the founder of one of Ethan's biggest fan clubs, who carried around in her wallet a lock of hair she insisted was his.

After this, Quinn had brushed up on his cyber skills and made a point of checking IP addresses.

Each time they advertised the position, the largest number of candidates was ruled out before the interview stage for their not-too-subtle fascination with death, with Ethan, or with Ethan's death.

He thought back to Vera, who'd been Uncle Kieran's secretary. Of motherly appearance and sharp wit, she'd eventually retired in order to spend more time with her grandchildren. At the time, Quinn had teased Kieran about getting a hot young new girl for the front desk, and his uncle had just rolled his eyes and said, "Lad, if you hire based on appearance you're too dumb to run this place."

Quinn ran his mind over the succession of applicants they'd had following Vera's departure. Several had made film noir references, which was to be expected when dealing with a private detective—he even did it himself sometimes—but not five times in one interview.

They got a lot of goths, or emos or whatever he was supposed to call them now. Quinn hadn't seen a predilection for black eyeliner as a problem, until he realised how far along the goth scale they were. The last one they'd interviewed had filed her teeth into fangs and hissed at the sunlight. Quinn instituted a new rule: nobody obsessed with death. It was distressing enough to him, let alone the clients.

And of course there were the fans. Ethan had only just progressed from small roles on *Midsomer Murders* and *Poirot*, but he was fast becoming a heartthrob. When the first episode of *Devilborn* aired, Ethan's tortured, charming, and possibly-but-only-maybe-evil character, Young Nick, made him a star. Quinn hadn't expected that would be a problem, but he'd reckoned without the power and determination of the average fan in the Internet age.

News that Ethan Sullivan had an identical twin didn't take long to get around, and thanks to an off-hand comment Ethan had made in an interview, the fans had tracked Quinn down. If they couldn't have Young Nick, they'd settle for his brother.

"You're brooding," Tessa said, and he glanced up, startled, to see her in the doorway. She already had her coat on.

"I amn't. I was thinking."

"Same thing, with you. I'm off," she added, nodding at the clock. Quinn hadn't even noticed it was clocking-off time. "She said yes to the job, by the way."

"Grand," said Quinn, wondering what was wrong with this one.

"I don't know what's wrong with me," Jen said, staring at the phone in her hand.

"Where do you want me to start?" asked Alice.

Jen wrinkled her nose at the ghost, who was lounging six inches above the sofa. "I just said yes to that job." To a job at Sullivan Investigations. *Sullivan*. It was pure coincidence—she'd looked it up and there were about twenty thousand people with that surname in the UK. Hardly uncommon. Perfectly normal. A coincidence.

And besides, Ethan Sullivan had been Irish, and Wirpness was probably as far as you could get from Ireland without leaving the British Isles.

"The detective one? Good for you. We could be like that TV thing where the detective's dead partner still helps him solve crimes. Ramsey and Hobbs."

"*Randall and Hopkirk (Deceased)*," Jen corrected absently. She tilted her head at Alice. "Do you really think I should work in a place that's haunted?"

"Who better?"

"But what if he turns out to be really annoying? Remember Whitby?"

"I don't know what you were thinking. Whitby, for heaven's sake. Every black dog a vampire in disguise."

"There's no such thing as vampires."

"Dear, you're talking to a ghost."

Jen ignored her. "I can't deal with another lonely, overfamiliar spook. He was creepy."

"He was dead."

"You're dead, you're not creepy." Honesty forced her to add, "Most of the time. And you don't come on to me like he did." She shuddered at the memory. Alice's touch was like a cloud, cold and insubstantial, uncomfortable but rarely unpleasant. Wrestling with the suicidal teenager who professed love for her two decades after hurling himself off a cliff was like being assaulted by a dead octopus.

"And then there was that woman in Ludlow. With the children. Do you remember?"

Alice made a face. "She kept trying to adopt me. But this Danny isn't going to be like that."

"Not like her, no, but I bet he was a regular Lord Flashheart before his plane came down. Girl in every airbase. You can tell it, looking at him. The good-looking ones are always trouble." She stood up, mentally totting up the laundry she'd need to do this weekend. Most of her work clothes had been crumpled up in boxes and suitcases for weeks.

Alice shrugged. "I'll have to take your word for it. Now, please tell me you're going shopping tomorrow? I saw a place on the High Street, they had some darling skirts with flowers on them, and—"

"I don't do floral."

"Well, something in a solid colour, then. Perhaps a nice green. You wear green ever so well."

Jen crossed her little living room and opened the door to the stairs, which had more or less been built into a cupboard and weren't much more than a ladder with a backboard. She'd had to pay the removals men extra to get a mattress up them. "Alice, stop it."

"I just can't bear to see you in all those greys and blacks. You look like you're already dead."

"Didn't people go into mourning for years in your day?"

"Yes, and it was ridiculous. Mam used to say a body'd never be out of black when the typhus was in town."

"Well, I like black. And grey," Jen lied. "They're... dignified." They're *safe*.

"They're boring. You used to be so much more fun,

Jenny."

"Well, I grew up."

"Oh all right, rub it in."

The narrow landing at the top of the stairs had a door to each of the bedrooms, the smaller of which was basically a storage room with a futon in it, and to the bathroom, which Jen thought might be the smallest space to ever have a bath, toilet and sink wedged into it. The place had been a weekend cottage before she bought it, not commercially rented and therefore terribly old fashioned.

The bath suite was pale pink and the tiles were chipped, but the shower was new enough to be usable. Jen leaned over and switched it on.

"I thought bathrooms like this went out with the ark," Alice said, peering at the shell-shaped toilet lid.

"People who grew up with tin baths and outside toilets don't get to throw stones at other people's bathrooms," Jen said, reaching for the hem of her sweater and pausing.

"Stones would be an improvement," Alice said.

"Are you going to watch me take a shower?" Jen said pointedly, and Alice rolled her eyes.

"Don't be such a prude. Remember when we used to take baths together?"

"Yes, when you were still older than me. Alice. Please. I shouldn't have to keep asking."

Alice made a noise like a huffy teenager and drifted back into the hallway. "It's nothing I haven't seen before," she called as Jen shut the door.

Jen stripped off her sweater and looked at the thin red scars on her stomach. "Wanna bet?" she murmured.

The first few days at Sullivan Investigations were relatively painless. Tessa explained the office quirks, showed Jen where the kettle was, and remained blissfully unaware of Danny Jones's leering over her cleavage. The boss—Tessa just called him Quinn—was currently away, so the place was quiet. Jen fielded calls, answered emails, and did her best to ignore Danny leering over her own cleavage.

"Come on, old thing," he complained. "This place has been an office for seventy years. Haven't seen totty with her top off for yonks."

"And you're not going to," Jen murmured, while Alice loudly informed him he was disgusting.

"I'm not disgusting, Alice, I'm a chap. I bet it's been a long time since you enjoyed a... er, what do you enjoy?"

"Adult conversation," Alice replied cuttingly.

"But you're just a sprog! You should be out enjoying wholesome sprog stuff. You know, running around getting grubby with kids your own age."

Alice gave him a look that was far too old for any nine-year-old to have mastered. "My own age? You mean, a hundred and fifty nine? Rather a lack of them about."

"No, I mean..."

"You mean living children? They get a little bit creeped out by oogly-booglies," she said, waggling her fingers at him and making her eyes all big and dark.

"I didn't," Jen murmured.

"You're weird," Alice replied, but her tone was fond.

"No, look," Danny said wretchedly. "Aren't there any other ghosts your age? Children, I mean?"

Alice blinked slowly at him. Then she put on a high, whining voice and moaned, "'I died when I was seven and it's ever so tragic. Mummy and Daddy will never get over me!' Trust me," she added in her usual scathing tones, "they are really, really boring. And/or creepy. Remember that one, Jen, who was so possessive over her parents that she killed all the children they tried to have

31

after her?"

Danny shuddered. Jen shrugged. "Sucks to be you," she said.

"Sucks to be who?" said Tessa, sticking her head round the office door.

"Oh... just... text from a friend," Jen lied, waving the phone that had precisely zero friends' numbers saved in it. *All my friends are dead.* "Feeling sorry for herself. You know. Uh. Not that I'm texting my friends or anything. Um."

Tessa gave her a look that said she was entirely unconvinced, but said nothing. Alice rolled her eyes at Jen. "Lame," she said.

"Listen, the boss'll be back this afternoon," Tessa said. "He's been on a job in Manchester. Took longer than he expected, and he's a grumpy old bugger at the best of times, so just a heads-up. If he comes in here and starts snarling at you, it's probably not your fault."

"Probably?"

Tessa shrugged. "Or he might not like how you've rearranged the paperclips. It's hard to tell, with Quinn."

"Forewarned is forearmed," Jen said, and Tessa smiled at her.

"Just thought I'd warn you—my mum can't pick the kids up this afternoon, so I've got to go and get them. I don't know why it's so complicated, it's not like it's a surprise it's a school day," she grumbled, refilling her coffee and disappearing back inside her office.

Jen just nodded and smiled as if this wasn't a daily occurrence. Half her phonecalls this week had been from Tessa's mother, enquiring about childcare arrangements. Tessa, while pleasant and efficient as a boss, seemed to be in a continual flap when it came to family matters.

She tried to imagine her own sister forgetting to pick the kids up from school. Nope. Charlotte never forgot anything, and she was never late, and everyone did exactly as she told them to. Other people's inefficiency struck her as a personal insult.

She waited until Tessa was far enough away behind the frosted glass to be unable to see her before she mouthed, "What's he like?"

"Who? Quinn?" Danny shrugged. "All right, I suppose. Hasn't cracked a smile in all the time he's worked here—"

"Although I suppose if you spent all day trailing cheating wives you wouldn't either," Alice cut in.

"Good point, well made. I say, Jenny my old chum, don't suppose you could find me any reading matter, could you?"

"I am not getting you top-shelf magazines," Jen muttered. A fine start to her residency in Wirpness if she marched into the newsagents to buy a load of porn.

"What? No! Nothing like that. I'd never ask a lady to find me something like *that*!"

Jen had never seen a ghost blush before.

"But you'd ask a chap, would you?" Alice said sweetly.

"I, er, I was thinking the odd novel or two. Used to like a bit of Biggles, back in the day."

"Biggles?" Jen felt her eyebrows shoot up. "Really?"

"Top stuff. Tales of British derring-do. Haven't you read them?"

"Bit before my time," said Jen, charmed despite herself.

"Hope they're still in print. Can't really go too far, you see," he explained. "Library's a bit out of my range."

"Are you stuck here, then?" Alice asked, as Jen attempted to turn her attention back to the report she was supposed to be typing.

"Well, I can go outside a bit, but much further than the end of the road and I start to get a bit confused and end up coming back here."

"Is this where you died?" Alice asked.

"Alice. Tact?" Jen said.

"Oh, pish posh. Death's too short. Did you?"

"No, no, miles away actually. But I lived here, y'see. Before it was an office, obviously."

"Did you stay for a reason? Not everyone does."

"Oh, I…" Danny trailed off. "I suppose not, really. Just not ready to move on, perhaps. I try not to think about it. What about you?"

Alice shrugged and glanced off disinterestedly. "I had more of the world to see."

"Perhaps you could toddle off and see some of it now," Jen said pointedly. "I've got work to do. Website to update, emails to answer."

"What *is* a website?" asked Danny, and she groaned.

Autumn in Wirpness was marginally quieter than summer, but a sunny day still made parking nearly impossible. Quinn drove around the block a few times before giving up and parking outside his own house, where he at least had a designated space. Tessa had reminded him several times that there was a disabled bay just over the road from the office, but Quinn usually had to remind her right back that you needed a blue badge to park in it.

"Then apply for a badge, you idiot," she said. "They give them to people who have trouble walking: I think having one leg qualifies you."

"I can walk just fine," he replied.

"Yes, on days when your leg isn't giving you gyp and you don't walk like an old man, or when you have to get a new leg or liner or whatever it is, and you're hopping about on crutches—"

"If I'm on crutches, I'm not driving," he reminded her. "It's kind of hard to do with one foot."

At this point Tessa would usually throw up her hands in disgust, and end the conversation. Quinn grinned to himself as he dropped off his overnight bag in the front hall. It was fun to annoy Tessa.

He shouldered his laptop bag and picked up the camera case. He could do without carrying it all to the office, but he didn't have the equipment at home to upload all the data he'd got in Manchester. At least it was a nice afternoon.

You couldn't see the sea from his house, or from the office—which was what made both of them affordable —but its presence was always there. In the crab nets sold outside the corner shop, in the vaguely nautical names of the cafés, in the ship's figurehead that sat above the pub door.

And in the air. It smelled like home, here on the other side of the British Isles.

Automatically, he glanced up at the agency's window, up above the flower shop. A shadow moved behind it, too tall to be Tessa. Maybe a client, or maybe their new receptionist or office manager or whatever the feck he was supposed to call her.

He put down the camera case, opened the door, wedged it with his foot, picked up the camera case, started up the narrow stairs, and then sighed as the door at the top opened and Tessa started down towards him. He squinted at his watch. Right: school run time.

"Bad luck to pass on the stairs," he told her, moving back, and she smiled, because she knew as well as he did that he didn't believe in superstitions.

"How was the trip?"

He shrugged. "Ah, you know. As expected."

"Quinn, it took two days longer than you thought."

"Well, that was because I had to hang around giving police statements."

"Didn't punch anyone, did you?"

Quinn bit his lip. Tessa sighed.

"Look, he was after putting MDMA in his grandmother's tea. He could've killed her," Quinn added. "He was asking to be punched at the least."

"Well, I agree with you on that one. How did the police take it?"

"I told them it was self defence. Look, I've this great big bruise here," he angled his face to show her the mark on his jaw.

"He hit you?" Tessa said, surprised.

"Well, technically it was his grandmother who hit me, but she thought I was a giant rabbit called Bonzo at the time."

Tessa's lips twitched.

"All right, you can laugh. You can also carry this camera up the stairs. I'm a cripple, remember, and I need your help and support."

She snorted at that, but took the camera and started back up. "All right, but then I really have to run or I'll be late."

"Sure. How's the new girl settling in?"

Tessa pushed open the door at the top of the stairs, heaving the camera ahead of her. "Why don't you ask her yourself? Jen, this is my partner—well, technically, since he owns the place, he's my boss, but don't let him hear me say that."

Quinn pushed past her and held out his hand to the girl rising from her desk, smoothing down her grey skirt and flicking her blonde curls out of her eyes.

"Hi, I'm—" he began, and her eyes rolled back in her head as she folded to the ground in a crumpled heap.

"Jenny, Jenny! I'm so sorry, I didn't know, I looked in his office and—"

"Crikey, old thing, you didn't faint when you saw me, and I'm much better looking."

"—there's no family photos, it's a different name, I didn't *know*—"

"Did she hit her head? Jen, can you hear me? Are you diabetic or anything?"

"And I'm a ghost, too. This one's flesh and blood. I mean, you have met chaps of the male persuasion before, haven't you?"

"Been a while since I had a fainter," came a fourth voice, cutting through the jumble of voices and hands and the jabber of emotions pushing at her like an incoming tide.

Ethan. He's a ghost, he's a ghost, and he's found me
—

"I'm sorry," Jen managed to gasp, trying to focus. Alice hovered over her, literally, gabbling on about how she'd have warned Jen if only she'd known, and through the ghost's slightly transparent form she could see Tessa, face tight with concern, running through a list of medical conditions Jen was pretty sure she didn't have.

It's a bad case of Seeing Ghosts, I'm afraid. Chronic and incurable.

Above her glowered the tall dark figure who looked exactly like Ethan Sullivan. He scowled at her, and Jen wouldn't have been surprised to hear a thunderclap accompanying it.

"I'll be in my office," he growled, and stalked out of her vision.

"Jenny, it's not him, it's his brother," Alice said, and suddenly the real world rushed back in.

"His brother?"

Alice wrung her little hands. "I didn't know there were any White Lady survivors here, I mean the odds are…"

Survivors. *He's the brother who survived.* Jen looked up at Alice's pale, anxious face, and exhaled. *She thinks that's why you're upset.*

Tessa sat back on her heels and sighed. "You're not part of the fan club, are you?"

"Whose fan club?" Danny said. "Who is he?"

Jen blinked, and raised herself up on her elbows. Her head swam. "He's the boss. The James Quinn listed on the database."

"Yes." Tessa bit her lip.

"Who appears to be the living image of Ethan Sullivan."

"Who?" Danny said to Alice, who just looked uncomfortable.

"They're twins." Tessa winced. "They were twins."

"With different surnames?" Danny said. "Sounds a bit *Irish*, if you ask me."

Alice rolled her eyes. "He is Irish, you halfwit."

Jen sat up, rubbing her arm where she appeared to have used it to smite the desk. "You said Sullivan was the previous owner. He was a relative?"

"Yes. Their uncle, on their mother's side. Ethan used it as a stage name. And Quinn... Quinn usually does what he can to disassociate himself from his brother."

When Jen blinked, she saw the two men sitting at the table in the White Lady. Ethan, relaxed and smiling, his brother tense and unhappy.

James Quinn, the one who lived. The Quinn twins. The Quinn, solo.

"They weren't close?"

Tessa shrugged. "He doesn't talk about it. He's quite a private person. I mean, he's great once you get to know him, but..."

"What happened to his brother?" Danny wanted to know. Alice shushed him.

Jen nodded tiredly. "Right. Well, I suppose I've some apologising to do." And some explaining. Maybe some explaining.

"You've got nothing to apologise for. He's just

touchy. Leave it a while. Sit and have a rest. Have some tea," Tessa said, gesturing to the kettle.

"Tea cures everything." Jen managed a smile. "I'm fine, it was just a shock. How embarrassing!"

"It happens. We get all sorts. Some of his fans are just insane."

"I'll bet. Well, I'm not a fan. I mean, I liked some of his stuff, but I'm not… I mean, he doesn't need to worry…"

Tessa was eyeing her warily. Jen found a bright smile and applied it to her mouth.

"I'll just make that tea," she said.

Tessa left shortly after, in her usual 'I mean I wouldn't normally leave you but I've got to pick the kids up and my mother's got the car today' flap. Jen stared blankly at her computer screen, utterly unable to remember what she was supposed to have been doing.

"I say, old bean," Danny said, "what was all that about with the fainting? Alice won't tell me."

Alice doesn't know. Not all of it. Not the worst of it. It wasn't easy to keep secrets from Alice, the person who had always been there and knew everything about her, and Jen guarded them jealously. Especially this one.

Slowly, she opened a new document, and typed, *Long story*.

"His brother was a famous actor," Alice said. "He died a few years ago. Jen thought she saw his ghost, didn't you, Jen?"

Apparently not that long a story, Jen typed.

"Although that doesn't usually make you faint. I'd've thought you'd be used to it by now."

Jen's fingers tensed above the keyboard and she typed, *I've never seen anyone from the White Lady.*

"No," said Alice shortly. "Yes, well."

"The…?" said Danny.

"It doesn't matter," Alice said. "You know, I'd've

thought it was the dead one too. They're spookily alike."

"Ah. I did wonder. Some of the other girls used to swoon over him a bit."

Other girls?

"Who worked here before you. Loads of them. Never stayed long."

Jen and Alice exchanged faintly panicked looks. Had she walked into a doomed job? What did Quinn do to these girls?

"How many?" Alice asked.

"I dunno, never counted. Used to be an old bird, then lots of pretty young totty. Few of those dreary girls who wear too much black."

"Goths," Alice said dismissively.

Emos, Jen corrected distractedly. *Why did they leave?*

"I don't know, I didn't pay that much attention."

"To a bunch of pretty girls? You've had your tongue hanging out ever since Jen walked in," Alice said.

"Yes, but they couldn't see me," Danny explained. "Takes all the fun out of it."

They didn't leave because of James Quinn?

"Well—er, what d'you mean? Because he was fed up with them mooning around? I expect so."

Alice opened her mouth, but Jen shook her head wearily. Paranoia again. James Quinn was probably a perfectly nice man who had simply suffered a devastating tragedy and was trying to cope with it. A troupe of girls obsessed with his dead brother would be the opposite of what he needed.

"You're not going to turn into another one of them, are you?" Danny asked, his tone anxious, and Jen glanced up at him. "It's just… you're the first person I've had a conversation with in seventy-odd years."

Alice caught her eye, her gaze a hundred and fifty years old. A hundred and fifty lonely years.

Don't worry, Jen typed. *That's the last thing I'm going to do.*

Quinn skulked. There was no other word for it, and he knew it. He was skulking. He couldn't even upload the heat detection footage from Manchester, since Tessa had left the camera out in the reception area and he wasn't about to go out there and retrieve it.

This time, he was definitely being a coward.

He typed up his notes, he glanced at the appointments the fainting girl had made for him next week, he heard Tessa leave, and he avoided any and all reflective surfaces. He didn't want to see what she'd seen.

He faffed about online, and then he gave in and looked Jennifer Hargrave up. As Tessa had said: very little. She certainly hadn't been using her Facebook page to announce to the world that she'd just got a job with Ethan Sullivan's brother and it was surely only a matter of time before he fell madly in love and married her, which was what Chloe or Leah or Alison had done.

Speaking of… Quinn glanced at the frosted window, as if his new secretary would be able to see through it, then logged into a chat forum where there were still a few Ethan conspiracies going around. He checked out the new members, made sure none of them had IP addresses matching the office, or the home address Jennifer Hargrave had given, and sat back.

Among the list of topics on the Ethan Sullivan Memorial Wall was one pinned to the top: "Who was the Woman with Blue Hair???"

Quinn pretended to himself that he wasn't going to read it. There were two new replies. Probably just more craziness. Angry girls trying to implicate innocent people in Ethan's death.

Then he clicked on it anyway.

The introductory post was so familiar now that he

hardly needed to read it. One of Ethan's neighbours had seen a woman with blue hair coming out of the apartment building on the day he died. She'd remembered it because the woman was dressed so brightly in pink and purple. The police hadn't released any footage from the camera across the street apart from one small clip, in black and white, which showed a woman exiting the converted warehouse and turning the corner. They hadn't been able to track her after that. Her face wasn't clear from that angle.

Quinn knew there was another snippet of footage, of the woman entering Ethan's apartment not ten minutes earlier. She'd paused on the street, dug in her pocket for something, then dropped a bit of paper in a doorway. The police had speculated that it was a note or an address, but they'd never found it.

The replies included even more excessive punctuation and atrocious spelling than the original post, but no more useful information. Quinn skimmed them. The last two posts, the new ones, added nothing new. One asked why there wasn't footage from the entryphone, and the other answered that according to a police statement there hadn't been one. The camera across the street held data for 48 hours, and there were no other sightings of her in that time. Nothing Quinn didn't know. Nothing new.

For all he knew, Ethan's neighbour might have hallucinated the blue-haired woman, or the figure on the CCTV was just an innocent visitor to another apartment. Bloody hipsters with their ironic drugs.

Still, he Googled it, as if he was going to find out anything new. As if a woman with distinctive hair who'd possibly been implicated in Ethan's death and remained hidden for five years might have just slipped up recently and posted about it on her blog.

As if Ethan's ghost might have popped up at the

coroner's court and given them a rundown of the day's events.

All Quinn found was the endless recycled transcripts of news and court reports. The coroner's verdict. The state of Ethan's body. The DNA evidence that he'd had someone, a woman, in his apartment, in his bed. As if this was unusual for Ethan. The strands of blue hair found in corners. Shoreditch was full of women with stupidly coloured hair.

"Fucking hipsters," Quinn muttered, and closed the search window before he turned into a proper conspiracy eejit.

Eventually he ran out of make-work. He braced himself, got up and opened the door into the outer office. The new girl sat at her computer, typing industriously. Dressed in grey, her hair pale, her whole demeanour colourless. She glanced up, flushed, and immediately closed the document.

Don't take it out on her. It's not her fault.

But the irritation rose in him anyway.

"I just need my camera," he said, and strode over to where Tessa had left it by the door.

"Sure, yes." She hesitated, then said, "You have some new appointments. Tessa said you'd be best for these cases, so I've—"

"That's grand."

"—they're in the system. I don't know if you—"

"I saw, thanks a million."

"Right, good."

He picked up the camera case. Turned. Glanced at her from under his hair. She sat chewing her lip and looking monstrously uncomfortable.

"Look, I'm sorry about earlier. I—it was just a shock, and—it won't happen again—"

"I'm not my brother." His knee throbbed.

"No. Obviously. You're not. It's just…"

43

Quinn lost his patience. "I look like him. I sound like him. Jaysus, go to Dublin, everyone sounds like him. I've a cousin in Dalkey who wears the leather trousers and shades from *Devilborn* just so he can get the girls. But I am not my brother. Do you understand? I've heard all the conspiracy theories. I am not Ethan. I'm not an actor, I'm a detective. And just in case you're in any doubt," he set down the camera case, put his left foot on it, and pulled up his jeans leg.

She stared at the metal of his prosthesis, her face expressionless.

"I believe Ethan had two legs. I had mine blown off by a bomb."

Jennifer Hargrave just stared. At the metal of the leg, at the sock that lay baggy around the ankle joint, at the socket that fastened over his knee. Her lips were white.

And just when Quinn thought she was going to stay silent, she said, "I know. I was there."

CHAPTER THREE

The White Lady: immediately after

There is snow everywhere. Jen remembers working in a
card shop one Christmas that had one of those trees
which sprayed fake snow everywhere. She thinks that's
what has happened here. It's snowed. Indoors. In July.

Alice is screaming at her, little mouth opening wide,
the sound coming from three inches away over a great
distance. All Jen can hear is a roaring noise, like
standing under a waterfall. Her hand is wet. The snow
keeps falling. The heat presses in on her, like standing in
front of an oven.

"You have to get up," Alice shouts above the roaring.
"You need to move."

Jen stares at her, blank. The words make no sense.

"Get up before the ceiling falls in on you!" Alice
screams, her misty hands plucking ineffectually at Jen's
white t-shirt. Funny, she'd been wearing a pink one
earlier.

She moves her hands, her feet. Hauls herself to her
knees. Grabs at the bar to stand up. The wood is

splintered and beer is everywhere. She's broken a pipe or something on the way down.

"It's snowing," she says.

"It's ash," Alice says, her voice returning to normal levels. The roaring slides away, and in its place comes the moan of sirens, of alarms, of people.

Beyond the bar is a warzone.

Jen stares at the shattered remains of chairs and tables and people. All the glass in the windows has blown out, the front wall has collapsed, and the partition by the fireplace is the only thing holding the ceiling up. There are bodies. There are pieces of bodies.

The ash falls gently on it all, a soft blanket of white covering the red and black. From under it, spirits rise.

Alice stands beside her, watching the souls float up from the bodies and slowly walk away towards an unseen horizon. Maybe a dozen of them. They don't look back.

In their slipstream, the air is icy cold.

"They need your help," Alice says.

"I can't help them now," Jen says, watching the shades fade away. One of them has long blonde hair, straightened and highlighted to within an inch of its—

"Not them. The living." Alice begins sticking her head into cupboards, zooming right through the broken wood. "There's fabric in here. For bandages. Tourniquets."

Jen can't tear her gaze from the departing ghosts. They're fading away somewhere she can't see. "Where are they going?"

"I don't know, but they won't be the only ones unless you help. Jenny! Pay attention."

Jen stumbles to the cupboard and grabs a handful of England football flags. "I don't know what to do," she says, tripping over a fallen table leg and falling to her knees beside a body.

"Not that one. He drifted away. This one. He's bleeding to death. This one, Jenny, over here…"

CHAPTER FOUR

He stayed skulking in his office, ostensibly uploading the heat detection footage to send to the Manchester police, but really just hiding out from Jen Hargrave.

I was there. Well, sure, there had been a few dozen people in the pub and not all of them had been blown to kingdom come. And of the survivors, not all of them came to those meetings the counsellors had set up. Quinn had only been to a couple.

Maybe he should have gone to more. Because meeting Jen Hargrave, the girl who'd tied a tourniquet above the shattered remains of his leg with a football flag then calmly gone on to save several more lives, had left him feeling more shocked than he could remember since he heard the news about Ethan.

The Angel of the White Lady, the papers had called her. None of the people she saved knew her name, and only two had any memory of her presence. They'd said that she looked like an angel, all haloed in white, but Quinn's more rational mind surmised that she'd just been covered in ash like the rest of them.

One woman remembered the Angel walking calmly

towards two men who lay perfectly still, and barely even glancing at one before stooping to treat the second. "I don't know how she knew which one was alive and which wasn't," she said.

No one knew what happened to her after that. She never came forward to accept the praise and rewards offered to her when the victims started talking about her. None of the emergency services knew who she was.

And now she was here, the Angel of the White Lady, doing his accounts and answering his phone. She looked completely normal. Average height and weight, hair a wavy blonde, pretty in a non-threatening way, didn't wear much make-up and her shoes were perfectly sensible. Dressed like a woman twice her age…

Didn't want to be noticed.

He glanced at the frosted glass separating her from him. She'd saved his life, several lives, and then vanished.

He drummed his fingers on the desk. Glanced at the clock in the corner of his computer screen. Nearly five o'clock. The footage was nearly uploaded now. Five minutes more and he could escape.

All he had to do was send the email to Manchester, walk out, maybe nod at her or something, and go down the stairs. He'd be home free.

Which made it all the more inexplicable when he sent the email, walked out, and said, "Fancy a drink?"

It was mild for October, and the benches facing the street outside The Admiral were all taken, mostly by people with dogs or buggies or both. Daytrippers, with their backpacks and Bugaboos and children called Horatio and Tallulah.

"They have some seats out back," Quinn said, not looking at Jen. "Go and get us a table and I'll get the drinks."

When Jen nodded she had the distinct feeling she looked like a nodding dog. It was all she'd been able to do since he'd stomped into the outer office and asked her for a drink.

What does he know? What does he want *to know?*

"What'll you have?"

"Uh," said Jen, who hadn't quite managed any answer more creative than 'okay' since they'd left the office. "Uh. Lager."

"Pint or half?"

Most men didn't ask. "Pint," said Jen, who figured she might need it.

Quinn nodded and disappeared inside the dark pub, apparently assuming she'd know where to go. It so happened that Jen had been inside The Admiral, as with all the other pubs and cafés around the place, to see if there were any spooks propping up the bar. All she found was a couple of advertisements for extra bar staff, which she'd studiously ignored.

The Admiral was an old coastal pub, low-ceilinged and beamed, with warped, scuffed floors and charts on the walls showing the locations of local shipwrecks. A jaunty figurehead looked out onto the street. Inside were pictures of Lord Nelson and one or two bits about the Battle of Sole Bay. In one corner was some nautical device with a complicated-looking dial on it.

It was nothing like the White Lady, which had London Pub written all over it. And besides, she couldn't avoid pubs for the rest of her life, could she?

Jen picked her way through the back garden and found a table with a couple of chairs. The back fence had been painted to look like a row of Wirpness's famous beach huts, and the wall of the pub held a couple of jaunty fake lifebelts painted with the name of the pub.

"I have to ask," Alice said at her shoulder, "is this the sort of situation where you want me around, or not?"

Jen weighed the balance. Alice there as moral support, or as distraction?

"Not," she said. "But thanks."

Alice shrugged and faded away, just as Quinn came out of the pub with two pints and some crisps. Jen watched the reaction amongst the other drinkers, and picked out which ones were local and which ones were tourists by their reactions. Some of the locals nodded in recognition. Some ignored him.

Amongst the daytrippers, there wasn't one who didn't turn to look. A couple even snapped pictures.

Jen leaned back and regarded him. Even dishevelled and unsmiling, he was handsome. Although if she was honest, the scruffy brooding thing probably made him more handsome. Unkempt dark hair fell around his collar, he clearly hadn't shaved for days, and his eyebrows were drawn down over his dark eyes in a perpetual scowl. He looked like a vampire in a bad mood.

Unbidden, she remembered Ethan saying, "I'm not scowling. This is just my normal face."

She shook herself. Quinn wasn't Ethan. Ethan would rather have been seen dead than in jeans with a hole in them, a tattered old flannel shirt, and fingerless gloves. Fingerless gloves! No wonder Tessa called him a hobo.

Jen sighed. A Hollywood hobo, maybe. Quinn might not have the rockstar glamour of his brother but he still exuded a kind of brooding sexuality, all dark intensity and wounded heroism. *It's a really good job I'm not interested, or I might make a fool of myself over him.*

He saw her watching as he put the drinks down, and perhaps deliberately mistook her interest. "Nine times out of ten, they hear the accent and ask why I'm not drinking the black stuff." He hooked the chair out with his foot and sank into it. "I've drunk more Guinness since I moved to England than I ever did in Ireland."

"Do you like it?"

"Happily," he took a sip, "yes."

"Well, that's all right, then."

He gave her a glimmer of a smile and added, "Tastes different here, of course."

"Really?"

"Sure. Back home it's made with the black waters of the Liffey." He pushed the crisps in her direction. Jen shook her head, not entirely sure if he was joking.

They both sipped at their drinks. Jen's foot jiggled under the table.

Eventually Jen said, "How long have you lived in Wirpness?" at the same time Quinn said, "Why did you move to Wirpness?"

Her face flooded with heat. Quinn gave the closest thing she'd seen to a smile so far, and took another gulp of Guinness, gesturing to her to go first.

"How long have you been in Wirpness?"

He tilted his head. "Ah… five years. Give or take."

Since before the bomb or after it? Yeah, that was how to make small talk. "And you took over the agency from your uncle?"

Quinn regarded her, and Jen felt her stomach drop. Ethan had been known for his intense, brooding gaze, but it was nothing to having Quinn's attention focused on you. Dark, fathoms deep, deep as eternity, and so intent it made her feel like a butterfly skewered with a pin.

"That's what Tessa said," she added in a squeak.

"My uncle Kieran," Quinn said, releasing her gaze and taking another sip. At this rate they'd be pissed as farts by six o'clock.

"On your mother's side?"

Again the intensity. She tried not to squirm.

"Yes."

"Hence the different surname."

"Yes."

Quinn took a long drink. Jen watched his throat work, which wasn't exactly a hardship. Quinn had a beautiful throat.

When he put his glass down, it was more than half empty. Jen took a big swig of hers to keep up, and then nearly spat it out when he said, "I wasn't sure you'd be all right with the pub."

How did he know she had to check every damn hostelry for ghostly regulars? How? She slammed down the glass, coughed a bit, and said, "Why wouldn't I be?"

Quinn blinked hard. "The, er, last time we were in one together, it…"

Blew up. "Right," she said, relieved. "Yes. No. I mean, it's fine. Not that pub, obviously."

"It's been rebuilt."

"So I hear."

"Little memorial plaque by the bar. A few people pushed for more, but, you know."

"Dignity."

"Right."

Jen drank half her remaining lager in one go and wondered if the lifebelts would be any help to a woman drowning in awkwardness.

"I'm sorry I gave out at you," Quinn said abruptly. "I thought you were one of the fan girls."

"I'm not," was all Jen could think of to say.

"I get…" he ran his hands through his hair, seeming surprised at how much of it there was. "I get it all the time. People who think I'm Ethan."

"What… like a… ghost?" Jen said, with a smile meant to persuade him that, haha, she didn't believe in any of that, haha, kind of rubbish.

"No such thing as." He paused. "Besides, if anyone was going to see his ghost, don't you think it'd be me? No, they think I'm actually him."

Jen frowned, opened her mouth, then shut it again. "Really?"

"Sure. Go online, there are conspiracy theories and everything. I'm Ethan, and it was my brother who died. Or I faked my own death. Or I'm Ethan, and there never was a brother, just one of me. Like Batman and Bruce Wayne."

"That's stupid."

"Of course it is." Quinn made a noise that coming from a happier man might have been a chuckle. "We used to laugh at that joke about thick Paddies. 'Was it you or your brother who died?'"

"Less funny now," said Jen.

"A lot of things are." He took a big gulp of Guinness. "You know, it was bad enough before. Even when we were kids, people could never tell us apart."

"You're completely identical?" Jen asked, and winced. *Were.* Were completely identical.

"Genetically speaking. Even our mother had trouble sometimes. We used to play it for laughs. Freak people out with pre-prepared answers when they tried to get us to read each other's minds. Had one teacher at school who genuinely didn't realise there were two of us because we were in different classes. He thought we just really liked chemistry."

"He sounds smart."

Quinn's brows quirked. "He brewed beer to demonstrate the process of... actually, I can't remember what, I think we were too busy drinking the beer."

"I revise my opinion."

Quinn smiled, his gaze far away. This was just as well, since the effect Quinn's smile had on Jen was akin to being slapped in the face with a rainbow.

He can't be identical to Ethan. He's better-looking.

"When they found Ethan talking like a wet wellyboot, he told them he was me. O'course, when they

55

called home and told our parents James was drunk, we both pretended to be Ethan. He argued very eloquently that you couldn't punish an innocent man, and since nobody could work it which of us it was who'd stolen all the beer, we both got off." His smile widened to a grin. It was breathtaking. "I used to say we'd never go to jail with that logic."

Jen tilted her head, her smile fading. *Alice made me do it. The other little girl made me do it!*

"Does that defence hold up in court?"

Quinn shrugged. "I was a garda, not a lawyer." He picked up his drink, and seemed surprised to find it empty. "Another one?"

"I should probably…"

"Ah, g'wan. Your boss won't mind."

"How do you know? He might be a right miserable old sod."

Quinn's gaze warmed. "He is, but he's worse when someone stops him drinking."

"Got to live up to that film noir cliché, eh?"

"Too right," said Quinn, and disappeared back inside the pub.

CHAPTER FIVE

The White Lady, an hour before

"Running late," says the text from Ethan. "Desperate for a drink. Get me one in willya?"

Quinn dumps his bag on the floor of his brother's stylishly ugly rented apartment and stretches. Despite the flight from Dublin only being just over an hour, he's been up since six and it's only lunchtime now. Ethan was supposed to have finished this morning's interviews by now and be back to meet him here.

London is disgustingly hot. Quinn is getting desperate for a drink, too.

"Where?" he texts back.

He has to wait for a reply. Idly flicking through a magazine on the uncomfortable sofa, he comes across a large picture of Ethan, staring moodily at the camera, his dark eyes menacing. He's wearing a sheer black shirt and leather trousers, and managing not to look ridiculous.

Despite being physically identical to his brother, Quinn knows he could never pull this look off.

He tries to remember the name of the pub a few streets away where they went last time he visited, but then he remembers Ethan telling him it'd been turned into a hipster joint selling nothing but champagne and hotdogs. He drags Ethan's laptop over to search for local boozers, but not before he's already noticed an email about negotiating a new contract for the next series of *Devilborn*, one which will see a significant payrise for Ethan.

There's a browser tab open to a property website. Ethan has been looking at flats with even more exposed brickwork, metal beams and weird-shaped windows than this one.

His phone rings. "Hey, how's it goin'?," Ethan says, as if he's speaking to a casual acquaintance and not someone he once shared an amniotic sac with. "Are you in London yet?"

"I'm at your flat." Ethan gave him a key last time he was here, but never bothered to check he still had it. His building doesn't even have an entryphone. Quinn calls this kind of security shocking.

"Grand. Listen, get a cab up to the studios, will you? By the time you get here I'll be done. Sure, darlin'," he adds in response to a feminine voice in the background. "Great to see you. No, I'm meeting my brother, or I'd love to. Sure. Yeah. No, he's very private. Hates publicity."

Quinn rolls his eyes. He can't count the number of requests he's had from various media types who want to do a photo shoot or interview or vlog or whatever with him.

"Why don't you say yes, and pretend to be me?" he says to Ethan.

"I can't pull off that 'miserable bastard' thing you do," Ethan says.

"Call yourself an actor?"

"I'm not that good."

"Your mouth to God's ears," Quinn says. He moves to put the laptop down on the industrial steel table, but dislodges a pile of papers and files as he does. Moving to pick them up, he finds himself looking at a picture of a young woman wearing a t-shirt with a picture of Ethan on it. *Be Bad To Me Baby*, it says in letters made to look like they're dripping blood.

"There's a boozer round the corner," Ethan is saying. "The White… something. Can't remember. Hey, Jimmy, what's the name of that place we went for the football? Real dive…"

Quinn is only half listening. The girl's picture is part of a police report. Having been a garda since he was eighteen, Quinn knows what he's looking at. She's been cautioned several times for harassment and public disorder. The report is attached to a letter from a lawyer, advising on a restraining order.

"Ethan, who's this girl?"

"What girl?"

"The one you want a restraining order against."

"Oh." Ethan's voice changes. "Just a fan, I guess. They get a bit overexcited."

"It says here she sent you some of her blood."

"Yeah. I get that a lot. Well, it's not always real blood, but—"

"Eth, she has a history of mental illness." Quinn flicks through the paperwork and tries to decipher the legalese. "Self harm. Attempted suicide. Jesus, why didn't you say anything?"

"Chill, man, all right? She's just a fan. I get a lot of crazies. For some reason the paranormal stuff brings 'em all out."

Quinn looks at the girl's face. Pale, both with make-up and the pallor of someone who doesn't get out enough, with dyed black hair and too much eyeliner. She has a soft, doughy, unhappy look about her. On her forearms are thin red scars. She looks like she needs some sunshine and a hug, not a restraining order.

"Look, you have a dangerous stalker, and you didn't think to tell your brother—your fucking twin, for God's sake—who just happens to be a garda—"

"Yeah, a garda. In Dublin. Not the Met Police, is it? Look, I don't want to talk about her," says Ethan.

"Tough. What's the name of that pub?"

"The White Lady," says Ethan, and hangs up.

CHAPTER SIX

Quinn made it into the office late the next day, barely awake, and fairly sure he was sweating whiskey. He'd woken on the sofa, fully dressed, as the sun came in through the open curtains of his living room. Beside him was a half-empty bottle of Jamesons. On the TV, breakfast news burbled.

His new secretary had gone home after the second drink, but Quinn had stayed on, sitting out in the increasingly chilly beer garden until he'd run out of cash. Whereupon he'd stumbled home, switched on the TV and continued to get horribly drunk.

But all the drinking in the world couldn't drown out the memories of the White Lady.

Goddamn bloody Jennifer Hargrave for coming back into his life. He'd been building up a gradual tolerance for reminders of that day, from attending the survivors meetings to not biting the head off anyone who mentioned Ethan. But a daily reminder? A person he had to see every day? He wasn't sure he could cope with that.

Could he fire her for being an unpleasant reminder of

a traumatic event? No, he couldn't. And she wasn't unpleasant, either. Once she'd stopped fainting and relaxed a bit in his company, she'd been fun to hang out with. Almost like having a friend.

Quinn wasn't really sure about that last bit. He'd never been very good at having friends.

He slunk past Jen where she sat at her computer, returned her polite greeting with a grunt, and shut himself in his office. Uncle Kieran used to keep a bottle of whiskey in the bottom drawer of his desk, something Quinn had made fun of as a terrible cliché, but now he was starting to come around to the idea.

His leg was bloody killing him. Sleeping with the prosthetic on wasn't advised, and especially not on the damn sofa. The twisted muscles throbbed in time with his head, and he was reasonably sure he'd got blisters forming from wearing the same liner too long. Eventually he gave in and removed it. It'd have to go back on when he walked home, but for the rest of the afternoon he figured he could get by on one leg. If that freaked out Jen Hargrave, she'd just have to lump it.

His mood wasn't improved by a phonecall a few hours later from Georgia Wright. Desperately, he hopped out of the office, calling for Tessa. "You take it!"

"She's not here," Jen said. "Gone to the Records Office." Her gaze flickered over the trouser leg he'd knotted below his stump, and she said nothing.

"Bollocks." He really didn't want to take this call.

Jen regarded the phone he was holding out as if it might give him a communicable disease. "You'd better answer soon or it'll go to voicemail."

"Then let it," Quinn said pleadingly, gripping the edge of the filing cabinet to stay upright.

"Don't be a wimp," Jen said, and took the phone from him. But instead of making excuses or dropping it in the bin, she answered and said smoothly, "Sullivan Investigations, James Quinn's phone, how can I help you?" She tapped at her computer and he saw Georgia Wright's file come up. His heart sank. "Yes... yes, I see. He's right here."

He dealt her a murderous look. She smiled brightly and pressed the phone into his hand.

Quinn leaned against her desk, blew out a breath and spoke into the phone. "Georgia. Sorry, I was... out."

"It's all right," she gushed. "I know you're, like, so busy."

"Yes. Very busy," Quinn said quickly. "Rushed off my feet. Foot. Got to run—"

"But before you do," Georgia said, an irritating thread of steel in her voice, "when are you going to come and set up the recording equipment? I spoke to Ms Adams yesterday and she said it was available now."

Quinn hopped across to the ratty old sofa and collapsed on it, scrubbing his hand across his face. He was tired, he was hungover, his leg was still throbbing, and even if he'd been in the best of moods he still wasn't equipped to deal with a teenage crush.

"Well, I'll have to check," he began, feebly, cursing Jen where she sat all serene and unruffled, focused on her computer screen. He saw her lips twitch. What was so funny about a teenager wanting to investigate some ruins in her school grounds?

Oh yeah, the fact that the teenager, along with her best friend, had discovered that Quinn was a dead ringer for Ethan Sullivan, star of their favourite show, and the fact that he was now a brooding crippled private detective only made them obsess about him harder. He'd made the mistake of checking Georgia Wright's Twitter feed the other week. It was mostly pictures of Ethan smouldering and links to a Tumblr account full of *Devilborn* animated Gifs.

Quinn grimaced as he recalled a few comments he might have added to the file on his computer. Comments which included words like 'vapid' 'irritating' and 'enough perfume to make an elephant sneeze'.

"If she wants the night vision and heat recording stuff," said Jen, evidently reading it off the screen, "then it's right over there."

He glared at the pile of cases, then at Jen, and then winced as Georgia shouted excitedly, "So when can you come over? Tonight?"

"Ah, no, I'm busy tonight—" Quinn began.

"Well, when then?" Georgia said impatiently. "Can't be at the weekend, I'm on exeat. I had to get some time off," she added in a more dramatic tone of voice, "that thing has just been freaking me out!"

Georgia thought she'd seen a ghost in the ruined cottage that was supposed to be out of bounds in the extensive grounds of her expensive boarding school. Said school, St Hilda's, was an hour or so away from Wirpness, and the most Quinn could say for the establishment was that it supplied smarter-than-average sixth formers to work in the various hotels, bistros and upmarket shops on the local High Street.

Unfortunately, it also supplied girls like Georgia Wright and Aimee Swinton-Hill, who were both blonde and pretty and believed this gave them the right to harass men like Quinn.

He caught Jen's eye. "Go and get it over with," she stage whispered, and Quinn nearly growled out loud.

"Georgia, could you give me a minute, please?" he said, and covered the microphone of the phone with his hand.

He fixed Jen with the sort of glare Ethan used to do on publicity photos. She raised her eyebrows, evidently unimpressed.

"She wants me to go over there tonight and set up the

recording equipment," he hissed.

"So? Go and get it done. It's money in the bank."

"It's a pair of over-entitled teenage girls who wear short skirts and far too much make-up—"

"Kids these days," Jen murmured.

"— and trip and fall into my arms or pretend they're terrified of ghosts so they've got an excuse to rub up against me, and—this isn't funny!"

She was giggling, damn her. "Of course it's funny. They fancy you, Quinn. That's funny."

He glowered even harder. "Right, and will it still be funny when they get discovered on school grounds in the middle of the night, with a man twice their age? Will it still be funny when their teachers tell their parents and they start asking all sorts of questions about why I thought it was appropriate to hang out with their teenage daughters and a video camera?"

Her giggles subsided. She glanced at the screen again. "Technically speaking it's outside the school grounds."

"Technically," he growled.

"You're being over pessimistic."

"Like hell I am." He narrowed his eyes at her as an idea occurred. Removing his hand from the phone, he said, "Sorry about that, Georgia. Yes, I'll be over tonight, and I'll be bringing my assistant. Her name is Jennifer."

Jen's eyes went wide. She started shaking her head rapidly.

"You don't need to do that," Georgia said, sounding put-out.

"Well, there's a lot of equipment to carry," Quinn began, watching Jen make throat-slitting gestures. "And I'm a little concerned about what your teachers might say if they found me in the woods with you alone, late at night."

"They won't know!" Georgia said. "I told you, come in via the service entrance, and—"

And then you put it on Twitter, and everyone finds out, and there goes my reputation, Quinn thought. "Why don't we ask one of your teachers to chaperone us?" he said.

There was a long pause. Georgia whispered to someone. Jen looked resigned.

Quinn smiled at her.

"All right," Georgia said. "But you have to agree to stay all night."

"Standard procedure," he agreed dispiritedly. His leg throbbed. "And what pretence are we there on?"

"Um," said Georgia.

"Should the faculty discover us on the school grounds with recording equipment, don't you think they'll ask questions?"

"They won't find us," Georgia said dismissively.

"I'm a pessimist. We need a pretence."

He let her sweat for a bit, then said, "All right, Georgia. I've an idea. This is what we do…"

"Come on, he got you fair and square," Alice said.

Jen glared at her computer.

"Shouldn't have laughed at him," Danny added.

"He should be able to cope with a couple of teenagers," Jen hissed, but she was uncomfortably aware that Quinn had a point. He might not reach the levels of adoration that his brother once had, but considering that those levels of adoration had resulted in multiple deaths, he was probably wise to be leery of teenagers with crushes.

"I'll come with you," Alice offered, and Jen nodded gratefully. Then she groaned.

"No, you can't. He's doing heat detection, remember? You show up and the thing'll go haywire."

"I don't make it that cold," Alice said, offended.

"I'm still wearing my coat inside the office," Jen pointed out.

"Yes, but you're always cold."

Jen opened her mouth, then shut it again.

"Quinn always said it was cold in here," Danny mused. "D'you think that's me?"

"I can't believe you two have been dead for a cumulative two-hundred odd years and you still don't know that ghosts make things cold."

Quinn's office door opened and he stomped out, looking his usual miserable self, only a bit more hungover. He'd put his leg back on, but he didn't look happy about it. "Where do you live?"

Jen blinked. "King Street," she said. "Near the post office."

He grunted at that. "Pick you up at nine-thirty then. Wear something warm."

Jen saluted him with her gloved hand, and he glowered at her and clomped out.

"Look at it this way," Alice said into the resulting silence. "You've got a second date with a man who looks like a movie star."

"A movie star with a hangover," Jen said, and turned back to her computer.

The drive to St Hilda's took just over an hour, for most of which the only sound came from the radio. Inside Quinn's car, Jen took off her warmest coat, scarf and gloves, barely glancing over at the man in the driving seat.

"Too warm?" he said.

"No, it's fine."

He glanced at the pink crocheted scarf on her lap, then at the rest of her clothing, which was plain and dark. His gaze went back to the scarf. It was very pink, the pinkest of pinks. The definition of pinkness.

"What?" Jen said.

"No, nothing. Nice scarf."

She patted it defensively. "It is nice."

"It's very… pink."

"Gosh. I can see why you became a detective."

His lips twitched. "Did you make it?"

Jen looked at the uneven loops and knots in the lurid yarn. She'd tried crochet once, years ago. Occupational therapy. She hadn't been allowed to pick up knitting needles. Her fingers still remembered the feel of the plastic hook, and even the thought of it made her recoil now.

"No. My niece." At least, that was what her sister had said. Jen wasn't entirely sure a not-quite-five-year-old possessed the fine motor skills to master a crochet hook, but then again her niece already spoke conversational French, so maybe kids were more advanced these days.

"Oh. Well, it's…"

"The only scarf I could lay my hands on," Jen said honestly. "I haven't unpacked everything yet."

"Ah. Well, I like it. Pink is nice on you."

That felt like a compliment, and Jen wasn't sure how to take it. She made a noncommittal noise, and vowed to find or buy a more sensibly coloured scarf before the winter set in.

Neither of them said anything more until they passed the main entrance to St Hilda's. "Service entrance is down here," Quinn said, the sound of his voice unexpected over the low hum of the radio.

"It won't be locked?"

"Apparently not. I think this is how the kids sneak in and out."

But the large gate, when they arrived, was locked. Quinn parked in front of it and got out his phone. "We're at the gate," he said into it. "Oh. Yeah, I like to be early.

All right then."

He ended the call and said to Jen, "Ten minutes."

She looked out at the trees shielding the main part of the school from view. "How big is this place?"

"Huge. They keep building new bits, too. Opened a new swimming pool last year, generously allowing the public to use it when the school doesn't need it."

"For an equally generous fee, I assume?"

"Of course."

Into the following silence, Jen said, "So what are we supposed to be doing here tonight? Just setting up equipment?"

"And monitoring it, and making our own observations."

"Such as?"

"Well, if you spot any transparent people going 'woo' that'd be a start."

Jen gave him a sharp look. He quirked his eyebrows at her, but said nothing.

"Have you ever seen a ghost?" she asked.

"Nope. Seen lots of excuses for ghosts. Have a look through the case files, it's like Scooby Doo."

"But the people who ask you to investigate, they genuinely think they're being haunted?"

Quinn ran a hand through his hair. He was still wearing his fingerless gloves. "People see what they want to see. Usually a bit of digging reveals they've been recently bereaved, or don't want to let go of someone, or sometimes they're just lonely."

Jen thought about Alice. You'd have to be pretty bloody lonely to invent a sarcastic nine-year-old.

"So you don't believe any of them have ever been real?"

He blew out a sigh. "I believe some of the people I've met believe they're real. But more often than not it turns out they have mental health problems. Psychosis.

69

Dementia. One poor guy was perfectly fine apart from his brain tumour."

Jen, who'd been thoroughly checked for all of those things and more, said nothing.

"They're here," said Quinn, pointing to an eldritch glow in midair, which revealed itself to be the torch on a smartphone.

Georgia and Aimee were indeed both blonde and pretty, and quite unsuitably dressed for a late night in October. They both at least wore wellies, but seemed to believe that a pair of shorts or a miniskirt were appropriate to the occasion.

Both of them regarded Quinn as if he were the Second Coming, whilst flicking glances of extreme distaste at Jen.

"Did you do what I asked?" Quinn said.

"Yes," said the one in shorts. "Aimee distracted Mrs Whishaw and I put the letter on her desk."

"Did you bury it?"

"Right under a pile of other stuff. Come on, it's this way. How quiet is your car?"

"Quiet enough," Quinn said, turning off the headlights. "Hop in."

They seemed disappointed not to be allowed to sit in the front next to him, and Jen couldn't help feeling like she and Quinn were the parents and Aimee and Georgia were the kids in the back.

They were directed down a muddy track around some woodland, to the accompaniment of Georgia and Aimee's running commentary.

"Oh my God, that's where Brooke threw up doing Cross Country."

"Yeah, did you hear her going, 'Oh, it's just exhaustion, I'm so stressed?'"

Jen compressed her lips together.

"Like everyone doesn't know she's totally mia."

"Dillon started a rumour she's knocked up."

"No way. Totes a virgin."

The disgust in her tone had Quinn glancing over at Jen, eyebrow raised.

"I know, right? Oh my God, did you hear about Blake and Chelsea?"

"I know they've been told off for snogging."

"Yeah, try shagging. In the Modern Languages lobby."

Quinn's shoulders were shaking.

"No! She is such a slut. Oh my God, who caught them?"

There was a dramatic pause. "Like, Mr Muirhead."

"Oh my God!"

"I *know*, right?"

Finally, they were directed to stop, which was just as well because Jen couldn't look at Quinn for fear of snorting with laughter. Aimee and Georgia got out of the car, still gossiping about who had what variety of eating disorder, and one of them—possibly Aimee—said over her shoulder, "We have to walk from here. Can you, like, climb over the fence?"

Said fence was of the picket variety, and didn't look to Jen like it was going to do a very good job of keeping anyone out of anywhere.

"I'm sure my old bones will manage," Quinn said gravely.

"You're not, like, that old," Aimee said, surveying him head to toe.

"Old enough to be your father," Quinn said. "Now help an old man out and carry some of this stuff, will you? And careful with it, too."

Jen surveyed the pile of cases in the back of Quinn's car. "I'm not sure my old bones will manage to carry much."

The two girls ignored her, then picked up the smallest

boxes and set off.

"Oh Quinn," Jen mocked, "you're so big and strong, you can surely carry all of these yourself."

"Shut it," he warned. He picked up a sturdy plastic crate which turned out to have wheels and a handle, and handed it to Jen. "They haven't figured out they've got the heaviest boxes."

She snorted at that, and set off after him, pulling the crate behind her.

The preliminary report compiled by Tessa had told Jen that Georgia first contacted the agency a couple of weeks ago about strange lights just outside the grounds of the school. On enquiring with her schoolmates— which Jen decoded as 'having a probably tipsy gossip'— she discovered that she wasn't the only one to have seen them, and that they were in fact famous for being spotted over the years.

At this point, Georgia recalled her older brother— who was at present, regrettably, uncontactable—telling her about them, a convenient fact that had made Jen laugh out loud when she read it.

Aimee Swinton-Hill, who had been described by Tessa as Georgia's 'best frenemy' had then upped her game by saying that she'd actually seen the ghost out in the abandoned cottage. Further enquiry as to what she was doing out there on her own in the dark revealed only coquettish giggling, and a refusal to yield the name of a paramour. Jen surmised that this meant she'd seen nothing but whoever she'd been trysting with.

Tessa had attempted to speak to other members of the student body, but whilst everybody knew the place was haunted, nobody would admit to being in the woods after dark. On enquiring amongst the faculty, she'd discovered that the students were expressly forbidden to go there at any time, due to the abandoned cottage being deemed unsafe.

"None of the students go outside after dark or leave the school grounds unless accompanied by a member of staff," was the official line, which neither Tessa nor Jen —nor, she suspected, Quinn—believed.

"First things first," Quinn said as the girls set off into the woods, their only light coming from their phones. He brought out a heavy duty flashlight and handed it to Jen.

"Oh good. So if the ghost comes after me, I can brain it with this."

"Don't be silly. It's zombies you brain."

She smiled at that, climbing over the fence and holding out her hands for one of the bags. "But only if, like, they're not totes shagging in Mr Muirhead's classroom."

Quinn snorted. "Were teenage girls this crazy when we were kids?"

"Yes," Jen said. "Of course. You just had too many hormones to notice."

"I mean, all that stuff about one girl being a virgin and another being a slut. You're damned if you do and damned if you don't."

"Pretty much," Jen said.

Quinn handed her a crate, frowning. "And what was the stuff about the girl being mere?"

Mere? Jen began to shake her head, and then an old memory surfaced. *Bony faces, jutting bones, hair thin across the scalp.* She flinched. "Mia. Short for bulimia."

His brows shot up. "And they're joking about this?"

"'Fraid so. For a lot of girls it's a badge of honour. There are pro-bulimia websites. Anorexia, too."

"Jesus."

"Yep."

He whistled as he handed her another case. "How do you ever grow up sane?"

Jen's fingers tightened painfully around the handle. "You quite often don't."

They hefted rest of the equipment over the fence and Quinn took a camera from one of the bags. Lifting it to his shoulder, he switched it on. "Night vision," he told Jen. She nodded, following behind him with the flashlight pointed down.

"How's your leg?" He was limping a bit and trying not to show it.

His shoulders stiffened. "Fine."

"Earlier, I thought…" He'd taken the prosthetic off in his office. Was that something he normally did? And she'd seen his hand rub over the joint of his knee as if it pained him.

"It's fine," Quinn said firmly.

"Oh good," Jen said, rolling her eyes in the dark. "That's fine then."

They walked on a bit more in silence. Then, "Are you okay?" Quinn asked softly, glancing over.

"Just cold."

"You're not afraid of the dark?"

"I'm more afraid of what the grown-ups will say when they find us out here in the dark."

She could've sworn she heard a soft chuckle from him. "I'm not scared of detention."

She found a smile. "Or writing lines on the blackboard."

"They might tell our parents," Quinn said.

"Worse, they might make us run laps. Until we're sick."

"Ah, I've an automatic dispensation from that."

"I'll say you made me do it," Jen replied.

Quinn smiled back at her. Her breath caught. *He could probably make me do anything.*

"By the way," he said, "if—"

"Shh!" hissed one of the girls. "We're almost there."

Jen squinted through the trees. Up ahead was a dark shape, craggy against the sky. The remains of a house, most of the roof gone, the windows just empty holes.

Despite knowing that nothing hiding in the shadows could hurt her, she still couldn't help be creeped out a bit.

"Quinn," she said softly.

"Yeah?"

"What if there is someone there? I mean... like a homeless person or a druggie or something?"

"Then I'll see them through the camera first."

"And? I mean... what if they're dangerous?"

"You have your flashlight."

"Seriously."

"We run like hell and bill the girls for any damaged equipment."

Slightly disappointed, she said, "You don't have a gun or anything? A taser?"

"You've seen too many movies," Quinn said. "I find it helps when one works alongside law enforcement to actually stay on the right side of said law. No guns. No tasers. Just flashlights." He flashed a grin at her and nodded at his false leg. "I could always kick them in the crotch."

Georgia and Aimee led them around the side of the house, where a broken wall gave them access. Quinn motioned to them to wait, and did a sweep of the place with the camera before stepping back.

"There's no one there. Although I do see some blankets and empty bottles."

"Homeless person?" Jen said, glancing at the girls, who studiously looked away.

"So what now?" Georgia said.

"Now we film every bit of the place, set up the heat sensors, then settle down for a wait."

"Wait?" Jen said. "What for? Won't the cameras record overnight?"

"Sure, but there's nothing like a bit of personal

observation," Quinn said. "Most sightings have been during the hours of darkness, correct?"

The girls nodded.

"Then we stay out here 'til it gets light."

"We can't stay out all night," Aimee began nervously. Despite her short skirt and grown-up make up she looked very young.

"We'll be missed."

"And I've got a maths test tomorrow, so…"

"Then you can go back any time," Quinn said equably.

They glanced at each other, clearly weighing up a night in the cold and dark, getting into trouble, versus a night spent with Quinn. Jen couldn't really blame them. In the darkness he looked like he was going to drink your blood, and what's more you'd really enjoy it.

"We can stay a *little* while," Georgia said.

"We won't be disturbing the… you know, spirits?" Aimee asked, whispering the last word.

"They've been seen by enough people that I don't suppose a few more will disturb them," Quinn said almost cheerfully. "Now, unpack that crate, and do it carefully. Any breakages will be added to your fee."

CHAPTER SEVEN

Aimee and Georgia huddled round the light of their phones, shivering. Quinn watched them for a while, smiling to himself, and tucked his scarf tighter around his neck.

"You're doing that on purpose," Jen said beside him.

"What?"

"Being warm."

"Hey, it's not my fault they decided to dress for a summer stroll on the beach."

Jen cocked her head to regard the two girls. "People wear wellies on the beach where you come from?"

"Have you been to Ireland in the summer?"

She snorted. He glanced at her, seated with her back against the wall, wrapped up in the kind of gear more usually seen on sports reporters for the Winter Olympics. Except for that bizarre scarf. "You warm enough?"

"Dude, this coat has seen off temperatures of minus twenty. It can cope with October in Suffolk."

"Minus twenty?"

"Skiing in Colorado. Well, I say skiing. More like

falling over whilst small children laughed at me."

"A snow-proof coat is a wonderful thing," said Quinn, who had never skied and was terrifically unlikely to take it up now. He thought back to Tessa's report on Jen before she'd been hired. Private school. Small inheritance. "You ski a lot?"

"God no." At his surprised look, she clarified, "That was the first time. I only went to make up the numbers after someone else dropped out. My sister's the skier. Went with some friends when she was twelve and got hooked." She said the last word with a flourish of jazz hands.

"You weren't invited?"

"Er... no." Jen chewed her lip. "Charlotte is one of the cool kids, you know? Swishy hair, good at sports, makes friends easily. Cares terribly what other people think of her." She indicated the coat, which had an expensive brand name on it. "Never wears the same jacket two years in a row."

Quinn nodded slowly. Charlotte would probably have got on really well with Ethan.

Jen rested her head back against the crumbling wall and closed her eyes. She wore a—sensibly coloured—beanie hat over her curls, which made her look as young as Georgia and Aimee. He wondered if she cared what other people thought of her. She seemed far too remote for him to be able to tell.

It's your job to observe people, Quinn, he told himself. *Observe Jen.*

He observed how her hair cascaded over her shoulders, how her lashes fell dark upon her cheeks, how her lips gleamed with some sweet-scented stuff she'd applied a little while back. He observed how even the thick downy coat didn't hide the rise and fall of her breasts.

He observed that he wasn't really taking this

seriously.

Right then a crackle of twigs caught his attention, and he looked up sharply. But it was just Georgia, huddled into her inadequate jacket, picking her way over to him.

"We're gonna, like, go back to bed?" she said. She had her arms wrapped tightly around herself. She looked miserable.

"Good idea," Quinn said gently. "See if you can get a hot drink when you get inside."

Georgia nodded, and stumbled off after Aimee, who gave them a feeble wave.

"Poor kids," said Jen, watching them go.

"By what measure are they poor?"

"They just wanted to spend some time with you."

Quinn glared at her, and levered himself to his feet to check the cameras. "Giving themselves hypothermia in the process."

"Well, you were pretty cold to them."

"Funny."

Quinn checked everything was working, then sat back down beside Jen and handed her a flask from one of the bags. "Tomato or vegetable?"

She blinked at him.

"Soup," he added helpfully.

"Oh. Uh, you didn't have to…"

"I made you come out here. Least I can do is buy you dinner."

She smiled, accepting the vegetable soup. Quinn unscrewed the lid of his flask and inhaled. Tomato soup, his old friend from many a stakeout.

"I've a wee drop of whiskey too, now the kids have gone," he said, stretching out his aching leg.

"I'm not much of a whiskey drinker."

"You will be around three am, trust me."

She sipped at her soup. Quinn watched her lips kiss the neck of the flask. Heat that had nothing to do with hot soup and everything to do with being alone with a pretty woman warmed his belly.

Dangerous territory, Quinn, he told himself. *Don't let yourself think about it.*

But he couldn't help it. Jen was pretty, and funny and smart, and she was sitting right next to him, and it had been a long time since Quinn had been with anyone. A really long time.

A really, achingly long time.

"What?" Jen mumbled, brushing a drop of soup off her lip.

"Nothing," Quinn said, far too quickly, taking a gulp of soup and nearly choking on it. He wanted to lick that drop off her lip. Dammit, what was wrong with him? Why now? Why her?

He'd met plenty of pretty girls in the last five years. Clever girls. Funny girls. One of his physical therapists had been a part time model, and yet Quinn had no more than a casual appreciation of her looks. Like admiring a painting, or a lovely view. Beside her, Jen was quite plain, and yet here he was, obsessing over her mouth.

There was probably a name for it, he decided, drinking some more soup. Like when patients fell in love with their doctors. Jen had saved his life, after all—or at least she'd saved about 60% of his leg. He'd been told that without the tourniquet she'd tied, he might have lost the whole leg or even bled to death.

Yeah, that was it. He was just feeling grateful. And there was all the… whatever it was soldiers felt after they'd survived a warzone. Camaraderie. Probably. He didn't know. He couldn't think.

"What?" Jen said again. "Go and do that brooding intense thing somewhere else, will you?" Her voice was breathy, slightly high.

She drained her soup and handed him the flask. Her gloved fingers touched his and he grasped them, suddenly urgent.

"Quinn," she breathed, and he saw her pupils, huge and dark. Her lips were parted. Her thumb caressed his through gloves that suddenly felt impossibly thick.

"I—I shouldn't—" she began, leaping abruptly to her feet. Quinn, his fingers wrapped firmly around hers, lurched after her, his bad leg giving way. He stumbled, and she caught him, her hands going to his shoulders.

Quinn looked down at her, shocked at the weight of her body against his, at the flush in her cheeks, at the breath fluttering between her beautiful lips, and he was lost. His mouth met hers in a kiss that was as bruising as it was delicious.

She gave a little moan and fell against him, her arms wrapping around his neck, tearing off her gloves, her fingers sliding into his hair. Quinn grasped at her, greedy, resenting the thickness of her coat. His hands shoved it up and away so he could cup her buttocks, pulling her closer to him. Jen's hands dug under the collar of his coat, touching the bare skin of his neck, her fingers kneading his flesh.

"Oh God, Jenny," he groaned against her mouth, sliding his hands up under her coat, desperately seeking bare skin. She bit gently at his lip and he actually whimpered.

Quinn fumbled with her jacket, nearly tearing the zip apart as he unfastened it, shoving her silly pink scarf away and feasting on the naked skin above the neck of her sweater. He nipped and sucked at it, his hands sliding up under her clothes to feel as much of her as he could. Jen's hands were trying to unfasten his jacket, her lips uttering little cries as he found a nerve ending she particularly liked.

Then she suddenly shrieked, "What the *hell*?" loud enough to startle Quinn into raising his head.

"You don't like that?" he asked muzzily.

She was staring at something behind him. "You need to stop right now," she said, and his head whipped round so fast his neck made a snapping sound.

"No, keep going, keep going, that's good stuff!" panted the female ghost as her lover fondled her bare breasts.

Cold air rushed into the void Quinn had left, chilling Jen's damp skin. She stared at the two naked ghosts writhing together a few feet away, and grabbed her coat tight around her neck. *Where Quinn had been making sweet love to a nerve cluster that had been neglected for too long—*

"Jenny?" Quinn said, his voice low and rough. She couldn't look at him as she tugged her clothes back into place. He hadn't touched her there, he wouldn't have felt —it was too dark to see—he didn't *know*—

"No, don't stop!" wailed the male ghost.

"Is someone there?" Quinn said.

Jen darted away from him, frantically trying to rearrange her clothing as she hid her burning face behind one of the thermal imaging cameras. Oh God, had they been caught on their own film? This was mortifying!

"Over here?" Quinn asked, walking over to the ghosts. He looked a little unsteady.

"Oh, yes please, handsome!" cried the female ghost, reaching out to him.

"No!" Jen yelped. On the thermal imaging screen, the blobs of bright colour went crazy.

"Jen, are you okay?" Quinn said, looking over at her with real concern. He was a few inches from the horny ghosts. She didn't know what would happen if he got any closer.

Oh God, she'd been kissing him. No, she hadn't even been kissing him. She'd been practically eating him alive. *Snogging* him. As if she was a horny teenager and he wasn't—wasn't—

Suddenly she felt sick. Lurching away, knocking over the camera as she went, she stumbled out of the ruined cottage.

"Jen!"

The woods were dark, full of hidden dangers, but at least they didn't contain Quinn. Jen ran blindly from tree to tree, tripped over something, went down on her knees and retched.

"Jen, for God's sake, tell me what's wrong?"

He was there beside her, kneeling down, his hand on her back. She shrugged him away.

"No, don't. Please don't."

He raised his hands in a gesture of surrender. "I'm sorry."

She shook her head. "No. I'm sorry. I just..."

She paused, glanced back at the cottage. From it she could hear the riotous shrieks of two ghosts shagging frantically.

Quinn grimaced and eased the weight off his left knee. "Did you see something? Was someone there?"

What the hell could she say to that? *Yes, there were two horny ghosts and I think their influence was making us randy?* Yeah, that was going to sound great. *I only kissed you because a ghost made me do it.*

"I don't know," she said weakly. "I thought I did."

Quinn rubbed his hands over his face, ran them through his hair. The hair she'd had her fingers entwined in a few minutes ago.

"Look, maybe we shouldn't have..." he waved his hands awkwardly. His really really nice hands.

Jen glanced up at his face, his beautiful face, his dark intense eyes, his drawn-down brows, and wanted to cry.

"We really shouldn't," she said.

CHAPTER EIGHT

The White Lady: some hours later

She's not sure how she got to the hospital. She's not even sure which one it is. She's been herded around from one room to another, been poked and prodded by more people in a few hours than in the rest of her life combined, and now she's sitting on a chair in a corridor looking at watercolours and posters about depression.

Things sound kind of muffled, but she's not sure if that's the same as her ears ringing. People keep asking her things and she's having trouble concentrating. There's a dressing on her arm, which is the only clean thing about her. She smells of ash. She wonders if she should go and find the smokers terrace, where people won't mind so much.

She's been told to sit down and wait, although she's not sure what for. People seem distracted and horrified. Alice isn't here. She disappeared some time before Jen left the White Lady. She remembers looking back and seeing a charred wreck, something from a disaster movie, something that isn't real. She remembers blood and splinters of bone and bits of bodies that should never see daylight.

She doesn't want to remember any of it.

A phone trills somewhere. A person sits down next to her, and Jen automatically shuffles aside so all the dirt and ash and blood won't make a mess of her neighbour's nice clean clothes.

She glances disinterestedly at the floor. Sees a dusty red sneaker and grey jeans. What's the term? Acid-washed. Or maybe it's ash. They're torn and streaked with blood. One leg has been cut open to the knee and there are fresh sutures on the skin beneath.

Something cold reaches in and clutches at her stomach. She presses her hands together in her lap.

Then fingers touch hers, bare hands, the first she's felt since the explosion. No latex gloves.

"Can you walk?" he asks.

She doesn't really know what he's asking. She looks up and left at his face, but he's looking down and right, at her legs, and all she can see is a tangle of hair, grey with ash. Or maybe just grey.

"They said there was only one other. One walker. Everyone else is…"

His fingers tighten. Jen twists her hand around so she can grasp his in return. She still can't see his face. She looks at his hand, which has a white plaster on it. His nails are filthy.

"They keep talking about fatalities. Quiet, when they think I can't hear."

"How many?" Jen asks. She both wants to know and desperately doesn't.

"I heard thirty. But I also heard twelve."

Jen stares hard at a crack in the floor. The White Lady wasn't so full as that. Was it? She can't think.

"The ceiling came down," she remembers. "It—there were some trapped. They might be…"

But they both know what those people might be. Crushed or trapped under burning rubble.

They've already gone away.

"There must be others. People who can *walk*, I mean…" Walking is basic. Everyone can walk.

"It's just us." He finally turns his head, looks up at her from under his hair. He's coated in ash and grime and there's blood on his face, but she knows who he is. His lips are tight and his jaw trembles but the beautiful lines of his face are so familiar. His brows are drawn down, his eyes are dark and intense. And frightened. Very, very frightened.

"It's just you and me," he says.

CHAPTER NINE

Quinn took her home, both of them silent in the dark car. He didn't speak until they reached her little cottage.

"Don't worry about coming in tomorrow. Today. Get some sleep and I'll see you Monday."

She wanted to say something, wanted to explain, but how could she explain this? Any of it? Even Alice didn't know most of this stuff.

"Right," she said, and stumbled from the car instead. She didn't look back as she let herself in, but she didn't hear the car move away until after she'd got inside.

"Good night?" asked Alice from the shadows.

I can't deal with you right now. "Cold and boring," Jen said shortly. She straightened and unwound that stupid pink scarf. "I'm going to bed."

As she brushed her teeth, as she got undressed and avoided the mirror, as she curled into a ball and wished she had a hot water bottle, she could feel Quinn's mouth on hers. His hands on her body. The tightening of her stomach as her excitement leapt—

Why him? Why of all the men in the world did it have to be him?

She thumped her pillow, and tried to think of something else.

Sleep eluded her most of the night, memories of the White Lady and what came after mixing with each other until she gave up, switched on the light and tried to read a while instead. She finally dozed off around the time she'd usually get up in the morning, and was woken a few bare hours later by her phone ringing.

Oh God, it's Quinn, telling me not to bother coming in Monday either. But the display said Charlotte instead.

"Hello?" she yawned.

"You're not still in bed, are you?" said her sister.

"Yeah, I had a bad night—"

"Really? What happened?" asked Alice, popping up beside her so suddenly Jen was glad she was already lying down.

"For God's sake!" Charlotte said, so Jen didn't have to. "I wish I could sleep until lunchtime!"

Jen peered blearily at her watch. "It's hardly lunchtime…"

"Well, it feels like it. I've been up since six," Charlotte told her proudly. "You don't get to lie in when you have kids."

Jen slid Alice a sideways glance.

"I hardly wake you up for midnight feeds," Alice said tartly. The sunlight filtered through her pale face.

"Now look. Mildred's birthday party," Charlotte said. Jen tried very hard not to groan out loud. "You're bringing the hummus and olives, right?"

"Yep," said Jen, who intended to get them from the supermarket near her sister's house.

"The *home-made* hummus? Because I promised it would be an organic party."

"Absolutely," Jen said. "I'll knit it myself."

"You can laugh," said Charlotte, "but if one of those mums gets a hint I've bought it from the shops I'll be a laughingstock."

"And God forbid anyone should laugh at her," said Alice, mirroring her thoughts so exactly Jen clapped her hand over her mouth, before realising she hadn't said it herself.

"Now. They've all got a thing about cake pops at the moment," Charlotte went on. "I don't suppose you could bring some of those?"

"I don't even know what they are," Jen said.

"Yes, you do," Charlotte said, as if Jen was being unhelpful on purpose. "Like cake lollipops."

Alice's eyes got all wide as she listened. "They sound amazing. Say yes."

Charlotte, it's a child's birthday party, so long as she gets to wear an Elsa costume she really won't care, Jen wanted to say, but what she actually said was, "Charlotte, I've got to come all the way by train, I can't bring a lot of stuff."

Charlotte sighed at the impossibility of dealing with her sister. Bad enough Jen thoughtlessly lived so far away, but she couldn't even drive.

"You're twenty-nine. You really need to learn to drive."

Alice pressed her lips together, watching Jen's reaction.

Jen took a deep breath and let it out. Charlotte had learned to drive at seventeen, taking half a dozen lessons and passing her test first time. Jen had been banned from driving a car before she was even old enough to learn. She supposed the restrictions might have been removed by now, but she'd never really checked.

"Is it stubbornness, or fear, that stops you trying?" Alice asked.

Jen glared at her. "I can't afford to right now," she said. "I did just sort of buy a house."

"Stop moving and get a proper job," was Charlotte's

response. "Yes, Mildred? No, have a satsuma instead. Well, I don't care how many pieces of chocolate Florence is allowed. You're not Florence."

Jen sat up and reached for her laptop whilst Charlotte argued with her nearly-five-year-old about what her friends were and weren't allowed to eat. When she'd been packing up her old flat, she'd found some organic carrot chewy bar things from when her niece and nephew had last visited. As she recalled, they hadn't been very enthusiastically received.

"Listen, young lady, do you want a birthday party this weekend?" Charlotte said threateningly, whilst Jen Googled 'cake pops' with one hand.

"Oh, they look niiice," said Alice.

"Don't drool on my computer," Jen muttered.

"Ghosts don't drool," Alice said loftily.

"Fine, don't get ectoplasm on me—" Jen began, as Charlotte said, "What?"

"I said, I... I'm making plans," Jen said, glaring at Alice.

"Good. What time can you get here? The party starts at eleven but we've got a lot of prep to do. It's a nightmare."

Jen thought back to the few childhood parties she'd attended. Prep had involved blowing up some balloons, opening some bags of crisps, and arguing over who got to stop and start the tape of Take That when they played musical chairs.

"I mean, you should see the parties some of these kids have. It's astonishing. You know Mildred's friend Elsie?" Jen didn't, but this didn't make any difference to Charlotte, who barrelled on regardless. "She went to this place, I looked it up, it's a grand just for the venue hire. And on top of that there's the food, the entertainer... it's madness."

Jen refrained from pointing out that her sister wanted

her to bring organic hummus to a five-year-old's birthday party.

"And it's all so fake. The entertainer wasn't even funny. I just want her to have something chilled, you know, laid back. It's much more fun that way."

Alice started giggling.

"How many children are coming?" Jen asked, although she knew the answer was immaterial. Mildred was five. She would fight 'chilled' with everything she had.

"Not sure yet, it's as if people don't know what RSVP means. About twenty, maybe twenty-five. Most of the class, I expect."

Jen closed her eyes and wondered if she could contract a stomach bug before tomorrow.

"And there are the children from swimming and Little Tots. Could be more like thirty," Charlotte added smugly. "She's very popular and busy."

"I'm sure she is. Look, I'll have a look at the trains later and—"

"Aren't you coming this afternoon?" Charlotte interrupted sharply.

"No," Jen said. "Tomorrow morning, like we said."

"No, Mum's coming tomorrow morning. You're coming down this afternoon."

"When did I say that? I never said—"

"I need you to pick up some stuff for the party!"

What, in this car I don't have and am not allowed to drive? "I have a job," she said. "I work during the day. I can't come down—"

"Then why are you in bed in the middle of the day? Nice try," said Charlotte.

"I was working late. I got the day—" Jen began, and cursed herself. "Off," she spat.

Alice gave her a slow-hand clap.

"Well then, you can come down this afternoon. Do

you have a pen? I need you to pick up some bunting, and it has to be plain, not patterned, but all in different colours, okay? And then we need balloons because the ones I ordered look really cheap. Are you writing this down?"

Jen closed her eyes, and wondered if it was too early to start drinking.

Tessa looked disgustingly chipper when Quinn finally made it in on Friday. "How'd the stakeout go?"

Quinn shot her a hard look as he flicked the kettle on. "Fine."

"No… shenanigans?"

"No," he growled, avoiding looking at Jen's empty desk.

"Really?" Tessa spooned some coffee into her mug. "How did those girls keep their hands off you when you're so sunny and friendly?"

Oh. "Just natural caution, I guess." He chucked a teabag in his cup.

"Any good footage?"

"How would I know? I only just brought the stuff in. I've been awake all night, Tessa, give me a break."

She raised her palms. "All right, all right. Look, I'd've gone, but I had a thing with the kids, and…"

"I know." The kettle finally boiled and he sloshed some hot water into his mug. Added another teabag.

"That's going to be some strong tea," Tessa commented mildly.

"Maybe I want strong tea," he retorted, spooning three heaped teaspoons of sugar in.

She watched him bang about in the fridge for milk, then said gently, "Are you sure nothing happened last night?"

"Nothing at all," he snarled, and stalked off to his office, spilling half his tea on the way.

He collapsed into his chair, unbelievably weary. The footage he'd recorded last night needed to be uploaded but he wasn't sure he had the strength. Those cameras had covered 90% of the interior of the cottage—there was no way they wouldn't have caught him snogging the life out of his secretary. Or her running away in horror.

Still, at least they wouldn't have caught her throwing up shortly afterwards, which was some mercy.

He slumped in his chair and wondered what the hell had come over him. It simply wasn't like him to behave like that. He'd never gone after a girl that ferociously, and never that quickly either. How long had they known each other? A day, a day and a half? Jesus, if Ethan was here he'd wet himself laughing. When Quinn was seventeen, it had taken him six months from admitting he liked Moira Henessey to actually asking her out, and another four after that to progress to anything more intimate than pecks on the cheek. In the end she'd dumped him, saying she'd like to lose her virginity before she took her Leaving Cert, thanks.

"You can always tell which Quinn Twin's which," he'd overheard her telling her friend Shona. "If it's Ethan, he'll be in your knickers before you've even said hello."

"If it's James, you'll be needing incontinence pants before he gets in them!" said Shona, and they'd both cracked up.

He'd been mortally offended at the time. Worse was to come when he discovered that Ethan had, in fact, got in her knickers, a bare week later.

At least that wasn't something he had to worry about with Jen.

Sighing, he slotted the memory card into the computer's reader and took a sip of tea while he waited for the files to upload. Ugh, Tessa was right, it was far too strong. He pushed the cup to one side, resolving to chuck it into the flower water when she wasn't looking.

The heat detection camera had been set to take photos at regular intervals. Quinn would've loved a camera that recorded video, but he figured he'd need to do a lot more expensive overnight jobs before he could afford one. The night vision cameras, however, recorded video and audio footage, which made them useful for cross-referencing.

The footage began with him taking a test of Jen standing in front of the camera, waving. Her warm face showed up bright yellow, her hair and clothes darker shades of red, the cold background a palette of grey-ish purple. Jen's hand was a reddish blur in the first picture, and then turned a warmer yellow as she removed her glove for the next one.

She laughed silently, her mouth going brighter as it opened, and he recalled one of the girls cosying up to him to look at the screen, and saying something about looking like Marge Simpson. Sure enough, the next shot had Jen miming Marge's beehive hair.

He skimmed through the pictures, watching as the colder, darker figures of Georgia and Aimee huddled together against the far wall and he and Jen sat down on the other side, easily distinguishable even in fuzzy thermal imaging: not only was Quinn's figure larger, but it also had only one leg registering as warm flesh. His prosthesis showed up as a dark purple blob.

He saw a small creature, orange and red, pass over one side of the cottage, which none of them had noticed at the time. Something appeared higher up, probably an owl by the shape of it. The purple trees moved a little in the wind. Periodically either he or Jen got up to adjust a camera. Eventually Georgia and Aimee left.

He both wanted to see what happened next, and dreaded it.

There he went handing her some soup. Her lips

warmed to white as she drank from the flask. He flicked faster through the pictures. They sat side by side, and then—

The camera didn't catch her hand touching his, but it did catch her leaping away from him, his awkward stumble on that invisible leg, both of them getting warmer in each shot. By the time they started kissing their mouths were white hot. Jen's skin flashed bright as he shoved her clothes away.

He was so engrossed in the flickering zoetrope of his own disgrace that he forgot he was supposed to be looking for whatever Jen had seen over his shoulder. It was only when she pushed him away that he saw the darker flash on the other side of the cottage.

He leaned closer to the screen. There was his overheated self, confused and ridiculously turned on, moving towards something that showed up on the thermal scan as pitch black. A misshapen blob. Nothing that had appeared in the cottage before. Nothing manmade, and nothing animal. Something colder than the fallen stones around it.

Quinn frowned at it, then scrolled through the next few pictures.

Abruptly, the angle changed, and when the camera refocused all he got were pictures of dark purple grass. Of course, Jen had knocked the camera stand, and he hadn't righted it for another ten minutes or so, after he'd taken her to the car and promised to drive her home.

He flicked on ahead, anxiously, but by the time he'd reset the camera to something approximating its original position, the darkness had gone.

Quinn scrolled back to the picture of himself reaching out to the darkness. He wasn't a man to spook easily, but…

…he was spooked.

He opened his mouth to call for Tessa, then thought

better of it, and reached for the night vision camera.

The footage seemed bland and wan after the bright colour of the thermal imaging, but at least it had sound. He put his headphones on—God only knew what sorts of noises he and Jen had been making—and began watching it on a second screen.

His gaze crept back to the photo of the darkness more than once.

CHAPTER TEN

"Do you remember," said Alice on Saturday, "that time you asked me about heaven and hell?"

"No," murmured Jen, staring in horrified fascination at her niece's birthday party.

"You were about Mildred's age."

"Right." Jen couldn't even tell which one Mildred was any more.

"Well, I said I didn't know what either one was like."

"Uh-huh."

"I was wrong. This is what hell looks like."

Charlotte had hired a village hall, which Jen had spent the whole morning decorating with fairy lights, floral garlands, fabric swags, and three kinds of bunting, most of which had become detached and was being worn by someone three foot tall and screaming. There were seven Elsas and at least six other Disney princesses, plus a Spider-Man and a dinosaur, despite it not being a fancy dress party. The cake pops she'd bought from Emma & Jo's irritatingly twee bakery on Wirpness High Street for an absurd fee had been fashioned into a sort of wedding cake shape, which had been demolished as soon as it was brought out.

The olives and hummus—also bought from the Wirpness deli, and hastily repotted into dishes from home—had remained untouched until one of the few dads present had attacked them, out of desperation.

"What d'you mean, there's only squash to drink?" he'd asked, before searching every bit of the tiny kitchen just to make sure there wasn't any beer hiding away.

"Organic squash," Jen clarified. The poor man looked like he was about to impale himself on a cake pop stick.

She looked around to see if anyone was watching, then ducked under the counter for her handbag, in which was hidden a small bottle of gin. She slugged some into a glass of squash.

"Try that," she said, and he did.

"Oh God. Marry me."

Jen laughed at that, which drew Charlotte's attention, and resulted in a whispered dressing-down during which she learned that the dad in question was going through Domestic Troubles, and so it was Very Irresponsible of Jen to flirt with him.

Jen privately thought that anyone with four-year-old twins and a six month old baby probably desperately needed both gin and flirting, but she gave her sister the apologetic smile she'd perfected as a child, and carried on serving cake to overexcited children.

"Is there sugar in that?" demanded one mother.

"Er, yes?" Jen said. "It's cake."

"Abraham, *no*," said the mother, smacking her son's hands away, as Jen wondered whether she'd misheard 'sugar' instead of 'hashish'. "He can't have sugar," the woman added in an accusatory tone of voice.

"Oh, I'm sorry. Is he diabetic?" Jen asked, wondering if she had time to nip out and fetch more gin.

"No," she was told, and offered no explanation.

Two minutes later, Charlotte marched up. "Jen, don't

tell them it has sugar in it. That's the sugar free cake."

"How the hell do you make sugar free cake?"

"With xylitol."

"Isn't he a villain in a comic book?" Jen said. Alice laughed. Charlotte did not.

"And watch your language," Charlotte said. "*Pas devant.*"

"Yeah, like they don't all speak French," Jen muttered.

"And don't let Edith, Agnes, or Donald have sugar either. They're not allowed it."

Jen started to ask why, then got overwhelmed with giggles at the thought of a five-year-old called Donald.

At least it's a distraction. She'd spent the train journey trying to think about what to say to Quinn on Monday. What she wanted from him. Well, she knew what she wanted, but she was pretty sure she couldn't have it.

She couldn't let him in, couldn't let him see… He was a detective, for Christ's sake, the minute he saw her with her clothes off he'd start putting things together and then he'd figure it out. He'd know, and he'd hate her, and she'd have to leave…

And she liked Wirpness. She liked the agency, and Tessa, and God help her she even liked Danny.

You like Quinn too, said a sly little voice in the back of her mind.

Yes, she did. And because she liked him she had to keep him at arm's length. It was the only way this could work.

She sighed, and went back to serving terrible cake.

Very shortly afterwards, she overhead a shrill argument between one of Charlotte's friends and a woman who was convinced the gluten free cake had gluten in it because it had risen too well. "You know I'm trialling Ermintrude on a gluten free diet and it's just not fair on her if Winifred has it when she can't."

"Jesus God, take me now," Jen muttered.

Beside her, Alice started to shake with laughter. They watched as Charlotte organised a game of musical chairs, which was not comprehended by several of the younger children, who simply burst into tears.

"Nora's very upset. I don't know why you can't take the needs of the littlies into consideration," said one of the mummies. Jen genuinely had no idea which one she was. They all wore skinny jeans and tops in the same seven shades of blue. One woman had a complicated outfit that allowed her to breastfeed whilst glaring at another mother giving her baby a bottle.

"Can you believe Courtney's still breastfeeding Bertha?" Charlotte said, following Jen's gaze. "She's nearly two."

"Doesn't that mean, she, er, has teeth?" Jen said, and Charlotte pulled a face before going to separate a fight between two people called Myrtle and Howard who had a combined age of about eight.

"I mean, it's normal to me," Alice said.

"What, breastfeeding until the kid's at college?" Jen muttered.

"No. Children called Winifred and Myrtle. But I'm a hundred and fifty years old. It's rather like meeting small children born the same year as me, called things like... Temperance, and Mercy, and..."

"If-Christ-Had-Not-Died-For-Thee-Thou-Hadst-Been-Damned was always my favourite," Jen said. "Remember that priest, in Stamford?"

"Whose brother Judge-Not-Lest-Ye-Be-Judged perished at Kineton Fight?" Alice giggled.

"Whilst, ironically, his other brother, Fight-The-Good-Fight, turned his coat and was banished from the family?"

Alice began to reply, but her voice and form

suddenly disappeared as Jen's mother walked through her.

"Dear, who are you talking to?" she asked. Her frown had the crease in it that she always got when she caught Jen doing something a bit 'different'. Charlotte used to call it the Jenny Wrinkle, before she grew up and started getting embarrassed by her sister's differentness. Jen had even developed a special Mum Smile to placate her.

"Oh, just thinking aloud," Jen said easily. "Making a mental list. Shopping, things to be done around the house."

Her mother winced almost imperceptibly at the word 'mental'.

"You... have taken your medication, haven't you, dear?"

"Of course," Jen said, and gave her the Mum Smile.

"You lying hound," Alice said, extricating herself. "When you take that stuff you can't see me."

"The medication is an excellent idea," Jen said loudly.

"Oh good. And are you settling in at your new place? When can we come and see it?"

"Oh," said Jen. She thought about her little house, with its kitchen from the 1980s and its bedroom papered in anaglypta wallpaper; and then she thought about her mother's house, which was huge and brand new and decorated by someone else; and her sister's house, which was Victorian and elegant and shabby chic. "Er... I'm still doing a lot of work on it."

"Don't work too hard," said her mother anxiously. "Doctor Ebury said tiredness could exacerbate your condition, remember?"

Jen didn't remember. Not specifically. Doctor Ebury was one of countless specialists her mother had taken her to see, who had diagnosed her with one of countless conditions.

"I'm not working too hard," she said, fixing the Mum Smile on her face.

"If you need any money, Robert could—"

"I'm fine," Jen said, and added quickly, "Is Robert here?"

"You don't think you'd have noticed a sixty-year-old man in a room full of yummy mummies and toddlers?" said Alice.

"No, he had a golf match, couldn't reschedule it. Charlotte was not very happy about that."

"Why?" Jen said. Her stepfather was quite a nice man, especially considering he had one control-freak stepdaughter and one who'd spent half her childhood in mental institutions. "He sees Millie and Eddie most weeks, doesn't he?"

"He's very good with Mildred and Edgar," said her mother, "but Charlotte felt he could have made a bit more effort to support her. I'm not getting in the middle of it," she added, raising her hands. "Now, have you applied for any jobs yet?"

"I've got a job. I've been there two weeks," Jen said, her head beginning to throb. "I emailed you about it."

"Oh, I never check that thing. Charlotte said you didn't have a job."

"Well, I do. It's—"

"She said you were still in bed at lunchtime," her mother added, as if this was concrete proof.

"And no one who stays in bed late could ever have a job, could they?" Jen said, her patience snapping. "How do you know I don't work shifts?"

"There's no need to shout, dear," said her mother, against the evidence of thirty small children having a party. "Stay calm. Doctor Wu said—"

"Yes, I know, Mum," Jen said, making an effort to control her voice with every word. Beside her, Alice made a face. "I do have a job, okay, but I had the day off yesterday. Not that it's anyone's business but mine what hours I work."

Her mother glanced over at Charlotte, who had been an actuary all of her boring adult life, working nice safe regular office hours with time off only for maternity leave and holidays on farmsteads in Dorset.

"I bet Charlotte gets up at sparrow's fart to weave organic lunches for Mildred and Edgar," Alice mocked.

Jen fought a smile.

"What sort of job?" her mother asked, the Jenny Wrinkle back in place.

Jen thought about saying: *I work for a really hot Irish detective with a tortured past, whose brother was a famous actor and whose life I saved in the worst civilian disaster to hit London in decades.*

Instead she said, "I'm an office manager."

"You mean a secretary?"

"I mean an office manager." Jen thought about trying to explain the difference, and decided she really hadn't had enough gin for that.

A cool, bright Sunday found Quinn standing outside the pub, breathing in secondhand smoke and trying to watch the rugby through the window. In front of him on the windowsill was a packet of cigarettes and a pint of Guinness, only one of which he was partaking of.

It was a test. He'd given up smoking three times in his life, and if he could stay off them when they were right there in front of him, he was winning.

Which was more than he could say for the Irish rugby team. He folded his arms and squinted at the score. Ah, feck it, someone had converted a try. The lads might as well go home now.

Leaning against the back of the nearest bench, he picked up his pint and was hit with a sudden memory of standing in a London pub with Ethan one afternoon, watching Ireland lose dismally to England and trying not to say anything that would betray their nationality.

"Can I buy you a drink?" a pretty redhead had asked Ethan, and he'd smiled at her and said in a passable London accent, "Sure, love, and one for me bruvver too? We're twins."

For the rest of the afternoon, Quinn'd had to keep his mouth shut. He was appallingly bad at accents. The redhead had thought he was so weird he'd overhead her asking Ethan if he had 'special needs'.

"What are you smiling at?" someone asked at his elbow, and he nearly dropped his pint. Jen stood there, half her face hidden by huge sunglasses, her hair whipping in the wind.

"Just… ehm, smiling," he said lamely. *Oh, brilliant, Quinn. Perfect. Witty.* He picked up the cigarettes and stroked the packet comfortingly.

"Who's winning?"

"The cigarettes, at this rate," he said.

"What?" They stared at each other, or at least Quinn stared at Jen's sunglasses. "I meant the rugby."

"Oh. Not us. Why'd you think I'm standing outside?"

"Because you can't smoke inside?"

They both looked at the unopened packet of cigarettes.

Jen gave up and peered through the window. "It's Ireland v New Zealand."

He nodded stupidly. She had on that pink scarf again, and her hair seemed to have glitter in it. *Maybe she's one of the Fair Folk. That would explain a few things.*

"Then isn't the rest of the pub neutral?"

He rubbed his forehead and tried to explain. "Now sure, if I was a Kiwi, and everyone else was English, then they'd all support Ireland. You follow?"

She nodded in understanding and smiled. "I'll go and get the drinks then. Same again?"

Puzzled, he nodded, and watched her weave her way through the crowded pub. A few people turned to notice her, mostly men who gave her curves an appreciative once-over.

Quinn glowered at them. It was about all he could do, at least until he knew where he stood. 'Back off lads, she's my secretary' didn't have quite the ring he was going for.

He scrunched up his eyes and wished he wasn't so out of practice with this. He flirted with a girl, kissed her, she kissed him back—and then she ran away screaming. *Sure you've got a great technique there, Quinn.* The last he'd seen of her she'd practically run into her house and not looked back.

Now here she came with his drink. He drained the last of his previous pint and accepted the new one. Jen leaned against the bench next to him, sipping her cider. Neither of them spoke. Her hair fluttered in the breeze, catching the weak sun and sparkling in the edge of his vision. *Definitely a fairy. Or a mermaid.*

Eventually, just when the silence was getting so unbearable Quinn was about to invent some rugby knowledge just to impress her, Jen said, "Look, I'm really sorry about the other night."

"Don't worry about it," he said, like the eejit he was.

"Well, of course I worry about it. I work with you. Er, I... do still work with you, right?" A note of worry crept into her voice. "You're not going to fire me for taking the day off, are you?"

"I gave you the day off," Quinn said.

"Right, but I just wanted to check that wasn't Irish for getting fired."

He gave her a sideways look. She stared ahead, impassive behind her shades.

"You're still in employment. That's why I said, 'come in on Monday'."

"Actually, you said you'd see me on Monday. You might have meant at the shops or something."

"Ah, great, you've an eidetic memory," Quinn said. That was exactly what he needed, a girl he'd disappointed romantically who remembered every second of it.

"A what?"

"Photographic memory."

"No, of course not." She shuddered. "Imagine."

He was imagining. It was horrible.

His left hand squeezed the packet of cigarettes very hard.

"Look, the thing is," Jen said in a rush, and then paused. She drank some more cider. "I'm not really after... that is, I... look, Quinn, you're a really great guy, but—"

"Sure," he said. "I'm a real catch."

"No, you are," Jen said, finally taking off her glasses and looking up at him. She looked tired. Pale, no make-up aside from that hair glitter. "And you're a great kisser too, so stop feeling sorry for yourself."

Quinn smiled down at her. He couldn't help it.

"And stop that. Don't you try charming me." She whipped her sunglasses back on as if they blocked charm as well as UV rays.

"I wasn't trying to charm you," he said, although the idea held some appeal. Dammit, Ethan would've been brilliant at this. That is, Ethan would've been brilliant at it, if he'd ever had to face a girl he'd snogged the face off who'd then run away. Which Quinn would bet pounds to pennies he never had.

"I worked out what to say, you know," Jen said. "And I've forgotten it all."

"It was just a kiss," Quinn said, looking at her mouth.

Jen snorted. "I don't know about you, mister, but there was no 'just' about that kiss. That wasn't 'just' anything. That was…"

"Oh, it really was," he agreed.

"A bad idea. Bad. And I don't think we were ourselves. It was a bad idea," she repeated. "We're not doing it again."

"Sure about that?"

"Yes. Very sure. Stop doing that Big Bad Wolf thing. I'm off the menu."

Quinn realised he'd been leaning closer to her. He abruptly straightened up. Off the menu. He wasn't going to push this, no matter how much he wanted to. "Okay," he said, and took a gulp of his drink to cover his nerves.

"Okay?" Was it his imagination, or did she sound disappointed?

"Sure. It was a great kiss, I'm a great guy, but you're… ah, shite," he groaned as a thought occurred to him. "Are you gay?"

"No," she said, sounding preoccupied. "You don't kiss all your secretaries like that, do you?"

"Thought you were my office manager?"

"Yes, but. Do you?"

Quinn wasn't sure how he'd got the upper hand here, but he liked it. "Well, there was that fling I had with Vera…"

"Oh God."

"But then her grandkids walked in and it all got very awkward."

"What?" Her sunglasses swung in his direction. Quinn looked down at his pint and tried not to smirk. "Oh, funny."

He took a sip and smiled at her. "No, I don't kiss all my office managers like that. You're the first."

"Right," Jen said. "Well, good. But that's the last time. It's not going to happen again."

Quinn stared unseeing at the crowded pub. "Why not?"

"You ever hear the phrase 'it's not you, it's me'?"

He groaned. "Ah, come on. Don't I deserve something more original?"

Jen bit her lip. "I had a really bad relationship," she blurted. "It ended really, really badly. I'm just not... it wouldn't be fair. On either of us."

Quinn started to say that he wasn't looking for a relationship, and then stopped. Partly because he didn't know if that would make it worse, and partly because he didn't know if it was true.

"I have to go. It's going to take all afternoon to get this sodding glitter out." She tugged at her mermaid hair in disgust.

"I like the glitter," Quinn said, and Jen managed to confer a glare even through her massive sunglasses.

"Then you can go to my niece's next party. I'm sure you'll look just darling with a bit of sparkle."

She handed him her drink and straightened up. Quinn, unsure how he'd got from flirting to being handed half a pint of cider, looked after her in confusion.

"What'm I supposed to do with this?"

"Try black velvet," she said, and walked away

CHAPTER ELEVEN

The White Lady, just before

The pub really is a dive, but Quinn kind of likes that in a boozer. The smell of stale beer and smoke that's been lingering since before the ban reminds him of sitting outside pubs with Ethan when they were kids, waiting for their da to bring out a bottle of Coke to share.

Ethan isn't there yet, so Quinn orders himself a drink. He hesitates over what to get his brother, whose tastes have become more sophisticated since moving to London, then he figures if Ethan doesn't want his pint, he can just drink it himself. God only knows it's hot enough inside the pub to need it.

He sits down at a scuffed table and gets out the folder of care home information he's brought to discuss with Ethan, but his mind keeps skittering away from it, back to the girl in the police report. The cuts on her arms, the fervour in her eyes. She's a mess, and he doesn't expect anyone's really done anything to help her. She's exactly the type of person who could go over the edge and do something really terrible to herself, or to Ethan. Or, and

Quinn has to admit the possibility is frighteningly real, to himself.

He quite deliberately dresses differently from his brother, or at least from his brother's character on TV. The wardrobe department on *Devilborn* appears to have a job lot on black dye, leather and tight denim, which are all things Quinn has no problem avoiding. He's cut his hair shorter, too, and he's clean-shaven. Still, the barmaid is staring at him.

Quinn ignores her. He's not looking for female company. He's not long since split with Fidelma, his girlfriend of just over a year. Delma kept haranguing him to apply for a promotion or suck up to the Chief Superintendent, but Quinn just can't seem to find the enthusiasm. Lately, Uncle Kieran's casual offer of employment in the private sector has been looking more and more appealing.

He glances up as a tall dark figure comes in through the door, pausing to survey the room. If Quinn were being charitable, he'd say this was because it's dark inside compared to the bright sunshine, and that Ethan is looking for him. But in reality, he knows it's because Ethan likes to stand and be admired when he enters a room.

He waves, as if it's possible Ethan won't have spotted him. His twin comes over, drops into a chair and takes a sip of Guinness. He peers at Quinn.

"God, I look ugly today."

It's an old joke, and Quinn just shrugs in response.

"How's filming going?"

Ethan sighs. "Ah, it's the wrong kind of filming. We have to do blog diaries, little clips of us fooling around and answering viewer questions. It's that and press stuff this week since we can't get on location for a couple of days. I mean it's all traffic to the site, but bejeesus it's boring. I'd rather get back to pretending to be the devil."

Quinn refrains from commenting on that. "Why can't you get on location?"

"Oh I dunno, some migrating toads or something." Ethan yawns. "Ninety percent of acting is just hanging around."

"Policing isn't much different. Now, listen. We need to talk about Mam."

Ethan eyes him over his drink. "Why, what's she done now?"

He seems to think she's just being eccentric. Quinn doesn't know how to tell him how serious it is. "Last week one of her neighbours came home late and found her out in the garden, pulling up weeds and decapitating the sunflowers."

"So she's just leaving the gardening 'til it's cooled down a bit," Ethan says with a shrug. "Sensible of her."

"It would have been nearly three am. She was in her nightie. When Mr Hooley asked her what she was doing she had no idea where she was. Eth, this isn't the first time. When I started asking around half of Dalkey had a story on her. Most of it's little stuff, like going out in her slippers or forgetting what a teapot is called, or giving out at the postman for not collecting the rubbish. Don't laugh!"

"Ah come on, it's a little bit funny."

"Is it funny that she forgets to eat? Or wear her glasses when she's driving? You know she's blind as a bat. How she's escaped a serious accident I don't know. I called her doctor and she hasn't been in for any of her repeat prescriptions."

"Well, there you are then. Get her back on those and she'll be fine," Ethan says breezily.

"No, you're not getting it. I went round to see her and check was she taking her pills. 'Sure I don't know what pills you mean,' says she. I found them in a drawer. She said they weren't hers and started accusing me of trying to fit her up."

"Well, you are a cop," Ethan says. He's not taking this seriously.

"Ethan. Please. Half her food had gone off. The bin was overflowing—"

"Because the postie hadn't been round to empty it?"

Quinn's jaw is clenched. "She's not paying her bills. She can't even remember to clean her teeth. She can't take care of herself any more."

"She's just—"

"If you say 'eccentric' I'll tell the press how you wet your bed until you were seven."

"I did not!" Ethan says hotly.

"Sure, will they believe you?"

His twin looks away, eyeing up the barmaid. Avoiding the conversation. He signals to the barmaid that he wants another drink, even though he must know full well this isn't the sort of place that does table service. But Ethan just gives her one of his lazy, come-to-bed smiles, and she giggles and blushes and starts pouring the drinks anyway.

"She needs proper care." Quinn gets out the leaflets the doctor gave him. "She needs reassessing and then we can work out where to go from there. It might be that she has carers round a couple of times a day—"

"What, strangers coming into the house? She'll hate that. You know how she likes her independence."

Quinn shakes his head. "I think she's been telling us that so we won't interfere and see how bad it's got. Like when alcoholics hide their drinking and make excuses for it."

"She's not an alcoholic. Is she?" Ethan asks with a sudden flash of vulnerability. Might he actually be feeling guilty about how little attention he pays to his only parent?

"No. She has dementia, Ethan. We need to face up to

it."

Ethan says nothing. He takes a large drink of his Guinness and frowns at the far wall, where a tatty poster advertises a band called West African Zombies.

"Is this because I moved away?"

Quinn can only stare at his brother for a moment.

"I can't go round there every week, Jim." Ethan is the only person who has ever called him Jim. "I can't stay in Ireland. The land where nothing ever fucking happens. I need to be here. Do you understand that?"

Quinn takes a breath and tries to calm down. Rationally, he knows that this is true, but Ethan's self-absorption is breathtaking.

"She needs more than visits once a week. She needs constant care. You think I go round there every day?"

"You only live around the corner," Ethan says belligerently. "Maybe you should."

"I don't live around the corner, I live in Donnycarney." There's the whole of Dublin between him and his mother.

Ethan snorts. "Why would anyone live in Donnycarney?"

Quinn could say the same for Ethan's choice of neighbourhood, but he doesn't want to turn this into a fight. "It's not about who lives where. Even if we both lived next door we couldn't give her the care she needs."

Right then the barmaid wiggles over with their drinks. Quinn notices her ironed-straight hair and freshly-applied lipliner. Ethan seems to be noticing her breasts.

"There you go," she says. "Anything else you want, just ask me."

"Thanks a million," says Ethan, giving her a megawatt smile.

"I mean it," she breathes. "Anything."

Ethan lets his gaze trail over her, then he looks back

up at her face and does the bedroom eyes thing. Quinn can barely keep himself from groaning.

"I'll bear that in mind," Ethan drawls, and the barmaid turns pink.

Quinn is about to intervene when the door opens, and he automatically glances over. A young woman stands there, wearing a bulky parka that is at odds with the relentless summer heat. She looks familiar but out of context, and his mind is too full of his mother to to work it out. Like that time he met Ethan in the Groucho Club and had a half hour conversation with one of the actors from *Eastenders* before realising who he was.

"Ethan," says the girl, and Ethan looks up, his smile freezing on his face. And in that instant Quinn knows where he's seen her pale, unhappy face before. It's on the police report in Ethan's flat.

"Not you," Ethan says, and the girl steps forward. Quinn's on his feet rightaway, reaching for the Garda radio he doesn't have. She's dripping with sweat, but as he looks closer he realises some of it is tears.

"I think you need to leave," he says, as firmly as he can without being harsh.

She just shakes her head and doesn't speak. Behind Quinn, he's vaguely aware of a commotion at the bar, but he doesn't turn to look because the girl in the parka is reaching for something inside her coat. Horror ignites in Quinn's brain and he dives to the ground, dragging Ethan down with him.

A second later, the world explodes.

CHAPTER TWELVE

"I still don't understand, old thing," Danny said. "Why d'you want to know about the school?"

Jen sighed. Alice said bossily, "Because Quinn doesn't believe in ghosts and therefore will never find an explanation for the strange goings on at the cottage."

"What kind of goings on?" Danny persisted. "What happened last week?"

Jen avoided the gaze of both ghosts and typed, "*It's been freaking out teenagers. I think it's a make-out spot, but they've been reporting weird stuff. I thought probably most of it was made up, but there were definitely ghosts there.*"

"Then why can't you go and ask them?"

Because last time they made me incredibly horny and if I'm around Quinn that won't end well, Jen thought, but she typed, "*Because I'd look majorly weird going there by myself and talking to thin air, okay? We were just lucky on Thursday that the school swallowed Quinn's excuse about doing a geological survey.*"

Her email pinged just then. Her heart leapt a little when she saw it was from Quinn, who so far had mostly ignored her today. The email was entitled 'St Hilda's', which didn't exactly reassure her.

She opened it, hoping neither of the ghosts would read it over her shoulder, and was almost disappointed to read the two line message. "Please print and file the enclosed. Report has been sent to Georgia."

She opened the attached document and scanned it, but it was mostly a summary of the data from the cameras they'd set up. It very carefully didn't include anyone making out with anyone, but it did include a mention of a dark spot on the thermal imaging camera.

"The black area is indicative of a cold spot, which could account for the chill reported by several people. There are several explanations for a cold spot, such as an underground spring, but a more detailed geological survey would be needed to find out if this is the case."

Jen translated this as: If you want me to come back, you'll have to pay me a lot more.

She set the document to print, then quickly Googled how to locate an underground spring. Most of the answers revolved around looking for running water— well, duh—or certain types of greenery that thrived in such conditions.

She looked at the night vision stills. There was a tangle of ivy over a couple of the ruined walls, but no other greenery.

"Why are you even looking?" Alice said over her shoulder. "You know it was ghosts."

"Good point," Jen said, and closed the search window.

"What is?" asked Tessa, making her jump.

Jen reflected that being startled by humans and not by ghosts was something of a sad indication of her life.

"Oh… I was just looking at the report for Thursday night. The school hauntings. Or, apparently, the school underground spring."

Tessa flicked on the kettle and picked up the sheets of paper still whirring from the printer tray. "Ah yes, the old underground spring. Quinn's usual fallback."

"Fallback?"

She shrugged. Danny watched the motion with interest. "He knows no one is really going to commission a geological survey. They're more likely to use dowsing rods."

"So... he finds these cold spots a lot?"

"People are always certain they've felt one. Usually he can prove it with a thermometer, but if there actually is a cold spot there are always other causes. If it's indoors, it's a draft caused by bad insulation, or possibly an underground well and a crack in the foundations. Since most of the ghost stories come from old buildings, that's reasonably likely."

Danny, peering at the report Tessa held, suddenly frowned and muttered something under what Jen would have to call his breath, if he had any. She ignored him.

"And I expect it usually gives the owners something bigger to worry about than ghosts."

"Exactly." Tessa looked wistful for a moment. "Sometimes I wonder what would happen if a client actually did do the survey and found there was no spring. No explanation whatsoever for the cold spot."

The door to Quinn's office opened and he said, "I'd do nothing, because that won't ever happen. No such thing as." He went over to the kettle and poked at it.

"There are more things in heaven and earth—" Jen began, as Tessa rolled her eyes. Quinn banged his mug down loudly on the tray and groaned.

"Jesus Christ, if one more person quotes Hamlet at me I'll go insane."

"He hates being called Horatio," Tessa confided.

"Who's Horatio?" Alice said.

Danny looked up. "Jenny, old bean, this school. Used

to be Adderall Hall, according to this report?"

"What?"

"The school," Danny repeated, whilst Tessa, misunderstanding, explained who Horatio was in Hamlet.

"Oh I see," Alice said. "Not much call for Shakespeare where I came from."

Jen nodded distractedly at her and tried to concentrate on what Danny was saying.

"...the school, it was called Adderall Hall. I know exactly the place, and the cottage in the grounds, too."

He hesitated expectantly. Jen raised a hand to him to wait a minute, then hurriedly turned the gesture into smoothing her hair.

"So what?" Alice said to Danny.

"The rumour about the ghosts isn't new. They've been there since I was a lad."

"Are they real?"

Jen nodded, pretending to be engrossed in her computer.

"Ooh, can I go and play with them?"

Jen looked up in horror. Alice and the nymphomaniac ghosts? "Uh, no," she said.

"Sorry?" Tessa glanced over at her.

"Ah, you know what, I'll have a coffee too," Jen covered.

Tessa shrugged. She spooned some coffee into a mug for Jen, and then added an extra spoonful to her own.

"That's a lot of coffee," Quinn said, spooning twice as much sugar into his mug.

"I'm doing Mrs Mac's family tree," Tessa said. "I need all the caffeine I can get."

"How far have you got?"

Tessa took a draught of coffee before answering. "1797. Patricius Macanally married Alicius Gorman in Liverpool."

"You know that's just Catholic church-speak for Patrick and Alice, right?"

"I certainly hope so," Tessa said. "Thanks for the census advice, though. I had an absolute breakthrough on the 1841 census where some idiot transcriber didn't realise 'Wm' was short for William. I won't tell you what they made of Christopher."

"Chrispr," Quinn said, without even pausing in his tea-making.

"Like the box at the bottom of the fridge?" Jen said.

"Beautiful name," Tessa said, and went back into her office. She paused in the doorway, and said, "D'you mind if I go home a bit earlier today?"

Quinn shrugged. He glanced at the calendar, as if she might have arranged this in advance.

"No, it's, um…" Her cheeks coloured, and Jen flicked a glance at Quinn, who looked utterly puzzled. "I just… I'm meeting this girl."

"Right," said Quinn.

Tessa hesitated, her gaze sliding away.

"Oh," said Jen, catching on. "Right. Sure, and you want to go and get changed, do the hair and make-up thing."

"Yes," said Tessa, relieved. "I wouldn't usually, but Mum said she could have the kids and it was the only day we could both do, so…"

Quinn blinked at her. Then he nodded abruptly. "Sure. Go and… meet your girl," he said. Jen thought his cheeks might be a little pink too. "Have fun."

"I will," Tessa said, and escaped.

"What was that about?" Danny asked, as Quinn frowned at the kettle.

"Oh Daniel," said Alice, world-weary. "So much you don't know."

Well, I'm not explaining it, Jen thought firmly.

Quinn made his tea, but instead of leaving the outer

office, he leaned back against the counter, left leg crossed negligently in front of the other, and surveyed Jen.

She tried not to notice him, which was pretty much impossible. Even just leaning there drinking tea, he exuded a sort of scruffy sexuality.

Eventually he said, "So what's your explanation?"

You're sexy and you know it. "What?"

"For the cold spot?"

Jen blinked. Alice giggled. "Uh… I don't know. I'm not a geologist."

"Right. Just so long as you're not going to try and convince me it's really a ghost."

"I don't *think* it's a ghost," Jen said, which was strictly speaking true.

"Good. 'Cos there's no such thing."

Alice floated up behind him and blew on the back of his neck. Quinn shivered, and Jen hid a smile.

"How do you know? I mean, you can't prove that something doesn't exist."

Quinn smiled. "Ah, the elephant in the room argument."

"If I asked you to prove there wasn't a ghost in this room, could you do it?"

"No," said Danny, waggling his eyebrows, "because there are two of us. See? Not one. Two. See?"

"Shut up, Danny," Alice said.

Quinn regarded her for a moment through narrowed eyes, then he broke into one of those breathtaking smiles. "No one can prove that something doesn't exist," he said. "But there are always other explanations and until someone comes up with concrete proof that ghosts are real, I won't believe it."

Jen cocked her head. "Which is a bit like saying you'll believe in God when he turns up at your front door."

He saluted her with his mug. "That's exactly how I feel about it, yes."

"If you have faith, there are no questions. If you have no faith, there are no answers."

"Is that from the *X Files*?"

"Yes, Mulder, that's exactly where it's from." Jen rolled her eyes.

"It's that Jewish feller, isn't it? Rabbi Something Chaim," Danny said. When Alice gaped at him, he clarified defensively, "A lot of our pilots were Polish and Czech, you know."

"And every one of them a philosopher," Alice murmured.

"If you bring an *I Want To Believe* poster in, that's a fireable offence," Quinn said.

"What about *The Truth Is Out There*?" Jen said.

"I might consider that one." He took a sip of tea. "Except I'd need one underneath it that said, *And It's That Cold Spots Are Caused By Nature.*"

Jen shook her head. "Isn't there anything you believe in?"

And with that she watched his face shut down. The smile that had lingered around the corners of his mouth faded. His eyes went cold and blank.

"Whoops," Alice said.

"No," Quinn said, and abruptly swung back into his office.

"Well done," Danny said.

"What?" Jen hissed. "What am I supposed to know about his beliefs?"

"One assumes they've been challenged of late," Alice said. "I remember the priest saying to my mother that some find faith when a loved one dies, and some lose it."

"I can hardly see him as a regular church-goer," Jen muttered. "He's far too cynical."

"He is now," Danny said. "Listen, forget about that.

This thing at Adderall Hall."

Jen had to stare at him for a moment before she worked out what he was talking about.

"It's a school now, yes? Lord, what a stupid idea."

"Why?"

Danny stabbed a finger at the report Quinn had ignored. "Here. The reports are of ghosts. Over the years, it says. What if I told you there were rumours about them when I was alive?"

Jen felt her eyebrows go up. Even Alice looked intrigued.

Pleased at the attention, Danny took a seat on the visitors sofa and crossed his legs. "Do you want to know the full story?"

"Don't tease," Alice said. "You know we do."

He grinned at them, the sort of grin Jen imagined worked quite a bit of magic back in the day.

"Right. Your St Hilda's School used to be an old pile called Adderall Hall. Owned by the Adderall family for donkey's years. After the Great War, it fell into decline, and was eventually sold on as a school. You see, Old Man Adderall had four sons, and all of them died during the war."

"How awful."

"Not an unusual story. Fact is, young lads from good families often washed up as junior officers, and they were worst hit. First over the top leading the men, you see. Nasty business. Especially since death duties were so fearsome in those days. It wasn't enough a family would lose their husbands or fathers, but then they had to pay for the privilege. Man like Adderall, his estate wound up being inherited by some distant cousin, which meant the duties were even worse—the further the degree of relation, the more you had to pay. Poor beggar inheriting Adderall Hall could never hope to pay the taxes on it. Same story up and down the country. I remember reading about it in a pamphlet. I was quite the socialist in my youth."

"This is fascinating," drawled Alice, "but what does it have to do with this report? Were the dead sons the ghosts Jenny saw?"

"Doubt it," said Danny, sharing a glance with Jen. "The ghosts at Adderall Cottage were always a couple. Male and female."

"So, one of the sons then," Alice said, losing interest.

"No. Their sister."

"Don't tell me, she went off to the Front too."

"No, but her lover did. You see, my old mother lived around here all her life. Knew everything about everyone. And she said that young Millicent Adderall had been having it off with the gamekeeper's son."

"Ah," said Jen. Alice floated off to inspect the weak-looking pot plant on the windowsill.

"Now, the gamekeeper's son, Edward I think he was, got conscripted halfway through the war. The story goes that he'd pledged to marry young Millicent and she'd rather taken him at his word. And so she soon found herself in the family way. But Edward had already shipped off to Flanders Field, and so all she could do was hope it really would all be over by Christmas."

"Which it wasn't."

"Indeed not. Increasingly desperate, and with news rolling in every day of more devastating casualties, Millicent somehow becomes convinced that her beloved is never coming home, and takes her own life. Although my mother always maintained it was an accident."

Jen couldn't help the flicker of pain shooting through her at his words. She glanced around guiltily, but Alice wasn't paying attention, and Danny seemed to think her unease was at the dreadful scenario he was painting.

"So poor old Adderall lost his third child in as many years, and the other two never came home either.

Imagine his anger when the one boy to return to the estate was young Edward, the gamekeeper's son, the boy who'd caused the death of his beloved daughter."

"Ouch," Jen murmured, a tad automatically.

"Now, no one's quite sure what happened next. Some say old man Adderall shot the boy. Some say Edward killed himself out of remorse. But the upshot was that his father found him dead in the cottage. Poor man left the estate and never came back. Not long after that, the rumours about the ghosts started."

"You think they're Edward and Millicent?" Jen whispered.

"Oh, I'm pretty sure of it, old thing." Danny gave a rueful smile. "Y'see, this might have all happened when I was a nipper, but pop forward ten years or so and the place was already in ruins. The idea of this haunted cottage out in the woods was just far too exciting for any red-blooded young man to ignore. Every chap I knew took girls out there. They always said a girl never said no at the ruins."

"Oh, I see," Alice said, drifting back over, "dark spooky place, all alone, snuggling up for comfort…"

Jen closed her eyes. *Oh yes please, handsome! That's good stuff!*

"Never said no?" she murmured. *Well, you certainly didn't*, her conscience reminded her.

"You're too young for this part of the conversation," Danny said.

"Oh please. I'm twice your age," Alice replied.

Danny frowned at her, but he sighed and told Jen, "Let's just say I never ran short of luck there. It doesn't surprise me in the least that it's popular with the St Hilda's crowd."

"So, the ghosts are… what, making people… er…?" Jen glanced at Alice and tried to think of a way to phrase her enquiry.

"Oh for heaven's sake. I'll be back when you've stopped behaving like blushing schoolgirls," the little ghost said, and vanished.

"Making people hot to trot," Danny said promptly. "Yes. Never really occurred to me until now, reading that report. I expect it's quite the Lovers Lane down there, yes?"

"Something like that." Jen frowned. She looked down at the report for Georgia Wright. Looked back up at her computer screen. There, appended to Quinn's email, was Georgia's address.

Jen drummed her fingers on the table. "Did you make all of this up?" she asked Danny. "Is there proof of it?"

"I didn't make up anything! I'm sure there are records."

Yes, like the ones Tessa was searching for Mrs Mac. Jen drummed her fingers again, then swivelled in her chair and opened one of the big filing cabinet drawers.

Here it was, in the accounting files. A list of annual and monthly subscriptions taken out by the company for purposes of research and investigation. She scanned down it until she found what she wanted.

The username and password for the genealogy website were the same as for everything else. Jen hesitated, then copied the information down.

She didn't dare look anything up at work, and the wait until she got home seemed unbearable. Tearing into the house, she booted up her laptop before she'd even taken off her shoes.

Alice floated in through the kitchen door. "What are you doing?" she asked, a warning tone in her voice. "You've never been interested in family history before."

"Not my family," Jen muttered. "The Adderall family."

"You think Danny really did make it up?"

"Yeah, but people like proof," Jen said, typing in the

Adderall name and searching dates during the First World War.

She got a hit on Millicent Adderall immediately. The 1911 Census listed the occupants of the estate, their ages, occupations, and relationship to the head of the household. Adderall, Millicent Elizabeth, daughter, aged 13. She did indeed have four brothers, the youngest of whom would have been conscripted only in the last year of the war. And under the family members were the rest of the household, including Beckett, Bertrand, groundskeeper; and his son, Beckett, Edward B, aged 14.

Jen did a bit more digging and found birth records for Edward and Millicent. A death record for Millicent, in the first quarter of 1917. There was no cause of death listed. The website told her she'd need to send off for the death certificate in order to find the cause of death, which seemed like going a bit far.

There was no death record for Edward. She searched under every possible permutation of his name she could think of, for several years either side of 1917, and found nothing. The website helpfully suggested military records. Jen found his enlistment into the Royal Fusileers in early 1916, listing the Adderall Estate as his address and his father as his next of kin. Under this was a brief record of his service abroad, and a note that he'd fractured his tibia at some point.

She found a list of parish registers and searched for burials. There was Millicent's father, buried in 1919, and mother, two years later. Neither Edward nor Millicent appeared to be buried in the parish.

"Suicide," Alice said quietly. "She wouldn't be buried in consecrated ground."

"What about Edward? Does this mean he killed himself, too?"

"Maybe. Or maybe Old Man Adderall killed him, and hid the body."

"Danny said Edward was found by his father."

"Then maybe the father buried him. Maybe he's still there in the cottage. Rotting under the floorboards."

Ew, right where Quinn and I were making out. "After a hundred years I doubt he'd still be rotting," Jen said, sitting back and rubbing her neck. She'd been at the laptop for hours. Her tiny living room was dark but for the blue light of the computer, and she leaned over to flick the standard lamp on.

It illuminated a room half moved into. Boxes of CDs and DVDs she'd probably never unpack, a drop-leaf table to assemble, an armchair that didn't really fit and would probably have to be replaced with something smaller. The walls all needed painting, and the only picture she'd hung on the wall was the family portrait taken when her dad was still alive.

"You could always ask them."

"I suppose." But what did it even matter? It was nothing to do with her. Unquiet spirits were hardly news to Jennifer Hargrave.

Unless the reason they were unquiet was because they hadn't been laid to rest.

She blew out a sigh. "Hey Alice, where are you buried?"

Alice stiffened, as much as someone non-corporeal could be said to stiffen. "What's that got to do with anything?"

"Just curious. You must have a grave."

"I suppose I must. Rather macabre to think about."

Jen reached for the computer, and Alice suddenly flashed in front of her, pale face even more eerie than usual in the screen's blue light. "Don't," she said.

"Why not? Might be nice to go and see it. Pay my respects."

"You can pay them to me now. Jenny, please don't go looking for my grave."

Jen tilted her head questioningly.

"I just don't…" Alice looked away. Through her, a website ad featuring a stern Victorian family glowed. "It'll make me more… dead to you."

Ah. "You've always been dead to me, Alice," Jen said, as kindly as she could.

"Not always." Alice looked up at her from under her hair. "When you were little you thought I was real, remember?"

Jen choked back a laugh. "Oh yeah. Remember the trouble I got into for that? 'The other little girl made me do it!'"

"I never made you do anything," Alice said innocently. "You required very little coercion."

"Yes, well, I was too young to know any better," Jen said, turning away from the laptop and heading for the kitchen.

She didn't miss the look of relief on Alice's face, but she pretended she had.

CHAPTER THIRTEEN

The rest of the week went by in predictable fashion, with Tessa by turns bored and flustered, and Quinn consistently surly and efficient. He made no more mention of snogging her brains out, and Jen didn't know if she was annoyed or relieved.

"How was your date?" Jen asked, and Tessa just gave her a smile. She went home early on Friday, too.

Georgia Wright failed to follow up on Quinn's dry assessment of the situation at St Hilda's, and little else of interest turned up. Jen answered the phone, sent emails, printed and filed reports, sent out invoices and filled in expense sheets.

And whenever she thought no one was looking, she looked for more information on Edward and Millicent. But short of going out there and talking to them, she couldn't find any more leads.

She sighed and closed the search window. The day was overcast, dull and rainy, the sky yellowish with a coming storm. Rain spattered the window. Tessa had already left, and Jen was clock-watching. She remembered light like this from interminable winter afternoons at school, when Alice used to loll around making fun of the other kids and getting Jen into trouble for laughing.

Alice. Jen reached for her computer mouse, then withdrew her hand. No, she'd said she wouldn't. Or... had she actually said it?

Anyway, it'd be pointless. She didn't even know Alice's surname. All she knew was that she'd died around the age of nine, about a hundred and fifty years ago. Not much to go on. Her efforts this week had taught her that such scant information really wasn't going to get her anywhere.

She'd just stood up to make herself some coffee when Alice zoomed in through the wall like the Ghost of Christmas Best Forgotten, and shrieked unintelligibly at Jen. Who, startled, leapt backwards and tripped over her chair.

"Ow!"

"Jenny! Listen to me!"

"Did you have to scare me like that?" Grumbling, she picked herself up and tried to peer at her own elbow.

"You have to—" Alice began, at the same time Quinn crashed out of his office and demanded, "What was that?"

"Nothing." Giving up, Jen dusted herself off. "I tripped over my chair, that's all."

He scowled at her. "Are you all right?"

"Jenny! You have to come downstairs, now. Elizabeth is in trouble!"

Alice didn't seem to think any more information would be needed. Jen limped in an exaggerated fashion over to the kettle and glared at Alice over her shoulder.

"From downstairs! The flower girl. A man is threatening her."

At that, Jen turned her head.

"Get Quinn to come too. He's big and angry, he'll

help. Come *on*!"

"I—" Jen glanced at Quinn, who stood with hands on hips, eyebrows raised, evidently waiting for an answer. "Did you hear that?" she said desperately.

"Hear what?" He glanced at the window. "All I hear is rain."

"Uh... a noise from downstairs. Er, is the flower shop still open?"

"What? I dunno. Why?"

"Early closing," Alice said, and snapped her fingers at Jen.

"Early closing," Jen repeated. "Someone's down there."

"Probably Beth. Jen, are you sure you're all right?"

"I'm just going to check," Jen said, and lurched toward the door.

Okay, so his office manager appeared to be hearing voices now. This was just grand.

"Are you sure—" Quinn began, but Jen was already out the door. "...you haven't lost your mind?" he finished, but all he got in reply was the sound of her footsteps pounding down the stairs.

He stood for a moment, listening. How could Jen have heard anything from downstairs? The rain was spattering against the window. Through it came the sound of an occasional vehicle passing in the street. There was the hum of Jen's computer and the overhead light and the groan of the ancient central heating. If anyone had made a noise that could be heard over that, well, then he'd have heard it too.

"She's mad," he said out loud. "I am not haring off after her."

Then he grabbed his coat and did just that.

The downstairs door opened onto a small side alley leading back to the yard where they kept the bins. Beth's shop had a door leading directly to the yard and her van, which blocked the view from the High Street. Passers-by, tucked under their umbrellas, wouldn't see or hear much over the rain.

The yard was full of shadows. Too many shadows.

Quinn heard a sob as he rounded the corner, and started to move faster, almost colliding with Jen. Through the open doorway to Beth's back room he could see movement. A figure too big to be Beth, pushing someone exactly Beth's size against the rough brick wall.

"Help," Beth said, her voice almost lost in panic.

And then Jen, the bloody eejit, ran in and tried to grab the guy. "Hey! Get off her!"

The big man shrugged her off, and with one meaty hand he shoved her across the room. Jen hit the table and crashed into a box of stationery. Staples cascaded over her, and a box of cards.

"This ain't your business," he said. A big man, broad shouldered, tattoo on his neck. He had Beth by the wrists, pinned against the wall above her head. The skin of her hands was bloody, and her face was drip white.

"The lady asked for help," Quinn said calmly, one eye on Jen as she struggled to her feet. She picked an oblong of card out of her hair. *With deepest sympathy.*

"It's just a game. Innit, Beth?"

Beth opened her mouth, and the man's fingers tightened visibly on her shoulders.

"Let me go," she whispered.

"There you are now. She wants you to let her go. Are you going to do that?" Quinn asked in his most reasonable tone as rain pattered on his bare head. Jen edged towards him. Her hand was curled into a fist.

"We're just having a discussion," the man said.

"Then you can have the discussion without touching her," Quinn said. "Just step back, okay?"

"Who the fuck are you?"

"A friend."

"Yeah? Well, I'm her boyfriend."

Beth shook her head rapidly. Her attacker's attention swung sharply back to her, and Jen took the opportunity to scuttle out into the rain. Quinn reached for her, drawing her behind him with one hand and miming a telephone with the other. "Police," he mouthed, and pointed upstairs.

Jen shook her head. Quinn glared at her.

"Babe, don't be like this. Don't listen to him, yeah?"

"I'm sorry, Paul," Beth whispered. "I didn't mean to… to give you the wrong idea."

Paul slammed her hands back against the brick again. Beth's whole body flinched.

Jen ran.

"Look, just fuck off, mate," Paul said to Quinn. "Me and Beth've got some stuff to talk about."

"No," squeaked Beth.

"She said no. Beth, would you like him to let you go?"

She nodded frantically. "'es!"

"You heard her, Paul. Let her go, please."

"Or what?" snarled Paul.

Or I'm going to get the shit beaten out of me, Quinn thought, but he said, "Or I'll have to intervene."

Paul, who was several inches taller and several stone heavier than Quinn, looked him over and started laughing. Quinn smiled politely and began strolling forward.

"Alas," he said, "I don't have my nightstick on me. And despite repeated pleas to the *Dáil*, I was never allowed a gun on duty."

"The what?" Paul's brow furrowed as his brain caught up with his ears. "You a copper?"

"Well," Quinn said, flexing his fingers in preparation

for making a fist, "not any more."

"Then piss off."

"Of course, not being a copper any more does have one distinct advantage. Shall I tell you what it is?"

"Look mate, I don't care, just—"

"It means I can't get into trouble for doing this," Quinn said, and while Paul was looking at his fist he used his metal foot to slam into the side of the guy's knee. As he went down, howling, Quinn jabbed the heel of his hand upwards into Paul's nose.

"Move," Quinn said to Beth, who obeyed instantly, dashing out into the rain. "Upstairs. With Jen. Lock the door. Go."

The back of the flower shop was full of rolls of paper and ribbon and sharp knives, which Quinn was grateful Paul didn't seem to have noticed. He grabbed a ball of twine and set about lashing the man's hands together before he could work out what was happening. When he knelt to tie Paul's ankles together, he got a kick in the face for his troubles.

He shook the pain off. "Nice," he said. "Kick a disabled man, will you?"

He got a stream of invective for that.

"Shut up, or I'll have to improvise a gag out of ivy. I hear it's poisonous. Want to test the theory?"

"Who the fuck are you?" Paul snarled.

"I the fuck am James Quinn. And that," he cocked his head, "is the police. You kick me again, it'll be one more item on your charge sheet. Stay still, it'll go easier for you."

He went out into the rain to greet the uniformed officers, who by this point were known to him, and watched as they wrestled Paul into the back of the car.

"And the victim, sir?"

"Upstairs. At least, I really hope she's upstairs."

She was, thankfully, being fussed over by Jen, who

was busying herself making enough tea for a small army and muttering under her breath.

"Do we have a first aid kit?" she snapped at Quinn as the police followed him in.

"Cupboard under the kettle," he said, and took Beth's hands gently. The skin on her wrists was raw and angry. "Maybe you should go and see a doctor," he said, "get this cleaned up."

"It's fine," she said. Her hands shook.

"There's bits of dirt in there," he said. "You don't want an infection." And with any luck they'll give her something to calm her down, he thought, looking at her wild eyes and bitten lips. "Look, is there someone I can call, to meet you at the hospital? A friend, a relative?"

Beth began to shake her head, and then her shoulders slumped and she let out a sob. "My mum," she said.

"All right. D'you have her number handy? Is it in your phone? Grand. I'll give her a call. Just you go and get those cuts seen to, and everything will be fine."

He prattled on until she was finally led away by a very patient police officer.

"Will you be wanting statements from us?" Quinn asked the officer as the car door closed on Beth.

"Just pop in tomorrow," the woman said, looking him over. Quinn's cheekbone was beginning to throb. "They've got special forms with your name already printed on them, you know."

"Nothing like the personal touch," Quinn said, and waved them off.

Then he trudged up the stairs, threw himself at the visitor's couch, and said to Jen, "Do me a favour. Fetch the whiskey from my desk drawer, would you?"

Jen nodded somewhat mechanically, but stumbled into his office and came back with the bottle of Jameson's. She started looking around for something to pour it into, and stood staring at all the undrunk tea she'd made. Nodding, she proceeded to empty them into a pot plant.

Quinn opened his mouth, shut it again, and reached out to take a mug from her. It slipped, the rim cracking as it hit the cupboard, and Jen went absolutely white.

"Ah, feck it," Quinn said. "The cleaners are in tomorrow."

She stared at the cracked mug. "It's broken."

"Yeah. It's not important. We've got others. It wasn't a favourite." It was some promotional thing from a stationery company. It had literally cost nothing. Why was she so appalled?

"I'll fix it," she said, and he said, "Jenny, no," but she was already going to the cleaning cupboard for the dustpan and brush.

Quinn shook his head and dialled Beth's mother. He was halfway through the conversation before he realised he didn't have to do this. He wasn't a policeman any more.

"Is she all right? It wasn't that awful Paul, was it?"

Quinn's brows went up. "He's threatened her before?"

"He was a friend of Stuart's," Beth's mother sighed. "Not a very good friend, obviously. He always had designs on Beth. I think he sensed a moment of weakness with her and moved in."

"Stuart being her…boyfriend?" He watched Jen rub at her forearm, her hand, and realised she was bleeding.

Oh, hell. He took the whiskey bottle from her and set it aside, motioning to her to sit beside him.

"Well, he was." A pause. "You didn't know then? That he died?"

"Ah. No." But it explained quite a lot.

He eventually sent Beth's mother off to the hospital, assuring her that her daughter was mostly just upset and not badly hurt, and finally turned to Jen, who was dabbing ineffectually at her palm with antiseptic. The broken mug had been swept up and carefully laid out on her desk.

"What happened?"

"Uh. The staples." She stared at her hand. "I think. It's fine."

"Right," said Quinn, looking up at her white face. "Fine. Okay. Just humour me," he took the cotton wool ball from her, "and let me take a look?"

The cuts weren't bad, once he'd cleaned away the blood. He paused to pour them both some whiskey into a cup that tasted of tea, and waited until she'd sipped hers before continuing.

The antiseptic stung her palms. She flinched, but let him carry on.

"It was brave of you," he said, "going in there like that. Stupid, but brave."

She gulped. "Someone needed to. I didn't think you'd followed me."

"Ah, sure, if there's a hint of a fight I'll be there. Us Irish can't resist a good brawl."

Her gaze flew up to meet his. He winked, and hoped she hadn't heard the crack about the forms with his name on them.

He didn't get involved in fights that often. He just... well, he supposed he didn't exactly mind getting punched every now and then. He'd had his leg blown off, a punch in the face was nothing.

He ignored the little voice that said putting himself in the way of a fight on purpose was basically self harm.

"Is it the policeman thing?" she asked. "You know, protecting the peace and all that?"

"The Guardians of the Peace, where I come from," he said. "Mostly it's that I don't like to see people being attacked. Neither do you, I guess."

Jen was silent a moment. Then she said, "I don't like

bullies."

He waited to see if any more was forthcoming. It wasn't.

"Did you know about her boyfriend?" Quinn asked. He didn't know if she and Beth were friends. He'd purposefully kept out of Jen's personal life.

"That he died?" She nodded. "Last year. Some kind of cancer."

"That's rough. He can't have been more than, what, twenty-five?"

Again that sense she was listening to someone else. "Twenty-three. They'd been together since they were sixteen."

"And this Paul fella. A friend of his?"

"I think," Jen began, and frowned. Some of the tension began to leave her shoulders. "He used to be a friend of Stuart's. Like, from school. I think when Stuart started to get ill a lot of friends dropped out. It happens. People don't know what to say or do. They get scared of saying the wrong thing."

"That doesn't seem to be a concern of Paul's."

"No." A bit of pink came into her cheeks. "I mean in general. When things go wrong."

"You lose your fairweather friends," Quinn said, and he knew he wasn't the only one speaking from experience.

"Yes, exactly. Beth didn't seem to think much of Paul. He wasn't there through all the hard stuff, just turned up when he thought it made him look better. Like, publicising charity drives and stuff. Offering to carry the coffin." She paused. "Being a shoulder to cry on."

Quinn exhaled. He knew exactly how this one had played out. "Let me guess. He's always fancied having a crack at Beth, he senses a weak moment, moves in not long after the funeral, gets her a bit drunk, she cries upon his shoulder, they end up in bed. He now reckons this gives him the right to do whatever he wants to her, whenever he wants."

Jen blinked at him. Quinn realised he'd crushed the ball of cotton wool between his fingers.

"I wish it was the first time I've seen this," he said.

"She said she just kissed him, and realised her mistake," Jen said.

"Still probably all he needed to give himself permission. If I've heard the words, 'she led me on' once, I've heard them a hundred times."

"Kiss a man once to see if you fancy it, and he thinks he owns you," Jen said. Then she went bright red. "I mean—remember the girls at St Hilda's? How they were either sluts or frigid?" Her voice had got fast. "You can't win either way. What is it you, er, they used to say? The woman has to be above reproach?"

Quinn tilted his face, watching her. She was fiddling frantically with the plasters and tape in the first aid box. *It was just a kiss.*

"I don't think I own you," he said gently. "And I don't think you owe me anything either."

Her blush got fiercer.

"Here, let me," he said, taking a plaster from her hand and smoothing it over one of the small cuts on her palm. He did this twice more before she spoke.

"That wasn't what I meant. I wasn't talking about you."

"Sure. Just making it all clear," said Quinn, when what he really wanted to say was, *Are you sure? If you want to make really sure, we could kiss again. And again, just so you're absolutely certain. Maybe we should go to bed. This couch looks comfy. I want you to be absolutely sure you don't want anything from me. Try before you buy.*

He concentrated on smoothing the plaster over the back of her hand, his thumb stroking back and forth, trying not to say anything that would make him sound as pathetic as he felt. Jen's skin was warm and smooth. He could just see the edge of a small scar on her arm, and a bruise forming further up where Paul had thrown her against the wall.

Pathetic is the right word, you worm. He opened his mouth to remove all doubt, and then Jen's phone rang, and the moment was broken. She inched back, her hand sliding from his to fumble for the phone in her pocket.

"Go ahead," Quinn said when she frowned at the display. "I don't mind."

She glanced at him, then stood up, answering the call. "Charlotte... Actually, I *am* at work. My boss is glaring at me."

Quinn glanced at the clock, which said neither of them should still be in the office, and spread his hands innocently. A slight smile touched the corners of her mouth.

He wanted to see more of that smile. Dammit, why couldn't he manage to get this right? He kept saying the wrong thing or doing the wrong thing—*that kiss sure didn't feel wrong, Quinn my lad*, said his libido—and making her feel awkward.

"What, this weekend? I—I might be free on the Saturday, but... well, where are you going to stay?" She blanched. "Char, I've only got two bedrooms... No, it's got a single bed in it and I haven't finished unpack—I've been busy! Um, with my job?"

He sat back and watched Jen pace up and down as Charlotte talked at her. Even if Jen hadn't mentioned her sister last week, he'd have been able to work out the relationship. Only siblings had that much exasperation with each other.

He blocked that thought out, but the one that replaced it wasn't particularly welcome either. Why did he keep getting things wrong with Jen? He managed to find the right things to say to Beth, and to her mother, and even to that thug Paul, but he couldn't say the right things to Jen.

Maybe you should kiss her again, said his body, but then his brain caught up with him. *It was just a kiss.*

It's not you, it's me.

It ended really badly.

Ah, feck. Things could indeed have ended *really badly* for Beth tonight. *It was just a kiss.*

"And Hell is just a sauna," Quinn muttered. Jen glanced at him, and he gave her a distracted smile.

Someone had hurt her, and Quinn was damn well going to figure out who he was and what he'd done, and then he was going to find a way to fix it.

CHAPTER FOURTEEN

The White Lady: a few hours later

She doesn't even know where his apartment is. She can't quite remember getting there, just a blur of running through the hospital, away from people with cameras and microphones, leaping into a cab and clutching at each other, not quite able to cry or to laugh but able to grab and kiss and tear.

She doesn't know who started it, or even when. The fear and the numbness and the pain hasn't stopped, not after the first time or the… whichever time this has just been. At some point they've made it to a bed, which she's assuming for now is his bed. It could be a bed in a furniture showroom for all the notice she's taken of her surroundings.

"Uh," she manages. Beside her, he rolls his head in her general direction. He's still catching his breath too. "Where are we?"

"My place."

"Oh." It's dark. Orange light glares through the window and illuminates part of a tree and part of a building outside. Shadows stretch across the floor. They could be anywhere in London.

Conversation exhausted for the time being, it takes a while before he speaks again. "You okay?"

She's not sure. Parts of her have begun to throb.

"Think so." Politeness makes her add, "You?"

"Yeah."

That seems to be it. He sits up, works his shoulder as if it hurts. Gets to his feet. She can see scratches down his back, dark with dried blood.

"Drink?"

She nods, and he wanders naked out of the room. He's limping a bit.

She sits up, and takes stock. She's going to be limping a bit, too. Her back feels like someone's taken a cheese grater to it, and after a moment's recall she remembers the fashionably bare brick wall in the living room.

She's in worse shape than she was after the bomb went off.

When he comes back in, he's got a bottle of something clear and syrupy. The label appears to be in Russian. Or maybe she's lost the ability to read.

He hands her the bottle, which is so cold it shocks her awake a bit more. She takes a swig, and yes, it's vodka, straight from the freezer.

Something occurs to Jen, and she glances around. But Alice isn't there. She hasn't seen Alice since—since—

She watches him cross to the window and pull the blind. Then he switches on a light, and she can see he's filthy with ash and dirt and blood and sweat. So are the bedsheets. So, she realises when she holds out the bottle to him, is she.

He takes a swig, looking at her over the bottle, then another. "I don't even know your name."

"Jen." That's all she gives him.

"I'm—"

"I know who you are."

He makes a sound like half a laugh, but there's nothing funny about it.

"You're bleeding, Jen."

She's not surprised. Sensation is returning all over, and she's not sure she likes it. Her back prickles with pain. Her thighs. Her wrists. The bandage on her arm, the one clean thing about her, is smeared with blood and sweat and God knows what else.

"So are you." She kneels up and touches a long scratch on his shoulder. "Did I do that?"

He nods slowly, his eyes on hers. He tilts the bottle to her lips and she drinks.

"And this?" His fingers trace a graze on her cheek. Sensation shoots through her. She's not sure if she likes it or not.

"That was you."

He touches a bruise on her breast.

"Yes."

"And here?" Her hip.

"Yes."

He's breathing hard again. So is she.

"You're filthy."

"So are you."

His gaze doesn't leave hers. He tilts the ice-cold vodka and pours it onto a scratch on her arm. Jen flinches. "Yes." He licks at the spilled liquid. "Yes. Yes."

It's all she says for some time.

KATE JOHNSON

CHAPTER FIFTEEN

"So, you kissed Quinn?" said Alice, and Jen squirted bleach right through her. "Good job I'm incorporeal," she remarked.

"Don't sneak up on me like that!" Jen grabbed a cloth and started mopping down the bathroom mirror. "Now look what you've done. I'll have to go and buy some more bleach."

"Dearling, you've only been here a few weeks. The bathroom can't possibly need cleaning this thoroughly."

"It can if Charlotte is coming to visit."

"Ugh. I think I shall make myself scare over the weekend if that's all right with you." Jen didn't know how to tell her it was nearly always all right with her. "I can't believe you let her bully you into this."

Jen gave her a dark look. "You've met Charlotte, right?"

"Maybe I should throw some things around the place," Alice mused, sniffing at the bleach and shrugging. "Make some oogly-boogly noises. Rains of blood, that sort of thing. They'd jolly well stop coming to visit then."

"Yes, and then I'd have blood to clean up instead of limescale," Jen said, wringing out the cloth and starting again to scrub at the sink.

"Moan moan moan. Why didn't you tell her you were busy?"

"I did." Jen went to rub at her tired eyes, and then stopped, mindful of the bleach. She'd started cleaning as soon as she got home on Thursday evening after the incident with Beth, despite being bone-deep weary with the aftermath of adrenaline.

Everything in the kitchen had been scrubbed, and then she'd noticed some mildew in the corner of the back door and spent ages trying to clear that up, and then she'd washed all the soft furnishing covers because last time Mildred had complained they smelled funny, and Charlotte had sniffed them and said, "Honestly, Jen. It smells like an old church in here. Don't you know what sort of spores live in unwashed furnishings?"

"Charlotte has a full time job and two small children and still finds time to wash her cushion covers," Jen told Alice. "She doesn't believe anyone else can be truly busy unless they have as much to do as she does."

Alice snorted. "One day, you will just say no to her."

"And the skies will fall and the oceans will rise, and my mother will never speak to me again."

"Your mother will." Alice thought about it. "Charlotte won't. What *is* her problem?"

"You want me to just pick one?" Jen said lightly.

But there was just one. There had always been one. Charlotte wanted everything to be perfect, and Jen wasn't.

Quinn didn't even really know why he was doing this.

She'd probably made up the thing about a bad relationship as an excuse. One of those polite ways of brushing someone off. Jen was probably looking for a new job already. She'd been quiet all day, after he'd taken her to the police station to make a statement about what had happened with Beth. Pale, tired-looking. Maybe the thing with Beth had brought up some unwelcome memories.

She'd left promptly at five, murmuring that she had a lot to do this weekend. Judging by the conversation he'd overheard yesterday, her sister had decided to visit. He guessed she'd be shopping or cleaning or something. And even if she wasn't, it was a Friday evening. She was very unlikely to come back to the office for any reason.

Quinn glanced at Jen's computer, sitting quietly on her desk, and drummed his fingers. It was unethical to go through her browser history, but then she was his employee and he was a damned detective.

He switched the machine on and went to make some tea.

The broken mug had been washed and carefully mended with superglue. Quinn knew it wouldn't withstand being used again, so why had she bothered? The cracks were barely visible.

The report Tessa had made when Jen first applied for the job was sitting on his desk. "But those are just the facts," he said to the empty office, having re-read the whole lot. He'd searched online for stories about the Angel of the White Lady, and found nothing conclusive. Plenty of people claimed to have seen her, but every story was different. Witness statements always were.

He'd discovered her address back then, in a small flat a half hour bus ride from the White Lady. Apparently she lived there alone and moved soon after. Well, who wouldn't? She'd gone to the Lake District, and a year later had moved to Ludlow. After that, the moves had come faster and faster.

But before the White Lady, she'd barely moved house at all.

"Who are you running from?" he asked her computer. It didn't answer.

Her browser history revealed little of interest. She'd gone searching for the Adderall family, the ones who'd lived in what used to be St Hilda's. Probably trying to find some claim that there were, indeed, ghosts there. Good luck with that, he thought. Generations of that family had lived and died there. Anyone could find a grisly story if they looked hard enough.

She had almost no presence on social media. Well, fair enough, not everyone did. Quinn had never bothered, although occasionally he'd get an email from a cousin about some old school photo that had been unearthed, and could he kindly identify which Quinn Twin he was, please?

He searched for her name on popular sites. She had one profile that had fallen into disuse years ago—round about the time of the bomb, he surmised—and no one seemed to have tagged her in anything for years.

There was an old photo of a New Years Eve party from seven or eight years ago. Some bozo had his arm around Jen. A bit of research found his name, a Jonathan Blake. This guy was all over the internet, posting pictures of stag dos and parties, his own wedding two years ago, his baby son. No further mentions of Jen.

Jonathan Blake had, it seemed, suffered a terrible car accident about seven years ago, after which he'd been told he might not walk again. Quinn knew this because there were more recent posts about how far he'd come since then with the love of his new girlfriend, now his wife, and how she'd believed in him to the extent that now he was running marathons and…

Blech. Nauseating.

Blake wasn't particularly security conscious. Quinn had his address in about five minutes flat. Without a single thought for scruples, he called up a contact at the

Criminal Records Bureau and asked to have Blake's name run through the system.

Then he sat back and contemplated being underhand.

By the time her sister arrived on Saturday morning, Jen had cleaned everything the family might use, and hidden the rest. On Friday as he'd driven her to the police station to make a statement, Quinn had asked solicitously how she was feeling, and Jen lied through her teeth and said she was fine.

"Any plans this weekend?" he'd asked.

"Family stuff," Jen said, and mustered a smile from somewhere. Far be it from her to complain about her sister when he didn't even have a brother any more.

The first thing Charlotte did when they arrived in Wirpness was call to accuse Jen of not having any parking outside her house.

"And if you had a car, she'd complain that it was in her way," Alice said, as Jen traipsed up the road to carry all the things Millie and Eddie simply *had* to bring with them. She'd moved house with less.

"This house is so small!" Mildred proclaimed as soon as she set foot inside. "Mummy, look I can run from the front to the back before I've even finished saying Muuuuummy. Mummy, look! Muuuummeeeey!"

"Hello Jennifer," said Charlotte's husband Oliver, dumping several large shopping bags in the doorway, as Alice stepped pointedly out of the way. She poked at his leg, and he scratched it vaguely. "Horrible journey, whatever made you move to the middle of nowhere?"

"Can't think," Jen replied, watching her niece and nephew scramble up the steep, almost spiral staircase.

"Eddie, careful!" Charlotte shrieked. "Jen, those stairs are a deathtrap! I can't have them running up and down them like that!"

"Guys, be careful," Jen called ineffectually, her voice

drowned out by Edgar and Mildred's cries of dismay that they had to share a room.

"There's just nowhere to put anything in this kitchen," Charlotte complained, opening the door to what Alice had christened the Hidying-Up Cupboard. "My God, how do you ever find anything?"

Jen cast a desperate glance around, wishing like hell she'd hidden some gin in the newly-washed sofa cushions.

"Oh, this is going to be a long weekend," Alice said grimly, and promptly vanished.

It was another hour before Jen got them out of the house, promising a nice long healthy walk, which Oliver approved off and his daughter didn't. She started dragging her feet before they'd even got to the end of the road.

"Look, there's an ice cream stand on the front," Jen said. "Let's walk there and I'll buy you an ice cream!"

"No," said Charlotte, looking at Jen as if she'd promised the child crack cocaine. "Not before lunch."

"Well, then how about we go for lunch? There are some lovely pubs. The Admiral has a nice garden—"

"Always full of people smoking," Oliver said disapprovingly.

"Right, well, there's supposed to be a really nice place if we cross over the estuary. I think it was mentioned in The Times as a great coastal pub. Lots of organic food," Jen said temptingly.

Charlotte's ears almost visibly pricked up. "Organic?"

"And local. And sustainable," Jen fabricated.

"Well, that sounds nice. Which way?"

Hussah! Jen pointed down the Common. "That way. It's about an hour's walk," she added, and watched Millie and Eddie's faces fall.

"That's *miles*!" Mildred said.

"Er," said Jen.

"No, that's too far," Charlotte said briskly.

"We could take the car?" Jen said.

"We won't all fit in," Charlotte said. "Not with the car seats. No. Is there a tea room or something here?"

"Sure," said Jen, shrugging in defeat. Better to let her sister pick a place, and then if she complained about it, it wouldn't be Jen's fault.

They walked down the pretty High Street, with its oddball collection of individual shops, and Jen relaxed a bit as Wirpness started to work its charm. Charlotte stopped to admire a skirt in one window, Millie and Eddie pressed their noses up against the window of the sweet shop, and Oliver looked longingly at the houses in the estate agent's.

"I can see why you live in such a dolls house," he remarked. "Not cheap around here, is it?"

"No," Jen said. "But it's very nice."

"It's boring," pronounced Mildred.

Thus the basis of its appeal. She glanced around, but Alice seemed to have made good on her promise to make herself scarce. Alice never had really liked Charlotte that much.

Her gaze came to rest on the frontage of Beth's shop. It'd been closed on Friday, but now it appeared to be open again, which Jen thought was a good sign. Above the shop, there was a light on in Quinn's office. Workaholic, she thought, and turned away before he spotted her staring at him.

"How about this place?" said Oliver a few minutes later as they arrived at The Admiral.

"You didn't want to sit outside because of the smokers," Jen said.

"Yes, but we could sit inside. Is there a children's menu?"

"I have no idea," Jen said, giving up.

There wasn't a children's menu, but they promised to make smaller portions of their ordinary food, which was pronounced healthy enough by Charlotte. Jen got in a round of drinks, including a large glass of wine for herself, and had just settled down next to Mildred when a shadow darkened the window to her left.

"Shall we play Hangman?" she asked her niece, and the shadow tapped on the glass. Expecting Alice, she ignored it.

"Auntie Jen, that man wants you," said Mildred.

Jen turned slowly and looked up. Quinn was waving at her. In the crook of his arm he held an enormous arrangement of flowers.

"Who's that?" Charlotte said.

"Quinn," Jen said, watching in bafflement as he pointed to the door of the pub. She spread her hands in confusion, but he was already gone.

"And what," Charlotte asked, "is a Quinn?"

Before Jen could think of a way to answer that—*he's my boss, he's someone whose life I saved once, he's a really good kisser*—he was by their table, the flowers even more impressive close up.

"Er," said Jen.

"Sorry to interrupt." He gave his most charming smile. "I saw you walking by, but you'd gone too fast for me to catch up. These are for you, now."

Jen felt herself go hot, then cold, as he presented her with the enormous bouquet. She couldn't look at her sister. "What—what for?" she stammered.

"To say thank you." He let her squirm for a moment, then added with a cheeky glint, "They're from Beth."

"Oh," said Jen. Then she spied the card tucked into the flowers. "Oh." And she felt rather stupid.

"Jen, aren't you going to introduce us?" Charlotte said pointedly.

"James Quinn," said Quinn, before Jen could say a

word. "And you must be Jen's sister."

"Charlotte," she said, holding out her hand for him to shake. Quinn did, and then shook Oliver's hand, and smiled and waved at the children.

"You do look familiar," Oliver said. "Have we met?"

Jen froze, but if this bothered Quinn he didn't show it. "One of those faces," he said easily.

"Quinn's my boss," Jen said loudly, and they all stared at her.

"Sure, but we're not at work now, are we? Are you having lunch here? The burgers are good."

"You're not having a burger," Charlotte said immediately to her children, who in turn began protesting loudly that it was all they wanted to eat.

"Quite right too," Quinn said smoothly, "full of fat and nonsense."

"I'm sure I know you from somewhere," Oliver said, frowning. "Where are you from? Can't quite place the accent."

By the glint in his eye Jen half expected Quinn to say he was Dutch or Japanese, but instead he said, "Just outside Dublin."

"Oh, I love Dublin. Great city." Oliver, Jen seemed to recall, said this about every city, whether or not he'd actually been there. "Been there a few times on business."

"Ah. And what kind of business are you in?" Quinn asked politely, as both Jen and Charlotte signalled frantically to him not to ask.

"Well, it's interesting you should ask. I started off in marketing, I used to work for a company specialising in online marketing, and in fact we pioneered the use of…"

Jen tuned out, as she always did when Oliver started on about his job. She still had absolutely no idea what he actually did. The explanation went on for so long that she'd never actually listened to the end of it.

"You might as well go and get poor James a drink," sighed Charlotte.

"Who?"

"James. Your boss?"

"Oh." Jen looked up at him. Somehow he didn't seem like a James. He seemed like a Quinn. "Sure."

She'd fetched his pint of Guinness back before it occurred to her to ask him what he wanted. He accepted it with a smile, already seated at the table.

From then on, lunch went an awful lot more smoothly than Jen had expected. Quinn seemed capable of great charm if the whim took him, chatting easily with Oliver and Charlotte and entertaining Millie and Eddie into the bargain. He sat beside Jen, his thigh brushing hers, that ludicrous bouquet of flowers on the windowsill behind them.

"Sure I only said to Jen the other night, kids just aren't the same as they used to be. Now, I went to a Catholic school, and there was just no way we'd have got away with half the behaviour kids do now," he said, leaning forward over his burger and chips as Charlotte nodded vigorously and launched into a detailed and frankly baffling explanation of the choices she'd had to make about Mildred's school.

When Oliver asked Quinn if he followed any sports, he replied that he watched the rugby whenever he could, "Like last week, you'd just come back from a visit with your family, hadn't you Jen? We watched a bit of the rugby here. Bit of a shower from Ireland, wasn't it?"

He even managed to engage Mildred and Eddie in conversation about the pencil and paper games they were playing while they waited for the grown-ups to finish talking. By the time they left the pub to go for a walk along the seafront, the entire family was in love with him.

"Just out of interest," Jen said as her sister stopped to

look at a beach hut for sale and Oliver led the kids in a race along the beach, "if my mother was here, would you ask for her advice on knitting patterns?"

Quinn glanced at her over the massive bouquet of flowers he was, at her sweet insistence, carrying. "Your mother knits?"

"Badly. Why are you doing this?"

He shrugged eloquently.

"Is this some detective thing?" She eyed him suspiciously. "I'd almost think you wanted to pump them for information, but I haven't the slightest idea what any of them might know that you'd be interested in."

Quinn caught her hand in his. "You," he said, and Jen stiffened and pulled away.

"Then ask *me*," she said.

"Oh sure, you're just an open book."

"I know myself better than they do," she said, and chewed her lip. She turned to face him so no one else would see her speak. The wind blew her words away. "Listen, there is one thing. Do me a favour and don't mention the White Lady."

He gave her a quizzical look.

"They don't actually know I was involved in it," Jen said urgently.

"What do you mean, they don't know?"

"I mean I sort of never told them." As Quinn's expression turned to something she could only call flabbergasted, she added hurriedly, "They don't need to know. No harm was done. Just... keep it to yourself, okay?"

Quinn glanced over her shoulder and she looked back to see Charlotte approaching. "Okay," he said in Jen's ear, "but you can explain this to me later, yes?"

Jen opened her mouth to tell him she didn't owe him any kind of explanation, but the voice she heard was her sister's.

"Sorry to intrude, you two," Charlotte said, somewhat slyly, "but the kids are looking for ice creams. Is there anywhere along the front we could get one?"

Quinn's dark eyes met Jen's, and for a long moment she couldn't look away.

"Later," she said to him, and turned back to her sister. "I think there's a café just after the next set of beach huts…"

Quinn's eyes felt hot on her back as she walked away.

He heard her muttering to herself before he even opened the front door that night. Something about a really bad idea.

"What is?"

Jen blinked up at him. She had a rucksack over her shoulder. "My sister," she began, and tailed off. "She seems to be under the impression you, er… that you're my…"

Quinn propped himself against the doorjamb and tilted his head. He knew exactly what impression Charlotte was under. He'd been insinuating it all day.

"And there's no room at my house because it's the size of a shoebox, which I did *tell* her, but she seemed to think I was exaggerating, and my sofa is really too short to sleep on. And I have… you know, nightmares, sometimes, about the White Lady and…"

He waited.

"Look, can I stay here tonight? They're driving me crackers."

Quinn had made up the spare bed as soon as he got home after their walk, when Jen had told him *she* was going home with *her* family and she'd see him *later*. He'd have made a pretty rubbish detective if he hadn't been able to work out what was going to happen.

He hadn't even bothered to take his leg off. She'd arrived later than he'd guessed, but he was still awarding himself mental points for getting it right.

"Sure," he said, and stood back to let her in. "But I'm quite a poor man, so I've only the one bed. You'll have to share it with me."

She stilled for a second, then blew out a sigh as Quinn grinned at her. "That could constitute sexual harassment."

"Not once you took me up on the offer."

"Drop it, all right?" She rubbed her forehead tiredly and turned back for the door. "My sofa isn't that uncomfortable."

"Neither is my spare bed," Quinn said gently. "I've put clean sheets on." At her raised eyebrows, he said, "I had a feeling you were coming. Call it a policeman's hunch."

"Isn't that what you get from ill-fitting trousers?" Jen muttered, and he laughed as he gestured her to go up the stairs ahead of him.

The spare room was furnished mostly with the same furniture Uncle Kieran had left in it. Quinn had spent so long in this house while he was recovering from the White Lady that he'd come to think of it as his own long before he actually bought it from his uncle. It was a little too big for just one man on his own, but it was pleasant and comfortable and it at least meant his uncle had somewhere to stay when he visited.

"Have you eaten?" he asked as Jen put her rucksack down on the bed.

"Yes." She rolled her eyes. "Charlotte brought all the ingredients for a lasagne with her as she didn't expect me to have anything in."

"Bathroom's that door." He pointed, and she nodded and followed him back down the stairs. "Did you have anything in?"

"Yes, all the ingredients for a lasagne. But apparently they were the wrong ones."

"How can they be the wrong ones? Pasta, mince, red sauce, white sauce…"

Her eyebrows went up, as if surprised he knew what went into a fairly basic recipe. Quinn made a mental note to brush up on his cooking. "Well, my pasta was white, not wholewheat, my mince was beef not lamb, I didn't have any carrots—"

"There are carrots in lasagne now?"

"There are if you're my five-year-old niece. Apparently she won't eat it otherwise. So then Charlotte assembles the lasagne, and it takes too long to cook because my oven is too slow and not nearly as good as her Aga, and then half of it didn't get eaten because Eddie was too tired and wanted to go to bed, because the food had been too slow…"

Quinn went straight to the cupboard and got her a wineglass.

"…and then I left because the only alternative was killing them all and that would just result in extra cleaning."

He grinned and held out the glass. "Red or white?"

"I don't care, so long as there's lots of it."

He poured her some red and gestured her through to the living room, flicking the TV off as he did.

"Now," he said, watching her curl up at the far end of the sofa like a cat, "how much of that is the reason why you haven't told your sister about the single most dramatic thing to ever happen to you?"

"How do you know it's the single most dramatic thing? My life could be full of drama."

"Oh, so nearly getting blown up is just an every day, boring occurrence for you?"

"Hey, I didn't nearly get blown up, I got nearly blown up."

Quinn blinked at her.

"Anyway," he said. "Why doesn't your sister know?"

"Well, the basic reason is that she was heavily pregnant with Millie at the time, and I didn't want to send her into premature labour or anything."

"And the complicated reason?"

She sipped at her wine. "It's hard to explain. Charlotte and I aren't that close. There's five years between us so we were never at the right age to do anything together when we were kids. Whatever I wanted to do, she'd grown out of already."

Quinn had the distinct feeling that Charlotte had probably grown out of it thirty seconds after her little sister wanted to do it.

"I told you, she cares terribly about what people think. And her family reflects on her. 'Cos, you know, none of us do things for ourselves, we all do it to make Charlotte look good. When I was younger I used to dye my hair bright colours, and she basically stopped talking to me. Like, I was just too embarrassing to be seen with."

Quinn cocked his head, beginning to understand. "Ah yes, the universe revolves around her."

"Exactly."

"Ethan was the same. Not a shred of empathy in him. If you asked him to walk a mile in someone else's shoes, he'd say he'd got far too much to do, and then berate you for not considering his busy schedule."

"Yes!" She smiled, but it quickly faded. She fiddled with her wineglass. "And here's the thing. My dad died when I was eleven. Charlotte was sixteen."

Quinn knew without asking that Charlotte had been high school queen bee. Polished and blonde, slender and perfectly made-up. Not as pretty as her sister but he bet people seldom noticed that. "And she made something of it?"

"No, that's just the thing." Jen sipped thoughtfully. "She didn't like being reminded of it, I think, because then she could pretend it hadn't happened and get back to normality. Like, she had to prove it didn't define her or something. I asked her once why she was getting on with life as if Dad just had never existed, and she said she didn't want to be an April Williams." Before Quinn could ask, she explained, "April Williams was this woman my mum was friends with. Her husband came home after ten years of marriage and told her he was having a baby with his secretary."

"Cliché," Quinn murmured.

"Right, and of course it's a terrible thing to happen. But I swear, I never had a conversation with April where she didn't shoehorn that little nugget into the conversation. No one did. She was famous for it. In fact Charlotte and her friends used to make fun of her for it. When Dad died she said she didn't want to be like April Williams."

"And you thought if you told her about the White Lady, then she'd just think you were being an April Williams?"

"Dining out on it. Yeah. Especially when I got off so lightly, compared..." She waved her hand, her cheeks turning pink.

"Compared to me and my leg. It's all right, you can say it."

Quinn took a few swallows of wine, considering what she'd said. Charlotte was so like Ethan in so many ways. He bet if she found out her own mother had dementia she'd be more worried about what the neighbours thought than how to get the right treatment for her.

But... but reasons for rifts in families could be very complicated and not easily explained to outsiders, or even to oneself, so looking for a more black and white explanation might just be tilting at windmills, but...

But… he'd bet dollars to donuts there was still something Jen wasn't telling him.

She rubbed absently at her forearm, where a faint pink scar lingered. She usually wore long sleeves in the office—where admittedly it was usually chilly—but even if she hadn't, he'd have had to know the scar was there to notice it.

"What about the rest of your family? Do they know?"

"No. My mother is a massive worrier. She'd have conniptions if I told her."

"And… you have a stepfather?"

Jen gave him a knowing look. "My, you are thorough." She drained her wine. "No one knows. I don't want this to be something that defines me. Look, you don't go around telling everyone about your leg the minute you meet them, right?"

"Well, not random strangers, but my family knows." Well. Uncle Kieran knew, and he was family. "I could hardly keep it a secret."

"I guess." She chewed her lip. "Does it hurt?"

Like you wouldn't believe. Quinn rubbed his knee. "Sometimes. But I survive."

"Why didn't you tell him the truth?" Alice asked after Jen had retired to the slightly old-fashioned spare bedroom. A grey cat was curled on the bed, much to Alice's delight. She petted just above its fur and it purred at her. Cats loved Alice.

It had been Alice who suggested she went to Quinn's in the first place. Jen slightly suspected she was being set up with him.

"Because I didn't want him to know."

"I'm sure he'd be quite sympathetic. I mean, he's had it a bit rough too, you know."

Jen squeezed her eyes shut. It had taken her most of the walk from her house to Quinn's to work out what to tell him—enough of the truth, with the reality of it left out. She thought she'd done a decent enough job.

"All his scars are on the outside," she muttered.

"What's that?"

"Come on, Alice, you know as well as I do. People are sympathetic to physical injuries. It's the mental stuff they have a problem with. What d'you think Quinn would say if he found out I spent half my childhood in mental institutions?"

"Maybe you could tell him, and find out."

"I'd lose my job."

"Aren't there laws against that these days?"

Alice was at her most annoying when she remembered how the modern world ran. Jen turned out the light. "Can I go to sleep, please?"

"Suit yourself. But I think you're coming up with reasons to keep him at a distance. Come on, Jenny. He's quite a nice man."

"I'm not interested," Jen said.

"Liar," Alice replied.

I know, thought Jen, and turned over.

CHAPTER SIXTEEN

I told him about my hair.

The half-asleep thought brought Jen to sudden, appalled wakefulness. She'd told him she used to dye her hair silly colours. Oh God, what if he remembered that and put two and two together and made... blue?

She sat up, feeling slightly sick in a way that had nothing to do with the wine she'd drunk last night. It'll be all right, she told herself. He'll never consider it. Too much of a coincidence.

He's a detective, her conscience screamed at her. It's his job to line up coincidences.

"Oh look," murmured Alice, drifting through the wall and over to the window. "The cavalry's here."

"Wha'?"

"Charlotte and the brats. Toodles," said Alice, and vanished.

Jen leaned over to the window and twitched back the curtain. Sure enough, there was her sister and the family, traipsing merrily along the road in co-ordinated Boden. God dammit, why did Quinn have to point out his house yesterday as they walked past? Charlotte had admired it,

167

because she approved of Edwardian semis with original features. Especially if they weren't quite as nice as her own.

Jen looked at her watch. Ugh, who got up for a walk this early on a Sunday?

She crawled out of bed, opened the door and looked around the small upstairs hallway. Both the bathroom and Quinn's bedroom door stood open—and like any normal person she took the opportunity to peek inside his room. Bed unmade, clothes draped over a chair in the corner, furniture that looked as if it had been here since the 1970s. A pair of crutches were propped in the corner next to a treadmill and weights machine.

Running up the side of the steep Edwardian staircase were fixings in the wood and discolouration on the paintwork, which Jen worked out was probably the ghost of a stairlift. Quinn seemed so able sometimes, it was easy to forget his prosthesis.

She heard his tread on the stairs just in time to duck out of his doorway and pretend to be heading for the bathroom. One normal footfall, one heavier, clunkier one. He paused when he saw her and smiled the sort of smile that was like being hit with a hundred-watt beam and made Jen clutch onto the doorframe for support. He was dressed casually, his hair wet from the shower. He smelled of lemons and mint.

"Ah, there you are. I wondered did you want some coffee?"

He already held the mug in his hand. Jen knew without looking that it'd be white, one sugar, just the way she liked it. Her warm feelings towards him evaporated. *He's too observant.*

"Yes, thanks." She reached down and took it, careful not to touch his hand.

"Look." Quinn jammed his hands in his jeans pockets —deliberately staying a few steps down, she realised, to give her some distance. "I'm sorry about yesterday. I... came on too strong. Didn't mean to make you uncomfortable."

He looked up at her with puppy-dog eyes. Jen gripped the coffee mug hard.

"It's okay," she said. He probably wasn't used to getting turned down.

"It's just I'm... a little out of practice. I haven't..."

He rubbed the back of his neck and looked away. Jen waited.

Quinn gestured to his leg. "Since this. I haven't..." He trailed off again, as Jen felt her jaw drop. "Confidence, is what I lack."

She tried to gather enough of her wits to ask if that could possibly be true, but then the doorbell rang and she winced.

Quinn glanced at his watch and frowned.

"It's Charlotte," Jen said. "I saw them coming down the road."

"Ah." He turned, and if she hadn't been watching for it she'd never have noticed the slight awkwardness in his gait as he went back down the stairs to the front door. Too late, Jen realised she was still in her pyjamas, still clearly rumpled from sleep, and there was no way her sister would believe she hadn't just rolled out of Quinn's bed.

She also realised, as Millie and Eddie zoomed into the house, that it was far too late to start protesting now. Might as well just style it out and pretend they were a couple until Charlotte went home which, please God would be quite soon.

Then she could let rip against Quinn.

She trailed down the stairs, drawing the attention of Charlotte as she stripped off her gloves and shoes. "Jen! Only just got up?"

Jen hugged her coffee mug closer and glanced

through into the kitchen where Quinn was attempting to find something suitable for the children to drink. He bent down to listen to them, and his t-shirt rode up, exposing a pale sliver of his back. "Late night," she said, and for once let her gaze linger on him.

"Oh I see," Charlotte said slyly, and to Jen's amazement actually winked. When her husband was out of earshot she whispered to Jen, "He is pretty scrummy."

Jen didn't have to manufacture her blush.

"We thought we might go for that walk out to the pub you mentioned yesterday," said Oliver as his children bombed past him.

"I thought it was too far?"

"Too far for the afternoon," Charlotte said vaguely. "Oliver's got the BabyBjorn if Eddie gets tired."

Judging by the way Eddie was racing around Quinn's house, that wasn't going to happen any time soon.

"Did you want some breakfast, Jen, if we're going for a walk?" called Quinn. He was standing in the kitchen, looking into one of the wall cupboards. Jen swallowed some more of her coffee and sauntered in to duck between him and the counter.

Quinn blinked down at her. She was flattened against him, only a couple of layers of thin cotton between them. His body was hot, and very hard.

"I suppose I could use some extra energy," she said, looking up at him from under her lashes. Memories of that kiss in the woods washed over her and she pressed against him involuntarily.

He swallowed. "Right then," he said, slightly hoarsely.

Damn, he felt good. And he smelled good. And this close up he looked really, really good. Jen felt herself relax against him, give into what her body wanted, tell the voices in her head to shut up and let her just enjoy something for once.

"Maybe some toast?" she murmured, as his lips seemed to get closer to hers. "Or some cereal? Maybe some bacon?"

"Bacon," he breathed, nearly kissing her.

"We were hoping to get off fairly soon," said Oliver, much closer than Jen had realised.

Quinn froze for the tiniest fraction of a second, then he broke into a rueful smile and whispered in Jen's ear, "So was I."

She choked back her own laugh as she turned away from him.

Quinn made bacon sandwiches while Jen hurriedly got washed and dressed, and they ate them standing up in the kitchen while Charlotte and Oliver went through the apparently endless process of getting the children ready to go back out again.

"What was all that about?" Quinn murmured while no one else was listening.

"Hey, you started it. I'm just giving them something to gossip about on the drive home."

He gave her a look she could only describe as smouldering, despite having a smear of ketchup on his lip.

"Don't tease a desperate man," he said.

"Like you've ever been desperate," Jen snorted, and turned to put her plate in the sink.

"Jenny, you have no idea," he muttered.

The day was fine and bright for October, and Jen had to squint at the map on her phone to make sure they were going the right way. The estuary had divided Wirpness from the neighbouring hamlet of Blybridge for centuries, flanked by woodlands. The path between the two was marked by a deep scar in the pine forest, a dip in the otherwise flat Suffolk landscape, which Tessa had told her flooded sometimes in the winter.

"Are you okay walking this far?" Jen asked Quinn,

glancing at his leg.

He rolled his eyes. "Fine. It's just like having a normal leg, most of the time."

"When is it not?"

He shrugged, half an eye on Charlotte and family, who were walking ahead. "It's not great for running—generally you want something with more give. Can't swim in it, what with it being metal, or walk on the beach."

"Can you shower with it?" Jen asked before she could stop herself. An image of Quinn in the shower, soapy and wet, made her stumble.

He grinned and caught her by the arm, sliding his hand down to take hers. "No. And in case you... your sister asks," he amended, giving her another smouldering look, "I balance on a plastic stool. Or you offer me assistance, whichever you think she'd prefer to hear."

"Haha," Jen said weakly.

His hand was bigger than hers, and his gloves were, as ever, fingerless. She could feel their light pressure through the wool of her own gloves.

For a few minutes neither of them said anything. The sun dipped behind a cloud and Jen willed herself not shiver, but it didn't work and Quinn slipped his arm around her shoulders.

"You do know this is just for show," she said.

"I know." Then, "It doesn't have to be."

Oh God, I wish it wasn't. "We've been through this."

"Well, in a manner of speaking," Quinn said. "You weren't exactly forthcoming."

"I shouldn't have to be."

His fingers dug in through her coat momentarily, then he stopped walking and turned her to face him. His dark eyes were serious. "Whoever he was," he said in a low voice, "I'm not him."

And Jen looked up into his beautiful, beautiful face, and couldn't say a word.

She drew back, and he let her go, frowning. Dammit, what had he said now?

"I won't hurt you, Jen. I never will. Not in any way," he said, his voice rising as she stepped back even further, all intimacy gone. "Jenny, please. Talk to me."

"No. Not you—I don't want to talk about this," she said tightly, and started walking fast to catch up with her sister.

Quinn took in a deep breath, reminded himself that there were children present, and very carefully did not swear. He pretended to bend down and tie his bootlace to give himself a few minutes, then he looked up and found Charlotte regarding him.

"Lover's tiff?"

He could still feel the shape of Jen's hand in his. Remembered the heat of her body that morning in his kitchen, the wicked gleam in her eye, the way her lips had parted. Quinn had never accounted himself an expert on women, but he wasn't an idiot. He knew what she wanted, he just didn't know why she wouldn't take it.

Past Charlotte, he could see Jen walking with Millie's hand in hers, pointing at a flock of birds in the sky. She avoided even looking in his direction.

"Ah, no, she just wanted to walk with the kids."

Charlotte gave him a knowing look and held out a hand to pull him to his feet. She was probably stronger than he was.

"My sister," she said drily, "never spends any time with children that she doesn't have to."

Quinn frowned at her. "She's great with them."

"She's getting better," Charlotte conceded, and started walking again. Quinn followed, dreadful ideas unspooling in his mind.

"Why wouldn't she want to see them?"

Charlotte sighed. "Jen never played well with others. No idea how to talk to children."

"Well, not a lot of people do, if they don't have their own."

"You're great with them," Charlotte said with more perspicacity than he liked.

"Irish Catholic," Quinn replied quickly before she could accuse him of hiding away a love-child. "Lots of children in my family."

She quirked an eyebrow at that, but said nothing.

"Look, Jenny's great," he said. "I really like her."

"Good. Don't mess her about."

It was said mildly, in a semi-automatic older-sister-being-protective way, but it gave him the opening he needed. "Why? Who else has messed her about?"

Charlotte gave him a sharp look.

"She's never said anything," Quinn admitted, "but I… well, I'm a detective, what can I say? I can't help noticing a thing or two."

"Like what?"

"That there's something she's not telling me."

Charlotte frowned and fiddled with the zipper on her coat—a newer model of the one Jen had worn that night in the woods, he noticed. He'd looked them up online and the price was staggering for something that was basically a padded jacket.

"It's not a man," she said eventually, "if that's what you're thinking. At least, if it is, she's never said anything to me."

Quinn knew with absolute certainty that Charlotte believed nothing ever went on in her family that she didn't know about.

He waited, like any good copper, for her to incriminate herself.

"Look, if Jen has her issues then… you should ask

her about them," Charlotte said eventually.

"You're saying she has issues?"

"You must've noticed she's a bit odd." At Quinn's enquiring look, she waved her hand and said, "You know. Talks to herself a lot."

That was her definition of 'a bit odd'? Talked to herself and didn't know how to communicate with children who only ate wholewheat pasta? Quinn was beginning to see why Jen hadn't told her sister about the White Lady.

"She doesn't care about fitting in," Charlotte said, frowning as if this was a really difficult concept to understand. "She used to dye her hair the most stupid colours and wear fluorescent purple. It was like, how do you not realise how ridiculous that makes you look? I mean I try to give her old things of mine so she's got nice things to wear, but... well, it's only in the last few years she's stopped dressing like a teenager."

She broke off abruptly, as if she'd just realised she was ranting. Jen really hadn't been kidding about her sister caring what other people thought.

They both regarded Jen, walking into a small wood with Oliver and the children, wearing jeans and boots and Charlotte's own cast-off discreetly designer jacket. From here, he might think she was any one of the yummy mummies they'd passed that morning.

"She just tries to be weird on purpose," said Charlotte of the one person Quinn had ever met who seemed to be trying very hard not to be weird at all.

"Ah, but that's one of the things I like about her," he said easily. Charlotte looked at him as if he was demented.

"Well, if that floats your boat," she said, in a tone that clearly indicated two such weirdoes deserved each other.

"It certainly does," Quinn said. Charlotte shook her

head in wonder.

"Charlotte, come and look at this," called Oliver from up ahead, and she began walking faster. Probably, Quinn thought with amusement, to get away from him.

He caught up with them near the old, rusting semi-cylinder of corrugated iron that had so excited Oliver.

"It's a Nissen hut, James, look!"

Ignoring the 'James', Quinn pretended to look impressed. Truth was he'd walked past this a hundred times on his way to the pub at the harbour. It was just the remains of an old pig shelter, or a cheap barn for farm equipment. Resting in a gully, it resembled a cylinder on its side, partly sunk into the ground. It was pretty much derelict, the windows at the nearest end just empty holes and the door skewed off its hinges, obscuring the interior. On one side, a tree had fallen and broken down a section of the roof.

"I thought Nissen huts were smaller," Charlotte was saying.

"No, no those are Anderson shelters," Oliver explained. "These were more often used for housing troops."

"Why would you house troops in the middle of a wood?" asked Quinn idly, looking around for Jen.

Oliver appeared not to know the answer to this, so he busied himself looking for the children, who'd got bored and gone to splash mud all over their pristine outdoor wear. Charlotte, noticing this, immediately ran over to make them stop.

"Where's Jen?" Quinn asked, and Oliver pointed off to the side of the hut where the tree had fallen in. Quinn sauntered round, as much as one could saunter when one had a trick leg that gave out slightly on uneven, slippery surfaces.

He heard her first, talking in quiet whispers, before he saw her in the shadows, the darkness of her coat blending with the moss covering the rusted metal.

He paused, straining to hear.

"So that's why there's a gully. But didn't anyone come to look? Whoever owned the hut? Oh… I see. That's awful. So you're still here—"

She broke off suddenly, and her head whipped round, face pale in the gloom. For a flash of a second she looked guilty, caught out doing something she shouldn't, and something odd settled in Quinn's stomach.

"Who're you talking to?" he asked, moving closer.

"Oh… myself. Just muttering on, you know. Nonsense."

Quinn willed himself not to look at the dark space she'd been addressing inside the hut.

"Have you been inside?"

"It doesn't look very safe."

"Sure it'll be fine." He stepped closer. "I'm not afraid of a few spiders."

"I mean structurally. Quinn, it doesn't look safe."

"Is that concern for my welfare?" Quinn said, grinning back at her and ducking his head under the torn metal.

There were quite a few things inside the old hut. A concrete floor scattered with dead leaves and fox poo, a few scuttling things that might have been mice, quite a few spiders and something covered in flies which had probably recently been a rabbit.

It did not contain anybody Jen could have been talking to. He'd half expected to see a homeless person or even a stray cat or something, but there was nobody.

"Quinn, please get out of there. It really doesn't look safe. If you cut yourself on that rusty metal you could get tetanus."

"Technically, tetanus is something you develop, not something you get," Quinn said, backing out.

Jen rolled her eyes at him, but there was a slight

tightness around her eyes and mouth that bespoke concern. Of course, right now he wasn't sure what she was concerned about.

He glanced around but only saw Charlotte and her family moving off along the path. "Who were you talking to?" he asked Jen.

Her gaze followed his, and hardened when she saw Charlotte. "Why, what's she been telling you?"

"That you talk to yourself."

"There you are then. I was talking to myself."

"About no one coming back? About still being here?" He stepped closer to her and she stepped back. "Jenny —"

"Are you two coming with us or not?" called Charlotte, and Quinn blew out a sigh.

"One day, we will have a conversation no one interrupts," he said, and Jen snorted.

"We really must leave as soon as we get back," said Charlotte as they left the admittedly very nice pub, which Jen translated to mean they'd spend hours faffing about trying to find something Millie had probably hidden on purpose. A headache had stolen up on Jen during lunch, and she didn't think she could cope with any more from her family.

"Oh, well, I'd better say goodbye to you straight away, because Quinn and I have that thing," Jen said, trying to signal to him with her eyes.

"What thing?"

"You know. The *thing*. That we do on Sundays." She held his gaze and saw a smile tug at the corners of his mouth.

"What thing?" Millie wanted to know.

"A grown-up thing," Quinn said, his eyes hot on Jen's. *Don't get excited, mate.* There was a bed in Jen's future, but she was going to it alone, with some paracetamol and the blanket over her head.

"What thing?" Eddie echoed, and his mother hurriedly pointed out a bunny rabbit in the fields.

"What thing?" Quinn said as he took Jen's hand and began walking with her after them. Oh, but it was nice to hold his hand. No one had held her hand in ages.

"A thing that means I don't have to listen to my niece and nephew not wanting to go home for hours."

"Ah, and here I was thinking you just wanted to spend time with me," Quinn said as his phone rang. "Oh hey look, a Thing."

She had to smile at that, but it quickly faded as she watched his expression. "What? How? Jesus. When? I'll be right over."

And just like that the day seemed to cloud over.

Quinn quickly ended that call and started dialling another number.

"What's going on?" Jen asked. He shook his head briefly and said into the phone, "Yes, can you pick me up ASAP, please, from the Earl of Sandwich pub in Blybridge Parva. To Halesbridge. Extra pony in it if you get here in the next five minutes. Name of Quinn. Grand."

He ended the call and turned to Jen, his eyes serious. "Something's come up."

"No kidding. What? Is it Tessa? Is she okay?"

"Not Tessa. Something else. I have to go."

"But—it's Sunday afternoon. What the hell happens on Sunday afternoons?"

Quinn glanced over at Charlotte and Oliver, who'd paused by the coastal path and were looking back at them. He lowered his voice. "Paul Dunlop gets found dead by his neighbours, that's what."

"Paul—?" The name rang a bell. Jen's eyes widened as she realised where from. "The guy who attacked Beth?"

"Yeah. I want to get there and see before Plod messes it up too much."

"Plod? You mean it's murder?" She whispered the last word. Her head throbbed.

"Clearly some foul play if they're involved, yeah."

"But," Jen began, about to ask what this had to do with Quinn and why he had to go right now, when the answer came to her. "Oh God, you think it's Beth, don't you?"

"I don't think anything." His mouth was a hard line. For the first time, he kind of scared her.

"Will they let you in?" She knew he was friendly with some of the local police—it helped when you were a private detective—but surely they wouldn't let a civilian in?

"Don't know yet."

It couldn't have been Beth. Jen couldn't think of anything more out of character. But would the police believe that?

And will they believe you when you ask his ghost who did it? she asked herself. It had to be worth a shot.

"Is everything all right?" called Charlotte, coming towards them, and before Quinn could interrupt, Jen said, "We have to go."

"We?" Quinn said.

"Aren't you even coming back to Wirpness with us?" Charlotte said, looking annoyed.

"No. The… thing started early. We have to go."

Charlotte came closer. "What thing is this?"

"A work thing," Quinn said, and added to Jen, "You don't have to come."

"What work thing? It's a Sunday."

"Not everyone works nine-to-five, Charlotte. I'll come and say goodbye to the kids now."

"Jen," Quinn hissed, but she was already on her way.

"You'd have left without me if he'd got here thirty seconds earlier," Jen said accusingly as the taxi sped away from the pretty pub.

"Too damn right." He glared at the achingly pretty village, still busy with tourists even in October. "Do you really want to escape your family that much?"

"No, of course not," Jen said, but she paused as if she was considering it. "I want to come with you."

"Why? A hankering to see a dead body?" He kept his voice low so the driver couldn't hear over the radio.

"I've seen enough of those," Jen said quietly, and he winced, because she'd probably seen more than he had, and all in the same day.

She took a deep breath. "I want to come to help Beth."

He glanced over at her. "What do you mean?" he asked carefully.

"Because three days after he assaulted her he's found dead. I don't have to be a detective to see where the natural suspicion is going to fall."

Quinn rubbed his face. *You had to be giving the come-on to a girl who uses her brain, didn't you? Why couldn't you fancy someone stupid?*

"True, but modern policing also uses more than just suspicion."

"I know, but... look, if I can see anything or... find anything that might help her...I know she didn't do it."

"Oh? And how do you know?"

"It's just not in her nature."

"Ah, the old 'nature' argument," Quinn said. "Never fails to stand up in a court of law."

"Oh bite me, Quinn. Of the two of us which one spotted the White Lady bomber in time to duck?"

There was a dreadful silence.

"I'm sorry," Jen said. "I didn't—"

"It's fine," said Quinn, although it wasn't.

"I didn't mean—"

"I said it's fine," he said firmly.

"Just let me have a look, okay?"

Quinn, who wasn't even sure they'd let him in to have a look, just shrugged, and neither of them spoke for the rest of the journey.

Halesbridge wasn't far, although it damn well felt like it. The DS who'd called Quinn had given him the address, which turned out to be a small modern-ish house in a development of small modern-ish houses. It wasn't hard to work out which one from all the crime scene tape already all over it. On one side it was joined to its neighbour, and on the other it shared an alley filled with wheelie bins.

"This is as far as I can go, mate," said the driver as he was stopped by a PCSO at the end of the cul-de-sac. Quinn paid him, including the extra twenty-five he'd rashly promised, and waited until Jen had already got out before quietly asking the driver to wait around the corner for ten minutes. He reckoned it'd be less than that before Jen chickened out.

"DS Coulson asked me to come," he said to the PCSO, who relayed this via her radio, then, looking surprised, held out a sign-in sheet and lifted the police tape for them.

"Sure about this?" Quinn said to Jen, who had a set look about her face, as if she was bracing herself for something unpleasant. Well, she was going to get it. Coulson said Paul Dunlop had been hanged, and that was always a lot more unpleasant than whatever they showed on cosy prime time TV mysteries.

DS Coulson met them at the front door of Paul Dunlop's house. A tall woman in her thirties, she'd once confessed that her previous boss had been invalided out of the Force after an incident involving a suspect ramming his car, so she had some sympathy for Quinn and his unasked-for civilian status.

"Who's this?"

"My associate, Jennifer Hargrave," Quinn said before Jen could open her mouth and incriminate herself.

"Associate, eh?" Coulson handed them gloves and blue baggies to go over their shoes. Jen looked uninspired, but complied.

"Sure it'll do her good to see the darker side of the job," Quinn said, leaning against the wall to put his shoe protectors on. This was always extra fun with a prosthetic leg.

"Just make sure she doesn't touch anything," Coulson said, giving Jen a disparaging look before sweeping inside the house. Quinn followed, and Jen trooped after.

"Quinn," Coulson paused in the doorway. "Are you sure about this? Do you really want to see him?"

Quinn gave her the sort of look Ethan used to pull for publicity posters. The DS raised her hands and backed away.

The front door opened straight onto a kitchen with cheap fitted units, a bin stacked with pizza boxes, and a load of dishes sitting unwashed on the counter. The small table by the door held a comprehensive toolbox, spilling its contents everywhere, and there was a pair of heavy workboots sitting by the door.

"What was his job?" Quinn asked.

"Construction. General labour."

Quinn translated this to mean someone who'd do anything for a few quid under the table. Don't make assumptions, he told himself, almost hearing his instructors telling him the same all those years ago at Templemore.

"Who found him?"

"Neighbours saw him through the window." She pointed in the direction of the alley side of the house.

"You can't see him from the street, but he's clear as day from halfway up their stairs."

The kitchen opened into a living room, which was about as typical of a bachelor pad as any Quinn had ever seen. Dominated by a big TV at one end and a sofa at the other, it was under-furnished and lacked any sort of personal touch. By the TV were several games consoles and a complicated-looking sound system.

Scattered heaps of videogames surrounded the TV, which Quinn would have taken as more evidence of Dunlop's slovenliness had it not been for the fact that the TV itself was smashed, the cheap curtains had been torn down and the only other piece of furniture in the room, a side table, had gone flying, spilling its contents of beer and crisps everywhere. A plate smeared with ketchup had been broken in two.

Quinn took all of that in with a few glances, the same way he knew DS Coulson would have done. Behind him, he heard a soft inhalation of surprise as Jen looked around.

"Don't touch anything," Coulson reminded her sharply. To Quinn, she motioned to the staircase in the corner. He knew what was coming. A house like this, with standard-height ceilings, wouldn't have anywhere else high enough to hang yourself from. A glance out the patio door revealed there were no trees substantial enough to manage it in the pocket-sized back garden.

A hanging. It had to be a damn hanging, didn't it?

He saw Dunlop's feet first, bare and unkempt with ragged toenails. Then bare hairy legs—*sweet Jesus please don't let him be naked, I've just eaten*—then, thank God, baggy boxer shorts and a t-shirt, his arms hanging loose, hands dirty. The rope around his neck was a blue nylon affair. If he did general building work he probably had reams of the stuff lying about.

He turned to ask Coulson if anyone had made it past

the body swinging above the stairs, because it was fairly clear the man had come recently from bed, but then he saw Jen on the other side of the room, her eyes wide and her face so white he knew she was going to faint.

"Jenny," he said, and rushed to catch her, as behind him, Coulson let out a sigh.

She crumpled in his arms, but when he'd have expected her eyes to roll back in her head they instead snapped open and shone at him with a sudden, terrifying brightness.

"Jen?"

She straightened away from him abruptly, moving like she wasn't in control of her own body, and stared around wildly.

"Why did you bring her here?" she said, and Quinn went very cold because while that had been Jen's voice coming out of Jen's mouth it hadn't sounded a bit like Jen at all.

Coulson said something behind him but Quinn's attention was riveted on Jen, who glared at him wildly, unnervingly, before suddenly lurching towards the kitchen. Quinn lunged after her.

"Breathe, breathe," Jen was muttering to herself as she stumbled towards the exit on legs that she didn't seem able to control. "Quinn, help!"

He grabbed for her again, steering her through the front door and narrowly missing knocking over Dunlop's muddy boots on the way.

"If you're gonna throw up, love, do it away from the crime scene," said one of the coppers outside, and Quinn glared at him as he dragged a shambling and mumbling Jen away from the house. Two doors down she abruptly turned to him and said in that same clear, unnatural voice, "Get her away from here. Somewhere quiet and warm, and give her gin. Understand?"

Horrified, he nodded, and she sagged in his arms like

someone had cut her power supply.

CHAPTER SEVENTEEN

The White Lady: just after

She walks among them like a ghost.

Quinn watches her through the ash that falls like snow. She steps over some heaps on the ground and stops by others. She glances at something he can't see. Quinn turns his head, sees a man sitting up and holding out an arm that stops at the elbow. He looks appalled. He's opening his mouth as if he's screaming, but he's not making any sound.

Quinn really isn't sure what's going on.

He sits up, watches the woman in white as she steps over another person on the ground. She looks down at Quinn, then she speaks to someone he can't see and gently pushes him back down to the floor.

"What's going on?" Quinn asks her, attempting to get up and failing. "I'm an officer of the law." But there isn't any sound.

She reaches for something and ties it around his leg. Quinn tries to see what it is she's doing. His foot's gone kind of numb.

Beside him, something icy brushes by, someone walking past him on cold, silent feet. He remembers that feeling for the rest of his life. It's the only thing he does feel as he's lying there, not quite able to move. It's like a dreamworld, soft and quiet, with no one crying or shouting.

He wonders if he's had too much to drink. He imagines he can see people moving in the corner of his eye, but when he turns his head there's no one there. Just a pile of charred clothes and some dead flesh on the floor. Were they having a barbecue?

He tries to get up again. It's still not working.

It's not until men and women dressed in garish yellow and green start trying to get him onto a stretcher that he realises this is because he's missing a significant portion of his leg.

CHAPTER EIGHTEEN

"Jenny? Jen? Wake up. Stop messing around now. It isn't funny."

"She all right?" asked the cabby, which Quinn thought was a particularly stupid enquiry given that Jen was a crumpled heap of limbs in the back seat only held upright by the seatbelt he'd buckled around her.

"Just get us back to Wirpness quick as you can," he said, and repeated his address. There was no way he was taking Jen back to her house and risking running into Charlotte.

She talks to herself. Was this what Charlotte had meant? This wasn't talking to yourself, this was... this was...

He had no idea what this was.

He was just debating whether or not to call a doctor when Jen's eyelids fluttered and her head stirred.

"Jen? Can you hear me?"

She blinked, as if the light hurt her eyes, and said, "Quinn?"

"Yeah. It's me. Hold tight, we're going home."

Jen sat up a bit straighter and rubbed her face.

"What…?"

"Jenny, listen to me. Have you taken any drugs?"

She looked at him for the first time and her eyes were their normal blue, tired-looking and confused. "No," she said.

"Are you sure? I need to know. Anything at all? Even if it's prescription?"

"What kind of question is that? Of course not." Her speech was slurred as if she was very drunk or very tired. "Half a glass of wine at lunch. You were there. I went onto Coke because I had a headache." She frowned. "Is this still Sunday? Quinn…" She looked around the cab and out at the passing streets, and down at her own clothes, and he saw when she registered the protective bags on her feet and the latex gloves on her hands.

"What the hell is going on?"

There, that sounded like Jen. He sighed in relief.

"I'm hoping you can tell me. Look, we're nearly there. Wait 'til we get inside, yes?"

She glanced uncertainly at the cabby, who was now earwigging furiously, and nodded.

The last five minutes seemed to take forever. Quinn thrust some money at the driver and bundled Jen into his house before Charlotte took it upon herself to pop round uninvited again.

He installed Jen on the sofa, went to run her a glass of water, then changed his mind and got the whiskey out.

He found her removing her shoe protectors and gloves with mechanical precision. Her face was full of some dreadful sorrow.

"Sorry, no gin," he said, handing her the glass, which she regarded as if it might be full of cyanide.

"Gin?"

"You said you wanted gin." *Give her gin.* Who the hell was 'her'?

"Why would I want gin? It's the middle of the day."

Quinn sat down on the coffee table in front of her and said gently, "You said gin."

Jen regarded the whiskey, then she handed it to him. "Tell me what I said," she said calmly. "Exactly what I said."

He had an excellent memory for details. Quinn told her word for word, watching her face get paler and paler until he thought she'd faint again. *At least she's already on the sofa. Oh God, what if she goes mad again?*

But she didn't faint. She closed her eyes, squeezed them tight, and something like a sob escaped her. "Oh God, Alice," she whispered.

"What?" said Quinn.

Jen opened her eyes as if afraid he'd still be there. "I spoke about myself in the third person and I asked for gin?" she said. He nodded tentatively. "Oh God."

She covered her face with her hands.

"Jen, who's Alice?" She gave a muffled sob. Quinn hesitated, then winced and asked, "Am I talking to Alice now?"

Her hands moved. Her brows went up. "No, you're talking to me. Alice is… well, she's…"

He waited, more afraid than he'd ever been. *Charlotte said she's not very good with children. Oh God, I hope I don't know where this is going.*

"Alice is a ghost. She's been with me forever. She's nine years old, and has been since the nineteenth century. Other children have imaginary friends. I have a ghost," said Jen, and Quinn gaped at her for a moment.

So I didn't know where it was going.

Thank God.

"I think she took me over or something when we were at Paul Dunlop's house. She's done it before." Jen took a deep breath. "How do you think I survived the White Lady?"

"A ghost?" Quinn said finally. "You believe in ghosts?"

She gave a sad smile. "I don't have to believe in them. They just exist. It'd be like believing in… this table. It's just there. It exists."

He looked down at the table, the one he was sitting on, and then back up at her. She looked, of all things, resigned.

People who told him they believed in ghosts didn't usually look resigned.

Georgia and Aimee had been full of bright excitement. They'd wanted to believe. Jen didn't.

She started to get to her feet.

"Where are you going?"

"Home." Then she realised, and sat down heavily. "Oh bollocks, I can't, can I?" She looked at her watch. "They're probably not even back there yet, let alone packed up and ready to leave." She rolled her shoulders tiredly. "D'you mind if I stay here a while? Just an hour or two. I'll get out of your way. I could do with a lie down."

She rose to her feet again and slipped past him. Quinn didn't know what to do.

"Jen," he said, and she paused. She looked weary beyond belief.

"It's all right," she said. "You wouldn't be the first person who didn't believe me."

After she'd gone back upstairs, Quinn sat for a long while on the coffee table, sipping the whiskey she'd left behind.

When she'd named Alice, he'd been so sure about what was going to come next that her confession had slightly floored him. Charlotte telling him Jen never spent any time with the children. Jen's bad relationship.

He'd begun to suspect there had been a small,

dreadful coffin somewhere in Jen's past. Just not that far in the past.

Draining the whiskey and pouring more, he settled on the sofa and pulled his laptop over. Jen had been searching genealogy sites for the Adderall family tree— did she think she'd seen ghosts there?

Had she seen ghosts there?

Those shadows on the footage…

No. That was ridiculous. She might believe in them but that didn't make them real.

He searched online for belief in imaginary friends. Most of the results came from parenting forums. None of it suggested that having an imaginary friend was a problem, and one site even went so far to say that adults with imaginary friends were probably novelists.

He started to search for people who believed in ghosts, but stopped. He'd done enough research into that kind of phenomenon.

Quinn sipped his whiskey and drummed his fingers on the laptop. Jen might have described Alice as some kind of imaginary friend she'd never grown out of, but that didn't explain her behaviour this afternoon. The way she'd moved, as if someone else was controlling her body. The bright, feverish light in her eyes. The voice that had been hers but not hers.

She'd sounded like a frightened, angry child.

Despite himself, Quinn shivered.

It wasn't as if he had no experience dealing with mental health issues. Quite apart from the mandatory counselling that followed losing both a limb and a sibling, he'd had years to watch his mother decline.

And yet Jen didn't act like a person with dementia. She wasn't muddled or confused like his mammy. Jen was calmly certain that what she—and only she—had seen was real.

And she'd behaved like she was possessed.

He sipped more whiskey. He opened a private browser window so none of his search history would be saved. Then slowly, straining his ears for any sign of movement from Jen upstairs, he typed in the word schizophrenia.

What he read made him go cold.

No less an authority than the National Health Service described schizophrenia as hearing or seeing things that didn't exist, believing in things that clearly weren't true, and displaying changes in behaviour.

Such as believing you were followed around by a small Victorian ghost and that she'd taken over your body for a few minutes.

He read on, fascinated and appalled at the same time. Episodes could be triggered by stress, and Quinn couldn't think of much that was more stressful than a bomb blast. Or, come to think of it, seeing the corpse of a recently hanged man.

There were various types of therapy. Plenty of antipsychotic drugs. A person could even be admitted to a psychiatric ward.

He read it all through, followed the links to mental health charities, looked up similar diseases. Psychosis. Brain tumour. He didn't want it to be any of these things. Dementia in the young. Alzheimers.

At this point he ran out of whiskey and made himself sit back and evaluate what he was looking at. Alzheimers was pretty unlikely in someone aged 29.

"Why are you even looking?" he muttered to himself, and shut down the laptop.

"Looking for what?"

He glanced up to see Jen standing in the doorway, looking wary. She was back in her pyjamas, but this time she'd put on a sweater which covered up the skinny vest she'd worn this morning. She'd pulled the sleeves down over her hands like a child.

"Uh, something to watch on TV. Did you sleep?"

She shrugged. "A bit. Then Charlotte texted me to say they'd just left and woke me up."

He moved the laptop and patted the sofa for her to sit beside him. She did, keeping to her own side and eyeing him distrustfully, as if she knew he was trying to figure out a way to get her to go and see a doctor.

"You didn't tell me you had a cat," she said.

"I don't," said Quinn, and saw her face shut down. "I mean—no, he's not mine, he just lets himself in sometimes. Belongs to a neighbour."

"Oh. Does he have a name?"

Quinn winced. "Um. I call him Ghost. On account of being grey and not always here. Um."

"Cosmic," said Jen. She looked appallingly weary. "I thought I'd come down and tell you the truth before you went around detecting it," she said.

"The truth about what?"

"About what happens when you see ghosts and people think you're crazy." She pulled at the frayed hems of the sleeves on her sweater. "Can you access my medical records?"

Dammit, how did she know? "Not without your permission. If I tried the doctor would contact you anyway."

She nodded. "Thought so. Well, anyway."

She thinks I'm going to fire her, he thought, watching her chew her lip anxiously.

"You don't have to tell me anything," he said.

"But you'll probably find it all out. You're a detective after all." She sighed. "You didn't believe me when I told you why I hadn't told my family about the White Lady. Well, what do you think happens to little girls who insist they can see someone who isn't there?"

"I've never given it much thought," Quinn lied.

"They get taken to doctors. Special doctors. Ones

who talk to you a lot, and then hold consultations with your parents. And you tell the truth, like a good girl, and somehow that makes it all worse."

She was pulling at a loose thread in her sleeve now. Quinn didn't think she knew she was doing it.

"It was just Alice before the White Lady. I hardly ever saw any others. Then... that day..." She looked off at the distance. "I saw the dead rise and walk away," she said, and Quinn shivered despite himself. *Walking away on cold, silent feet.* "You think my family wanted to hear that?"

"Well," Quinn tried, "trauma..."

"Doesn't make you see dead people." Jen sighed again. "I told you Charlotte cares desperately about what people think. She gets that from my mother. She's a worrier. Always has been. The slightest thing that isn't normal and she freaks right out. And I wasn't normal. So off I went to the doctors. All the doctors."

"How old were you?" Quinn asked softly.

"I don't even remember. Old enough that I should have grown out of having an imaginary friend," Jen said, as if quoting someone. "Some of the doctors told my mum it was normal, and my dad kept saying it was nothing to worry about, but she was convinced there was something really wrong. It wasn't until I was much older that she told me about all the other women in my family who'd gone crazy and been sent to loony bins. Right back to the Victorians, and some poor woman who'd been lobotomised as part of her treatment. Runs in the family, she said."

She looked so bleak Quinn reached out and touched her hand. But he couldn't help thinking that he'd just read how some people were genetically pre-disposed to mental health issues.

"I wasn't sent away until after my dad died," Jen said. She hadn't moved her hand, but neither had she moved to take his.

"Sent away?"

"They call them clinics now, not asylums, but they're still the places where you send the crazy people," Jen said. "The ones you don't want. The ones that… don't fit in or get in the way. There are specialist units for children. The ones with eating disorders or severe bipolar, or the ones who like burning stuff. The ones who are dangerous."

"Were you dangerous?"

"No. But I was… in the way. It was easier for Charlotte and my mum to tell people I was ill than that I was crazy."

She was quiet for a while, and Quinn didn't interrupt.

"I'd have some therapy, I'd take some new course of drugs, I'd pretend Alice wasn't real and then I'd get sent home for a while. And then a little while later Charlotte would catch me whispering to someone who wasn't there, and the whole circus would start up again."

"What a little fucking snitch," Quinn said before he could stop himself.

Jen looked at him then with something like wonder on her face.

"Well, she was. Christ, I mean it's my job to snoop on people, but that's just…" Horrible, he wanted to say. Emotional abuse, that was another one.

"You know," Jen frowned, "this one time, I was in there over Christmas. Can't remember which year. And she gave me bubble bath."

Quinn's incomprehension must have shown on his face, because she continued.

"You don't get to take bubble baths in mental health clinics. You get showers. And if you're really lucky and you've been a good girl, you get to take them unsupervised."

That *bitch*. Quinn pulled Jen into his arms and

hugged her tight, because she might have severe delusional problems but she didn't deserve such a bitch of a sister.

For a moment Jen seemed startled, and he realised she probably wasn't used to being hugged. She seemed to know her way around sexual wiles—boy howdy did she—but he'd bet dollars to donuts no one ever hugged her.

He cleared his throat and relaxed his hold slightly, trying to make it clear she was welcome to stay as long as she wanted. To his surprise, she tucked her head against his shoulder and made herself comfortable. "How long did this go on for?"

"Until I was eighteen. By then I'd given in. I just told them whatever they wanted to hear. I took their drugs and I took their counselling and I ignored Alice to such an extent that I didn't see her for… oh, six years. Not until that day in the White Lady when she made me get down." Jen's fingers curled around his. "I don't care what else you say, she saved my life. There was a beam that crashed right through where I'd been standing. I'd've been dead if it wasn't for her."

Years of accident and incident investigation had taught Quinn that narrow escapes were not usually half as narrow as the victim thought. But part of him wanted to look up the footage from the White Lady to see if what Jen said was true.

Not that this means I believe you.

"So when I tell you that my family doesn't know about the White Lady, it's not because I don't want to bother them or I don't think they'd believe me, it's because I know with absolute certainty that if I told them, I'd just be back in the system. And I don't ever want to be in that system again."

Quinn just held her close and thought about how much she was going to hate him.

Jen insisted on going home that night, despite Quinn's protests that she shouldn't be alone.

"I'm not alone," she said, glancing at Alice's transparent little face beside her. Not that the ghost was much comfort at the moment, ever since she'd reappeared looking pale and troubled, and Jen had hissed at her that her little stunt had got her into a heap of trouble.

Quinn stared hard at Alice, and frowned.

"I don't see anything."

"Of course you don't," Jen said wearily. No one ever did.

"I'll walk you home," Quinn offered after an awkward pause.

"It's fine. I know the way."

"Not the point," he said, and refused to let her go alone.

She couldn't stay with him. Not when he was being so kind and she felt so vulnerable. There was no telling what secrets she might spill. She'd already said too much, about Alice and about the clinics and about how crazy she was.

Well, I guess you don't have to worry about a relationship with him now.

They walked in silence along the dark road, quiet at this time of the evening. Behind the doors and windows they passed were families eating Sunday dinner, watching cosy autumnal mysteries and costume dramas.

Ghost the cat trotted along with them for a while, weaving around Alice's ankles and purring.

"Is he okay?" Quinn said. "He looks... drunk."

"He's fine. He likes Alice," Jen said gloomily. Alice stopped to pet the cat, her hand going right through him.

"Look, if you're not feeling up to it, you don't have to come in tomorrow," Quinn said, and her heart sank.

"And the day after that?" She looked up at him, ridiculously beautiful even in the ugly orange streetlight. She could still feel his arms around her, solid and comforting. When was the last time anyone had hugged her? "Do I still have a job?"

"Of course you do."

"Right up until he calls your doctor and tells him about today," Alice said glumly.

"Well, it's your stupid fault," Jen snapped.

"Pardon?" said Quinn.

"Not you. Alice." She stopped walking, closed her eyes and counted to ten. "You'd probably still think I was reasonably normal if she hadn't gone and…"

She opened her eyes. Quinn was looking at her with concern. The head-tilt and worried expression she'd come to know and dread.

"Do I have to find a new job and a new town?" she said. "'Cos you might as well tell me now."

"No, I told you. Job's yours. Why would you move?"

Jen raised her eyebrows. "Um, you think I'm crazy? Word gets around, you know." She started walking again.

"Do you really think I'd go telling people about this?" Quinn said, following her.

Not you. The ghosts.

Then, belatedly he added, "Of course I don't think you're crazy."

"Liar," she said.

"Anything you want to tell me?" enquired Tessa as soon as Quinn walked through the door on Monday.

Oh, bollocks. "Ehm, good morning?" he said. She raised her eyebrows. "You look nice today?" he tried.

Tessa folded her arms.

"All right, what?"

"My mum's neighbour, you know Sheila? Grey hair.

Lots of cats."

For the second time in as many days, Quinn realised this wasn't going where he thought it was going to go.

"Anyway. She babysits for her son's kids a lot and they live on Holly Road, just around the corner from you?"

Oh no, it *was* going where he thought.

"What is going on with you and Jen?"

Quinn opened his mouth without having a clue what he was going to say, and then he spotted Jen coming up the stairs and winced.

"Nothing," she said, and Tessa spun around guiltily.

"Jen! What is going on with you two? My mum's friend Sheila saw you two all snuggly and going out for cosy family walks! How come you never told me?"

Tessa, Quinn realised, was more upset that she'd been left out of the loop than that Quinn and Jen were seeing each other. *Pretending* to see each other, he amended to himself. She'd made that abundantly clear.

The one girl in all the world who might understand about Ethan and the White Lady...

Jen had frozen in the act of unwinding her pink scarf. She started up again, giving him a look like a rabbit trapped in car headlights, and he shook himself. What Jen needed right now was a friend, and he could be that.

"It's not what it looked like," Quinn said, and Tessa snapped her attention back to him.

"She said you were holding hands," she accused.

"I have cold hands," Quinn said, and held up his palms for emphasis. It was true, he did have cold hands. Especially in the office for some reason. Something to do with circulation, he assumed. Probably, getting a limb blown off was bad for circulation.

"Give me a break."

"He was helping me out," Jen said. She pushed past them and hung her coat up on the stand. "My sister came

201

to visit."

"And that necessitates pretending you're dating your boss?" Tessa said.

"Well—"

"It's my fault," said Quinn, at the same time Jen said, "You haven't met my sister."

Tessa tapped her foot.

"She's a Smug Married," Jen said, and while Quinn hadn't a clue what that meant, Tessa made a noise of understanding.

"You thought it'd get her off your back?"

"Yeah. And she'll go home and report to my mother, and everyone will be happy. All right?"

"I suppose." Tessa moved towards her office and then paused. "She said you looked good together," she added, and Quinn groaned.

"Not you too."

"Not going to happen," Jen said, sitting down at her desk and switching on her computer.

"You two are hopeless," said Tessa, and shut her office door behind herself.

Quinn rubbed his cold fingers and tried not to remember how soft and warm Jen had felt under his hands.

Jen kept her eyes on her desk, busying herself with organising pens and bits of paper that clearly didn't need to be organised. Quinn flicked on the kettle, took a seat on the sofa and waited for her to acknowledge him.

Eventually she looked up. "Something I can help you with?"

He leaned forward and asked quietly, "Are you okay?"

"Fine." Her eyes avoided his face.

"You've not been bothered by this 'Alice'?"

Jen let out a sharp breath and looked up. "No, but I'm being bothered by this 'guy'." She gave him a pointed look. "I'm fine, Quinn. Go away and continue your good work disproving the existence of ghosts."

He put on his most reasonable, policeman-talking-to-people-with-weapons voice. "I'm just saying, maybe you should talk to—"

"You finish that sentence and you can start advertising for a new secretary."

He stood up and spooned sugar into his mug. "Thought you were my office manager."

"Oh, bite me."

Quinn escaped to his office before she tried to turn him into a ghost.

Jen closed her eyes and counted to ten. Again.

"You confide one little thing," she muttered.

"He's trying to help," said Danny from the sofa, where he'd been sitting beside Quinn, making silly faces. Alice had vanished last night, looking contrite and upset. Jen didn't know if she was pleased about this or not.

She still felt... off about the whole episode. Tired, prickly, defensive, and quite upset that Alice had betrayed her like that.

"And you can bugger off as well," she said, turning her attention to emails.

"Charming. Look, I need to tell you something. Over the weekend, your chap Quinn was—"

"For crying out loud, he is not my chap!"

Danny dismissed this with a wave of his hand. "He was in here over the weekend."

"No he wasn't, he was pretending to be my boyfriend."

"Before that. I know he saw you out the window and went haring off with those flowers."

Jen paused and glanced over at him. "They were supposed to be from Beth," she said slowly.

"Oh, they were." He waved at a similar arrangement on the table. "He considered pretending they were from him though. I saw him take the card out and then put it back. No, listen. He was at your desk. On that... thingy."

"The computer?"

"Yes. He was looking at the same things you'd been looking at. Now, I don't know how these thingimajobs work, but it looked like he was trying to find out what you'd been looking at."

Guilt flushed through her before she realised she had nothing to feel guilty about. "Well, so what? He's my boss, and he's a detective. To be honest I'd be a bit disappointed if he didn't snoop through my browser history."

"He was also looking things up about you."

"What kind of things?"

"I don't know, I don't understand these things." Danny waved at the computer again. "I think he was trying to find out more about you."

"Well," Jen said, glancing involuntarily at Quinn's office. "Like I said. He's a detective."

"It's still bally rude of him to sneak around like that!"

He seemed so aggrieved on her behalf. Jen smiled despite herself. "It's fine. He knows the worst." The worst he could find out, she amended to herself. To distract Danny, she asked, "Hey, where did you die?"

"What? Oh, I don't know. Why d'you ask?"

"I met someone in the woods yesterday. An airman." She hesitated. "I wondered if you knew him."

"What was his name?"

"He didn't give it." She thought back to the ghost in the Nissen hut. Except that he'd been less of a ghost and more of an echo. Trapped in the repeating cycle of reliving his ghastly last hours. "He'd been badly burnt," she said quietly, more quietly than she'd already been speaking. "Said his crate had taken a hit and ditched him overland. He wasn't sure where it had ended up."

Danny was uncharacteristically silent.

"He was in a Nissen hut in the woods by the estuary. That sort of gully," she closed her eyes as she realised what had made the scar on the landscape in the first place. "Said he'd fallen through the trees. He had a wound that had gone bad. I could smell it."

Danny swallowed and said nothing.

"I think he died there, alone and in terrible pain. I heard him calling for morphine. I just wondered if you knew who he might have been."

This airman didn't know who he was. He didn't know anything except how much pain he was in.

"Probably after my time, old girl. I haven't left this place for seventy-odd years. Don't get to socialise with other ghosts. Speaking of, where's Alice?"

"No idea. Wherever you people go when you're not here."

She'd asked Alice once where she went, but the little girl had shrugged vaguely and said she didn't know.

"Ah. Oh well. Just you and me then, eh?"

"God shield it should ever be just me," Jen muttered, clicking through new client requests and forwarding them on to Quinn and Tessa. Five had come in over the weekend. She sent two infidelity cases to Tessa, one background check and a missing person to Quinn, and then opened the last one.

"My friend Georgia Wright recommended your agency," it began, and Jen snorted and sent it onto Quinn without reading any more. No doubt he'd bounce it back to Tessa, but she might as well torture him while she had the opportunity.

She was muttering to herself out there. Quinn could see through the frosted glass enough to tell that she wasn't on the phone and there was no one else there. Was she talking to this Alice again?

He began to edge closer to the glass wall, but of course then she'd see where he was and know he was eavesdropping. Dammit.

Maybe he should install a bug.

"Or maybe that'd just be shitty," he said, wiping his hands over his face. "Look, now I'm talking to myself."

Dragging his attention back over to his desk, he flicked on his voicemail and listened to the messages there. New clients would be directed to Jen's phone in the outer office, but she didn't seem to have got round to that yet today. The messages Quinn got were callbacks from references he'd checked or contacts he'd requested information from.

One was from DS Coulson, telling him Paul Dunlop's post-mortem was scheduled for later in the week and he could ring her to find out the results. He made a note of that. Coulson also added that she'd informed Beth of the incident. She didn't say whether Beth was being considered a suspect or not. She didn't even say whether she suspected murder.

A few messages down the line was one from his contact at the DBS, telling him Jonathan Blake had no criminal record. Quinn had to think for a moment on that one, before recalling that Blake was Jen's old boyfriend. The one he'd thought might have hurt her.

Had she just made that up? Had she made it all up? The sudden depressing thought came to him that there was no Alice, there were no psychiatric clinics, that Jen was just messing with him.

He stared through the frosted glass at her indistinct shape. Grey shirt today, with black trousers and her hair in a sensible plait.

He'd met some con artists in his time, but this was really taking the cake.

"Now who's imagining things," he muttered to

himself, and shook his head. He turned to his computer and started reading through his emails.

Ten minutes later he read an email from one Ellie Robertson which began, "My friend Georgia Wright recommended your agency," and groaned. But professionalism made him read on.

"Last summer my brother Max died in a diving accident on holiday. According to the inquest it really was an accident. For a while I thought it might have been something darker, but that's because of what happened afterwards.

"He used a lot of social media and I kept his profiles open so people could post messages about him. He was quite popular and loads of people said really nice things about him. But then I started getting messages from him.

"At first I thought it was a horrible joke. I couldn't understand why someone would hack my brother's account to send me messages like this. The first one I had is here: @Maxattack: *where r u??* And then a few days later: @Maxattack: *im cold*

"I reported the messages and changed the password details. He used the same password for everything so I changed everything. But then I got this two days later: @Maxattack *ellie why wont u answer me??*"

Quinn frowned and took a sip of his tea. Clearly it was a sick joke. He'd advise her to shut down the accounts and harass the site owners to up their security.

"I got kind of angry and started replying. I told this person they were sick and cruel and, well I won't repeat it but I swore a lot. Max didn't like swearing. He had this quote from George Washington on that he used to bring out like it made him sound super clever. He used it in essays and stuff. And the reply I got back from this person was '*foolish n wicked profane*'. Which is a thing from the quote."

Quinn Googled it. She was right. "The foolish and

wicked practice of profane cursing and swearing is a vice so mean and low that every person of sense and character detests and despises it."

Wondering where this was going, he read on through Ellie's email.

"I've changed passwords so many times I can't remember. I'm using random words from the dictionary and typing numbers by hitting the keyboard at random. I've had my laptop checked for viruses and keystroke loggers but it's clean. I've used computers at the library. I don't know how a person could be doing this.

"I started to wonder if it was a glitch and just sending fragments of old messages or bits that had gone stray from other people's messages. I emailed and phoned the site and they said no one else had accessed the account but me. And when I told the police they said if no one else had accessed it then it must be a glitch and there was nothing they could do. And then I got these every other day or so for a couple of weeks:

"Max Mobile: e*llie im trapped*

"@Maxattack: *cooold*

"Max Mobile: *cant breath*

"@Maxattack: *so dark here went too far*

"@Maxattack: *ells will u help me*

"Max Mobile: *foot hurts! black*

"Max Mobile: *want to come out*

"@Maxattack: *COO OO O OOO OOOLD*

"And it was the thing with the foot that really freaked me out. Because the thing is when Max was found it was because he'd floated to the surface and a ship's propellor had cut off his foot. That's not something we told anyone. We just said it had been a diving accident. No one else knew that about his foot."

Quinn sat back, chilled despite himself.

It was a good story. The kind of thing you'd tell around a campfire to give your friends bad dreams. The story of the haunted computer!

He drank more tea and read the rest.

"I deleted the account. I took his number off my phone and that really hurt because it was like deleting Max and pretending he never existed. And then I got this text:

"Unknown: *ellie where r u?*

"I don't know what to do. The police think I'm making it up. I heard Georgia and Aimee talking about hiring you to find the ghosts in the groundskeeper's cottage at school and I thought I'd try one last desperate attempt. I just want these messages to stop. It's ruining my life."

Quinn stared at the last sentence for quite a while before picking up his pen and making notes about who he needed to contact. Police. Website help staff. IT expert. He hesitated, then wrote Psychiatrist.

Either someone was messing with this girl or she was having some kind of breakdown.

He looked at Jen's silhouette again, standing by the kettle and tapping her foot.

Then he sighed, and opened up the next email.

CHAPTER NINETEEN

"I've just realised who he reminds me of," Charlotte said when Jen answered the phone. At least she'd waited until lunchtime, and Jen was on her way to the shops.

"Who?" Their mother did this too, began a conversation as if you'd already heard the first half of it.

"Your Quinn."

Jen didn't even bother to say he wasn't hers and never would be. "Who?"

"That actor! You know, the one who died."

She pretended her shiver was because of the temperature. "Might need to narrow it down a bit for me."

"You know, the one in that vampire show. Or whatever. I don't have time for television. But you know, it was that pub bomb a few years ago."

"Oh," said Jen. "Yes."

"That stupid, selfish girl who blew herself up. What is wrong with some people?"

Jen's fist clenched around the phone. She took a deep breath as Charlotte ran on.

"He is *exactly* like him. It's weird."

Jen stopped walking and looked around to see if anyone was listening. She had a very quick mental debate with herself. And she sighed.

"Okay," she said. "Yes. He does. You're thinking of Ethan Sullivan, right?"

"Right! The Irish guy. Such a shame," Charlotte added as an afterthought.

"Yeah. Such a shame. Listen, Charlotte, keep this to yourself, yeah?"

"Were they related?" Charlotte interrupted.

"Yes." Jen braced herself. "They were brothers."

"Oh my God. Really? I knew he looked familiar! Why didn't you tell me?"

"Quinn likes to keep it quiet. He doesn't really like being reminded of it."

"Didn't they get on or something?"

"No—I mean he doesn't like to be reminded his brother is dead," Jen explained. For someone so bright her sister could be very dumb. And a bitch, she thought, suddenly remembering Quinn's words from last night.

"Well, sure. Doesn't want to go all April Williams, right?" Charlotte tittered.

"Yeah."

"He was quite the heart throb," Charlotte mused, then added piously, "I mean he never did anything for me, but I know a lot of girls like that kind of thing."

Yes, because your tastes are so superior to mine. Jen wondered how she'd never noticed how passive aggressive her sister was.

"Yep. Well, anyway, I've got to get to the shops, my lunch hour is nearly over."

"Why don't you go after work?"

"Because out here in the sticks the shops shut at 5.30. And for some reason I was busy at the weekend."

"With your new boyfriend!"

Jen suppressed a scream and said instead, "No, with

you lot. And a murder investigation."

"Murder? Jenny—" there was a sigh from Charlotte's end, "are you making things up again?"

"No. A local man died. Quinn suspects foul play. You can look it up," she said, because Paul Dunlop's death would probably be on a local news site.

"Ooh, check you out, being all *Midsomer Murders*," Charlotte said, sounding peeved.

"Yep, gotta go, bye," Jen said, and hung up. "I'm very busy and important," she told the silent phone. It didn't seem impressed.

Later that afternoon, Quinn came into the outer office with his phone in his hand. He looked thoughtful as he leaned against the cabinet opposite her desk. "I just called DS Coulson," he said. "From yesterday?"

"I remember." She couldn't help her shudder.

"I don't have to go on if you—?"

Jen rapidly shook her head. "I'm fine. I, er, didn't mess anything up at the scene, did I?"

"No. But it is the mess they're interested in. Remember the TV was smashed and the food was spilled?"

"Signs of a struggle?"

"Difficult to explain in a suicide. They're running fingerprints but that might not mean anything. Apparently he regularly had friends over for gaming or football. Police are checking for alibis, doing door-to-doors."

"Does Beth have an alibi?"

Quinn hesitated. "I did ask," he said. "She claims she was with family all day. But…"

"But what? You think they're covering up for her?"

"I don't think anything," Quinn said, raising his palms. "I just… Ah, why is it my business anyway? I'm not a garda any more."

"You're her friend. Neighbour at the least," Jen said.

"Which means I should stay away from the whole damn mess." He scrubbed a hand through his hair, which, judging by the state of it, he'd been doing all day. "I've asked Coulson to keep me advised. She might want a statement from you, by the way. Just a heads-up."

"Great, and what am I supposed to tell her? I got possessed by an overprotective Victorian child?"

A smile caught the corner of his mouth. "You could just say you were overwhelmed by the sight of a dead body."

"Oh. Yeah. That sounds better."

He smiled more fully at that, and straightened up. "Oh, I meant to say. That case you passed on to me? The haunted computer?"

"The what?"

"The teenage girl whose brother is haunting her computer?"

Jen shrugged. "I didn't read them. I just saw Georgia's name and figured this one was yours."

"Oh." He looked a bit confused by that, but went on, "She keeps getting messages from him. Is that, uh, common?"

Jen cocked her head. "What, you mean is it common amongst people who see ghosts? I don't know, I've never met anyone else. And no, I've never heard of a haunted computer. But you do hear of ghosts being tied to objects that had meaning. He was a teenage boy, I guess he was never off his computer."

"It's actually her computer."

She turned back to her own, decidedly un-haunted computer and started clicking on things at random. "Well, I don't know. I'm sure it's just a hacker or something. Someone messing with her. Or she's making it all up. A cry for help. Attention seeking."

"I never said that," Quinn said quietly.

"You didn't have to." *Everyone else has.* "I'm sure

you'll find a rational explanation."

"Jen—"

Her fingers stabbed the keyboard. "I've got things to do. You're paying me for them."

She continued making work for herself until she heard him sigh and take a step.

"Let me know if DS Coulson wants to speak to me about my dead body inspired hysteria."

"Jenny—"

"I'll see you tomorrow," Jen said, as coldly as she could, and Quinn went.

Uncle Kieran called that evening, as Quinn was looking up mental health laws and feeling bad about it.

"Hi, howareya?"

"I'm grand," Quinn said, smiling. Sometimes it was just good to hear an Irish voice. "And yourself?"

"*Go maith.* Now then, when are you coming over next? Before your birthday or after it?"

The smile slid away. "I, ehm, I don't know." Not on the day. Please God not on the actual day.

"Your mother's after asking."

Quinn let out a harsh breath and turned his face away, as if that would help. All it did was show him his reflection in the TV screen.

"Ah, now. I know just how she's been asking, too."

"She wants to see her son," Uncle Kieran said.

Quinn let out a bark of laughter at that.

"Ah come on, Quinn. Make your mother happy."

"By pretending to be Ethan?"

When he'd been a kid, he'd hated sharing his birthday. Joint parties with Ethan's friends, who he didn't particularly like. Matching presents from people who thought it was cute. Or worse, joint presents from people who seemed to think they were actually one person in two inconvenient bodies.

But ever since his 28th birthday, he'd realised that there was something worse than sharing your birthday, and that was suddenly not sharing it.

"I never said you had to pretend to be him," Uncle Kieran said, wheedling.

"Just don't correct her when she assumes I'm him. D'you know, last time she thought I was him and then gave out that *I* never came to see her."

"I'm sure she just—"

"'I never see James,' she said. 'He's such a selfish boy.' Do you know what that's like? Can you imagine it?"

His uncle sighed. "It's not her fault, son. You know that."

"I know. But it's a bad enough day for me without having to do all that too." Childishly, he added, "It's not as if she even knows what day it is."

"She does and she doesn't. The other day she gave out at me for not visiting for weeks and I tried to pretend I'd been there last week. But do you know what she'd done? Only got herself a diary and written it down!"

"Ah, grand," said Quinn sourly, and felt even worse.

"Look anyway. Come over some time soon, willya? I'd like to see you, and I do know what day it is."

"Maybe." Quinn picked at a thread on his shirt, and relented. "It'd be nice. Everyone here is so… English."

His uncle laughed. "Well, you couldn't've got much further away, could you? Any further east and you'd be swimming."

"Don't be daft. I can't swim any more."

"Ah sure you can. Haven't you watched the Paralympics? They swim all the time with one leg, one arm, no arms…"

Quinn had, in fact, watched the Paralympics, partly out of a morbid fascination to see people with bodies like his. But the thing about parasport was that everyone involved in it had some disability. They weren't freaks surrounded by normals. They didn't get stared at.

"Sure, but the kids at the local municipal pool'd probably nick my leg and run around pretending to be the Terminator. That happened to someone I know, so it did."

"Sure you're making that up."

"I amn't, she told me." One of the women at the White Lady support group. That was what happened when you went swimming in Peckham, apparently. "Can't exactly run after someone when I've only the one leg, now can I?"

"You're being defeatist. Anyway. I know you can get on a plane with that thing."

"Oh, it's gas getting through airport security with a metal leg," Quinn said. The amount of times he'd had to hop back and forth through the scanner while they debated what to do with it. He wondered how Paralympians got treated.

"Whisht! Stop your complaining, son, and come over to see me. I've a case you might be interested in."

Quinn sighed and swung his feet—one making a soft thud and the other a hard clunk—onto the coffee table. "Uncle Kieran, you're not a detective any more."

"A good detective never really retires," said Uncle Kieran dismissively. "Now. I've a lady out in Rathmichael convinced her house is haunted."

"What a surprise," Quinn murmured. It was always hauntings with his uncle. The man was obsessed. What he'd do if he ever met Jen, Quinn didn't know.

He sat up straighter. Now there was an idea.

"I've been out there and I tell you son, there's something not right with that house."

"Then perhaps she needs a builder. Maybe a plumber?"

"You know what I mean. How about you come out

217

with all your fancy equipment and take a look at the place?"

Quinn rubbed his jaw thoughtfully. *How about I get Jen out there to look at the place?* She hadn't mentioned seeing other ghosts since the dead arising—ugh—at the White Lady. Was it just this Alice she saw?

Had she seen Ethan?

"I'll think about it, Uncle."

"You will?" Kieran sounded surprised, and guilt crept over Quinn.

"Sure. Be good to see you."

He said goodbye to his uncle and ended the call, staring thoughtfully at nothing. He could take all his cameras and recording equipment and Jen could take her... well, herself, and they could do a little test.

Whatever she saw, it wasn't going to match up with what he recorded. These hallucinations of hers couldn't stand up to actual science.

Friday morning, Quinn called DS Coulson for the autopsy report. "Asphyxiation caused by hanging," she said succinctly. "No recent wounds or bruising except the claw-marks to his neck."

Quinn knew that even in a suicide, sometimes the claw-marks were simply a reflexive action. They didn't necessarily mean that the victim was trying to escape the noose.

"Fingerprints? DNA? What was under his fingernails?"

"What is this, CSI?" said Coulson. "We won't have the DNA results back for weeks, you know that. There's not a lot to suggest it's anything other than suicide."

"I don't suppose there was a note?" Quinn asked hopefully. "No 'Goodbye cruel world' Facebook status?"

"Wouldn't that be neat and tidy?" Coulson sighed.

"I'll keep you posted."

Quinn hung up and typed a few notes into his files. Couldn't hurt to keep his eye on it.

Later that afternoon he received an email from Uncle Kieran about the haunted house he wanted Quinn to look at. Large period property—although no one quite seemed to know which period—in which dwelt a lonely widow convinced something was haunting her. Kieran had given Quinn plenty of tragic details about the death of her first husband in a riding accident—apparently the place had its own stables—and the second in a drunken fall down the stairs. Her daughter had also been widowed, and had also miscarried following yet another fall down the stairs.

"You need a carpenter, not an exorcist," Quinn muttered.

"Excuse me?" Jen said from the doorway, and he looked up.

"Ah, nothing."

She shrugged. "Your four o'clock is here."

"I have a four o'clock?"

Jen gave him a look of exaggerated patience. Today she wore grey again, her hair pulled back into a plait with all the stray curls ruthlessly pinned down. Quinn was surprised she hadn't taken to wearing granny spectacles.

"I put it in your online calendar."

His gaze travelled guiltily to the icon on his desktop. Then he glanced at the notes he'd made when Jen had last deigned to speak to him. "Ellie Robertson? Oh... yeah. The girl with the... phone thing."

"She's come by herself. Tessa's gone home so... do you want me to stay in the room?"

Quinn sighed. He understood the need for a chaperone, but he'd never really been satisfied by any interview conducted with one. All too often a younger person didn't tell the truth because they were embarrassed, or frightened to say it in the presence of a parent—or sometimes it was the parent who influenced what the kid said. The police had ways of dealing with this, using video interviews and social workers, but Quinn did not. Quinn had Tessa, and now Jen.

"I'll come out to you. But do me a favour and don't interfere, all right?" The last thing he needed was her sympathetically explaining that she believed in ghosts.

Jen shrugged as if it was all the same to her, and went back her desk. All week she'd been so coldly professional that Quinn had found himself checking the temperature more than once.

He stood up and shuffled through his notes. He'd exchanged a few emails with Ellie and checked out her social media profiles. She seemed reasonably sane, or at least as sane as anyone who thought their computer was haunted could be.

He wheeled his desk chair into the outer office, giving Ellie an encouraging smile as he did. She was a pale girl, even more wide-eyed and skinny than her online selfies suggested. She smiled nervously back at him.

"Hi, I'm James Quinn," he said, holding out his hand. She took it briefly. "You're Ellie, right?"

"Right," she said, and swallowed. She glanced at Jen.

"It's great to meet you. Now, before we start: Jen's going to stay here in the room with us while we talk. It's nothing personal, but you're under eighteen so we want to make sure there are no misunderstandings, all right? We also have security cameras," he pointed them out, "and I can give you a copy of the afternoon's feed if you want. All right?"

She nodded uncertainly.

"Now." Quinn sat down in his chair, facing her from a few feet away. "I've looked at all the data you've sent me, and I've spoken to people at the phone company and the websites you listed." He handed her copies of some of his notes. "Now, these are the IP addresses of computers you told me you've used to access Max's accounts."

She glanced at them, and then took out a notebook and made some comparisons. Quinn was impressed. She'd even sent him a comprehensive list of the dates and times she'd gone into Max's account.

He almost wished she hadn't.

"Yes," said Ellie. "Has anyone else accessed the accounts?"

Quinn hesitated, then handed over another list. "This is the data I gathered." It wasn't complete, and he'd had to use quite a bit of trickery to get some of it, including using DS Coulson's phone when she wasn't looking.

Ellie looked it over, then looked up at him with big grey eyes. "These are all devices I've used, aren't they?"

"I'm afraid so. Ellie, there's no evidence of anyone accessing those accounts but you. As you can see, the dates and times match up. Even if someone else was using your computer, the only times we have match the ones you gave me."

She was shaking her head. "There has to be someone else. Maybe the app companies didn't tell you everything."

"They told me the same thing they told you. I spoke to the police and got the same story. They can't do anything," he added gently, "because this isn't technically a crime."

Ellie's pale cheeks went pink. "Someone's hacking my computer and my phone!"

"There's no evidence for that. The only person to have accessed your devices is yourself. The data you've given me backs that up."

Ellie looked down at the notes in her lap. "So it's not

a hacker."

"It really doesn't look that way."

"So then... it's either a ghost or... it's me. Is that what you're saying?"

Quinn could feel Jen's eyes on him as he carefully worked out his response. "Ellie. Have you told anyone else about this? Friends, family, perhaps a teacher or a counsellor?"

She shook her head. "Who'd believe me?"

Jen would. He didn't look at her.

"I—I nearly told Georgia. At school. After she was going on about hiring you to look into the thing at the cottage." Ellie rolled her eyes, looking like a proper teenager for the first time. "She was so boring about it. You know she doesn't really believe there are ghosts out there? It's all, like, an attention-seeking thing."

"That's the conclusion I came to, too," Quinn agreed. "Ellie, did you take your computer to a different security expert like I suggested?"

She nodded, and reached into her bag to pull out a brand new laptop, tablet and phone. "They were checked for everything. I got them to run like five different checks for keystroke loggers. The phone is actually a new one. I only got it last month."

"And have you had any messages since then?"

She hesitated, then grabbed a sheet of paper tucked into her notebook. On it was a printed screencap of her computer screen with a message window open. He read:

"07700 900753 Unknown: ellie where r u?"

"07700 900753 Unknown: its me max i need to talk to u"

It was dated two days ago.

Quinn looked at the piece of paper. "It was a text?"

"Yes."

He looked at it some more. 07700 900753 Unknown. "Did you call it back?"

"What?"

Quinn looked up at Ellie. She'd gone white again. Quinn read the number out loud, faltering over the last three digits. "Did you call it back?"

"N-no."

Quinn drummed his fingers on the chair arm. Then he spun to his left and held out the print-out. "Jen, would you call this number for me, please? Put it on speaker."

"What?" stammered Ellie. Jen stared.

"Please," Quinn added, and Jen reached out for the paper. She smoothed it on the desk. She picked up the phone, and glanced over at him before turning it onto speaker.

Quinn gave her an encouraging smile.

Slowly, she dialled the number, whilst Ellie went whiter and whiter. Her fingers clutched her phone so hard he thought she'd break it.

At the final, cheerily rising tone of the number 3, a voice abruptly cut in.

"Calls to this number are not being connected."

It was a woman's voice, pleasantly modulated and obviously recorded. She went on to explain that the number was not available from this network, and then the call disconnected into silence.

Jen held the phone in one hand, apparently frozen.

"You see?" Quinn said to Ellie, who dragged in a breath and relaxed her fingers. "It's not a real number. It's a fake one, unassigned. Like in American cop shows where every phone number begins 555. They're set aside by the regulator."

Jen still hadn't replaced the receiver.

"A fake?" Ellie said.

"Yeah. Jen, you can put the phone down now."

"Huh? Oh." She hesitated, averting her eyes, then did.

"Ellie." Quinn leaned forward and gave her his most

approachable smile. It was not, he feared, very approachable at all. "Now, I know this is painful to think about, but last year when your brother died, were you assigned a counsellor or someone like that?"

Ellie seemed to shrink back into the sofa, her bony shoulders twisting and her face tilting away. Quinn recognised it for the involuntary body language it was. He was pretty sure he'd flinched away when people used to ask him about Ethan. He probably still did.

"Yes," she said, her voice almost lost.

"I'd like you to think about telling them this story. Whatever you say will be held in complete confidentiality. They don't have to tell your parents," he emphasised, which would be true insomuch as Ellie wasn't judged a danger to herself or others. He didn't think she was, any more than he'd been in those dark days after Ethan died.

"I'm not making this up," Ellie whispered, her eyes going pink and shiny.

"I'm not saying you are. But grief affects us all differently." He hesitated, and thought, *Ah, feck it.* "When I lost my brother I'd've given anything to hear from him again. To find a lost note or hear a voicemail. To pretend he hadn't gone."

A tear spilled out of Ellie's eye.

"And at the same time every reminder of him was so painful. Every time I saw a news item about him. I could never watch repeats of his show but sometimes just seeing the title of it in the listings was enough to send me over."

Ellie swiped at her eyes, sending mascara everywhere.

"Not to mention looking in the mirror," Quinn added, and Ellie sniffed and looked up at him.

"Does it get easier?" she hiccupped.

Quinn chewed his lip.

"It gets less hard," he suggested, and that drew a watery smile from her.

Later, after they'd seen Ellie into a cab bound for the station and were shutting up the office, Jen asked him off-handedly, "Is it true, about those fake numbers?"

"Sure. People use them for TV and such." Ethan had explained it once, when Quinn had asked if anyone ever dialled the numbers in *Devilborn*. He could still hear Ethan's voice, his own voice, reading one out. "Never tried to dial one before."

"So… you didn't know what you were going to hear?"

He watched her putting on her coat and buttoning it up. "Well, I didn't think it was going to be the voice of Max Robertson, did I?"

She shrugged.

"Did you?" Quinn asked, because talking to Jen about the whole ghost thing was like probing a sore tooth, but he couldn't help it.

She gave him a smile far too bright to be real. "I couldn't tell you what I was expecting," she said, and picked up her handbag. "See you on Monday."

Despite himself, Quinn's gaze lingered on the telephone.

CHAPTER TWENTY

"I heard it too," Danny said as Jen left the office. With Quinn watching, she said nothing, but gave a slight nod in his direction, and hurried down the stairs, repeating the bogus phone number to herself as she went.

As soon as she was out of view of the office, she dialled it.

"Calls to this number..." began the woman's recorded voice.

"...Ellie?" breathed a faint voice underneath it.

"Max, is that you?" Jen said, but then the recorded woman spoke again and if Max said anything else, she couldn't hear it. A car went past, the road noise drowning out any sound from the phone.

The walk home seemed to take forever, but once she was inside her own house, with the door shut against the world's noise, Jen turned up the speaker volume and dialled the phone again.

"Max?"

"—Not being connected—"

"...Ellie?"

"Max, can you hear me?"

The call cut out. Frustrated, Jen dialled again.

"Whatcha doing?" Alice said behind her.

"Listening. Be quiet."

"Ooh, sorry," Alice said, her tone so sulky Jen wondered briefly if she'd finally turned into a teenager.

The call cut out again. Jen turned to her little ghost. "Look—where have you even been this week?"

Alice shrugged. "Around. You've been ignoring me."

"You've been weird ever since the Paul Dunlop thing. The guy who hanged himself," she added when Alice looked blank. "I'm trying to contact this kid called Max who died last year. He's been sending his sister messages online."

"In my day we used seances," Alice said, regarding Jen's phone with suspicion.

"In your day you also used carrier pigeons. Look, all his accounts have been shut down but he's managing to contact Ellie using this fake number. Do you think it's possible he's got somehow... trapped in cyberspace?"

"I don't even know what that is," said Alice, which was something of a lie since she'd comprehended it perfectly well in the past.

Jen looked at her phone in her hand and realised she was still wearing her coat and boots. Taking them off, she reached for her laptop and flicked it on.

"All right, my little Luddite, how about this for an analogy. Imagine you did most of your communication by letter."

"Luddites went out of fashion years before I was born," yawned Alice.

"Pay attention. You wrote detailed letters to everyone in your life. You got stuck in such a pattern," Jen went on rapidly, thinking it through, "that you hardly ever spoke to real people. And when you died, the only way to communicate from the hereafter was not by appearing to your loved ones, but by writing to them. Are you with me?"

"He's stuck in Facebook," Alice said, and when Jen frowned, she shrugged and added, "I was just messing with you. So he's trying to contact his sister using the Internet?"

"And her mobile phone. Think about it. It's how most kids communicate these days. I mean, even I prefer to write texts and emails rather than actually speak to my family."

"That's because your family are perfectly horrid," Alice said. "All right, so this boy is haunting his sister through her mobile phone. What about it?"

Jen searched for Max Robertson on a few social media sites, but Ellie had been telling the truth when she said his accounts had been shut down.

"What if he's trying to tell her something?"

"Then he'd have told her."

Jen frowned at her computer for a few moments, trying to remember what had been in those messages. Her work email was only accessible from the office computer, and Quinn had all the files.

Quinn, who had never looked more genuine than when he said he'd give anything to hear his brother's voice again.

I could tell you the last things he said.

She shook herself. Maybe the things Max was saying were nothing more than echoes, bouncing around the airwaves, playing themselves out. Like that echo of an airman out in the woods. Only, hadn't Max mentioned having his foot cut off? That had happened after he died. That wouldn't have been an echo of anything he did while living.

She picked up her phone, and redialled. "Maybe he'll tell me," she said.

On Monday, Quinn arrived at the office to find Jen

already there, industriously typing away at something. She gave him a distracted smile and looked back at the screen.

"Morning," said Tessa, poking her head out of her office. "Listen, are you going home any time soon?"

"Well, I figured that come five o'clock or so…"

She rolled her eyes. "I meant Ireland. I've hit a brick wall with Mrs Mac."

"Ah." He flicked on the kettle. "Where've you got to?"

"1704. Only another fifty-five years to go."

At that, Jen looked up. "Why, what happened in 1649?"

"Siege of Drogheda," Quinn told her. "Your man Cromwell decided to go on the rampage and kill all the Irish Catholics he could find."

"On behalf of my country, I apologise," Jen said.

"Duly noted. I'll try not to hold it against you," said Quinn, and tried not to think about holding Jen.

"Mrs Macanally is convinced she's descended from one of the Irish commanders," Tessa said.

Quinn grinned. "One Arthur Aston, a man with whom I've something in common."

"What, did he never comb his hair, either?" murmured Jen, eyes back on her screen.

Quinn shoved a hand through his hair, scowling at her. "He'd a wooden leg."

"Yours isn't wooden."

"And you hopefully won't be beaten to death with it," Tessa put in, sounding amused. "Apparently the enemy soldiers believed his leg contained gold coins, although quite why that was a reason to bludgeon his brains out, I'm not sure."

Jen made a face. "I'd avoid Drogheda if I were you."

"Might be difficult," Quinn said. To Tessa he asked, "Aston did have children, did he?"

"Yes. But they mostly seem to have been born when he was serving in Germany and Poland. And rather than trying to trace forward from them, I figure it's got to be a damn sight easier to trace back from Mrs Mac."

"Not to mention you don't speak Polish," Quinn said.

"Not to mention. Look, I just wondered if you were heading over that way any time soon. You'll probably get a better reception than I will."

"This accent is a whole lot less charming over there than it is here," Quinn said, but he held his hand out for Tessa's notes. "I might be going over in a week or two. Uncle Kieran has something he wants me to look at, and I should probably go and see my mum."

Tessa's gaze flew quickly to the wall calendar.

"I'll be back before November," Quinn said shortly, and finished making his tea.

"Why?" said Jen, scanning the calendar for anything of relevance. "What happens in November?"

Tessa said nothing. Quinn looked at Jen for a brief moment, then away. "Ethan doesn't turn 33."

"Ouch," said Danny, as Quinn's door shut behind him.

"Well, how was I supposed to know?" Jen muttered, glancing sheepishly at Tessa. "Why doesn't he want to see his mum when it's his birthday?"

"Because she thinks he's Ethan." Tessa sighed and dropped her voice. "Kieran told me about it. You know he used to be my boss before Quinn took over? Well, he had to sort out everything after the... erm, accident. Not just about poor Ethan but about their mother, too."

Tessa glanced in the direction of Quinn's office and lowered her voice even further. "The reason Quinn was over in London in the first place was to talk to Ethan about putting their mother in a home. Dementia, apparently. Quinn was the only one who saw her regularly enough to know how bad it was. Kieran said he was shocked when he finally saw her. And now of course when she sees Quinn, half the time she thinks it's Ethan. I can't imagine how painful that is for him."

His mother had dementia? His father died, his twin brother died, and now his mother was sliding away too. Jen bit her lip and looked over at Quinn's office.

"But for God's sake don't breathe a word of this. Not to a living soul, you understand?"

"Oh, of course," Jen said, not looking at either of the ghosts in the room. "Not a living soul."

After Tessa had gone back into her office, Jen opened the search window she'd been using before she'd heard Quinn's tread on the stairs. Frustrated by a whole weekend unable to access the messages Ellie claimed to have received from Max, she'd been waiting outside when Tessa turned up this morning.

There they were, those messages. Max said he was trapped. He said he'd gone too far. He said he needed to talk to her.

He said he needed to come out.

Jen tapped Ellie's phone number into her mobile and started counting down the hours until she could escape the office for lunch.

"Jolly sad about old Quinn's mater, isn't it?" Danny said.

Jen cleared her browser history and shut down the window.

"It is," she said quietly. "Seems horribly unfair after everything else he's gone through."

"Good job he still has his uncle," Danny said.

"D'you remember him? Is he nice?"

"Oh yes, capital fellow. Rather Irish, but that can't be helped."

Alice rolled her eyes.

"I mean to say, I once knew a lovely Irish lass. Quite in love with her, I was. So you can't say I..." Danny trailed off, his frown deepening. "Really lovely lass," he said. "I wonder where she went?"

"She probably married someone who didn't die," Alice drawled.

For a moment Danny looked crestfallen. "Probably," he said. Then he rallied, as he always did. "Anyway. What's all this with the girl whose telephone is haunted? What have you discovered?"

"I'll tell you after I've spoken to her," Jen said.

Time dragged that morning, and she was practically dancing by the time lunchtime came around and she could leave the office without fabricating a ridiculous excuse. Making her way hurriedly to the seafront, where neither Tessa nor Quinn were likely to happen upon her, she found an empty bench and sat down to dial Ellie Robertson.

It went to voicemail. Jen nearly screamed. Then she reminded herself that if she'd been getting weird texts from unknown numbers she might not pick up either.

"Ellie, this is Jen Hargrave from the Sullivan Investigations agency. We met on Friday. I know you've had an official report from Quinn—that is, from Mr Quinn, but I wanted to talk to you myself. You see, the thing is—"she took a deep breath, "I do believe you. I think maybe your brother is trying to contact you about something and I wanted to ask you a few questions about what that might have been." She paused, not sure how much more to say. "So maybe you could give me a call back and we'll have a chat. Thanks."

She waited five minutes, but Ellie didn't call until Jen got up to leave.

"Ms Hargrave?" The girl sounded hesitant, and very young.

"Ellie. I'm so glad you called me back." Jen fixed her gaze on the weathered lifebelt fastened to the railings. Half the letters stencilled on it were missing or smudged away, so it seemed to read *Wird on-set.*

"Look, I'm not sure—Mr Quinn seemed to think it was all me doing this anyway."

"He believes there's always a rational explanation. Look, let's say it was you doing this subconsciously, okay? Without your own knowledge. Why would you want to talk to your brother again? Do you think there's something he wants to tell you?"

Ellie paused for such a long time Jen thought she'd put the phone down and walked away.

"I dunno," she said eventually, her voice slightly wobbly.

"Because I've been rereading those messages and there was something that occurred to me. Did Max have a girlfriend?"

"No," said Ellie, with such surprise that Jen believed her.

"Boyfriend?"

This time the hesitation was the convincing factor. "No."

"But was there someone," Jen asked as gently as she could, "who he liked? Someone he maybe didn't want anyone else to know he liked?"

A really long silence this time. "Maybe," Ellie whispered.

"And was this person with him on holiday? You see, I'm wondering if maybe Max got up the courage to tell this someone that he liked them, and got turned down, and maybe that's why he swam too far and dived too deep."

The ragged intake of breath from Ellie sounded like she was trying not to cry. "Will was with him," she said. "Will Blackbourne."

Jen closed her eyes and let out a sigh. It had taken her half the night to get a name from Max, syllable by syllable, and neither she nor Alice had been totally sure they'd got it right. 'Will' and 'black' weren't immediately recognisable as names.

"He said 'will you help me,'" she said gently.

"I thought he was asking me for help!" Ellie sobbed. "He wanted Will to help him? Oh my God, do you think Will killed him?"

"No," said Jen, although she really wasn't sure. "But maybe you need to talk to him. Clear the air. Maybe that's what Max wanted."

Ellie sniffed and cried some more, and then she said, "Do you really think it was Max? Not me?"

"I think either way you should talk to Will," Jen said, and then added, "but, er, don't take any risks or anything, will you? Maybe go somewhere public."

"Okay," Ellie sniffed.

Jen talked to her for a few minutes more, then hung up, and dialled Max's phantom number.

"She's going to talk to Will. She's not in any danger, is she?"

"No," came the faintest of answers, and then the line went dead.

Quinn had met Tessa a few days after leaving hospital and moving in with Uncle Kieran. She'd come round with a stack of DVDs 'in case you get bored', which was probably the kindest thing anyone had done for him since the Angel of the White Lady saved his life.

She'd had Jack in a pushchair and Emily on leading reins and a file of paper stuck under one arm, which rather predictably spilled everywhere. Quinn watched her pick it up, pinned helplessly to the sofa with the stump of his leg resting on a cushion.

"It's just a case I'm working on," Tessa said, flustered, scooping it all together. "For your uncle. I've been working part time for him."

"Anything interesting?" Quinn asked idly.

Within days, he'd started helping out with casework, reading files and searching the Internet. A few weeks later, he'd officially signed up to become Kieran's apprentice. In less than a year, he'd taken over the firm.

Which meant he'd spent a lot of time with Tessa. Which meant he knew when she was up to something.

He sneaked out as quietly as he could to make some tea whilst she was on the phone, but the damn kettle was being stupidly slow and he hadn't even put the teabag in his Kiss Me I'm Irish mug before she darted out to stand there as nonchalantly as possible, watching him.

"If you send me what you've got on Mrs Mac I'll see what I can find out," he said, not looking up.

"It's already on the server. When are you going to Ireland?"

"Probably next week. Haven't looked at flights yet." The kettle clicked off and he poured water in. "I'll let you know."

"Going by yourself?"

He flicked her a glance. Her eyes were all big and innocent. Quinn shook his head and got the milk out of the fridge.

"We don't need to both go."

"No, but we could probably spare Jen for a few days…"

The milk thumped down on the counter. "Tessa, if you've something to say, say it."

She leaned back against Jen's desk. "I'm just saying it might be nice to take her away for a few days. I hear Dublin is a beautiful city."

"It is."

"And very romantic."

Quinn poured the milk into his mug and ignored that last comment.

"Come on, Quinn. I am a detective. And I know you too well."

"Oh, do you? So are you comparing my behaviour with Jen to my behaviour with all my other girlfriends?"

"What girlfriends?" Tessa said.

"Exactly."

She frowned and folded her arms. "You like her," she said accusingly.

"Oh, for the love of…" What was it going to take? The truth?

Actually… maybe. Yes. The truth.

Quinn raised his palms. "Yes, all right, I do like her." *Even if she's totally gone in the head, I like her. Dammit.* "All right? Happy now?"

Tessa actually clapped her hands and squealed like a little girl. "Oh my God!"

"But before you go around picking out bridesmaid frocks," he wagged the teaspoon warningly at her, "you might want to bear in mind that she doesn't actually like me back."

Tessa stopped mid clap. "What? No. Rubbish."

"Swear to God. She's made it perfectly clear."

"But…" Tessa looked him up and down. "But… have you *seen* you?"

"Generally I try not to." Quinn saluted her with his cup of tea, wishing he had some whiskey to pour in it.

"Quinn."

"I don't want to see Ethan, all right?"

Tessa opened her mouth and then shut it again. Her head tilted in that specific way that usually meant sympathy was on the way.

"You're not your brother."

"No. Women usually fancied him back." He took a sip. "Look, the heart wants what it wants, all right? And hers doesn't want me. And that's fine. I'm not madly in love with her or anything. I just… think she's nice," he lied, as if he hadn't fantasised about what she wore under all those greys and blacks. "So don't go getting all overexcited about it, all right?"

"I just think you'd be really good together," Tessa said.

Quinn recalled the way Jen had felt pressed against him. The taste of her lips. The soft sound she'd made when he caressed her. *Oh God, we'd be so good together.*

And then he forced himself to remember she believed in all that spooky supernatural bollocks.

"No, we wouldn't," he said, and slammed his office door behind him as he left.

When Jen got back to the office, she found an email from Quinn forwarding on the details of his flight next week to Dublin. He'd appended: "I'll have my phone and laptop and wifi is generally quite good so I'll be able to stay in touch, but don't go sending me a lot."

She added the dates to the office calendar, then glanced at the rest of the month. Hallowe'en was coming up, which usually meant a load of Hollywood sanitised ghosty rubbish and silly scary movies, coupled with some genuinely unpleasant happenings should she be stupid enough to go near a churchyard.

And after that... when was Quinn's birthday? Should she send him a card? Would that be a normal thing to do, or something horribly cruel? Should she ask him when his birthday was, or ask Tessa, or—*no, wait, stupid.* It was a matter of public record.

Right then Tessa appeared with some reports to file, and then Danny drifted in and out, and it was late in the afternoon by the time Jen got her chance. Quinn's phone rang, and she saw him lean back in his chair as he answered it.

She quickly opened a browser window and googled Ethan Sullivan.

Born: 5th November 1985, Dalkey, Co. Dublin. Died

—

No, she didn't need to be reminded of that.

She started to type Quinn's birthday into her phone calendar, then stopped herself, snorting. "Remember, remember, the fifth of November," she murmured.

"Gunpowder, treason and plot," chimed in Danny cheerfully, emerging through the window from Quinn's office. "I say old girl, what have you been up to in your lunch hour?"

"What do you mean?" Jen said, as Quinn's door opened and he regarded her with his head tilted.

"I haven't said anything," he said.

"No. Sorry. Talking to myself." His eyes narrowed infinitesimally. "I got your email about the flights, by the way."

"Right." He hesitated, rubbing the back of his neck as if he was tired. "Listen, have you heard anything else from Ellie Robertson?"

Oh bollocks. She'd forgotten to tell Ellie to keep this to herself. She flicked a glance at Danny, who nodded and said, "Afraid so, old bean."

"Is that who you were speaking to?" Jen asked.

"Yeah." Quinn appeared to be trying to think of a way to say something. Eventually he said, "How the hell did you know he was gay?"

"Who?"

"Don't 'who' me. Her brother. Max. He was in the closet."

"The boy was a shirt-lifter?" cried Danny, and was ignored by Jen.

"Gosh. Must've been difficult for him."

Quinn's brows drew down, his eyes narrowing as if he wasn't sure whether to be annoyed or amused.

"What do you know about it?"

"Nothing!" Relenting, she explained carefully, "I just wondered if there was another side to the story. If Ellie was sending these messages to herself, then maybe she had a subconscious reason to. Look at all the things about coming out and being trapped. I just… wondered if she knew something she hadn't told us."

Quinn ran a hand through his hair. "Well, she did. Or she thought she did. Turns out Max wasn't alone when he went diving. He was with a friend. Will Blackbourne. Go on, look him up," he said, gesturing to her computer and muttering something that sounded like, 'if you haven't already.'

Jen had, of course, but she made a show of looking him up via Ellie's Facebook page.

"All Will said in his statements was that they'd got separated and he couldn't find Max, so he decided to raise the alarm," said Quinn.

"Aha!" said Danny. "So this Will did the deed, did he? Young Max does something to frighten the horses and William panics and holds him under the water!"

"You don't suspect foul play, do you?" Jen asked Quinn.

"Of course I do. Once a guard, always a guard." Quinn flung himself at the sofa, scowling. God dammit, he even scowled beautifully.

Jen opened Will's profile, and looked upon blue eyes and blond hair and wonderful cheekbones. "Oh, there he is." Just to annoy him, she added, "Wow, handsome boy."

Quinn scowled all the harder.

"D'you think there was some sibling rivalry there? They both fancied him?"

"Yes," said Quinn simply. "And maybe that's why Ellie never mentioned Will."

"To protect him."

Quinn nodded, and neither of them said anything for a moment. Quinn turned to flick on the kettle, and Jen made a quick throat-slashing gesture to Danny. Looking peeved, he vanished.

"The thing is, plenty of times Ethan and I fancied the same girl," Quinn said.

And did that girl ever try to kill you? Jen forced a smile. "Is that so?"

"Sure. And every bloody time, she went for him. Without fail. I mean, I know it was never a looks issue," he said morosely.

I think you're better looking than Ethan.

"Must just be your sparkling personality putting them all off," Jen said.

"Does it put you off?" he asked. "No, don't answer me. I'm depressed enough as it is." The kettle flicked off and he turned to tip a teabag into his mug, thereby missing the way Jen stared at the line of his jaw.

You cannot fancy Quinn. It's the worst idea in the world.

"You don't half drink a lot of tea," she said, trying to change the subject.

"Better than drinking whiskey all day," Quinn said, and side-eyed her. "Wait, are you saying you don't fancy me because I drink too much… tea?"

She felt her cheeks flush. "Don't be ridiculous. Look, what did Ellie say? What happened with Will?"

Quinn looked at her for a moment, chewing on his lip, then shook his head and said, "She confronted him about the day Max died. Asked if something had happened between them. And, cut a long story short, it had." He waved the coffee jar at her.

Jen nodded. "Will's gay too?"

"No. But it sounds like Max made his move anyway. Will was horrified, brutally rebuffed his friend, and swam away. He says Max swam the other way and that was the last he saw of him."

"Do you think he's telling the truth?"

Quinn finished making their drinks before he

answered. "I'd need to speak to him direct, really, but... I'm inclined to say yes. It has the ring of truth to it. I mean, for a lot of guys that's going to be kind of a shock. I'm not sure I'd've reacted well in the circumstances."

Jen sipped her coffee. "Poor Max."

"Poor Max," Quinn agreed. "And poor Will, too, maybe."

"What do you mean, maybe?" Jen's throat got a bit tight. "If all this is true then Will's been walking around knowing that what he did caused his friend's death."

"If he's telling the truth. For all we know he was so upset he held Max's head under the water 'til he stopped kicking."

"Or maybe he just tried to give it to him straight because he knew it was never going to work," Jen said, her fingers clenching on her coffee mug. "Does that mean he's guilty of murder?"

Quinn gave her a strange look. "No, of course not. Christ, imagine if you were held to account for everything someone did when you turned them down."

"Imagine." *Don't break this mug too.*

"Mind you, seems that's what happened with Beth and Paul Dunlop."

"Well, it's not Beth's fault that Paul hanged himself," Jen said tightly.

"No, I meant he reacted badly in the first..." he tapered off. "Are you all right?"

"Sure. Fine. Just a little chilly in here. Why is it always cold?" Jen babbled.

"God knows. The heating works fine and I've checked for draughts. It's why I drink so much tea." Quinn stood up and added, "Maybe it's a ghost."

Jen barely managed a smile at that.

CHAPTER TWENTY-ONE

The White Lady: two days after

The blood wells up shockingly fast, a thin red line that rapidly bubbles over onto her white skin. It's July, but Jen hasn't made an effort to tan and her midriff and upper thighs are still white. And now they're purple with bruises and red with blood.

This one, the one on her thigh, is the newest. She's scored it herself with nail scissors, which turned out to be pleasingly sharper than she expected. It stings, like lemon juice or tequila, a good sting, and one that lasts longer. When the sting fades it'll be to a throb, until she pulls the wound open again to watch it bleed.

She's been doing that with all the cuts he gave her. Poking at them, pushing until they hurt and then hurt a bit more. Making them bleed and throb and hurt. At the hospital they told her she might have some residual side effects from the bomb, like ringing in her ears or nausea or coughing, but the only thing she's actually felt in the last two days—has it only been two? Two days?—has been the sting and throb of the cuts and bruises that came after the bomb.

After the bomb, after the hospital, after that mad dash to his place. After the first time and the second time and the…

The blood is staunching itself, the flow slowing. She puts down the scissors and pinches the cut to make it bleed worse.

His sweatshirt is hanging on the back of her door. He lent it to her when her t-shirt fell apart in her hands. She's washed it, several times, so it doesn't smell of smoke any more. She's washed her hair, shampooed it three times in a row, scrubbed herself with soap that got into every cut and made it sting so hard it brought tears to her eyes.

She likes those tears. She needs them.

The sweatshirt is dark blue and hooded. A sombre colour for Jen, who likes pinks and purples. It's too big for her. She should probably return it.

She wipes the blood from her leg and stands up, getting dressed in a t-shirt and skirt that covers the new cut. The girls in the home always covered theirs up, too, and Jen never quite realised why until now. Because if anyone saw them, they'd ask what had happened, and she'd have to lie. Best not to show them. Nobody would understand.

She fastens her hair back so the heat won't plaster it to her neck. It's blue now. The dye had been sitting there on the shelf, remnant of a whim she'd forgotten about. She'd expected the familiar shock of seeing herself with new hair, but nothing seems to shock her right now. It'll fade soon enough.

His flat isn't far from the Overground station. She knows that because she tried to get home that way yesterday and her Oyster card wouldn't work. Her phone screen had shattered, and her Oyster had fused to its case, but her credit cards and house keys were fine. The contents of her handbag had been hit-and-miss. There was a lipstick in there Abby had left behind once. Jen had meant to give it back to her. But now it's melted into its packaging and Abby is in several body bags in a morgue somewhere.

Jen knows what brand it was. She'll never buy it now.

She buys a new Oyster now and travels to Shoreditch with her head down. The place is full of men with ironic beards and women dressed like their grandmothers. No one even glances at the strands of blue wisping from under the dark hoodie. The cut on her thigh stings privately as sweat runs into it.

She finds the right door, a black one, unmarked but for the graffiti in the corner. There's no entryphone. She just pushes the door open and goes up the stairs, noisy metal steps that are probably meant to look like they've been there since the warehouse was built.

His door is at the top. It's red.

He might not even be in.

But he is in, and when he answers the door she pushes back her hood and looks up at him. His hair is damp and his shirt clings to his chest. His eyes are dark and sunken.

"I brought your sweater back," she says.

"I said you could keep it," he replies, and stands back to let her in. As he turns to shut the door behind her, she notices a bruise on his neck. *I did that*.

"Take it off," he says, as she stands in the middle of the room.

She pulls off the sweater, and holds it out to him.

"I said you should keep it," he repeats.

"I know."

"Why did you bring it back?"

"Why did you ask me to take it off?"

He doesn't smile. His eyes seem to burn right

through her.

"It's hot," he says, and begins to unbutton his shirt.

Jen watches as his skin is revealed to her. Pale, then dark: purple and red and pink. When his shirt hits the floor she raises the hem of her skirt. The new cut glows there.

He closes the gap between them, falls to his knees. Licks the length of that cut. Jen tenses in anticipation, and his eyes meet hers. He's watching her as he nips the broken skin with his teeth.

Sweet pain makes her gasp. "Again," she says. "Do it again."

CHAPTER TWENTY-TWO

People didn't recognise Quinn half so much as they used to. When Ethan had first got famous, Quinn had taken a flight over to see him, and he hadn't got beyond the check-in desk before someone said, "D'you know, until I saw your passport I thought you were that feller off the telly!"

These days, thanks to the twin miracles of technology and not getting his hair cut, he could make it all the way through the airport without anyone putting two and two together. Now he took his seat on the plane, fell asleep and, given by the sniggering looks he collected, snored a bit, and washed up at passport control without anyone recognising him. Machines might recognise whether you matched your passport, but they didn't care if you looked like someone famous.

Now he joined the queue for Immigration at Dublin airport and saw, joy of joys, that they'd installed automated gates. Passengers were avoiding them like the plague, despite the half-hearted efforts of the young lad waving them on.

"Will I use one of these?" Quinn asked, and the kid

shrugged and said optimistically, "Ah, you can give it a go."

Quinn smiled, and stepped forward. The machine scanned his passport, the camera read his face, and the barrier opened.

"I bloody love technology," he said, walking forward into Ireland.

As he mooched towards baggage reclaim he remembered Ethan laughing with him after his first visit to America. "They shuffle you all forwards into this huge, big long queue, no cellphones, lots of angry looking staff and big American flags, and when you finally get forward to one of the booths there's this humourless eejit trying to make you feel like a criminal. They want to know every bloody thing about how long you're staying and what you're staying for, and God help you if you make a joke! And then, this is my favourite bit, they scan your eyes and your fingertips. And I asked what that was for, and the feller said, 'It's so we can identify you if you outstay your visa, sir.' And I thought, ah sure now! You and I could pull a nice one on them, eh Jim?"

By the time he reached the baggage carousel, his smile had faded into a scowl that had a small child running away from him. Quinn watched his hands unlocking a trolley, hauling his flight cases and holdall onto it, and pushing the whole unwieldy cart out into Arrivals. He looked at his fingers as he texted Uncle Kieran to say he'd arrived.

Somewhere on An Garda Síochána's database were the fingerprints of Quinn, James and Quinn, Ethan. They'd done it for fun, to settle a bet between some of Quinn's colleagues, a comparison between Quinn's meticulously collected prints and the smudged set Ethan had sent over in an envelope splattered with red wine and perfume. The analysis, not exactly a priority, had come back just a little too late to be funny. It sat on Quinn's desk for weeks before someone thought to forward it onto him as he convalesced in Uncle Kieran's spare room.

"Well, you're a sight for sore eyes."

Uncle Kieran stood there, arms held wide for a hug. Quinn leaned in, patting his uncle on the back.

"I wouldn't inflict me on anyone with sore eyes. Tessa says I look like a hobo."

Kieran held him at arm's length and looked him over critically. "Well now, you could be right. Awful ugly is what you are."

Quinn laughed. "I made a girl cry just now, so." He'd certainly upset Jen enough.

Kieran pushed the trolley towards the exit. "Good flight?"

"Not bad. Nearly lost the use of my arm to the drinks trolley."

"They serve drinks now?" Kieran asked with mock astonishment, turning towards the car park.

"Once you've taken out a mortgage for them." Quinn breathed in the diesel and petrol scented air of his homeland. "Thanks for picking me up. I'd've got the Aircoach."

Kieran flicked his hand dismissively. "Not a bother. Mind, they're after charging me three euro for parking. Three euro! For twenty minutes."

"It's a scandal," Quinn agreed solemnly, knowing he would offer to pay it later, and also knowing that his uncle would never let him.

"Now, your cousin Emer came by last week and I was after telling her you were coming over, and she said why don't we have lunch this week? Her youngest is at school in Dalkey, and she works up at the hotel, it's only five minutes into town, so…"

His uncle talked on as they made their way to the car

249

and loaded the flight cases containing Quinn's recording equipment into it. It kind of shocked Quinn, how much older his uncle seemed, talking on about people Quinn hardly remembered and giving out over the weight of one of the equipment cases. Somehow he'd managed to preserve his image of Kieran as the dashing private detective he'd visited as a teenager, all dynamic intelligence and charm, driving everywhere at thrilling speeds and winking at ladies who admired him in the street.

Uncle Kieran, the man who'd stepped in and taken care of them all when Quinn's father died. He'd seemed like a rock then. Calm, implacable, kind. The man who'd helped arrange the funeral, who'd fixed things around the house, who'd talked things through late at night with Ethan when he declared he wanted to run away to be an actor. The man who helped Quinn with his application to An Garda Síochána.

The man who'd visited Quinn in hospital, made inappropriate jokes, then arranged to have a stairlift put in his own house so Quinn could recuperate there. The man who'd settled his younger sister in a care home when one of her sons was unable to and the other one was dead.

You're not the only one who's changed, Quinn you eejit.

Quinn nodded at appropriate intervals as his uncle talked on. They were halfway down the motorway before he realised they weren't taking the coast road, as his uncle usually preferred, but the longer inland route.

"Are they digging up the docks again?" he asked at a break in Kieran's updating of what his cousin Aislin's kids were up to these days.

"They're always digging up the docks," his uncle replied easily, changing lanes at a speed which still had Quinn grasping the door handle after all these years.

"Right, but…" a road sign caught his eye, and Quinn sighed. "We're going to Rathmichael, aren't we?" To the house where people kept falling down the stairs.

Kieran looked somewhat shifty. "Well, it's almost on the way."

Quinn pulled down the vanity mirror and ran a hand over his jaw, which he'd probably shaved at some point in the last week, and through his hair, which looked like he'd been dragged through a hedge backwards.

"Don't I get the chance to freshen up? I look like a hobo."

"The beard is very fashionable these days. I do be seeing young men on Grafton Street with—"

"Uncle Kieran, there's a world of difference between a hipster beard and someone who's forgotten his razor." He sighed and put the mirror away. *At least you don't look like Ethan today.* "Will I not even have a cup of tea?"

"I'm sure Mrs Kelly has tea. Ah cheer up, son. What's the worst that could happen?"

With Quinn gone from the office, the place seemed a lot quieter. Tessa still whirled around the place, always looking for something or late for an appointment, and Danny and Alice still drifted in and out, being unhelpful, but the office still lacked something.

"A miserable old grump who drinks too much tea," Danny opined when she mentioned this.

"He really does drink a lot of tea. I thought the English were bad."

"Could be worse, old bean. There's a bottle of whiskey in his desk."

Jen looked up. "You think he's spiking his own tea?"

"No. I think he's drinking tea instead of whiskey." Danny drifted down to the sofa and put his booted feet up on the table. "I knew a fellow once, a mechanic chappie, frightfully good with machines so long as he hadn't had a skinful the night before. Eventually of course, once the war broke out he had to give up the booze. Can't be risking an aircraft to a hangover! So he took up smoking instead. I can hardly picture him without a fag in his mouth. What was his name now? Higgins, Figgins? Something like that…"

Jen frowned, no longer listening. It was true, Quinn did seem to have a pint in his hand a lot of the time. And yes, he'd brought out a bottle of whiskey when Beth had been attacked. *Let's face it, you'd drink if you were him.*

"It's just another addiction," she muttered, and as she moved her head a shaft of light caught the blade of the letter opener on her desk. *I know all about those.*

Her computer flashed up a new email, and she shook off that thought and started reading it. It was Ellie Robertson, thanking Jen for her help.

"I think I was scared that Will had somehow been the cause of Max's death," she'd written. "And I think Will was scared of it too. I knew he'd missed something out of the police report, but now I can see that he was just scared of telling people the truth about Max. Now we've talked it over and we think the best thing is not to keep it a secret any more. I think if Max was still alive he'd have come out by now, and if he'd stayed in the closet it would have made him unhappy. So we're going to out him and hope that makes him happy, wherever he is. I guess it's true that honesty is the best policy. I certainly haven't had any more messages from 'him'."

Ellie's Facebook page showed a picture of herself and Will smiling together at a school sports event.

"Another satisfied client," Jen said, as Tessa opened her door and wandered out to check the printer. "Ellie Robertson," she clarified. "Her phone appears to be no longer haunted." *But I'm going to call Max's number just to be sure.*

"I almost wished it was a ghost," Tessa said, peering at the printer, which was inscrutably not printing anything. "Be nice to find something Quinn couldn't explain away with science."

Jen shrugged. "He'll see what he wants to see," she said.

"He's so adamant about not believing in ghosts. Mind you, I can hardly blame him."

"Why?"

Tessa poked at the paper in the printer tray and frowned before replying, "Well, wouldn't you be? It's bad enough seeing Ethan every time he looks in the mirror."

It's bad enough for me too.

"You'd think he'd want to see him," Danny said from the sofa. "There are plenty of people I'd give anything to see again."

"But there was no bad blood between them, was there? I mean, they got on. And it's not as though Ethan's dying was Quinn's fault."

Tessa lifted the printer lid and tugged at a piece of jammed paper. "No," she agreed, "but you don't need a psychiatrist to see why he's messed up about it. Ethan is gone and Quinn's still here, hale and healthy. Well, mostly. Ha!" This last seemed to be aimed at the printer, which finally gurgled into life.

"Survivor's guilt," Danny said, nodding sagely. "Dreadful thing."

Jen said nothing. Tessa glanced over, and winced. "Ah, crap. I'm sorry. You probably don't... I keep forgetting you were, um, involved."

Jen's fingers tightened on the arms of her chair. *Bad choice of words.* "It's fine."

"Quinn never talks about it. I mean, if it wasn't for Kieran telling me about it I wouldn't know anything. I can't even imagine the trauma... how do you recover from that?"

Jen shrugged. "There was counselling. I wouldn't be surprised if a few people didn't take up drinking or drugs."

"Did you? You don't have to tell me," Tessa added hurriedly.

"No. Nothing like that."

"Don't suppose Alice would've let you," Danny said, looking at her with concern.

Alice wasn't there.

Of all the things Alice had ever done to Jen, abandoning her after the White Lady was still the worst.

"Well, anyway," Tessa said into the silence, "I've got things to do. Still going back into Mrs Mac's history."

"Is she still trying to find that ancestor from the seventeenth century?"

"Yep. If Quinn doesn't find anything I'll have to get back to her and explain this really isn't my field of expertise. I mean I could start going to Poland and trace back that way, but it will be expensive and very slow. Translators and the like. I think she's been watching too much *Who Do You Think You Are*."

Jen chewed her lip and fought the urge to look around for Alice. "How hard is it, to find one person? I mean, say, if they were born in the UK and you knew approximately when?"

"Not that hard. You can search the BMD records for free. Births, marriages and deaths," Tessa explained. "The actual certificates give you more detail, but you have to pay for them. Why? Are you looking for someone?"

"Just… an old family story, I suppose. A photo we have," Jen invented, "of a little girl in Victorian dress. It's labelled Alice." Danny's gaze met hers, suddenly sharp. "I've always assumed she's a relative."

"Is there a date? Do you know which side of the

family?"

Please don't let her turn up before I've told Tessa this. "Mid-nineteenth century. She died when she was nine, that's why we have the picture."

Tessa made a face. "It's awful how many child deaths you find when you start looking back. Mrs Mac has one relative who had seven children and they all died. The census lists it, you see, or it did then."

Awful, Jen thought, but useful. "So you think she shouldn't be hard to find?"

"The more data you have, the more accurate you can be. A child called Alice dying over a hundred years ago…you'll find hundreds of them, I'm afraid. Do you have a location?"

"No," Jen said slowly, "but I can find out."

"How's she been?" Quinn asked as he picked up the car keys.

Kieran raised his palms. "She ebbs and she flows. Sometimes seems to forget she lives there. Asks to come home." He paused. "Says she doesn't like this holiday."

Quinn rubbed at his forehead. He'd already got a headache and he hadn't even left the house yet.

"She ask after Ethan?"

"You know she does."

"And me?"

Kieran didn't look at him. Quinn couldn't blame him. Even asking the question was like poking at a wound.

"Not so much, son."

"Grand. Well, I'll see you later." He gathered up a cellophane-wrapped bunch of flowers. "Get us some beers in, willya? I'm going to need some."

It wasn't a long drive to the care home. It was off the road in a residential area, a hodgepodge of buildings added together and built over with hardly any room for parking. *Where you send the people you don't want. The ones that don't fit in or get in the way.*

Be patient with her, Quinn told himself. It's not her fault.

He got out into the light drizzle, looked over the uninspiring grey brick and steel-framed windows, and braced himself.

The dry, hot air hit as soon as the door was opened to admit him. God, it smelled like a hospital. *Why are they always so hot?* A woman in a tabard smiled at him and asked in a foreign accent who he was here to see.

Quinn found a smile for her, since she didn't seem to have recognised him. "Dervla Quinn. I'm her son."

She ran her finger down a list. "Mrs Quinn... She's in the day room. Upstairs. You want I take you through?"

Maybe Mum's stopped going on about her famous son. "No, I remember the way."

He passed the ground floor rooms and the lift, taking the stairs just because he could and wishing he hadn't when he arrived at the top sweating. His throat was dry. *It's just the heat.*

The day room was at the back of the house, positioned to take in the sunlight, should there ever be any. He paused and looked around at the overstuffed chairs, the walking frames and wheelchairs, all the unfamiliar faces, and for a moment panic swamped him because he couldn't recognise his own mother.

No, there she was. In a blue sweater and skirt, her feet neatly in slippers. Her hair had been styled into a candyfloss style that made her look like someone else and her lipstick was rather too pink.

Uncle Kieran wasn't the only one who'd got old, but at least he'd aged on his own terms.

"Hi, Mum."

For a moment her expression was blank as she looked up at him. Then it suddenly lightened. "Well, the dead arose and appeared to many!" she cried.

Of all the phrases.

Around her, a few other residents stirred and looked over. By the door, one of the carers looked up from his paperwork. His eyes widened when he saw Quinn standing there, and then his face clenched in pity.

"What's that?" said an old gent with an English accent. "Dead arising? Blasphemy!"

"Sure it's a common expression in Ireland, Colonel," said the carer. "It just means she hasn't seen him in a while."

"Ireland? We're not bally well in Ireland!"

Quinn tried to ignore them. He presented the flowers to his mother. "I brought you these."

"Oh, thank you, son!" She breathed them in as if they smelled of anything other than a petrol station forecourt. "Have you see what my son's brought me? Beautiful flowers! All the way from England."

"Only the best," Quinn murmured awkwardly, looking around for a seat. He'd been walking half of yesterday, around Drogheda and Naven, looking for links between Arthur Aston and Mrs Mac. It had been what his uncle would call a soft day, drizzly and overcast, and Quinn's bad knee was aching.

He pulled over a chair as his mother beamed up at him.

"Ah sure, Ethan, you've always been the best of sons."

Quinn's smile froze into place. The woman sitting in the chair beside his mother gave him a pitying look.

"Well, I try," he said.

The carer brought over a vase with some water in it and asked Quinn if he'd like a cup of tea. Quinn could have drunk the ocean dry at that point, but he settled for one cup as he watched his mother fuss over the flowers he'd bought for a few euro as if they'd been cut from the

Buckingham Palace gardens.

"James never brings me flowers," she said, and he nodded as if he wasn't dying inside.

CHAPTER TWENTY-THREE

The White Lady: Three days after

Waking up isn't something that happens to Quinn in one go. He drifts, unsure if he's dreaming or has woken into a nightmare. There are machines and lights, people talking, hands poking at him. Faces swimming in and out of vision.

By the time he thinks to ask where he is, three days have passed and where his left foot used to be is now a blanket lying flat on the bed.

"Twenty five stitches in that," says the surgeon as he checks the stump. "I did my best work on you."

"Like embroidery," Quinn says, watching as if it's someone else's leg. "What happened to my brother?"

The surgeon looks up. "I'll find out for you," he says. It's all anyone ever says.

Later that afternoon Uncle Kieran arrives. He looks shocked, but tries to hide it.

"Now who's identical?" Quinn jokes. It doesn't sound very funny to him.

"Have you heard from Ethan?" Kieran asks, and

Quinn shakes his head.

"No one will tell me anything. Is it bad? Is he hurt bad?" Quinn's fingers curl into the blanket. They feel stiff and unused. "Is he alive?"

"Oh Jesus, Quinn, did no one even tell you that? Yes, he's alive," says Uncle Kieran, and Quinn feels all the adrenaline rush out of him. He flops back on the lumpy pillows like a ragdoll. He can't even say anything.

"I couldn't even get through when the news broke," Kieran goes on, filling the silence. "Tessa comes running into the office, white as a ghost, asking if I'd heard. Heard what, says I, head full of a background check I'm doing. O'course, what with the Twitter and the Facebook, everyone knew Ethan'd been in the pub with you. I'm frantically trying to get through. Later they tell us phone networks were jammed with everyone else doing the same. I finally get a call from the gardaí, of all places. Scared out of my mind, I was, that it meant it was bad news."

"But it wasn't?" Quinn manages.

Uncle Kieran smiles and pats his hand. "No. They explained the hospital had found your warrant card and contacted them. Since you and Ethan are each other's next of kin, they'd been going round in circles before someone remembered me. Tracked me down via the Google, so they did." He pauses. "I called your mother."

Quinn looks up at him, fearful. "How did she take it?"

"Not well, son, not well. I managed to contact a neighbour to go and sit with her. They've got hold of your cousins Emer and Aidan and they've been taking care of her." He pauses again.

"She's not good, is she?"

Kieran shakes his head. "I know you were worried, but I hadn't realised... Ah look, we don't need to talk about that now."

"We do," says Quinn, trying to shake off the fog that's been over him since he woke up. He tries to lever himself more upright in the bed and pain shoots through him.

"Lie still," Kieran says, pushing him back down. "You've burns on your back. Not bad ones, as they go, but still."

Quinn closes his eyes, as if that's going to help at all. Kieran's voice comes to him, quiet now.

"What you did saved your brother's life, James. There's hardly a scratch on him."

Quinn lies there in the hospital bed, with half his leg missing and his back raw as a bloody steak, and tells himself that it's worth it, if Ethan is all right.

"I'm sure he'll come to see you soon," Kieran says, and they both know it's a lie.

CHAPTER TWENTY-FOUR

Finding out information about Alice without Alice finding out about it was proving somewhat difficult. Jen knew that strictly speaking, she'd only promised Alice she wouldn't go looking for her grave, but she remembered the alarm on the little ghost's face when she'd seen how easy it was for Jen to look up her family history.

She lived in fear of Tessa saying something while Alice was in the office. Even Danny was in on the conspiracy, after Jen had run though some alternative lies and eventually just gone for the truth, that Alice didn't want Jen to know.

"Why not?"

"I don't know. Where are you buried?"

"Not perfectly sure I am, old girl. Ditched over the water, you see. Don't entirely remember making land, and if truth be told, don't entirely want to. Perhaps that's why Alice doesn't want you to look. Dying when you're a wee nipper can't be a fun experience."

"Suppose not," Jen said. Tessa came in just then, so she focused her gaze on the computer screen.

"Will you check if I'm on the Wirpness memorial though, Jenny?" Danny asked, as Tessa fiddled with the printer and sighed.

Jen nodded, and Danny looked relieved. "I shouldn't mind, but… well. One can't help it."

At lunchtime, Jen put on her coat and left the office. Wirpness had more than one church, but Jen had put her money on the large Church of England edifice whose steeple she could see from most streets in town. The war memorial was, indeed, on the green opposite the church. Looking at the age of the place and the number of gravestones in the large churchyard, Jen was glad she hadn't had to venture any closer.

The memorial was a Celtic cross, with one plinth for the First World War and a second below it, for Danny's war. The men had been listed alphabetically by surname and initial, with no rank, so it wasn't hard to find Danny.

Jones, D. That was it. No rank, no service number, not even the branch of the military he'd served in.

Jen knelt and touched his name on the worn stone. "He should have a proper grave," she murmured.

"Plenty of them should," came a voice from behind her. She looked back to see a gentleman with a fine moustache standing just past the wall in the churchyard. He looked to be around sixty, slightly plump, and if the afternoon sun filtering through his body was anything to go by, rather dead.

Beside him stood a slightly transparent whippet. It trotted over to Jen and nosed at her hand hopefully. It was like being nuzzled by a lollipop.

"Beano, no. She doesn't have any treats," said the ghost.

"Can you even eat?" Jen murmured to the dog, who wandered off to cock its leg on the memorial.

"Beano! Bad dog!" shouted the man, despite the fact that the ghost dog, being a ghost, was having zero effect on the stone.

There was no one else around, so Jen said, "What do ghost dogs wee? Ectoplasm?"

The ghost looked somewhat surprised. Jen rolled her eyes. "Oh look, a ghost," she said flatly. "Woo, I'm so scared. Please save me someone."

"You can—"

"—see you, yes. I can also see a ghost called Danny Jones," she added before she got into the same old conversation with him. "He was in the RAF. I don't suppose you know him?"

"You think we all know each other?" said the ghost, who she'd have bet money was called Colonel something.

"I just wondered," Jen said, shrugging. "Never mind." She turned to go, counting under her breath.

"Wait!"

She'd got to three.

"Yes?"

"There is a chap out in the woods. That scar in the land. Pilot, I believe. Terribly burned. Shocking state of affairs."

Jen nodded slowly. "I've seen him. But he can't be Danny. He can't be haunting two places at once."

The ghost raised a supercilious eyebrow. "Can't he? Is that the rule?"

Jen didn't quite know what to say to that.

"Jones, you say?" mused the ghost, stroking his transparent moustache. The whippet wandered back over to him, and to Jen's amusement he took something from his pocket and fed it to the dog. "Hmm, well, common name. Seem to remember a Jones family in the village. Lived on the High Street. Think it's a shop now of some sorts."

"A florist?" Jen asked.

"Hmm. Maybe. Don't go up that way often. They did

have a son though. Believe he died. Can't remember the details. So many of them, you see."

Jen glanced at the war memorial. "Yes," she said. "I do see."

Alice turned up as she was on her way back to the office. "Where've you been?"

"Walking. I'm allowed to walk?" Jen said.

"All right, I was just asking." Alice sniffed. Jen glanced at her, trying not to let her unease show. Alice was… not quite the same, recently, and she couldn't put her finger on how.

"I went to see if Danny was on the war memorial. He's not sure where he died, so he might not be buried anywhere, but it's nice to know he was listed there."

"Why?"

"Well… so that people can recognise his contributions, I suppose. And if he had any family, they'd have somewhere to pay their respects."

"He doesn't though, does he? Have any family. Or you wouldn't be working in that office."

"What?"

"Wouldn't the Jones family still own it?"

"Not unless they sold it. Buildings change hands, Alice. People don't stay in the same house unless they're lords and ladies."

Alice shrugged. "I suppose."

They walked in silence for a minute or two. Jen smiled absently at a few passers by as an idea began to take shape for killing two birds with one stone.

"Remember when Charlotte was here?"

Alice gave a theatrical shudder.

"We went for a walk over by the estuary. There are some woods there."

"You were getting on very well with Quinn, so I hear," Alice said slyly.

Jen felt herself blushing. "It was all an act," she said,

and added quickly, "I met a ghost out there. In the woods."

"Did you?" Alice looked bored, twitching her skirts from side to side like a macabre can-can dancer.

"An airman. Like Danny. I wondered if he knew Danny, and how he died."

"So ask him," Alice said.

"I can't. I've got work to do, and these days it's dark by the time I'm done. It's not very safe. I did say I'd find out for Danny," Jen said, and gave Alice a pleading look.

"Oh, so you won't go out to the woods after dark, but it's fine to send me? I'm a child," Alice said, making her eyes all big.

"You're not a child, you're a ghost," Jen said. "What's the worst that could happen?"

What's the worst that could happen?

Two days later as he stood outside Fairview, the country house of uncertain vintage owned by Mrs Assumpta Kelly, Quinn was beginning to wonder.

"...and then there were the Quigleys in the early nineteenth century," his uncle was saying. "Terrible story, the Quigleys."

"Let me guess," Quinn said. "Fire, murder, accident, death?"

"Ah, so you have talked to Mrs Kelly?"

Quinn rubbed at his forehead, which hadn't stopped throbbing since they'd first arrived at Mrs Kelly's house. He'd asked her for a basic rundown of the events that had caused her to believe her house was haunted, and set up his equipment, and ever since then he'd been hearing stories of grisly deaths and miserable lives.

Back at Kieran's house, his uncle had got out his own notes on the history of Fairview, and the stories had got even worse. There barely seemed to be an owner untouched by tragedy.

"Did your machines find anything?" asked Uncle Kieran.

Quinn shrugged. "A few cold spots, but the house is a few hundred years old and not in the best repair. Lots of odd clicks and noises but, again, old house settling down."

"Did I ever tell you about the time I heard someone knocking on the inside of the hot press?" Kieran said as they began towards the house.

"The hot press? Where the boiler is? Sure it could never be anything but a ghost making knocking noises inside a cupboard full of hot pipes!"

Kieran shook his head sadly. "Ah now, Quinn."

"Don't you 'ah now' at me," Quinn said, shoving his hands in his pockets and starting up the house's grand front steps.

Mrs Kelly met them, a plump woman of retirement age who seemed to be under the belief that dressing in beige and wearing lots of coral lipstick would protect her from the screaming *bean sidhe* that seemed to have taken up residence in her house.

"*Ah Cíarán*," she said to his uncle, an inflection Quinn didn't miss. Kieran very nearly blushed as she kissed his cheek. *Like that, is it?*

"Mrs Kelly, how are you?" Quinn said, smiling his Ethan smile at her.

"I'm quite well, and yourself?"

"Grand. Now, do you think any of those machines recorded anything last night?"

"I couldn't be telling you. It's all I can do to work the television, so it is."

He'd set the equipment up in a different place each night, beginning with the former master bedroom, which Mrs Kelly had long-since vacated after feeling someone sit on the edge of her bed when she was alone in the house. Quinn had found nothing on his recording of that room.

The second night he'd angled the cameras and microphones towards the stairs at the back of the hall, where both the former Mr Kelly and his unfortunate daughter had taken tumbles. The stairs were built with a wide landing halfway up, and a couple of rooms leading back off it. The footage from those stairs had been dark and cold, undisturbed by so much as a mouse. He'd been working his way through the other rooms since.

"I'll upload all this to my computer," he explained, "and then we'll set up in the stables. Will you tell my uncle where it is you'll be needing us?"

This was his polite way of getting rid of her while he uploaded the footage. Mrs Kelly was a hoverer, prone to peering over his shoulder and asking him the most pointless questions about how the recording equipment worked.

With Kieran and Mrs Kelly off to inspect the disused stables, he settled back on the bench by the hall telephone and started uploading to his laptop. He'd go through the footage later, in private, as he always did. Having the owner point out utter irrelevancies was less than helpful.

At first glance, there was nothing useful. Quinn would bet good money there would be nothing useful when he looked through it all later, too, but professionalism made him keep that to himself for now.

While the laptop took its time, he got out his phone and sent a text to Tessa asking how things were going back in Wirpness. Her reply came ten minutes later, slightly mistyped in a way that usually meant she was dealing with her kids at the same time, that everything was fine. "have tou been tk drogheda yet?" she asked.

Quinn had, but he'd found nothing there relating to Mrs Mac and her supposed ancestor. He told Tessa as much and added that he'd send her a more detailed report that evening.

Five minutes later there came a more measured reply: "As I thought. Ah well. Everything's fine here BTW. But I think Jen misses you."

I miss her too, Quinn thought, surprised at himself. Yesterday he'd been driving along the coast road back to Uncle Kieran's house in Dalkey and found himself commenting on the sights as if he was showing them off.

So she thinks she sees a Victorian child. Everyone has their flaws.

"I'm sure her aim is getting better," he typed back, and the message had just sent when his phone started to ring. "Uncle Kieran?"

"Quinn, lad. Now what would you be saying if I told you Mrs Kelly has asked for another expert on the case?"

Quinn frowned at an error message on his laptop and reconnected the camera to begin uploading again. "What kind of expert?"

"The kind who sees ghosts."

He groaned. "Ah you haven't got Jen in on this, have you?"

"Jen? No, her name is Gobnait Ní Dhomhnaill. Will you have heard of her?"

"No," Quinn said distractedly.

"She's quite the following on the Internet. It's taken Assumpta all this time to coax her out of the Gaeltacht. She doesn't even have any English, can you believe it?"

Privately, Quinn wondered how much of a following she'd have if she really only spoke Irish, but he murmured, "Really?"

"People travel miles to see her. Lives on this tiny farm up on Inis Óirr. She'll be here the day after tomorrow. How's your Irish, son?"

"Fecking awful," said Quinn, who hadn't had cause

to speak a word of it since he'd quit being a garda.

"Better brush up on it now! Won't this be grand, you can see if your findings match up with hers."

"Sure," said Quinn. "Grand."

The shadows shifted in the hallway. A cold breeze whistled through.

Five minutes after he'd ended the call, Quinn picked his phone up again. "Jen," he heard himself say. "Are you free this week?"

"No, this week you have to pay," she said cautiously.

"Pay will certainly be included. Flights and hotel too. Fancy a trip to the Fair City?"

"Dublin? What... for?"

Because I appear to have lost my mind. "Listen, and hear me out before you put the phone down."

"Then don't give me a reason to put the phone down," Jen said.

"You've mentioned seeing this Alice. Do you ever, ehm, see... other ghosts?"

There was silence on the line.

"Jenny?"

"I've never seen Ethan," she said, her voice flat.

Thank God for small mercies. "I wasn't asking about that. I was asking have you seen any other ghosts? Because there's this house I'm investigating—"

"In Rathmichael," she said, computer keys clicking.

"—which is apparently haunted six ways to Sunday. Now just for research purposes," he crossed his fingers, "I thought you might come out here and tell me if you think you can see anything. Or hear, or, ehm... whatever."

Stop saying ehm, you bloody eejit. You sound like a tongue-tied child.

"Why?" Jen asked, her voice still flat. "You don't believe in ghosts."

"But you do." And so did this Ní Dhomhnaill woman

with her Gaeilge and her internet following. "Look on it as a holiday. All expenses paid."

"Nice hotel?"

"Don't abuse the minibar."

Was it his imagination, or did her silence get a bit more thoughtful?

"This isn't going to turn into one of those things where there's a mix-up at the hotel and we have to share a room, is it?"

I wish. "No, I'll be staying with my uncle in Dalkey. Bono lives there," he added, for no reason other than trying to impress her. *Which'll only work if she's a fan, you dope.*

"In your uncle's house?"

"Sure, in Ireland every home has a resident rockstar."

This time he heard the smile in her voice when she replied. "All right. Look… there's going to be a catch with this, isn't there?"

"No catch. Swear to God. Come out to this house and tell me what you can see. Meet my uncle. He can tell you all about the old days of the agency before I took over."

Another pause. Then Jen said, "All right, when shall I fly out?"

"What if it rains?" Alice said, watching Jen roll up a sweater.

"I'll take an umbrella."

"It rains all the time in Ireland."

"No, it doesn't."

"Yes it does. There was this Irish family down the street from us," Alice said, as if this put an end to the matter.

Alice had never been abroad. She had a working class Victorian scorn for Johnny Foreigner, believed the food would be terrible, and couldn't see the point of travelling when England clearly had the best of everything.

Holidays abroad were the only time in Jen's childhood she'd ever been away from Alice.

Jen stared at her wardrobe, trying to decide if more casual clothes would be appropriate. "And did they have webbed feet?"

"I don't know." Alice swung her legs. "Probably." She looked sideways at Jen. "Are you going to tell him?"

Jen took a grey t-shirt from the wardrobe and folded it over the pile of pink and purple knickers she'd just packed. "Tell who what?"

"Danny. What I found out. From the airman."

Jen shrugged. "I don't know yet. I don't know if there's enough to tell. I'll see what Uncle Kieran knows, maybe."

"I don't see why you didn't tell Danny."

Jen looked at her sharply. "That he was either blown up or drowned? Look, if this Sergeant Jensen was so badly injured he couldn't even tell what happened to Danny, then it must've been bad."

"He just said he didn't notice Danny wasn't there until it was too late. I mean, plane breaks up high in the air," Alice said, with the air of one who parroting what an expert has just told her, "bits of it are scattered all over the place, the debris field is going to be huge, even with a small craft."

That was the other thing. "He said he flew Spitfires," Jen said.

"Ghastly name."

"They're tiny planes. I looked them up. Single seaters. Why did he have a copilot?"

"Oh I don't know, Jenny, I'm just repeating what he told me." Alice poked at the contents of Jen's suitcase, her fingers pushing right through a green bra. "Why d'you have to go to Ireland?"

"Quinn asked me, and he's my boss."

"Does he desperately need some filing done?" Alice said peevishly.

"He wants me to look for a ghost. I know, I know," she raised her hands before Alice could interrupt, "he still doesn't believe in them. Research purposes is what he said. I guess we can always see if what he records and what I see match each other up."

"He'll make up some excuse why they don't," Alice said.

"Probably. But anyway. I'm kind of curious to meet Uncle Kieran. And I've never been to Ireland. And it's free."

Alice watched Jen tuck pairs of socks around the edge of the case. "Do I have to come?"

"Not if you're going to have that attitude. Look. Stay here, keep Danny company, see if you can jog his memory a bit with what Jensen said. But…" she chewed her lip again. "Just what Jensen said, yes?"

Alice gave her a military salute. Jen rolled her eyes.

Bored with scanning through last night's data, Quinn got out his phone and checked for messages from Jen. She'd explained slightly tersely that since she didn't have a car, she'd have to get the bus to the airport, which due to East Anglia's interesting aversion to motorways or direct routes of any kind, would take her over four hours. Still, he'd pointed out to her, at least she wouldn't have to arrive early to hand over dozen cases of sensitive recording equipment. Or, indeed, to enjoy the advanced waiting times that came part and parcel with taking a prosthetic limb through Security.

Her flight was due to land at around one in the afternoon, so by now she'd probably be waiting for a connecting bus in Lowestoft. He sent her a text and got one in reply.

"On time so far. Hope your weather's nicer than ours."

Quinn glanced at the bright autumn sunshine outside his uncle's house. "Sure the sun's splitting the stones," he replied, grinning to himself.

Five minutes later, Jen texted, "Stop being Irish at me."

He laughed a little at that and wondered if there might be a friendly Irish ghost around to help her translate.

Then his smile vanished, because now he was starting to think like her.

This weekend is a litmus test, he told himself. If she admits she's making it up about the ghosts, that's fine. If she insists she can see them and no one else can, then it's not, and I talk to her about getting help.

And what if she and this Ní Dhomhnaill woman see the same thing? asked a nasty little voice in the back of his mind.

Shut up, he told it.

A short while later his phone rang with Kieran's number. "Mrs Ní Dhomhnaill is busy with another engagement today, it seems. She'll be coming out to the Rathmichael house tomorrow night instead."

"Must it be at night?" Quinn asked.

"That's when most of the phenomena have been seen," Kieran replied.

"That's when it's easier to fake stuff," Quinn muttered, rolling his eyes at 'phenomena'. "All right," he said louder, "so Jen gets a day of sightseeing."

"If she likes ghosts Dublin has plenty," Kieran began.

"No. No ghosts. She can go to Temple Bar and Christchurch Cathedral like anyone else."

"Ah now, Christchurch has ghosts! Have you not seen the mouse and the rat from the organ? Stuffed inside it, they were. Mummified."

"That's disgusting," said Quinn, glancing over at Uncle Kieran's fat tabby, Billy, in the wooden bowl on the windowsill. His ears twitched as if he knew he was being watched.

"Yeah. Don't tell Billy."

"Look, she's had a long trip. We'll save the city for tomorrow, just go for a walk around Dalkey. It's quite a bit like Wirpness."

"Only with a better name," Kieran opined.

Quinn sent Jen a text that he'd meet her at the hotel, and finished uploading last night's data onto his computer. Flicking through the thermal images from the hallway, he came across one with a figure in it and for a second shock ran through him. Then he looked closer, saw it was body-temperature, short and plump. Mrs Kelly. She came down the stairs, disappeared in the direction of the kitchen and reappeared a few minutes later with her hand out as if carrying something.

Realising he'd just been spooked by the image of a woman fetching a glass of water, Quinn shook his head at himself.

Then he saw the black cold spot on the stairs.

"Probably left a window open," he muttered, but made a note of the time on the footage, and added a reminder to ask her about it.

The Aircoach from Dublin Airport took Jen along the coast road by the docks. She found herself sitting behind an American couple who read out every bilingual road sign they saw with wonder that increased in direct proportion to their terrible pronunciation. She particularly enjoyed them getting off the coach at Dun Laoghaire, especially when the bus driver gently corrected them and was totally ignored.

Quinn had told her to get off at the last stop, which

would be right outside her hotel. It was a huge and rather fanciful-looking building, a Disney castle of an edifice. Hopefully, it was entirely modern, and not full of the interesting kind of history.

She thanked the driver, stepped down into the car park, and looked around. The day was bright, the grass was greener than the tourist photos, and there were no ghosts around.

"Jenny!" Quinn shouted to her as she was trying to stop her suitcase from falling over on the sloping ground. Flustered, she looked up and saw him loping towards her, the wind tousling his hair, sunlight brightening his smile. He looked like a rockstar. Damn the man for even managing to turn a limp into a swagger.

"How's the form?" he asked, slinging an arm around her shoulders for a hug. Jen breathed him in for a second, then stiffened and pulled away.

"Good. Great. Form?"

Being home clearly suited him. "It's an expression. Will I help you check in?"

"I'm pretty sure I can manage," Jen said drily, but she allowed him to carry in her case and charm the receptionist. The poor woman faltered when Quinn unhooked his sunglasses, and temporarily lost the power of speech when he smiled at her.

"Reservation in the name of Hargrave," he said.

The girl gazed at him with adoring eyes.

"I have the paperwork," Jen said crisply, passing it over so the bedazzled receptionist had something to work from.

Quinn continued to smile at her until she'd upgraded Jen to a sea view room, and then he tossed a casual, "Thanks a million," at her as he picked up Jen's case again.

"I can manage this part too," she said.

"Now what kind of gentleman would I be if I didn't walk you to your door?" Quinn said, all innocence.

She eyed him as they got into the lift. "This is my room, isn't it? You're not staying with me?"

"You wound me, Jenny. As if I'd try such a cheap trick. A cheap, sleazy and above all unimaginative trick. It hurts," he said, clutching his hand to his chest.

"Yeah, well. Try it and something else'll hurt," she said, without much conviction. He laughed at that. *Handsome bastard. Stop being so charming.*

When they reached her room with its lovely balcony and views out over the bay, she excused herself to the bathroom to freshen up, and spent five minutes giving herself a pep talk in the mirror.

"You do not fancy James Quinn. He's a weirdo and a miserable bastard and he thinks you're insane, and besides if you did sleep with him you might give yourself away."

She pulled up her t-shirt and looked at the thin pink lines scoring her torso.

"You can't explain those," she told herself quietly. "He's a detective. He'll work it out."

She let her shirt fall back down, and avoided her own gaze as she fixed her face.

Quinn smiled at her from the balcony doors, the sun gilding his black curls like a halo. He looked unfairly handsome, and not at all weird or miserable. "You ready? Thought we'd go for a walk. The views are amazing from up on the hill."

Jen nodded. "Are you sure you don't want me to go and check out this house tonight?"

He shook his head. "No. Tomorrow's fine. Take a day off and relax, see the sights."

Jen regarded him for a suspicious moment. He was being almost too nice. "Okay," she said slowly, and he beamed at her and held out her coat.

It turned out he hadn't been exaggerating about the views from the hill, which were nothing short of breathtaking. At the top was a sea view, an obelisk, a step pyramid, and, almost inevitably, a ghost. He didn't seem to notice Jen, though, simply wafting around looking out to sea.

"What's with the pyramid?" Jen asked. Some teenagers were climbing on it and posing for photos.

"Why not?"

"Well, if you put it that way…"

Quinn grinned at her. "Story goes it was a relief effort. Providing work to men who hadn't any."

"Oh…yes, I met someone once who—" *was dead—* "er, who had an uncle or something, who dug ditches and filled them in again."

Quinn gave her a strange look. "In the eighteenth century?"

She winced. "No, during the Depression."

"Ah, right. Thought it was one of your ghosts."

"Hey, you're paying me to come out here and look at ghosts," Jen said.

Quinn rubbed at his forehead. "Indeed I am."

For a while they watched the kids messing about. "That used to be me and Ethan," Quinn said. "Minus the selfies, of course. When we were kids we'd run up here to play. All the kids did, much younger than this lot. Can't imagine anyone doing that now."

"Health and safety," Jen murmured, glancing back at the ghost. She fancied he was wearing a uniform.

"Sure. Then when we got a bit older we'd bring girls up here. Dead romantic at night. Well, so Ethan told me. They're called the Wishing Steps, you see, so… When I tried it she gave out at me for dragging her up a cold hill in the middle of the night, and made me take her back down again."

"Very romantic."

"I did try and offer her another way of warming up, but…" he shrugged. "As I recall, the next week Ethan tried it and," his mouth twisted bitterly, "'she warmed up nicely'."

"He stole your girlfriend?"

"Well. Not girlfriend so much as… girl I fancied. Story of my life," he sighed, and Jen said nothing. "Come on, then, before it gets cold and dark and you tell me to take you back somewhere more civilised."

He turned away, and Jen watched him for a moment, half wishing he'd offer to warm her up like he had that girl. As he approached the ghost looking out to sea, the image of the man seemed to blow away in the wind.

Behind her, the teenagers giggled and shrieked. She glanced back, watching a girl leap off the bottom step of the pyramid into the arms of a boy, who pretended to stagger and tugged her to the ground, still laughing. They rolled around, kissing, as their friends jeered and catcalled.

I remember that, Jen thought, smiling. The thrill of it all. Sneaking out from the clinic, hiding behind bushes and bus shelters, snogging like they'd just invented it.

Quinn stood staring off at the distant peaks to the south, his shoulders hunched, ignoring the kids having a good time. Back to his usual self. *How come even I managed that and he didn't? Was Ethan really that jealous, that self-obsessed?*

Her nails bit into her palm, pain stinging through her flesh. *Yes, yes he was.*

"Hey, Quinn," she said, catching up and touching his shoulder. He glanced back down at her, brows drawn down, unhappy with his memories. "You're not your brother."

He flinched at that. Jen's fingers tightened on a fold of his sleeve.

"I mean that as a compliment. He was… he sounds

like a bit of an arse."

That took him by surprise. "What?"

"He knew you liked this girl and he went after her anyway? That's just..." It was a lot of things, but she settled for, "Mean. Didn't he even have the imagination to try the whole, 'Hey, I was pretending to be you,' thing?"

A smile crept around the edges of his mouth. "He wasn't that bright."

"Right?" Jen tucked her arm into his and they started down the path together. "He'd have got on well with my sister."

"Nah. They need people to boss around. Anyone argues back and they don't know what to do."

"Yes, and they're always right."

"Oh God yes! Ethan never lost an argument. Never. He just won out by constantly insisting he was right, until you either gave up or belted him one out of frustration."

Jen found herself giggling. "Charlotte's the same. Only being so much smaller I could never hit her."

"And being the twin in possession of some actual morals, I generally didn't hit Ethan. Unless he really deserved it."

A cold wind blew in off the sea and Jen found herself leaning closer to Quinn. He felt reassuringly solid, substantial, unlikely to blow away. He smiled down at her, and in that moment she couldn't think of a single reason why she shouldn't invite him back to her hotel room.

"Look," Quinn said, pointing off ahead. "Can you see Dalkey Island out there? See the grey thing in the middle of it?"

Jen squinted, and nodded.

"It's a Martello tower. Built to look out for Napoleon. There's a handful of them along the coast, you might've passed them on the bus if you took the coast road. Now, you can't see it from here, but on the island there's also the remains of a church from the seventh century. Goats live in it now."

"The Father, the Son, and the Holy Goat," Jen said gravely, and she felt him shake with laughter.

"Indeed. Sacred, holy goats."

She smiled as they made their way down the path towards the town, Quinn pointing out a stone eagle on the hillside and something that might have been a seal in the bay, "but it might be a bit of garbage."

"How charming. I've always wanted to see garbage in the sea."

"There's dolphins out in the bay sometimes, but I haven't seen any yet. My dad used to say if we called for them, they'd hear us and come swimming up."

"Well, they're smart animals, dolphins. Too smart to be taken in by a couple of gullible kids," Jen added, and he grinned.

Eventually the path turned into a street with the occasional house, and then a steep flight of steps Jen was glad she was going down, not up, especially when they afforded such a glorious view of the bay. She stopped for a moment, captivated.

"Sunrise is the time to see it," Quinn murmured in her ear. "With us facing East here."

"It's pretty damn spectacular as it is," Jen said. Her gaze was caught by the view stretching along the coast road back into Dalkey, the light fading all the way.

"I can't believe you grew up here." She gestured to one of the houses enjoying the sea view. "How much would one of these set you back?"

"Damn sight more than it cost my parents when they bought their house. Back before it was fashionable," Quinn said. He glanced at another crenellated property and shrugged. "One of these? Couple of million."

"Euros?" Jen did a quick calculation into pounds and whistled. Seven figures whichever way you looked at it. Houses in Wirpness sometimes sold for that amount, but they were the huge, grand, old-money houses.

"Uncle Kieran told me a modern build out on Sorrento Road," he pointed up ahead, "was after being sold for four million. Four. Million. Euro. All glass and weird angles, he said. We'll have to see if we can spot it."

He took her arm again and led her along the narrow pavement, keeping between her and the traffic. Jen gazed out at the sea as the sun sank behind it, watching a ferry track its slow way across the bay.

At a turn in the road, Quinn turned her and pointed to the peaks she'd seen to the south. "The Wicklow mountains. Told you it was quite a view."

"You weren't kidding. How far away are they?"

"Ah now, you had to ask something I don't know." Quinn ran a hand through his hair and shrugged. "Maybe ten, fifteen miles away?"

"Looks further."

"Well, it's a small country, so."

The road began to slope back down to a junction, where Quinn paused and said, "How're you holding up? Want to walk further, or do you want to go for a sit down and a cup of tea?"

"You and your tea," Jen said. "I'm all right to walk further—if you are," she added guiltily, recalling his prosthetic.

He gave her a sideways look. "I'm sure I can stumble on." Limping theatrically, he towed her down the road.

"Cut that out," she said.

"Ah, I'm naught but a poor cripple," Quinn cried, dragging on her arm until she tugged herself free and ran, laughing, ahead of him. Quinn chased her into a small park and she darted away, shrieking like those teenage girls, up a wooded slope to a clearing where she'd have stopped to catch her breath if it hadn't been stolen from her.

Out to sea, the last rays of the sun turned the Martello Tower into a fiery crown on Dalkey Island. A ship crossed the horizon. Jen could have happily sworn she saw a school of dolphins out in the bay.

Behind her, Quinn caught her around the waist and she fell back against him, murmuring, "How could you ever leave this place?"

CHAPTER TWENTY-FIVE

She stood with the dying sun gilding her flyaway curls, cheeks pink from the cold and from running, gazing out at his favourite place in all the world as if she'd just fallen in love. Quinn was afraid to know if he looked the same.

Playfulness gone, she leaned back against him, which was almost too much to bear. "How could you ever leave this place?" she asked.

I wouldn't, if you were here. If she turned her head a little, he could kiss her. Kiss her while the wind blew around them and the sun sank behind the hills and she melted in his arms.

Quinn breathed in the scent of her hair, just like she'd done to him when he hugged her at the hotel. *People don't do that to people they don't fancy at all.*

And they don't pull away immediately, either.

He sighed, aching for her, and stepped back before he did something she'd hate him for.

"Well, it is getting a wee bit chilly," he said, and Jen blinked at him.

"Right," she said. "Yes. Chilly."

"Will we go and get something to eat?" He gestured back towards town.

Jen hesitated for a microsecond. Then she smiled and nodded, and held out her arm companionably.

Fecking *companionably*.

Quinn walked her back into town, pointing at houses on Sorrento Road and trying to work out of any of them might be worth four million. Jen asked which one was Bono's, and Quinn made a game of picking out the smallest houses he could and trying to persuade her.

They walked along the High Street, past the place where Quinn had attempted to learn to play the piano, past the pub he and Ethan had been thrown out of for underage drinking, past the newsagents he still knew only as 'the red shop' since it had always been painted the same colour. And they walked past people he'd known all his life, people whose kids he'd been to school with, people *he'd* been to school with. And he watched their gazes slide away from him, saw them murmur behind their hands or pretend not to have noticed him.

And he knew Jen saw it too. Her arm tightened around his, and she said with unconvincing lightness, "What's with all the castles around here? That's about the third I've seen."

"There used to be seven," he said absently. "What? Oh… well, it's a port, so." He pulled himself together. "Did you know Dalkey has the smallest working harbour in Europe?"

"Really? All of Europe?" This time her smile was a bit more mischievous. "I suppose that explains it then."

"Explains what?"

"All these massive houses and huge phallic towers. You're compensating for something."

Quinn slid her a look. She was waiting for him to laugh.

"The town may be," he said loftily, "but I'm not."

Jen snorted at that, but Quinn thought with some mixture of hope and longing that her expression got a bit thoughtful.

He took her for dinner at a café that hadn't been there last time he'd been in town, and where he figured he'd be less likely to run into someone he used to know.

"What d'you want to do tomorrow?" he asked. "We've most of the day."

"I'd be happy to hang around here," Jen murmured, looking out of the window at the street. "But I suppose Dublin has its merits."

"Bigger castle," Quinn said, and she smiled. "Couple of cathedrals, great museums. One of them has bog bodies."

"Bog… no, I don't want to know."

"Maybe not." He smiled and picked up his wineglass, wondering what might impress her. Probably not St Michan's Church, then, with its mummified crusader.

"I'm not great with museums," Jen said, and hesitated, before she said, "They're all just full of broken plates."

"Well, then there's Trinity College, the library there is spectacular. You'll have heard of the Book of Kells?" She nodded, to his relief. "They have it there. And the Book of… might be Durrow. Or the Lindisfarne Gospels."

"That's in the British Library. School trip," she added.

"Book of Armagh, then, it's one of them. If you've a liking for old books, there's Marsh's Library, where they used to put visitors in cages so they couldn't steal valuable books. No, it's true! Or there's the Chester Beatty Library, which has lots of ancient texts from all around the world." He smiled. "We went on a school trip and Ethan and myself spent months trying to learn hieroglyphics."

"Why? Don't tell me, there's an old document telling you where to find even more treasures than Tutankhamun's tomb."

"Even better." Quinn refilled their glasses. "Naughty poems."

Jen grinned. "Beats looking up swearwords in the French dictionary."

"It does, or would if they'd actually been in hieroglyphics. Turns out it was a totally different script and we were no closer to smut than we'd been if we'd stuck to the French dictionary."

She laughed out loud and took a swig of wine. "Hey, do you learn Irish at school here?"

"We do."

"Do you speak it?"

"*Beagáinín*." A little, but probably not enough to keep up with the Ní Dhomhnaill woman tomorrow.

One eyebrow went up. "I'll take that as a yes."

"Actually, there isn't a word for 'yes' in Irish. Or 'no'."

"Now you're having me on."

"Swear to God." He put one hand on his chest. "We just repeat the question in the affirmative or negative."

"So if I were to ask you if you're enjoying your meal…?"

"I am."

"Or if it's still daylight outside…?"

"It isn't."

She tilted her head. "Cop out. Say it in Irish."

Quinn groaned. "I can't remember most of it. Lived in England too long. *Níl Gaeilge mhaith agam*, there you go."

"What's that mean?"

"I don't speak Irish very well." He pointed his wineglass at her. "Useful phrase in any language."

After they'd eaten he walked her slowly back through the streets to her hotel. Jen kept nagging him for more words in Irish, which he didn't really mind since it was fun to watch her try to say them. *I could offer to kiss her for every one she gets right*, he thought dreamily, and nearly walked straight into oncoming traffic.

By the time they reached the hotel he was desperately willing her to ask him to stay up for a drink. But as proof, if it were needed, that psychic powers didn't exist, she just smiled and said, "How do I say good night?"

"*Slán leat.*"

Jen leaned in… and her lips brushed his cheek. "*Slán leat,*" she whispered, and was gone.

Jen was good at lying. Of course she was.

Of course she'd only pretended Alice was real. Of course she'd recovered fully from her illness. Of course nothing interesting had happened in that month before Millie was born, apart from those bruises and that scratch, haha, well that's what happens when you live in London, muggings and so on, that's why she'd moved out.

Of course, she wasn't interested in Quinn. Of course, of course, of course.

She made it to her hotel room before the emotion broke, and she truly didn't know if it was delight or horrible pain. She fell back against the door, hugging herself, trying to keep it in, trying not to let it show even if there was no one else in the room. Not even Alice.

Alice would be interfering right now.

The resentment hit her like a punch in the gut. Alice was her friend, her oldest and only real friend. Alice had always been there for her, comforted and consoled her, even saved her life. So what if she sometimes poked her nose into Jen's business? Friends sometimes did that, right?

Only with most friends you could tell them to bog off. With Alice...

The smile fading from her face, Jen pushed away from the door and started taking off her coat. With Alice —that was the rub, because she'd never be without Alice. Even those brief few years when she'd willed Alice away, she'd always known the little ghost was just biding her time. That she'd return, and she'd know everything about Jen and she'd... interfere.

Jen kicked off her shoes and watched them tumble over on the hotel carpet. She flicked on the TV and stared unseeing at an Irish talk show she didn't recognise.

She'd always assumed it was Victorian prudery, why Alice had never interfered with Jen's boyfriends. If you could call them that. A few furtive snogs behind the recycling bins at the home, a couple of faintly grubby one-night stands. She could count the men she'd spent more than a few hours with on one hand. Well, except that most of them had been boys, because she'd only been a girl herself, off her head on whatever antipsychotic treatment was currently in vogue or in such a state of denial over Alice's existence that the ghost could have danced a can-can and Jen would've ignored her.

Alice didn't know about Ethan. She couldn't.

And if she didn't know about him, then she wouldn't stop Jen from getting involved with Quinn. Nobody would stop her getting involved. There was no reason she couldn't call him right now, tell him to turn around and come up to her room. Greet him at the door with a kiss and lead him wordlessly to the bed, scattering clothes as they went.

If she called him, he'd come up. She knew that as sure as she knew anything. He hadn't been subtle about telling her. When he'd caught her by the waist out in the park, the dying sun setting them both ablaze, she'd been almost sure he was going to kiss her. And she was just as sure she wanted him to.

Her phone was in her hand. All she had to do was call him.

She went to bed instead.

The evening had turned proper cold by the time Quinn got back to Uncle Kieran's house. His face was cold, his shoulders tight and hunched, but there was heat inside him.

She'd nearly kissed him. Nearly. He'd watched her face as she stood in Sorrento Park and fell in love with his hometown. *Look at me like that. Please look at me like that.*

He paused with his key in his hand. He could call her, right now, call her and ask if he could come over. Tell her he wanted her with the distance of a phonecall between them, then if she said no he wouldn't have to try and persuade his face into pretending it didn't matter. Just his voice, and he could manage that. Probably.

Ethan would've just gone for it, he told himself savagely. His hand was on his phone in his pocket—

—and the door opened.

"Are you coming in, son?"

Billy twined around Quinn's ankles, stretching up to paw at his fake leg. Quinn scooped him up and smelled the smoke from the peat fire on his fur. Nothing in the world smelled like burning peat.

"Just getting the air."

"Sure they don't have air up on Killiney Hill?"

Quinn ignored that and stepped inside, releasing Billy to go back to his bowl.

"By yourself?" Kieran asked, peering out at the obviously empty street.

"I told you, she's up at the hotel."

"I thought you might have invited her back for a drink. Or she might've invited you," Kieran said, his expression far too innocent.

"No. She was tired. It's been a long day for her."

Kieran gave him a knowing look. "Ah, c'mon Quinn. Good looking fella like yourself, own business, most of his own limbs… you can't tell me she's not interested?"

Quinn's fingers curled in on themselves. "I can," he said, "and I will. Goodnight."

Quinn was waiting for her the next morning, leaning against a perfectly ordinary small car and somehow managing to look cooler than James Dean with his Porsche. Every cell in Jen's body ached with regret that she hadn't asked him up to her room last night.

He slid his sunglasses up on top of his head when he saw her, as if she might not have recognised him without them, and said, "Top o' the morning."

Jen laughed despite herself. "You did not just say that."

"Couldn't resist."

He didn't try to kiss her this time, for which she told herself she was grateful, just opened the passenger door for her and waited 'til she'd got in before he shut it. Don't be impressed, she told herself as he rounded the car and slid in behind the wheel.

"Now, Uncle Kieran wants a lift to the house in Rathmichael. He'll pick up the overnight data and see what else Mrs Kelly has to tell him. He's under strict instructions not to breathe a word about it to you, though."

Jen nodded.

"And in case you're wondering," he started the car, "yes, he could've come with me to pick you up, but he's a man of habit and if he doesn't spend at least an hour chatting to friends while he picks up the morning paper, his day is ruined."

"Fair enough."

He drove down the hill and the sea came into view, sparkling in the sunshine. Jen heard Alice's voice telling her authoritatively that it *always* rained in Ireland, and smiled.

"What?"

"Oh... nothing. The town looks pretty in the sunshine."

"Yes, you see us masquerading as a Mediterranean country today." He glanced at a road sign, swore, and abruptly shoved the car into reverse, whereupon it stalled.

"Fecking... not used to manual gear change," he muttered, restarting and reaching over to take hold of the back of her seat as he took the car backwards up the narrow lane. Jen breathed in and went very still.

"Been a while since I drove around here," Quinn explained as he turned down the road he'd missed. "I forget... one road looks pretty much like another round this bit of town. Still, at least it's not one of those tiny boreens down near the Rathmichael house. I got so lost round there."

Jen cleared her throat. For some reason, she'd always found it unbearably sexy when a man reached over the back of her seat while reversing. "Boreen?"

"Rural road. Lane. See the width of it?" He indicated the high walls either side of them. "There's an old law that the width of a road must be the length plus the width of a cow. Like this," he briefly made a T with his hands. "*Bó* is the Irish word for cow, so, *bóthar* and the diminutive, *bóthairín*." He pronounced it almost like 'boreen' but with a sort of imaginary H in the middle.

"You're having me on."

"Swear to God."

"You said you didn't speak any Irish."

"Much. I said I didn't have 'much' Irish." His eyes didn't leave the road, but he was smiling. Jen tried not to stare.

He drove her through town, past the restaurant where they'd eaten last night, pointing out the newsagents where Uncle Kieran bought his morning paper, and the school where he and Ethan had played twin pranks when they were kids.

He drove a little slower past it than was necessary. Then he sighed, and sped up again. At Jen's look, he shrugged and explained, "School sees some weirdo in black glasses drive by peering at the place, they're going to get a bit nervous."

"I'm sure they'd recognise you," Jen said.

Quinn said nothing.

He eventually parked outside his uncle's house, an unremarkable semi that stood a little way outside the town, although not, Jen noted, far enough that a trip to the paper shop could merit an hour's round trip.

"He should be back by now," Quinn said, and she followed him up the short garden path. Inside, Quinn was greeted by a man's voice coming from another room. Jen was greeted by a large tabby cat bumping around her ankles.

"Whisht, Billy, leave her alone," Quinn said, bending down to tickle the cat's ears.

"He's all right," Jen said, holding out her fingers for the cat to sniff. He purred and licked them, which seemed to surprise Quinn.

"Sure he doesn't usually like strangers," said a man coming down the stairs. Maybe in his sixties or seventies, he was greying but bright eyed and so familiar she'd have known he was Uncle Kieran without asking.

"Cats like me," she replied, bending down and letting Billy stretch up his paws to head-butt her.

"Ah," said Kieran, shrugging into his coat. "That'll

be the spirits."

Quinn groaned. "We've not even got into the car," he complained. "Can't you save all that for later?"

Ignoring him, Kieran scooped the cat up and deposited him in the living room, where Billy proceeded to jump into a wooden bowl on the windowsill. "Has Quinn told you of Billy in the Bowl?" Kieran asked as he followed them to the car.

"Uh... the cat? Or...?"

"When Uncle Kieran got him as a kitten, he curled up in that bowl. Hence the name." To his uncle, he added, "We're not going on a ghost tour."

Again, Kieran ignored him, and proceeded to spend the first part of the journey telling Jen an old Dublin folk story about a beggar called Billy, who was born with no legs and so propelled himself about in a large bowl on wheels.

"An option I looked into," Quinn muttered as he turned onto the main road, "and discarded in favour of a modern prosthesis."

"But see how many girls you could've got with the bowl!" cried his uncle. "Billy was famously handsome, Jennifer, with beautiful black curls all the girls loved. Just like our Quinn here."

"Except I'm not a murderous psychopath," Quinn interjected.

Jen sat back and enjoyed the ride. Kieran was a great raconteur, embellishing the story with little asides about eighteenth century Dublin and the outlandish people to be found therein, whilst Quinn muttered asides about realism and history.

"Sure you'll have to take her to the Leprechaun Museum," Kieran exclaimed.

"The what?" Jen said.

"There's a what now?" Quinn said at the same time.

"On Jervis Street. Next to Wolftone Park. I'm after

hearing the *seanchaithe* there are grand. Those are storytellers," he explained to Jen. "Tales of folklore and the like."

"Including leprechauns?"

"Of course including leprechauns! This is Ireland!"

Jen cut her eyes at Quinn. "So, ghosts you don't believe in, but leprechauns are fine?"

He quirked an eyebrow and looked like he was trying not to smile. "This is Ireland," he repeated.

They dropped Kieran off at the entrance to a large, grey house only just glimpsed through the trees, and Quinn pulled back onto the main road.

"Hear that?" he said as the car sped up.

"What?" There was nothing but the road noise.

"Exactly."

She smiled. "I liked his stories."

"Just remember, stories is what they are."

"So there wasn't really a Billy in the Bowl?"

"If there was, I'd lay money he wasn't the handsome charmer of the stories."

"They never are," Jen agreed.

They drove into the city, Quinn pointing out various landmarks along the way. "St Patrick's Cathedral," he gestured to their right. "And behind it is Marsh's Library, the one where the books are kept in cages. Said to be haunted by a bishop."

"We'll give it a miss."

Quinn's eyebrows quirked, but he said nothing.

The lights changed, and the car eased past the cathedral. Jen peered up at its high gothic towers. *Probably haunted too,* she thought glumly. It had the look of a very old building, not some Johnny-come-lately built in the Medieval style.

"Now for some that's the grandest in the city, but I prefer Christchurch."

"Is that far?"

Quinn switched lanes, rounded a bus, and said, "See for yourself."

Jen looked up at another huge medieval edifice, this one with a stone bridge spanning the road ahead. "Wow."

"We can go in if you like. There's a nice café in the crypt."

She tore her eyes away for a moment. "I'm sorry, did you say crypt?"

Quinn grinned. "Sure they weren't using it for anything else."

Like keeping dead people in. "I'll pass on that," she said.

"Sure? There's said to be the ghost of a soldier eaten alive by rats."

Jen shuddered. She'd glimpsed a ghost like that once, as a child, before Alice had scared him away. The memory of torn flesh and mad red eyes hadn't faded since.

"Are you all right?" Quinn said.

"Sure. Fine. Just… it's a horrible way to die."

For a moment Quinn was silent as he watched the traffic lights ahead. Then he said, "I've seen worse."

"As a garda?"

"That too."

For a moment she didn't know what he meant, and then it hit her.

"Most of the people who died at the White Lady died instantly," she said quietly. *I know they did. I saw their souls leave.*

"And the ones who died later?" Quinn said, his eyes on the traffic.

A memory assaulted Jen. A man with half his face missing, breastplate dented, leaning on his halberd. "Dost know what it means, to die of wounds?" he'd said to her. "It means thou dies slowly. Once that bullet, or sword, or aye, that flame does bite thee, thou art dead, but the dying may take days. Or weeks, or even years. The body may seem to heal, but the mind, child. The mind is dying. Th'art dead the moment the bullet hits thee."

She'd been ten.

"They were dead the minute the bomb went off," she said. Just like that old soldier. Just like Ethan.

She turned her head as they passed Christchurch. She didn't want to see a rat-eaten soldier gazing reproachfully at her from dead eyes.

Quinn said nothing as they turned down a narrow, curving street. On one side, the buildings were relatively modern, but on the other some concrete monstrosity reared up, and she focused her attention on that.

For a moment the concrete wavered, and she swore she saw lurching, crowded medieval buildings. Pigs foraged in the mud and a woman in green stared spitefully at Jen. In her hands she held the two halves of a broken plate.

Then Jen blinked, and the ugly modernity was back.

"This is an old part of the city," she said, looking up at the concrete.

"Fishamble? One of the oldest streets. You can tell by the shape of it. Viking, I think. God only knows what's under the council building there."

Abruptly, the road swung around and opened onto a thoroughfare running by the river. Quinn drove a few hundred yards, then parked the car on the street. He had to reverse again to do so, putting his arm on the back of her seat again. She breathed in the leather of his jacket and the heat of his skin and the faint tinge of soap. Thank God he didn't use the same aftershave Ethan did. She wouldn't have been able to cope with that.

"I'm sorry," he said, in the silence of the parked car. "About the ghosts and stuff. I didn't mean to… to tease you."

"It's all right." She looked out across the river, sun shining on the dark water.

"They say Dublin's full of ghosts."

"But you don't believe in them, so that's no problem," Jen said brightly.

"But you do."

No, I don't, she wanted to shout, but it was pointless, it had always been pointless. "Shall we go sightseeing?" she said, opening the door. "All those things you told me about yesterday. The castle, wasn't it, and the, uh, the library with the dirty poems, and maybe we can be total tourists and go to the Guinness brewery."

"If you like," Quinn said, and she got out of the car and pretended the wind was making her eyes water.

He said no more about ghosts, turning instead into the perfect tour guide. His knowledge of the city was minutely detailed, each street perfectly known to him. "Remember I was a guard nearly ten years," he said when she complimented him. "I've walked every one of these mean streets."

"They don't look so mean," Jen said, looking around pointedly at the tourists gawping at Dublin Castle.

"Try hanging around Temple Bar on a Saturday night," he said.

He walked her through the gardens to the Chester Beatty Library, where the Egyptian love poems were still on display. For once, Jen half hoped there'd be a ghost around to tell her what the naughty ancient Egyptian poems meant, but the only people she saw were flesh and blood ones.

Until they passed the garda station behind the castle, where Quinn said nothing and didn't look at the blue light or the rows of official vehicles. *There's more than one type of ghost*, she thought.

They walked on past elegant Georgian houses to St

KATE JOHNSON

Stephen's Green, past the Shelbourne Hotel where, Quinn insisted, he'd once been sent to break up an incredibly ribald party involving a footballer, two popstars and a collection of ladies whose affection was negotiable.

"But it looks so…" Jen began, looking up at the handsome building.

"Trust me. It's the fanciest hotels with the most filthy parties. That's why they cost so much: staff discretion doesn't come cheap."

"Who's the most famous person you've arrested, then?"

Quinn laughed. "I can't tell you that!"

"Oh, go on."

"No." Grinning, he looked down at her from behind his shades. "If I did, I'd have to kill you. Although I will tell you that my da once got called out to a party with George Best. Whole thing had got too out of hand and the gardaí had to be called in. Well, once they got there, all the undesirables cleared out and George bought the officers a pint as a thank you."

"I don't suppose they were able to accept?"

"Whisht," he scoffed. "It was the sixties."

Jen rolled her eyes, unsure if he was joking or not. "So your dad was a policeman, too?"

"Sure he was. That's why I joined up." Quinn hesitated, his expression inscrutable. "He had a heart attack when I was taking my Junior Cert. Didn't live out the year. I'd half an idea I wanted to follow in his footsteps. That cemented it for me."

Jen reached out to take his hand, then stopped herself. "I'm sorry," she said instead.

He gave a shrug that wasn't in the least bit convincing. Eyes utterly hidden by those damn shades, he said lightly, "Ah now. Everybody dies."

This time she did take his hand. "Quinn—"

"I know. Jenny, I know."

Words stuck in her throat. Quinn smiled down at her, a small smile but a real one, and then said, "Time for lunch? Or d'you want to see Merrion Square? Fine statue of Oscar Wilde. Or the Parliament buildings, they're just round the corner. It's a small city, so it is."

I want to keep holding your hand. I want to pretend this is real.

"Whatever you think is best. It's your city, after all."

Quinn squeezed her fingers, then let go, and guided her round to the imposing Palladian grandeur of Leinster House. "That's where our august and venerated elected officials make shite decisions," he told her. "Still. The building's nice."

"It's grand," she said, and he grinned at her use of the word.

He took her past Trinity College and insisted she had her photo taken with Molly Malone. "Although she's moved, the cheeky floozie. You nearly found the one thing in Dublin I didn't know about."

Jen looked at the bronze face of Molly, standing forever serene with her low-cut blouse and her cart full of fish, and wondered if she'd found the one thing in Dublin that wasn't haunted.

He took her for lunch at an upmarket restaurant, regaled her with non-confidential stories of his time as a garda, many of which revolved around drunk students from Trinity and even drunker tourists doing unspeakable things to poor Molly Malone.

"I'm glad I washed my hands," Jen said, and Quinn laughed.

"Ah, she gets washed by the rain. You'll be grand."

After lunch they crossed over the river and Quinn, looking slightly stunned to find it where Uncle Kieran had told him, presented the Leprechaun Museum.

"Appropriate enough it wasn't here last time I was on

Jervis Street," he said. "How dare the city move on without me?"

"Cities do that," Jen said. "And hey, look: something you didn't believe in is real! How about that?"

He frowned a little at that, but took her inside and did a great job of behaving like a tourist. As they sat around a wishing well to hear a tale of the leprechauns, his knee brushed hers. Jen tried to pretend she wasn't affected by that. She was pretty sure she failed.

All was going grand, in fact, until they passed through a small courtyard at the end of the tour and a huge black figure emerged from the wall. Taller than Quinn, sunk into the ground, and emanating cold, it seemed to be dragging chains with it like Marley's ghost.

Jen stumbled, stifling a yelp, and Quinn caught her.

"Are you all right?" asked their guide. "You look like you've seen a ghost!"

Quinn's arm tightened around her. "Just a dizzy spell, eh darling?" he said, and guided her to a bench.

Jen couldn't tear her eyes from the apparition as it clanked across the courtyard and vanished through the opposite wall. She supposed she sat down. Her heart hammered, her breath came short, and she'd just told herself to stop being freaked out because it was just another ghost—when the ghost turned to her, and from beneath its hood darkness seemed to suck at her soul.

"Jen. Jenny. Are you all right?"

The spectre disappeared through the wall.

Jen blinked. Quinn's face was very close to hers. She could feel his breath hot on her cheek, smell the mint he'd popped in his mouth at the restaurant.

"I'm fine," she said. "I just..." *Saw a ghost.* Godammit.

"If it's a leprechaun, they're meant to be good luck," he said. "Or weren't you listening?"

"Right," she said weakly. "Good luck. Uh huh."

She waved away his protests and busied herself looking at souvenirs in the shop. Might as well pick up something for Millie and Eddie while she was here. Quinn wandered off to talk to their guide, his voice low. He glanced over at her once or twice, frowning a little.

Jen felt irrationally jealous. *He can talk to whoever he wants*, she told herself. He was probably telling the woman how his batty assistant thought she saw ghosts. Probably flirting with her a bit. She was certainly flirting with him.

Not that I can blame her, Jen thought with a sigh, and selected a book of Irish folk tales for her niece.

Quinn watched her from the corner of his eye as they left the museum and he looked around for a coffee shop. He'd heard on the radio a while back that people had seen ghosts at the Jervis Centre, and—

Oh, what the feck is the matter with you, Quinn? Whatever she saw, it wasn't a ghost. And if he paraded her around the darkest corridors of the Jervis Centre in the middle of the night she still wouldn't see any. *There's no such thing.*

But still, he opted not to walk her past the row of gravestones propped up against the back wall of the Leprechaun Museum. Best not to stir things up. Not after what the *seanchaí* had told him.

Jen accepted the coffee, declined a pastry, and sat watching him stir sugar and milk into his tea. Her face was mostly back to its normal colour. Around them, ordinary people did ordinary things. A mixture of tourist voices babbled, a small child squealed, the radio played popular hits.

Quinn couldn't have identified a single one of them if his life depended on it.

Jen fiddled with the end of her plait. As it fell over

her shoulder, it brushed aside the neckline of her navy t-shirt to reveal a bright purple bra strap. Quinn startled at the contrast, rattling the teacup in its saucer, and her gaze darted up.

"Feeling better?"

She nodded.

"Tea's the best restorative, you know. Better than coffee."

"I'm fine with coffee, thanks."

He tapped the plastic stirrer against the cup and eyed her. "What happened back there? Were you ill?"

Jen sighed. She picked up her drink, put it back down again, and said, "What did it used to be? The Leprechaun Museum? What was in that building?"

Quinn frowned, trying to remember what Uncle Kieran had told him. "A factory, I believe. Corsetry. Why?"

"You know why." Her voice was resigned. "I saw a ghost."

He took his time in replying. After all, wasn't that why he'd brought her to Ireland in the first place?

"What kind of ghost?"

She looked up disbelievingly. "The woo-woo, dead kind! Big, dark, robed, dragging chains around like something out of Dickens. And don't tell me I imagined it or it was someone else playing a trick, because if anyone else had seen that you'd have damn well noticed it. And he walked through the wall. And the bottom of his robes were sunken into the ground. He was a ghost."

Realising her voice had gone up in tone and volume, she stopped talking, and took a sip of coffee, her cheeks pink.

"Which wall?" Quinn asked.

"What?"

"Which wall? Back inside the building, or out into Wolftone Park?"

Jen blinked, as if surprised he was even asking. "Uh… not the building. It…" She frowned. "Was there a park?"

"We went the other way. It's a small paved space with benches and trees." Quinn fiddled with the tea stirrer. "And gravestones," he conceded. "There are gravestones lined up against the wall."

She threw up her hands and glared at him. "Gravestones? So—what, the museum used to be a graveyard?"

"No, but the park did. There's a church at the other end of it," Quinn said desperately. "Look, I didn't know the place was fecking haunted, did I?"

Not until he'd talked to the woman at the museum who'd told him the shade of the hated Lord Norbury, the Hanging Judge, was known to drag his chains around the place. His gravestone was one of the markers pushed up against the wall of the museum courtyard.

"You don't think anywhere is haunted! You probably think the thing I saw was a—a visual disturbance or a tumour pressing on my brain, and if you say one word about seeing a doctor I will murder you." Her hands were shaking. "I have been tested. For *everything*."

Quinn raised his hands for peace. "I'm sorry. Look, maybe we'd better forget about tonight."

"No bloody way, mate. You got me out here to see ghosts and I've seen plenty so far."

"Plenty?"

She winced. "Around Fishamble Street. And on Killiney Hill. For God's sake keep me away from the sites of the Easter Rising or I might go completely mental."

Quinn made a face at the word 'mental' but Jen didn't seem to even notice. She was staring at her coffee as if she was angry with it.

"We'll avoid O'Connell Street, so," he said softly.

And anywhere else he could remember from his history lessons.

He leaned back in his seat and watched Jen drink her coffee. God help him, but he was starting to believe her about all this ghost stuff. Something had shaken her up, that was for sure. How could she have known Lord Norbury was buried in that graveyard, or even that there'd be a graveyard, or any of it? And if it wasn't a ghost she'd seen, then what? Was she faking the whole thing? Was she mad, or ill, or...?

He sighed and rubbed his hand across his face. What she saw tonight, that'd be the test of it. Quinn had his notes and his recorded footage, and he had Mrs Kelly's stories and the history he and Uncle Kieran had put together, and now it was time to see if any of it matched up.

If Jen saw nothing, then there were no ghosts. End of story. Which meant something else was affecting her. He really, really didn't want to have the conversation with her about seeing doctors. Not after all the ones she'd apparently already seen.

If she really had seen them. Maybe he should ask her sister about that. Even though that would amount to spying on her. Which also probably wasn't the way to win her heart.

And then... what if she did see something tonight? A ghost in the same spot he'd recorded a dark shape on the heat cameras? A voice where he'd heard pops and clicks? The shade of one of Fairview's many unfortunate former inhabitants?

What if she presented him with incontrovertible proof that there was really a ghost haunting Mrs Kelly's house?

"What's that face for?" Jen said, and he blinked, focusing on her face.

"It's just my face," he said vaguely, and ran a hand

through his hair, sitting up straight. "Are you about done? We should make a move, the traffic can be murder this time of day."

Jen shrugged and drained her cup. "Lead on."

CHAPTER TWENTY-SIX

The name on the gate said "Fairview", but Jen had an uneasy feeling the big grey house hadn't always been called something so innocuous. In the brightness of morning, she hadn't noticed any sense of foreboding, but then again maybe the dread stealing over her since they left Dublin had more to do with what she rather suspected was coming. It wasn't likely Quinn had been called in to see to a cheerful, happy spirit.

"It's going to be Ludlow all over again," she murmured.

"Sorry?" Quinn glanced over.

"Nothing." Her head throbbed just like it had the day of the White Lady. And the day Paul Dunlop died.

Today in Dublin the sun had shone, and she'd spent the day with a charming, handsome man looking at beautiful, interesting things. *Like a date.* And now… now it felt as if the morning had been a sunlit holiday, and every mile further from the city had brought them further into darkness.

She shook herself before she started imagining the Eye of Sauron in the sky.

"Is your uncle still at the house?"

He nodded, wheeling the car around a wide carriage circle to the front of the house. "He is. And, ehm, there's someone else coming too. Someone Mrs Kelly organised herself."

"Oh?"

Quinn stopped the car and sighed the sigh of the long-suffering. "Her name is Gobnait Ní Dhomhnaill. O'Donnell to you and me," he added with a roll of his eyes. "She's a medium or something. Big on the Internet, apparently. Will you have heard of her?" Jen shook her head. "Ah well, she's from the Gaeltacht. Where they mostly speak Irish," he added. "And as you heard last night, mine is fecking terrible, so I don't expect we'll become the best of friends."

"Plus, she's a medium, so you're not disposed to like her," Jen said. The big grey house seemed to be looming over her.

"Well, I like you just fine and you were after seeing a ghost this afternoon, so."

Jen frowned at him, but didn't say anything as Kieran came out of the house and down the steps, followed by a plump woman of middling years. Quinn got out of the car, so she did too.

"Mrs Kelly, this is my associate, Jennifer Hargrave," Quinn said, and Jen took the hand she was offered.

"Pleased to meet you," she murmured, staring up at the house. By the front steps was an old-fashioned streetlamp with three branches. It was lit with electricity, but Jen had an uneasy feeling she could see the flicker of gas flames on the walls. The wind swished the trees and her pulse throbbed in her ears. The grey walls seemed to suck at her.

There was something in this house, and she knew with reasonable certainty that she wasn't going to like it.

"Jen?" Someone touched her arm, and she didn't

flinch because ghosts don't touch people, and turned to see Quinn's dark brows drawn down in concern. "Are you all right?"

"Fine," she said.

He didn't look convinced, but turned her towards a woman getting out of a car Jen hadn't even heard arrive. She was tall, stately in black, and had a mound of greying curls piled up on her head. She was followed by a young man with a somewhat pretentious goatee.

Mrs Kelly rushed over and gushed something in Irish, at which the woman nodded in a regal sort of way.

They both regarded Jen in a way that made her want to straighten her clothes and brush her hair.

She was rescued by Kieran, who walked forward, offered his hand and said something in smooth Irish, which he followed up in English with, "And Jenny, this is Gobnait Ní Dhomhnaill, and her nephew Padraig. Mrs Ní Dhomhnaill also has the Sight."

You make it sound like a plague, Jen thought, smiling politely and shaking Mrs Ní Dhomhnaill's hand. "Pleased to meet you," she said.

She was rewarded with an expression of chilly disdain and a flurry of Irish that the young man translated as, "My aunt replies that she's pleased to meet you too."

There was a short, awkward silence. Jen's temples began to throb.

"Will we go inside the house?" Kieran said. "I don't know if either of you has a particular method...?"

Jen shook her head. A method? *Yes, pretending I'm absolutely normal and ghosts don't exist. That's my method.*

Mrs Ní Dhomhnaill said something Padraig translated as, "She will go into the house and see where the spirits draw her."

Jen gestured for them to go ahead, mostly so they

wouldn't see her rolling her eyes.

"You okay?" Quinn murmured as he followed Jen.

"Oh, I'm fine. I'm just dandy." Jen shivered as she crossed the threshold. No, there was something awful here, and she didn't want to meet it.

Quinn shivered too, pulling his scarf tighter around his neck. She noticed Mrs Kelly had on a rather thick cardigan and Uncle Kieran hadn't taken off his coat.

The pounding in her head grew louder. She pinched at the bridge of her nose, and nearly walked straight into Padraig, who stood just behind his aunt. Mrs Ní Dhomhnaill had gone very still.

"Does she see something?" Mrs Kelly hissed. Kieran put his finger to his lips. Jen edged around the rather substantial shape of Mrs Ní Dhomhnaill, dread building in her as she came face to face with the staircase.

It was a wide staircase, facing the front door directly, and it was wooden with a carpeted runner. Halfway up, it halted at a wide landing with several doors off it, before turning back on itself. Both the walls and the underside of the stairwell were panelled with dark wood. Save for a small table holding a vase on the landing, it was empty of people, animals, and furniture.

It filled Jen with absolute horror.

Over the thundering of her blood in her ears she heard Padraig translating his aunt's words. "… something terrible happened here," he said.

"No kidding," Jen muttered. She started shivering and couldn't stop.

"Close the—" Kieran began, then stopped on realising the front door was already closed.

"This is where—" Mrs Kelly began at the same time, but Quinn shushed her.

"Don't give them any clues. I want to know what they both see."

Jen shook her head. "Nothing. There's nothing there,

but it's… I can't describe it. I just don't want to go near those stairs."

Mrs Ní Dhomhnaill looked at Jen, and despite her apparent composure Jen saw the same dread in the older woman's face.

"*Ní mór dúinn*," she said softly.

"We must," Padraig whispered.

To Jen's surprise, Mrs Ní Dhomhnaill took her hand. Her fingers were like ice.

Quinn looked between them, his expression hard to read. "How about I go on ahead?"

Jen managed to nod, and he bounded easily up the stairs as if they weren't the portent of all that was evil in the world. Kieran followed, and then Mrs Ní Dhomhnaill started after him, which meant Jen had to follow.

With every step she felt the dread deepen, until her hands were shaking and her teeth chattering and she had to hold on very tight to this strange woman who seemed to feel the same thing.

They made the first step, and nothing happened. Then the one after it, and nothing more. Ten steps to the landing, and they were all like wading through a bog.

Quinn waited on the stair return, watching their slow progress. Jen took a decent breath, let it shudder out, and joined him there. Mrs Ní Dhomhnaill let go of her hand, and said something to Padraig.

"It's not the stairs themselves," he said as his aunt spoke on. "It's… the air around them. Above them."

"Under them," Jen said uneasily.

Quinn moved to the next section of the stairs, and Jen stepped after him, feeling a little lighter, and then she realised it.

Someone was still speaking Irish, and it wasn't Mrs Ní Dhomhnaill.

Jen stared for a second at her, then, dread oozing in through her pores, turned her gaze to where Mrs Ní

Dhomhnaill was staring, as if transfixed.

A woman stood at the top of the stairs, the landing visible through her body. Her dress was long and stained with blood, her hair was dark, and her face was a terrible greenish white. She was muttering feverishly, continuously, through grey lips.

Worse, her gaze was fixed on Quinn.

"What's she saying?" Jen whispered. Then when Mrs Ní Dhomhnaill didn't respond, she said it louder. "Padraig, ask her what she's saying. The ghost, there's a ghost," she gibbered, pointing for no good reason at the terrible apparition.

Mrs Kelly gasped and clutched at Kieran, who swore, then seemed to recover himself. "Can you describe it?" he said.

But Jen didn't get a chance. The creature swooped forward, screaming like a banshee, hands extended into murderous claws, and flew right at Quinn.

Jen shouted and ran at them, but not before the ghost had flung Quinn to the floor, crashing into the small table and bringing its vase of flowers down on his head. He tried to get up, but the fall seemed to have done something to his bad leg.

He looked around in confusion, trying to fix something at his knee, as Mrs Kelly shrieked, "It's the ghost!" and Padraig clutched at his aunt, who stood motionless, watching. Kieran started towards Quinn, but Jen was faster.

"Get away from him! Leave him alone!" Jen shouted, and the terrible creature paused in reaching out one clawed hand to Quinn's neck. "Yeah, I can see you. Get your filthy undead hands off him!"

The ghost straightened up, and regarded Jen with a sort of curiosity. She spoke, this time more loudly, and in the manner of a question. Her jaw didn't seem to be moving properly with her words, sliding around like it wasn't connected.

"I don't know what you're saying," Jen said, backing away, "but—"

This time, the ghost flew at Jen, so fast she had no time to react before the wave of ice slammed into her.

It was as if she'd been injected with utter fear and loathing. Disgust writhed through her veins like live maggots and she couldn't stop herself lurching forward, falling to her knees and grabbing at Quinn's collar with clumsy hands.

"Jenny?" he began, his eyes wide and dark, and the creature controlling Jen let out a terrible laugh.

Her own mouth spoke, but the voice wasn't her own and the words weren't in English. Through the swamp of terror drowning Jen she was aware of Quinn's mounting horror, as her hands scrabbled for a grip and yanked him to his feet with a strength that wasn't hers.

"Jenny?"

And the creature inside Jen laughed again and snarled, "*Brónach is aimn dom!*" before Quinn's fist connected with her face and she stumbled backwards, darkness closing in.

CHAPTER TWENTY-SEVEN

The White Lady: Three weeks after

The phone rings, and the name on the display is the catering company Jen used to work for. She's gone in and told them she's all right, which felt like walking and talking underwater, and now they've taken to ringing her. Probably with offers of a new job. Or maybe to tell her to go and see a doctor or a counsellor or one of those people Jen will never go and see. Not ever again.

She hasn't seen Alice since the bomb went off. That's probably a mercy, given what she's been doing.

She reaches out to the phone, and admires the cuts on the back of her hand. Then she stops, because if she answers and they have a job for her then she'll have to go for an interview, and then she'll have to explain why her hands are covered in cuts and her arms are permanently bruised and her neck has bite marks all over it. Nobody is going to employ someone who looks like an extra from *The Walking Dead*.

The phone stops ringing, and reverts to its usual screensaver. It shows a countdown to a date. The date is when Charlotte's baby is due.

Jen looks at that date, and at the calendar where she's circled it in red ink with lots of exclamation marks. And she looks at her hands, scabbed and scarred with cuts from scissors, forks and screwdrivers.

She will have to go and see Charlotte when the baby is born, and her sister might not notice but her mother will, and Jen will need an excuse for those cuts. A job in an animal shelter? A mugging? A car accident?

"I've been stabbing myself with household implements and allowing a virtual stranger to beat me up while we have sex," will be a one-way ticket back to one of those homes. And she will never go back there.

She gets up, slips her phone into her pocket, and leaves the flat. It's cooler now, and by the time she gets off the Tube in Shoreditch the sky has gone dark. She walks the same familiar route, but this time as she passes a wretched-looking girl begging in a doorway she pauses, digs out a fiver and passes it over. The girl stares, doesn't take it, and Jen lets it fall to the ground. She doesn't notice how it goes right through the beggar. She's already walking on.

She reaches the door, his door, the black one with the graffiti on it. She pushes it open and goes up the noisy metal steps that have probably been there since the warehouse was built. His door is at the top. It's red.

He might not even be in. But he always has been before, every time she's called round, just as she's been in whenever he's come to her place. Neither of them have anything else to do.

She knocks, and he opens it, standing there all dark-eyed and gorgeous. He looks like a rockstar or a vampire. A rockstar vampire. There's a bruise on his right forearm. She did that to him the last time... or maybe the time before that.

He stands back wordlessly to let her in, and the door

318

has barely shut behind her when he's grabbing her for a bruising kiss.

She pulls away, and for a second he follows until she backs up several steps. His dark brows draw down.

"What?"

"I don't want," she begins, then realises she probably should have worked out what to say before she came. "I don't want... that," she says lamely.

He looks puzzled, then his face clears and he begins to pull off his shirt. "You just want to get right to it," he says. His stomach bears the scratches from her nails.

"No," she says, and this time he looks really confused.

"Then what are you here for?"

Jen takes a deep breath and lets it out. The apartment smells stale, as if he hasn't even opened a window in weeks. There are clothes strewn around where he's obviously dropped them and forgotten. Piles of coffee cups in the sink and takeaway containers everywhere.

"We need to talk," she says.

He folds his arms and looks petulant. Talking has never really been on the agenda before.

"About what?"

"This," she says, and gestures between them. "It isn't healthy. What we're doing. It's not good for either of us."

He looks at her with those devil-dark eyes in that angelic face, and says in a soft voice, "It feels good."

Heat curls low in her belly. Damn him for being right about that.

"But it isn't. I think we need to end it."

He doesn't say anything, just looks at her with those damned eyes.

"I need to end it. I am ending this relationship," Jen says.

"What relationship?" he says, and a weight lifts from

her.

"Exactly," she says, and heads to the door. "Goodbye, Ethan."

He doesn't come after her.

CHAPTER TWENTY-EIGHT

"Go faster," Quinn said.

Kieran's little runabout wasn't really intended to scream down unmade driveways like a rally car, but one glance in the rearview mirror had him gunning the engine.

"Jesus, she's white as snow."

Quinn paused in trying to jam his prosthetic back on, and looked down at her. "I know."

Jen lolled beside him, apparently unconscious. Which had been Quinn's intention when he'd hit her. Well, sort of. She'd been about to throw him over her own head, which wasn't something that had ever come up in his garda training, and besides—

Besides—

Dear God, he'd never known panic like it.

As Quinn finally popped his stump into the socket, Kieran reached the end of the driveway and careened out onto the road. Behind them, Gobnait Ní Dhomhnaill's car followed. Quinn thought it contained the medium and her nephew and Mrs Kelly, but he wasn't sure and he didn't care.

He grabbed for Jen and she felt like a corpse in his arms.

"Is she breathing? Tell me she's breathing," Kieran threw over his shoulder as he took a turn at high speed.

"She's breathing. Pulse is fast and Jesus, she's cold. Jenny. Jenny, can you hear me?" *Jenny, are you in there?*

Fear beat strongly in him. What if the eyes that opened weren't Jen's? What if they still belonged to that... that... *thing*, whatever it was, that had possessed her?

"Did you hear what she said?" Kieran threw over his shoulder.

Brónach is aimn dom. "Yes," Quinn said, cupping Jen's cold cheek.

My name is Brónach.

"She was... oh, was it the eighteenth or nineteenth century?" Kieran said desperately. "She disappeared..."

Quinn's eyes burned. "Apparently she didn't go far," he muttered. He stroked Jen's hair back from her face, chafed her hands, held her closer as the car lurched over a pothole. Her forehead was pink where he'd hit her.

He'd hit her, and her eyes had rolled back in her head and she'd crumpled. And Quinn had dragged himself as near to upright as he could manage, looked around at the shocked company, and said, "We are getting the fuck out of here. Now."

Now the car rattled away from the house as fast as it could go, back towards light and civilisation and away from nightmares. "I believe you now, darling, I really do. Ghosts are real. No argument from me," he gabbled, tears in his eyes. "Wake up, Jennifer, please."

Her eyes slammed open and she sucked in a huge breath. Quinn tensed, his hands on her wrists, but the eyes looking up at him were blue and confused, and the voice that spoke was her own.

"Quinn? What—ow," she moaned faintly as the car hit a bump.

"Jen. Jenny." Quinn breathed out half a prayer he didn't even realise he still knew. "Are you all right? You're not still…"

She shuddered and curled closer. "I'm freezing," she gasped, her words slurring as if her tongue was too big for her mouth. "Oh God, what happened? Was it Alice?"

Her eyes were huge in her face, but they were her eyes, human and frightened, not the terrible bleak dark holes they'd become on the stairs. When she'd stared down at him and screamed.

When the bean sidhe screams, someone will die…

"I don't think so. I think it was whatever's been haunting that house. It took you over, like Alice did that time."

Jen looked up at him in horror. "It wanted to kill you. It tried to get me to—"

"But you didn't," Quinn said. His heart was pounding. He cuddled her closer, her icy face and hands against his chest. "You didn't hurt me. Everybody's fine. I've got you."

"Quinn," Kieran called from the front seat. "Will I bring you to the hospital?"

He hesitated. On the one hand, she was shivering uncontrollably and had just been hit in the face. On the other, she'd also just been possessed by an evil spirit, and he didn't think that would go over too well in the telling.

"No," she whispered, clutching at him. "No doctors. Please. I just need to get away and be… away."

Wasn't that what Alice had said when she'd taken over Jen that time? *Oh Jesus God, the last time Jen was possessed by a ghost*. Take her somewhere quiet and warm and give her gin.

Give her spirits. He almost laughed.

"No, not the hospital," he said. "Go back to the hotel. And turn the heating up, will you?"

Ghosts were real. Whatever that thing had been, it'd been real, and it had tried to kill him.

"You were right," he whispered to Jen, who only shivered in reply.

It couldn't have taken as long as it felt to get back to the hotel. Kieran parked the car recklessly and came round to help Quinn get Jen out of the car. She was so cold, her words slurring, and when Quinn let go of her she'd have slid to the ground were it not for his uncle's quick reflexes.

They met eyes, and Quinn sighed and scooped Jen into his arms.

"I c'n walk," she mumbled into his chest.

Quinn started towards the front door. "No, you can't. In fact, if I took off my false leg right now, I'd still be able to walk better than you. We're almost there now. Just hang on and I'll get you into bed."

She mumbled something that Quinn heard as, "I wish," although he knew he was just imagining things.

Uncle Kieran held the door open, which meant that Quinn was the first in and the first to be greeted by the receptionist.

"Good evening... uh, Quinn?"

He looked up into the concerned face of his cousin Emer. Great. *Totally forgot she worked here.*

"Emer, is it yourself?" he stalled desperately.

"Emer!" cried Uncle Kieran behind him. Then, like the wonderful man he was, he said conspiratorially, "Ah, don't mind them. Young Jenny's had a bit too much of the craic. She'll feel it in the morning!"

Emer looked over Jen's pale, shuddering form, and nodded uncertainly. Kieran beamed cheerfully and went on, "Will you be needing my help, Quinn, or do you—"

"No, I have it from here, Uncle, thanks a million."

Quinn strode gratefully towards the elevator and jabbed his elbow manically against the button until the door opened. "Oh… and will you check up on Mrs Kelly this evening?"

"I will that. *Slán!*"

"*Slán*," Emer, pride of Tourism Ireland, repeated obediently.

"Yeah, that too," Quinn muttered as the lift doors closed.

It took some manoeuvring to unlock the room door, but eventually he shoved it open and stumbled inside. He pulled off Jen's shoes and coat and tucked her under the covers, removed a bit of broken vase from her hair, then started opening cupboard doors until he found a spare blanket and draped that over her too.

She huddled in the bed, rigid with cold, and Quinn felt horribly helpless.

"D'you want a drink?" he said. "Water, or tea, or gin?"

"Gin," she stammered, and he almost smiled as he crossed to the minibar and started pulling out miniature bottles. Gin. Good.

Her hand shook as she reached for it. Quinn held it to her lips and she sucked it all down with a shudder.

"Better?"

She coughed and spluttered, then pulled the covers right up to her chin and nodded.

Quinn didn't know what to do now. He ran some water and put the glass by her bed. He turned off all but the bedside light and shut the curtains. He put her coat and shoes away neatly so she wouldn't trip over them on her way to the bathroom.

Then he stood and watched her a bit. The shivering had slowed down, but she was still white with shock.

"D'you want me to stay?" he asked, and she nodded. Quinn nodded too, regarding the armchair in the corner without much enthusiasm. Well. His back already ached from being thrown down the stairs and his head wasn't feeling great either. Added to which, it turned out that getting thrown into a table wasn't fantastic for the wrecked muscles of a half-amputated leg.

What more could a night in an armchair do to him?

He hung up his coat next to Jen's, pulled off his shoes and tried to ignore the domestic cosiness the two pairs presented side by side, and sat down, wishing there was another blanket. Or maybe he could fetch his coat back and—

A sudden gasp from Jen had his head whipping round so fast he was in danger of injuring himself for the second time that night.

"Jen?"

Her back was to him, shuddering with wrenching sobs. Her breath came in gasps. He lunged across the bed, pulling her by the shoulder to face him.

Her eyes were wet, her nose pink, a bruise forming on her temple where he'd hit her. She flung herself at him, her face crumpling. "Quinn, Quinn. It tried to kill you."

Quinn wrapped his arms around her, his heart pounding as the fear came back. "Ah now, Jenny. No harm done."

"N-no—harm?" Jen hiccupped. She writhed against him, snaking one hand out from the blankets to touch his face with cold fingers. "You're bleeding."

He frowned, touching his cheekbone. His fingers slipped against hers, touched soreness, came away rusty with dried blood. Well, then.

"It's nothing," he said distantly.

She pressed herself closer to him, cheek against his chest, breath hitching with sobs. "I couldn't stop her. I couldn't do anything."

"It's all right. It's over now." He rocked her gently,

holding her as close as he could. Tears were threatening again.

He'd had to *hit* her. She was hurt because of him. She was a shivering wreck because of him. If he hadn't started this, hadn't mocked and doubted and paraded her out here to—what? To prove she was lying, or mad, or…?

She wasn't mad. She was actually amazingly sane.

All this is your fault, Quinn you selfish bastard. He hid his face in her hair so she wouldn't know he was crying, held her close because she was precious and she was hurt.

She mumbled something, half asleep, and he pulled the blanket up over her back, reluctantly easing her back down to the mattress so he could cover her over. But she clung to him, pulled him with her and cuddled close like a child.

He glanced over his shoulder at the great expanse of bed she wasn't taking up. He looked down at her face pressed against his chest, lashes shadowing her cheek, breathed in her scent and felt her cool fingers at his neck.

And although it wasn't remotely the way he wanted to share a bed with her, Quinn crawled under the covers and pulled her into his arms. Just until she's warmer, he told himself, and didn't wake until morning.

Jen's dreams were awful, vivid and confusing. She dreamt of the White Lady, but instead of the smoky remains she saw the two brothers, laughing together over their drinks. Ethan gave her a saucy once-over but it was Quinn whose dark eyes lingered.

She dreamt of Alice, standing by her bed and laying cool fingers on her brow. "It's all right, it's over now," she whispered, and for a moment Jen wasn't sure who she was.

"Can Quinn see you?" she asked, and Alice shook

her head, smiling. Her voice was distant, muddled.

"He'll take care of you, my love. Remember that. He'll never harm you."

Jen shifted, trying to reach for Alice. The darkness was full of broken plates.

"Nothing will harm you," the ghost crooned. "Not while I'm around."

It was a lullaby, one Jen didn't like. And it wasn't Alice singing it. It was the thing, the creature, wailing a lullaby through a torn-out mouth and falling, falling...

There was Quinn, pale and bloody because she'd hurt him. But then his arms came around her, warm and strong, and she breathed in his skin. The faintest hint of soap and sweat and leather, and him. And him.

"You didn't hurt me. Everybody's fine. I've got you."

Exhausted with relief, she curled into him, and his voice echoed in her ear as warmth returned.

"I've got you."

And Jen dreamed of sleep, soft and welcoming, in his arms. Of the Sunday-morning pleasure of lying with him, half-awake, holding him close and being at peace. She dreamed of his skin, warm and enticing, the rough stubble on his neck teasing her cheek. Of the texture of that stubble against her lips, the surety of his hands on her back. Of her lips finding his in a soft, tender kiss, his hair silky against her fingers as she pulled him closer. Her thigh snugged over his hip, the heat of his body seeping through the layers of their clothes. Her foot slid over his knee, the bumps and ridges under the denim then the smooth hardness of his metal leg, and she smiled against his mouth because this was Quinn, her Quinn, holding her close and kissing her so tenderly.

His fingers touched the bare skin where her t-shirt had ridden up as the phone rang, and Jen made a small noise of pleasure that made him smile against her lips as the phone rang, and his fingers caressed her skin as the phone rang, and—

"Wha'?" she mumbled, confused. Why was a phone ringing in her dream? She was dreaming of kissing Quinn and now there was a phone ringing and daylight coming in through the curtains and his phone was buzzing on the nightstand.

Oh God, she wasn't dreaming.

"Jenny," Quinn murmured, sleep-tousled and unbearably sexy, and she scrambled back in horror. He blinked up at her, confused.

"You'd better answer that," she said, tangled in the sheets, and nearly fell out of bed in her haste to escape.

"Are you—?" Quinn began, but she bolted to the bathroom and locked the door. For a second she leaned against it, heart fluttering, and then the phone went quiet and Quinn, his voice disgusted, said, "Hi, Uncle Kieran."

Jen ran her hands over her face, then risked a look in the mirror. Hair all over the place, remains of yesterday's makeup lingering most unflatteringly, lips pink and swollen from kissing. From *sleep*-kissing. Sleep-kissing her boss. Who she had tried to kill last night whilst being possessed by an evil spirit.

A whimper escaped her.

She pressed her ear to the door, and heard Quinn stomping about the room. "Oh, she's fine. No, she's going home today. Well, her flight's booked so that's that," he snapped.

Jen slid to the floor, the warmth of the dream fleeing like mist.

He'd ended the call by the time Jen emerged from the bathroom, and sat at the desk, staring at his scribbled notes and hardly seeing them.

Jen had kissed him, really kissed him. Nuzzled his

neck and kissed his lips and wrapped herself around him, and then she'd made that noise, and he was utterly undone. A statue would have come to life at that noise.

And then she'd run her foot over his bloody prosthetic and suddenly stopped. Quinn wanted to cry. She'd been kissing him… and then she'd realised it was him.

"Ethan never had a fucking fake leg," he muttered, viciously stabbing his notepad with the pen.

Then the bathroom door unlocked and Jen emerged. She had her face washed and her hair brushed. She was still in last night's clothes, and damn him if he hadn't daydreamed about this exact scenario being played out in the exact opposite way.

"How's your head?" he said before she could speak. He couldn't look directly at her.

Her hand went up to her temple, which was blooming red and purple. "It's fine. Bit sore. Nothing a painkiller won't fix."

Quinn nodded and fixed his attention on the desk. "That was Uncle Kieran. He, ehm, he's been looking at some of the history of the house, and there was a young girl called Brónach who went missing around two hundred years ago. Her father owned the house and they seemed to live there mostly alone."

He picked up his notepad so he wouldn't have to look at her. "Now I don't know what you remember but the last thing you said was 'my name is Brónach', which I did understand, but…" He didn't allow himself to shudder. "The rest of it I wasn't sure of."

Liar. He'd understood enough.

"Now Padraig has been trying to put together the things you said and what his aunt remembers the spirit saying before she took you over, and it's kind of muddled but the gist of it seems to be that a man hurt her and she'll go on hurting him, hence why she came after me and Mrs Kelly's husband and all the others. She also seems, historically, to have a grudge against young women, especially those who are, ehm, pregnant. Three of them have fallen down those stairs in the last hundred years and maybe some of the others who died were expecting too, we don't know."

"Quinn—"

"Mrs Ní Dhomhnaill," Quinn went on, still not looking at her, "seemed to think the path of the spirit didn't coincide with the actual geography of the house, but we've the plans going back a fair while and it seems the stairs we stood on are only about a hundred years old, and in fact the whole return level there on the landing was added at the same time, being built over the old staircase leading down into the cellar which actually was the path of the spirit. Now Mrs Kelly claims she's never been down there and it seems to have been sealed off, but if we can uncover a door in that wooden panelling it might lead us to some answers."

That was the end of his notes. The rest of it he hadn't had to write down.

Jen cleared her throat. "I didn't know what I was saying," she said. "Or doing. Quinn, I'm sorry, I didn't mean to hurt you."

He swallowed past the lump in his throat. "Likewise."

She began forward. "If there's anything I can do—"

"Pack, maybe," he said, standing up abruptly. His leg protested. "Your flight is this afternoon, right?"

A moment's silence, then a very quiet, "Just after six."

Quinn collected his shoes and sat down to put them on, focusing on the laces. "Ah, well then. You'll need to be there about four at the latest, and the Aircoach is, what, an hour, hour and a half from here? So be ready to leave by half two. Whatever time the bus goes. They'll

331

tell you on Reception."

"Right." She forced a laugh. "Might need to apologise for last night, they probably thought I was drunk or something."

"Right. Yeah." He picked up his coat and swung it on. "Oh, there's a gin missing from the minibar. You seemed to be in need of," his voice nearly faltered on the word, "spirits last night."

"I'll pay for it."

"Put it on the tab. Company pays." His hand was on the doorknob. He was nearly away.

"Quinn," she said, and he paused, aching for her. For an eternity she said nothing, and he was just about to turn when she gave a little sigh and said, "I'll see you back at the office, then?"

Where I will spend the rest of my life in despair that I'm still not my brother.

"*Slán leat,*" Quinn said, and left without looking back.

CHAPTER TWENTY-NINE

Yesterday's sunshine had blown away, and drizzle misted Jen's hair as she climbed the path up Killiney Hill. Cold, clean air filled her lungs, her heart pumped, sweat beaded the back of her neck. She was alive and healthy, which was more than she could say for poor Brónach last night.

Her thumbs swiped at her eyes, and she told herself it was just the wind making her eyes water.

The view opened up ahead of her, the obelisk standing up against the bruised sky. Today there were few dog walkers around, and not many brave souls out for a jog. There were no teenagers fooling around on the step pyramid. Just one transparent figure, standing sentinel, staring out to sea.

"Hey," she said, hands in pockets.

The soldier half-turned toward her, his battered face surprised.

"Been here long?"

"I…" his voice sounded rusty. "I couldn't be telling ye."

She glanced over his uniform. A red coat, which put

him back a fair few years.

She looked at the pile of stones. The Wishing Steps. *I wish I could fix this with Quinn.*

Maybe she could. Maybe…

I could be with him. Just for a night. A weekend. Until I have to tell him the truth. Maybe, when we get home…

"Are you making a wish?" she asked the ghost.

He turned back to the sea. "Waiting."

"You'll be waiting a long wait."

"Aye."

Suddenly irritated, Jen flung herself down on the pyramid's steps. "What's the point?" she exploded. "Standing here on sentry for hundreds of bloody years, waiting and watching and waiting. Why? *I wish, I wish.* Whoever it is, they're never going to come."

The old soldier kept his eyes on the sea.

"Why don't you just give up? What's the point of being a bloody ghost?"

"I didn't choose it," he said calmly.

"No, nobody would choose it," Jen said. "Why would you ever doom yourself to this? Like being a, a broken record or a fly trapped in a bloody jam jar, or whoever that poor sod was who had to roll the boulder up the hill every damn day…"

"Sisyphus," came a voice behind her, and Jen nearly fell off the steps as she spun to see Quinn standing there. His collar was turned up against the damp, his hands jammed in his pockets. His dark hair blew in the wind, catching the burst bruise on his cheekbone. He looked like he'd just walked off the cover of a vintage rock magazine.

I wish…

She stared up at him, dumbstruck.

"It was Sisyphus with the boulder," Quinn said. "Or was it Prometheus?"

"His was the liver," Jen heard herself saying. "Being pecked out every day."

"By an eagle. That's right. For stealing fire." He brushed a curl away from his eyes. "What did Sisyphus do?"

She shook her head. "I don't remember." She glanced out at the ghost of the soldier, waiting his long wait. She looked back at Quinn and the Wishing Steps.

I wish…

"Dammit," she said, and got to her feet.

Dismay swept his features. "I'll walk somewhere else. I just—"

Jen put her finger on his lips, and he abruptly shut up.

"Look, I'm sorry," she said, because if she didn't say it now she'd be waiting as long as that damn soldier. "For last night, going all psycho on you and trying to, you know, kill you and stuff, but it wasn't me. I mean, I wasn't in charge. Of myself. Oh God, now you'll have me committed…"

"No, I won't," Quinn said, soft lips and hard stubble rasping against her finger, and her eyes flew open wide. He reached up slowly, took her hand away from his face, and held it between them. Just held the back of her hand in his palm, and looked down at her with those liquid dark eyes of his.

"I know. Last night, you didn't have the run of yourself. It was Brónach, or whoever the feck she was. We're still trying to figure it out. Spent all morning—but never mind. Jenny, do you think I'd have spent all night with you if I thought you were a danger to me, or anyone else? To yourself?"

"I don't—know…" Jen trailed off, because in all her embarrassment and misery she hadn't really allowed herself to think about it.

His gaze softened. "I was worried about you," Quinn said. "You were… what was that, a possession?"

Jen's fingers curled around his thumb. "You believe me?"

"I believe you. All of it. Ghosts are real," he cracked a smile, "and I'm an idiot."

She couldn't speak. Quinn's eyes were dark and earnest and fixed right on her.

"Ah Jenny. I'm sorry I doubted you."

She'd waited her life to hear that. By the pyramid, the old soldier smiled, and faded into the mist.

Jen's breath went out on a whoosh, her hand tightening around Quinn's poor thumb. "God, I could kiss you," she said, and his brows shot up. "But I—don't worry, I'm not about to—ugh, I didn't mean it like that —"

"Right, of course," Quinn said on a rush. "I didn't think—"

"No."

"No."

Awkwardness froze the air between them again.

I wish…

Jen cursed herself, and before Quinn could leave she said, "Actually, about that. This morning. I'm really sorry."

Quinn's gaze fell. He swallowed. "Right," he said, and the word sounded painful.

"It's just," she ploughed on, determined to clear the air now he was on her side, her ally, and didn't think she was mad as a sack of cats, "I was dreaming, well, I thought I was dreaming, at least I hope I was because some of them were bloody awful. Do you dream about the White Lady?" she said desperately, and Quinn looked faintly incredulous.

"The White Lady?" he said.

"Yes. No. I mean it was that and then it wasn't, and then Alice was there and she said she'd take care of me and then it was you saying you'd take care of me and I suppose I just got… confused. In the dream."

"You… thought you were kissing… Alice?"

"No, you idiot, I thought I was kissing you!" Jen blurted, then smacked her hand over her mouth. Unfortunately she was still gripping Quinn's thumb and nearly knocked her own teeth out.

"Jaysus!" Arm around her shoulders, he steadied her. The bastard was grinning. "Are you… did you say you were dreaming about kissing me?"

Jen felt her face heat up. "All right, don't go on about it."

"Are you sure it was me? Not anybody else?"

"Yes, it was you! Nobody else I know has a metal leg!"

He ducked his head, looked up at her from under his lashes, tried to hide a smile. Hideously embarrassed, Jen tried to twist away, but he grabbed her by the scarf, tugged her back in against his body, and his lips came down on hers.

She'd spent so long convincing herself that he didn't want to kiss her that it was a hell of a shock when he did, and for a second she couldn't do anything at all. Then she couldn't do anything but kiss him back.

Her arms twined around his neck, her fingers tangling in his wild curls as he pulled her closer and kissed her with laughter on his lips.

"Hold on," she made herself say. "This morning, you wouldn't even look at me."

"Well, that's because I thought you didn't want to be kissing me," Quinn said, exasperated.

"Why did you think that?"

His arms still encircled her. His hair was soft against her fingers. He smelled like himself. "Well, you did run away," he said.

"Oh." Her cheeks heated again. "Right. Can we… draw a line under this morning?"

Quinn's eyes went playful. He nuzzled her cheek. "Start again?"

"Yeah. With the whole," her breath hitched, "you don't think I'm mad, I wasn't trying to grope you in my sleep or anything—" he laughed softly against her neck "—type of thing?"

When he looked up at her, his eyes were pure sex. "I think that sounds grand," he said, and brushed his lips over hers. "More than grand." Another brush. "That sounds… class. Deadly."

"Are you being Irish at me?" Jen murmured against his lips.

"Maybe. D'you like it?"

"I like it."

"Deadly."

She laughed as he kissed her, and kissed her, and the wind and the rain faded around them and there was no one else but the two of them on the clifftop, kissing like they'd just invented it.

"Ah, get a room," someone shouted from behind Jen, and they broke apart to see a couple of teenagers passing with a dog on a lead.

That sounds like a really good idea, Jen thought, swiftly followed by, "Bugger. I just checked out of mine."

"Ah, now." Quinn's arms were tight about her, but he loosened one and reached for his pocket. He raised his eyebrows suggestively. "If you wanted it back, I could call Emer."

Her heart flip-flopped. *I can have this. Even if it doesn't last, I can have it.* "So long as you don't think I'll get into trouble with my boss."

Quinn gave her a crooked grin as he scrolled through his phone. "Your boss thinks it's an excellent idea."

Jen snuggled in close as he dialled his cousin. "He's a very good boss."

"He has his good points," Quinn murmured. "Howerya, Emer, it's Quinn. I've a favour to be asking you..."

It was raining full on by the time they burst back into the hotel, grabbed the room key from a deadpan Emer, and skidded across the lobby to the elevator.

"Will I be calling the airline then?" Emer called.

Quinn slid his arm around Jen's waist and called back, "Tell them something came up," just to feel the giggle go through Jen's body.

He grinned back at her, but his pulse felt a little sharp. On their way down the hill his foot had caught on a rough patch and he'd stumbled, caught by Jen who just smiled and kissed him again. His knee ached, and not just from the stumble. In the last twenty four hours he'd slept with his leg on and then been thrown into a wall, neither of which were exactly advisable. The twisted, scarred muscles of his knee and thigh had been protesting all day, and he'd just swallowed some painkillers and ignored them.

And now he was anxious. Jen knew all about his leg, of course she did, but knowing wasn't the same as *knowing*. What would she say when she saw it? Would she be repulsed—or worse, would she pity him? And how capable would it render him of... performing?

Jen led him into her room, and exclaimed, "They brought my case back up!"

To his consternation, she dropped his hand and went to her knees by the sensible black trolley case. He took off his damp jacket and sat down on the bed to watch her unzip it, wondering what was so important.

She pushed aside a grey sweater and a black t-shirt before pulling out a toiletry bag with pink cartoon cats on it. He was so intrigued by the incongruity that he didn't see what she'd extracted from it until she held it up and said, "Old habits."

Then he realised it was a box of condoms, and felt his cheeks flush. *Smooth, Quinn.*

"Oh... good," he said, because that hadn't even occurred to him and the one he had in his wallet had probably expired.

She tilted her head. "Are you all right?"

"Grand." His knee throbbed. Jen flipped the suitcase shut, stood and put the condoms on the nightstand, then came to stand between his knees. Her hair was drying into curls around her face and up close she smelled like fresh rain and hot skin. He reached up and played with the ends of her pink scarf, unable to quite meet her eye.

She read his face for a moment, then said quietly, "Second thoughts?"

"No." Quinn shook his head violently. "No. I want you," he slid his hands under her coat and smoothed them over her hips. He made himself raise his gaze to hers. "I've been wanting you for... I don't even know."

Jen kept her eyes on his as she stripped away her sensible coat and frivolous scarf, and then there was just a shirt and jeans between him and her skin. No more than there ever had been every day in the office, and yet somehow, suddenly hardly any barrier at all. The heat of her skin seeped through her clothes.

"Good," she said, "because I've been wanting you for 'I don't even know,' too."

"It's just," Quinn said, looking up at her lovely face, "it's... it's been a while."

Understanding dawned. Her fingers touched his hair, stroked his cheek. Quinn leaned into the caress like a cat.

"For me too," she said.

"Bet it's been longer for me," he said grimly.

"Oh yeah?"

"Put it this way," Quinn said, "last time I had sex I still had two legs."

She laughed softly, her fingertips doing unbearably pleasant things to his neck. "Well, I'm sure you'll remember how it goes."

She tilted his face up, leaned down and kissed him, gently at first and then with passion, heating his blood. He pulled her closer, body to body, and they fell back on the bed. His hand clutched at the cotton of her shirt then slid beneath to her hot, smooth skin. Jen made a noise—that same moan at the back of her throat she'd made this morning—as he caressed her waist. Her knee nudged his

——

—caught exactly the wrong spot, and made him grimace. He nearly bit her tongue.

"Sure you're okay?" she said.

Quinn closed his eyes and groaned. "Fucking leg," he said.

"Oh." He looked up to see her sitting there, hesitant. "Did I do something I shouldn't?"

"No—" he began, but she wheeled away from him anyway, kneeling on the bed with her shirt half unfastened and her hair all rumpled. God, he wanted her. "It's just—what with last night, and the stairs, and I shouldn't have been after sleeping with it on…"

"It hurts?"

"Just a bit. Not enough to stop me doing… er, stuff," he added quickly, feeling his cheeks heat again.

"Mr Big Tough Detective Quinn," Jen said, lips twitching with a smile, "are you blushing?"

"No," he said, a little too vehemently.

Jen smiled, leaned in and brushed her lips over his. "Show me," she said. "I want to see."

His heart pounded, but not with lust this time.

"I've seen it looking worse," she added dryly.

Quinn swallowed.

Jen pulled away, bit by bit, coming back for more kisses, before she knelt up and fumbled her shirt undone.

Quinn watched, his mouth dry, as she tossed the plain garment towards her suitcase and faced him in her bra. It was pink and blue, with little bows on it. And lace.

His gaze was so glued to the sight that he didn't see the faint pink lines on her stomach until her fingers traced them.

When he looked up at her face, she wasn't smiling any more. Her mouth was tense. "I know it's not the same," she said, "but no one's ever seen these, either."

Quinn looked down at the marks, like scratches but more... deliberate. If he could get his garda head back on he might try and guess that they were a few years old and had been caused by... he didn't know what. Something sharp and precise, scoring across her skin.

His gaze flicked up to her face again. Whatever had caused them, she was ashamed of them.

He stood up slowly and unbuttoned his jeans. Pushed them and his shoes and socks to the floor. Stood before her in shirt and underwear, the unsexy beige liner over his knee giving way to the composite socket, and then the metal shank, ball-joint and moulded foot that now comprised his left leg.

Countless medical professionals had seen him like this. Not once had he felt this vulnerable.

He made himself look up and meet Jen's eyes. They were... assessing.

"Can you take it off?" she asked.

He nodded, took a deep breath and sat back down. He pressed the release button at the bottom of the socket, pulled away at the ankle, and with the same vacuum-release sensation he got every time, his leg divided in two.

He stood the prosthetic on the floor, and didn't look up as he unrolled the gel liner, turned it right-side out, and lay it across his clothes.

Then, telling himself he'd faced much more

frightening things, he turned and lay the stump of his leg on the bed for Jen to see.

He watched her take it in, her gaze roving over the lumps and ridges of scar tissue extending well over his knee, the bony protrusion that was all that remained of his tibia, the misshapen muscles.

Her hand came out, fingers brushing lightly as she explored the monstrosity that used to be his left leg. He watched her face, the tiny changes around her lips and her eyes. Pain, he thought, and nearly turned away before it turned into pity. Which it inevitably did, but underpinned with a sort of fascination. Her lip trembled, her eyes shone, and for a second her fingers tightened as if she was angry. Then they gentled into a caress. Her lashes were wet.

I could watch that face forever.

Finally, she looked up, and her cheeks went pink when she realised he'd been watching her.

"Well?" he said, unable to bear it.

"Well," she said, stroking up over his scars and his ugliness until her hand rested on his bare thigh, suddenly reminding him he was half naked.

Emotion ruled her face for a moment, pain washing in to be chased by a half smile, and then a damp laugh as she said, "Aren't you just the sexiest thing on one leg?"

Quinn spluttered with unexpected laughter, and Jen moved in and kissed his open mouth. She pushed him back onto the bed, hands smoothing over his shoulders, stroking his chest. She tugged at the buttons of his shirt, baring his skin and kissing him there. His head fell back in bliss as she uncovered him, then she sat back and he watched her unclip that frivolity of a bra and fling it away.

Then she hesitated, vulnerable, and Quinn smiled and swept her into his arms, rolling with her on the bed and stroking all over her lovely skin he could reach. And when that wasn't enough, he pulled off the rest of her clothes and his too, and the shock of being naked together made his skin prickle.

The way she felt in his arms was too much and not enough, all at the same time. He needed to touch more of her than he had hands for, taste her everywhere. And when he finally slid inside her, all laughter gone, she clutched at him and gasped his name.

This felt right, more right than anything ever had. For a long moment he stared down at her, eyes bright and lips parted, and almost couldn't bear that this was real. Then her hand tightened on his neck, her thigh slid over his, and a smile broke over her face.

Quinn was lost. He moved in her, with her, and she laughed and kissed him and everything became a blur of heat and sweat and glory until she came apart in his arms and he fell with her, overwhelmed.

"Hey, Quinn?"

"Mmph?" His voice was muffled, his face buried in her neck. She ran her foot down the back of his left leg, letting her toes feel the twisted scars and dents, the abrupt rounding of his stump, and wrapped her leg around his.

She put her lips to his ear and whispered, "I think you remembered how to do it okay."

For a second, nothing, and then his shoulders shook with laughter. He raised his head, eyes wicked, and said, "Just okay?"

Her fingertips feathered over his spine. "Grand. Class. What was the other one?"

"Deadly," he murmured, kissing her and making her go boneless.

"Deadly," she repeated, as he eased away from her and sat up. She watched him deal with the condom, then go to stand up, and realise why he couldn't.

He really hadn't done this for a long time. "Let me," she said, holding out her hand, and when he hesitated she rolled her eyes. "I do know where it's been."

He flushed at that, and she kissed his cheek and slid off the bed to sort it out. She used the toilet, washed her hands, blushed at her own glowing reflection, and stifled a scream when Alice's face appeared between her and the mirror.

"Is it over?" Alice said, looking doubtful.

Jen clutched the countertop. "Jesus Christ, Alice!" She fumbled for a towel to hold between herself and the ghost. It bunched right through Alice's hair, and she swatted it like a fly. "How long have you been here?"

"Thankfully, not long enough. I could see where it was heading," the child said matter-of-factly.

Jen closed her eyes and tried not to freak out over the idea of Alice nearly catching her having sex. As far as she knew, Alice had never seen her having sex. She'd been drugged away when Jen was a teenager, and ignored away for the next few years. And since the White Lady—

"Anyway, you can get back to..." Alice made an elegant gesture with her hand. "I've got things to do."

"What things?" Jen asked. "You're nine and you're dead. You hardly have a packed work schedule."

"That you know about," Alice said primly.

Jen rolled her eyes and stepped back, trying to wrap the towel around herself. It didn't cover the fine pink lines on her thigh.

"I just wanted to check you were all right," Alice said, looking up at Jen's reflection. "After last night."

"How do you even know about that?" Jen said, and Alice looked puzzled.

"I always know when there's something wrong. I was here, don't you remember?"

Jen began to shake her head, then she remembered

her dream and stopped. "Dear God, isn't there anything I actually do dream any more?" she grumbled.

"Jenny," Alice said, looking at her curiously, "how did you get those scars?"

Jen wrapped the towel tighter around herself, suddenly feeling a little colder. *Don't remind me it has to end.* "I told you. It was the bomb. Look, what are you doing here? I thought you hated going abroad."

"I do, but you were hurt. I came as soon as I realised," Alice said, "but Quinn had already got you away. He was taking good care of you."

"Yeah," said Jen, not meeting her eyes.

Alice's gaze dropped too, then she looked up and said quietly, "He's a good man, Jenny."

"I know he is," Jen said, surprised.

"He won't hurt you," Alice said, and there was something in the way she said it that disturbed Jen. But she didn't get to ask what Alice meant, because Quinn called her name from the bedroom.

"Who're you talking to?"

Jen glanced automatically in his direction, and when she looked back down at Alice, the little ghost was gone.

She frowned, dried her hands and looked at the towel for a moment. Then she squared her shoulders, hung it back up and went naked back to the bedroom, where Quinn was spread out like a feast.

She stopped, took him in, and shook her head. "You're doing that on purpose."

"Doing what?" His eyes were dark and dreamy.

"Being all sexy." She climbed onto the bed, feeling somewhat unalluring beside all his manly beauty, and he raised himself up on his elbows, looking adorably confused.

"You don't have to flatter me," he said. "You've already got me into bed."

She pushed him down and snuggled up against him,

feeling his heart beat under her hand. "I'm not flattering you," she said. "You're—come on, you know you're gorgeous."

He was silent for a moment, his fingers playing with her hair, and then he said seriously, "No, Ethan was the gorgeous one."

Not from where I'm looking. "You were identical," she protested.

One shoulder shifted in a shrug. "But he was the sexy one. Wasn't I after telling you he got all the girls? Besides, we're not—we weren't identical. I had our fingerprints tested."

Jen opened her mouth and then shut it again. *Confidence is what I lack.* How did you grow up with a brother who stole every girl you liked, and then flirted his way through the TV screen into the hearts of millions?

Oh Jenny. Don't hurt this man.

She wormed around in his arms until she could kiss his neck, his beautiful neck, and then his perfect jaw and his delicious mouth, and then she said, "Remember when you said you'd been an idiot for not believing me?"

Quinn gave a bare nod.

"Don't be an idiot about this too."

CHAPTER THIRTY

It was going dark by the time Quinn's phone rang, and he somewhat guiltily recalled that he'd just gone for a walk several hours ago and not told Uncle Kieran when he'd be back. Disentangling himself from Jen, who'd fallen asleep while they were watching comedy reruns, he grabbed at his jacket and fumbled for his phone.

"Uncle Kieran?"

"Quinn, lad. Now I was thinking, I've that lamb in the fridge and it'll probably stretch to three if I put some potatoes on."

Quinn blinked. He glanced back at Jen, who was coming awake quite attractively. "What?" he said.

"You'll be wanting to invite Jenny over for dinner," he said. "Unless it's a restaurant you had in mind. The one at the hotel gets booked up weeks in advance, so it does."

Quinn scrubbed his hand over his face and tried to work out what was going on. Then he remembered Emer's knowing look as she handed over the room key, and groaned. Probably all of Dalkey knew by now.

"Ah," he stalled. "Give me a minute, would you?"

He covered over the speaker, and turned to Jen, who was watching curiously. "Ehm, Uncle Kieran wants to know would we be going over for dinner?" When she hesitated, looking confused, he explained, "Small town. News travels fast."

Her cheeks went pink.

"We don't have to go," he said. "We can eat somewhere else. Or," he tried to sound casual, "I can just feck off and you can do what you want."

She bit her lip and seemed to be weighing the options. "Can he cook?"

"He's not bad. There's lamb."

"Lamb sounds good," she said, and Quinn smiled, warm in a way he eventually identified as happiness.

They walked back through the streets to Uncle Kieran's house, and when Quinn dared to take Jen's hand she smiled up at him and held on. This time, when he saw someone he knew he waved until they were forced to acknowledge him.

"Who's that?" Jen asked.

"Domnall Ryan. We would have gone to school together. I think his sister went out with Ethan."

"It sounds like half the town went out with Ethan," Jen said.

"Felt like it, too." A memory occurred to him, and he laughed. "Aislin, I think she was. Last time I saw her she commiserated with me on the death of my brother."

"Oh?"

"Yep. Only she told me how very sorry she was to hear James had died."

Jen's hand went over her mouth.

"It's like that old joke. 'Was it you or your brother who died?'" He smiled, because it didn't hurt so much now. "I didn't think it was funny at the time."

"I bet." Jen hesitated, as if she was about to say something else, then stopped, and changed the subject.

"Did you say you wanted to get some wine?"

He didn't probe, but there was something in what he'd said that made her uncomfortable. Did talking about Ethan remind her of the White Lady?

He hadn't asked about those red marks on her stomach and her legs. She'd told him, back when they first met, that the scar on her arm was the only one she had from the bomb. Had she lied? But... no, the lines on her stomach, the scars on her thighs, couldn't have been caused by debris from the bomb. To make a scar that lasting they'd have practically disembowelled her.

He watched her dithering over two bottles of wine, and said, "Get them both. We all like a drink." She smiled and took them to the counter, where she was served by the man who'd been selling Quinn alcohol since he was almost old enough to drink it. He ducked his head and avoided conversation, thinking.

He'd seen plenty of different kinds of wounds in his time. Bar fights, muggings and deliberate attacks all had their own pattern, as did football and rugby brawls. He knew what stab wounds looked like—the scar on her arm for one, that she touched whenever the White Lady was mentioned. The others, though?

They have special units for children. The ones who are dangerous. Jen had never been a danger to anyone else. But what about herself?

"Do you have five euros?" Jen said. "Save me breaking a fifty."

He handed over the money without thinking about it, and she smiled and paid the man.

Straight, precise, deliberate cuts, where no one could see them. They weren't accidental. Someone had hurt Jen, and he very much feared—

"Come on," she said, handing him the bag and linking her other arm with his. "Don't want that lamb to get cold."

Quinn put his arms around her, the bottles clinking, and pressed his face to her hair, unable to ask the question that bubbled up in his brain.

"Hey," Jen said, turning her face and forcing him to look at her. Her blue eyes were warm. "What's this in aid of?"

I love you. But he couldn't say that either. *James Quinn, you're a fucking coward.*

"I just like," Quinn began, and ended truthfully, "you, Jenny. I like you."

She smiled, pleased but bewildered, and allowed him to kiss her while someone across the street wolf-whistled.

When they walked on, he kept his arm around her, and matched his step to hers.

Kieran greeted them warmly at the door. He took the wine from Jen, told her Billy was in his bowl if she wanted to say hello, and as soon as her back was turned, gave Quinn the most enormous wink.

Quinn rolled his eyes. "Emer told you?"

"I've eyes in my head, so I have! Anyone could tell which way the wind was blowing with you two."

"And here's me thinking I was being discreet," Quinn muttered, following his uncle into the kitchen.

"The heart wants what it wants," Kieran intoned.

"Well, mine's going to want some wine if you're going to carry on like that," Quinn said.

The food was good, although Quinn suspected his uncle hadn't found it in the fridge so much as driven to Blackrock and bought it from Marks & Spencer. Still, he appreciated the gesture. Kieran seemed overjoyed that Quinn had finally brought a girl home, and Jen clearly enjoyed his company.

He kept finding himself drifting off and just watching her speaking and listening, her eyes bright, her laugh ready. *Oh God, Quinn, you've got it bad.*

"So how on Earth did you end up becoming a detective in Wirpness?" Jen asked as she topped up their glasses. "It's not exactly a thriving metropolis."

"It reminds me of Dalkey," Kieran said, which was high praise from him. "The truth is, I went there in search of my father."

Jen frowned, her forehead wrinkling adorably.

"Uncle Kieran's only half Irish," Quinn told her, "but don't go spreading it around."

"Sure wasn't I born and raised here?" Kieran said. "My mother was Irish, God rest her, but she served in England in the WAAF during the war. Fell in love, so she did, with a handsome young pilot. He promised to marry her, as these young men promised so many ladies, but he went off and got himself killed all the same. Meanwhile my mother found herself in… difficulties, and no husband to take care of her. Discharged in disgrace, back to Ireland she comes, and doesn't she charm another fella into marrying her?"

"Did he know she was pregnant?" Jen asked.

"Well, I was born two months after the marriage, so I'd assume he had some idea," Kieran said, eyes twinkling. "Ah, he was a great man, my da. A brave thing, to take on another man's child, but you'd never have known I wasn't his, the way he raised me. They'd six more, including your man's mother," he indicated Quinn, who nodded. "And all this time I'd no idea he wasn't my real da."

Jen shook her head. "Amazing. How did you find out?"

"Well. What I didn't know, what my mother herself didn't know for years, was that my real father had made a will on joining the RAF. Short life expectancy for a pilot, so it was. And for all my mother giving out about empty promises, it turned out he'd amended his will so that everything he owned went to her. Perhaps he did intend to marry her after all. Now she didn't know about this for quite some time, it being taken up with lawyers and the like. His family fought and fought to keep their property getting into the hands of some filthy Irishwoman who didn't even know it was hers. But in the end it came to her, and then to me."

Jen tilted her head. She glanced at Quinn. "Let me guess, it's now the agency office?"

"And the shop beneath it. Brings in a nice rent. I went there to see about the house itself, found I liked the town. Setting up as a detective had always been my plan, and I thought now why not do it in England?"

"The rest is history," said Quinn, taking a sip of the wine Jen had chosen and watching her face.

"Quinn here took it over from me when I retired, and now you work there as well. Sure, it's a family business!" Kieran said, clinking his glass against Jen's. She smiled, but she seemed distracted.

"Don't be premature," Quinn said. Christ, they slept together once and Uncle Kieran was practically choosing wedding china.

"Ah you're made for each other," Kieran beamed. Quinn wondered how strong that wine was.

They were all more than a bit tipsy by the time he called it a night. Kieran asked innocently if Quinn would be wanting his old room back, and Quinn reminded himself that he was a grown man who ran his own business and had faced down angry football mobs with no more protection than a stab vest, but it still didn't stop him blushing.

"I need him to walk me back," Jen said, her fingers doing delicately wicked things to his. "And you should probably stay with me," she murmured in Quinn's ear. "You need to rest that leg of yours."

Quinn nodded with mock solemnity. "She's right, Uncle. For the good of my health I'll be staying at the hotel."

Kieran laughed and chased them out of the house, giving Quinn another outrageous wink as he did. Jen turned to wave goodbye, lost her footing and stumbled against Quinn, who enjoyed the excuse to yank her close to his body far more than he should have.

She rested her head on his shoulder as they turned up the street. "I like your uncle."

The warmth Quinn felt at that had nothing to do with the wine. "He likes you too. I'll have to watch him or he'll steal you from me."

She nudged him, and this time he stumbled and she had to hold onto him, laughing. "No one's doing any stealing," she said, and then for the briefest moment, an emotion he was too drunk to identify crossed her face. "There's not a man alive who could steal me from you," she added quietly, and Quinn knew he should have paid more attention to that.

Emer had managed to book them onto a flight leaving the next afternoon, which seemed frantically soon to Jen, especially when Quinn told her they'd have to arrive early at the airport in order for him to get through security with his leg. Once they left the hotel, their time left could be divided into chunks of travel until they were back in Wirpness, back to real life and away from this interlude.

Real life would come crashing down on them.

Quinn seemed oblivious to this, flirting with her over breakfast and kissing her senseless in the lobby while they waited for Kieran to pick them up. He sat beside her in the back of the car, playing with her fingers, acting every inch like a man in love. *And I'm going to destroy him.*

She watched as he patiently explained to the airport security staff about his prosthetic, then waited for a supervisor, who looked somewhat at odds and called a manager. Then they led him off to a private screening area while she sat alone with her handbag and waited, all the while telling herself that she was panicking over nothing and maybe everything would turn out fine.

Right, but he's a detective. It's his job to figure out the truth from small clues. And you've dropped far too many of those.

He has no reason to suspect me, she told herself. And he's super distracted right now. Maybe if I just keep on having really good sex with him he'll forget all about his brother.

Until next time he looks in the mirror.

Shut up. This is like talking to Alice.

Or the next anniversary rolls around. The sixth anniversary of the White Lady. Of Ethan's death. Of the inquest's findings. Remember all that DNA evidence they couldn't match to anyone on record?

Well, I still don't have a police record, so—

Yes, but you're leaving plenty of really good DNA around, aren't you? All those bodily fluids you've been exchanging.

He has no reason to suspect I have anything to do with it, Jen told herself firmly. He likes me. He might even love me. He is, as Alice said, a good man. He won't hurt me.

He won't get the chance.

"Now don't tell me," said Quinn, making her jump, "the airport has ghosts too?"

"What?" she looked up, sure her guilt was written all over her face.

"You were staring off into space."

"Oh, just... bored." She stood up. "Are you all done?"

"Yep. Managed to persuade them I'm neither a terrorist nor a drug dealer, and in only half an hour, too.

Come on," he linked his arm through hers, "let's go to Duty Free. I promised Tessa I'd bring back one of those huge Toblerones."

He bought his Toblerone and some whiskey, while Jen half-heartedly browsed the perfume section.

"You smell good enough already," said Quinn roguishly when he found her.

"Very smooth. I was looking for something for Charlotte, but I've no idea what she wears." She pulled herself together. "Something subtle, yet pretentious."

"Ah yes. The scent that says, 'I'm just a little bit better than you'," Quinn said. He picked up a bottle and sniffed, then made a face.

"The Boden of scents."

"Eau de Yummy Mummy."

"If Farrow & Ball made perfume, she'd wear it," Jen said, and Quinn laughed.

Her phone rang, and for a surreal instant she wondered if Charlotte had somehow overheard them, and then she shook off her paranoia and read the screen. "It's Tessa." Answering, she said, "He's got the Toblerone."

"Sounds like code," Tessa said. "Do I take it this means you're at the airport? Have you both finally decided to come back to work?"

"Hey, we have been working," Jen protested, then shivered as Quinn slung his arm around her and murmured in her ear, "For some of the time, anyway."

"Yeah, working on some Guinness," Tessa said. "Look, anyway, I've been looking for this Alice you asked me about, but I've not had much luck. I mean, there are plenty of Alices in your family tree, but none of the right age or era."

"Oh," said Jen, not sure what to do with that. It seemed so long ago she'd even asked Tessa to look.

"I thought I'd found her—Alice Riley, born 1851 in

Deptford, but I couldn't find a death date."

The thought flashed into Jen's mind that maybe Alice's death had been unregistered—if she'd been murdered, for instance, which would also explain why she was a ghost. *Poor Alice.*

"But then I found her marriage certificate. Her death was under her married name. Only twenty-one, poor thing. Are you sure your Alice died as a child?"

"Positive," Jen said, as Quinn pointed at some empty seats and steered her towards them. "Ah well. It doesn't really matter all that much. Thanks for looking."

"I just hate to leave a mystery unsolved," Tessa sighed. "Well anyway. I'll see you tomorrow?"

"See you then," Jen said, and hung up. Quinn was giving her a mildly curious look. "Never you mind," she said.

He gave a theatrical scowl, which suddenly turned into a real one. "Ah God, she's remembered my birthday."

Remember, remember, the fifth of November. "I can't say a word," she said.

"Don't let her do anything, will you? One year she tried fixing me up on a blind date."

"On your birthday?"

"Right. Nightmare. All I want to do on my birthday is get drunk and forget it's happening."

He flung himself down in one of the moulded airport seats and she sat down more carefully next to him.

"I'll pass the message on."

Quinn rolled his head on the back of the seat and looked at her. "I mean… usually that's all I want. It's not a good day for me, you know?"

She nodded, and Quinn reached for her hand.

"Will you spend it with me? I promise not to get really drunk," he added, doing that looking-under-his-lashes thing.

Jen sighed. If she said no he'd probably drink himself to death instead. "It's the fifth, right? Well, that comes five days after my worst day of the year."

He frowned, as if trying to remember what terrible thing she'd told him occurred at the end of October.

"Hallowe'en?" Jen prompted, and his face cleared. But before he could say anything, a young woman approached them, her phone in her hand.

"Excuse me, are you Ethan Sullivan's brother?"

Jen felt, rather than saw, Quinn tense. Hopefully, he was too aware of his own private hell to notice hers.

"I used to be," he said shortly.

"Wow. Oh my God, you look so much like him. Can I get a selfie with you?"

"You know what, I was having a private conversation," Quinn began, then sighed and said, "Sure. Just make it quick, all right?"

The girl leaned right over Jen as if she wasn't there and shoved her face next to Quinn's. Jen, contact abruptly severed, leaned over to one side and tried not to glower.

"Oh my God," the girl repeated as the flash went off, "this is so amazing. I was his biggest fan, you know." *Snap.* "I was, like, so devastated when he killed himself." *Snap.* "It was such a tragedy. I mean, he had everything—"

"Including a rope," Quinn said, abruptly shoving her away. "I think you should fuck off now."

"But—"

"*Go,*" Quinn said, eyes dark, face like a storm.

The girl scampered away, muttering, "Rude," over her shoulder.

Quinn put his face in his hands. Jen, feeling somewhat like she'd been punched in the throat, tried to breathe normally, but it was all knocked out of her when Quinn grabbed her in a fierce hug.

For a few seconds all she could do was hold onto him. His face pressed against her hair and his hands shook. She didn't know if he was angry or upset or both. She didn't know what she was herself.

"Are you okay?" she ventured.

"Yeah," he sniffed. "No. God, why do people think it's okay to do that?"

"I don't know."

"Just walk up and be all, 'Hey, remember how your brother committed suicide.' For God's sake."

Jen stroked his hair and held him. *It's worse for him*, she reminded herself. *It's terrible for him.*

It's not so great for me either.

"People are insensitive," she managed.

"Insensitive jerks," Quinn said, and lifted his head. His eyes were wet. Jen swiped away a tear from his cheek, and he gave her a terrible excuse for a smile. "Sorry. It just… sometimes it hits out of nowhere. And what with talking about his—our—birthday and everything."

Jen nodded and kissed his cheek.

"You're really not going to want to hang around on my birthday now, are you?" he said, a trace of humour back in his face.

And Jen said, "You're not going to want me to, after Hallowe'en."

CHAPTER THIRTY-ONE

The White Lady: Three weeks and one day after

It takes her hours with the colour stripper but finally her hair has lost most of its blueness. Jen lets it dry as she surfs the Internet for rental properties within her budget. Somewhere far away in the countryside. Somewhere no one will know her, and she won't stand out. Somewhere she can pretend to be a tourist for a while, until she finds her feet.

The Lake District pops up on a search result, and she finds a cottage available from tomorrow for two weeks. She's booked it almost before she thinks about it.

"Going on holiday?" says a voice behind her, and Jen spins to see Alice there. It's the first time she's seen her since the bomb went off.

"What are you doing here?"

"Looking after you, Jenny, just like I always do."

Jen opens her mouth to snap that Alice should damn well have been here over the last few weeks while she's been cutting herself and having rough, angry sex with a man who has only been using her to hurt himself—and then she closes it again. She can't explain that to Alice, who is after all only a child.

Alice hasn't been medicated away, or ignored like she has been for years. She's just popped up to save Jen's life then fucked off again. If she'd been here these last weeks—

But then who was it who sent her away in the first place, Jennifer?

"I could use a break," she says now, turning back to the computer which has just confirmed her booking. "I want to get out of London. Look for somewhere to live in the countryside. I've had enough of this place."

Alice nods. "I never liked London anyway," she says.

She doesn't leave as Jen re-dyes her hair, this time a sensible shade of mid-brown, the sort of colour that no one will notice. "I'm tired of looking like a silly kid," she says, and Alice nods.

"I always thought you only did it for attention," she says.

Jen almost smiles at that. She's never done anything for attention, but people always liked to find excuses for her behaviour, so the first time she dyed her hair, she gave them one.

She spends the evening packing every suitcase she can find and going to the supermarket for boxes. She's only booked two weeks away, but she knows she won't be coming back.

In the morning she goes to the catering agency office and tells them she no longer requires their services. The girl on reception barely recognises Jen's face. After that she gets on the Tube and goes to Westminster, crossing over the river to the hospital on the south bank. She sees people loitering there in old-fashioned dress, the sunlight filtering through them. It seems she's seeing ghosts everywhere these days.

Alice hasn't come with her. They're still uneasy

about their new relationship. Jen has asked her for peace for the time being, and Alice has gone off to make sure there aren't any undesirable spirits hanging about Jen's holiday cottage.

This means she's alone as she navigates her way around the hospital. It's not the one she was brought to after the White Lady. It's the one Ethan mentioned, just the once, as the place his brother went to have his leg amputated.

She finds him eventually, the brother. It isn't easy because she knows the second she gives them her name they'll have her up in front of a shrink for some sort of post-traumatic counselling, and once they see her name and bring up her record...

No. She's never going back into that system.

But she finds Ethan's brother, the one who saved his life at the White Lady, the one who lost his own leg in the process. The news has been full of it. Jen can't escape it no matter how much she's tried.

She finds him lying asleep, or unconscious, on a bed next to a wheelchair. He's dressed in t-shirt and shorts, which means she can see the ruined stump of his leg. A few inches under his knee it ends with a seam of dark stitches. The flesh is puffy and swollen, streaked with dark burns and cuts. On his other leg there are scabs and abrasions. His face is bruised.

He both looks exactly like Ethan and not at all.

Jen doesn't know what to say. She doesn't really know why she's come. She reaches out, then withdraws her hand, and then defies herself to touch his fingers. He stirs a little but doesn't wake.

Jen gently covers his fingers with her own. They're cold. When the warmth of her palm hits them he stirs again and she freezes as his eyes open.

She tries a tentative smile. He blinks at her and opens his mouth, but then the door opens and Jen abruptly snatches back her hand, her nerve deserting her.

"Sorry," she says, and scrambles back. She darts past the nurse about to enter with a muttered, "Wrong room," and escapes. The last thing she sees is the man who isn't Ethan, watching her.

That afternoon she gets on a train to Penrith, and the man sitting opposite her is reading a newspaper folded back to reveal the headline all in capital letters.

ETHAN SULLIVAN FOUND DEAD.

CHAPTER THIRTY-TWO

Jen left his house early that morning to get ready for work. "You don't have to," Quinn said. "Wear jeans and a t-shirt, I don't care."

"I do," Jen replied, pulling on the dark, tailored jeans she'd worn the day before. Her knickers were pink today, with yellow trim, and she wore the bra with the ribbons again. Ghost the cat batted at her grey jumper as she picked it up.

Quinn lay back in bed and watched her. "How come," he asked, "you cover up all that prettiness with grey and black?"

"Because I'd freeze if I walked around in my underwear," she replied, smoothing her jumper over the scars on her stomach.

"I mean, how come your underwear is brightly coloured but the rest of your stuff is…" he waved his hand, trying to indicate 'bland' without saying it.

"Professional? Conservative?" Jen gave him a knowing look. "Boring?"

"I wasn't going to say that," he protested.

Jen shrugged. "I don't feel the need to be noticed,"

she said. Ghost head-butted her, purring, and she scratched his grey head.

"But you have the prettiest underwear."

"Well, that's just for me. And you, now, I guess."

"Damn right," Quinn said, sitting up and reaching for her. She was warm and soft and curved in all the right places. He kissed her and she made that soft little sound, sinking against him, then pulled away.

"I have to go and shower and do my hair and cover this up," she said, indicating the bruise on her forehead. "You might not care about what I look like but we do have clients, you know."

"If we're lucky." A thought occurred. "You know that haunted mobile phone?"

Jen looked shifty.

"Was it?'

She picked up her bag, chewed her lip, and eventually said, "Might have been."

Quinn flopped back on the bed. "Christ, is there no end to it?"

"Just you wait," Jen said. She leaned over and kissed his nose. "I'll see you later."

"Can't wait," he said, and watched her go.

Ghosts in haunted mansions, a ghostly guardian angel, and now a haunted mobile phone? He shook his head. It probably made sense, in a weird way. Kids these days spent their lives on their phones. Where else would one go after he died?

He found himself opening up the office early, anticipating Jen's arrival. They'd been parted for less than two hours and already he missed her like hell. He was verging on pathetic now, and he didn't care.

"Focus, man," he told himself. "You've got a business to run." He'd probably got a million emails to go through and God only knew what system Tessa had been using for phone messages. Might as well make a start now, before Jen came in and he spent all afternoon staring at the curve of her cheek.

After half an hour, Tessa came in. He heard her busying around, hanging up her coat and switching on the kettle, humming to herself. Then her curly head popped around his doorway. "Morning."

"Morning." Quinn smiled: she only had one earring in and wore a Captain America t-shirt which was so out of character he'd bet good money she hadn't spent the night at home.

"You're cheerful. Want some tea?" She didn't wait for an answer before flitting off. "How was the romantic weekend?"

Quinn stood up, stretched and wandered out after her. "Well," he said, wondering how much to say before Jen arrived, "…romantic."

Tessa nearly dropped the mug she was holding. "You're kidding? Please tell me it was Jen."

"Tell you what was Jen?" said the woman herself, opening the door.

Tessa went scarlet. Quinn grinned.

"I told her we had a romantic weekend," he said.

"Oh." Jen went a bit pink, and spent more time taking off her coat and hanging it up than she needed to. Quinn closed the gap between them, grabbed her by the waist and tugged her against him. "Oh! Are we—I guess we're…"

"Telling Tessa," Quinn said, unable to stop beaming. He wanted to tell everyone.

Jen looked up at him, then Tessa, who was gaping at them. "So I guess we're telling you," she said.

At that point Tessa came back to life with a squawk, and rushed over to hug them both, babbling about how great and wonderful it was and how she just knew they were meant for each other and hadn't she been telling them both?

"And you said you were just friends," she scoffed.

"Apparently not," said Jen, who was starting to look uncomfortable.

"All right," Quinn said, disentangling himself. "Maybe we should just have some tea and calm down."

When he let go of Jen, her fingers lingered against his. He smiled, one eyelid flickering in a wink, and she smiled back before her attention was caught by something... that wasn't there. Right. Alice, he assumed.

He made the tea, sent Tessa to her office to get some work done and stop dancing around grinning at them both, then perched on the edge of Jen's desk to make a nuisance of himself while she started up her computer.

"Sorry," he said, jerking his head in Tessa's direction. "Did you mind?"

Her smile was a fraction of a second too late. "No. I mean... it's not like it's a secret, right?" A pause. "Alice has just reminded me that even she knows."

Quinn couldn't help looking around for Alice, and shivering slightly. It had got colder in here. *I cannot believe I'm having a conversation with someone who is having a conversation with a ghost.*

Then a horrible thought occurred to him. "Please tell me she wasn't there when we—" He gestured frantically with his hands, too appalled to continue.

"God no," Jen said quickly. "That would scar us all."

A shudder nearly made Quinn spill his tea. The thought of being watched by a spectral child while he tried to make love to Jen was too hideous to contemplate.

"If it's any help," Jen said, "she's as revolted by the idea as you are."

"Ugh," said Quinn. "Good."

His phone rang then, giving him a fantastic excuse to end the most disturbing conversation he'd ever had.

"Uncle Kieran," he said. "Did you get my text?"

He'd promise to let his uncle know when they'd got home safely.

"Yes, son, thanks a million. Now listen. I'm at the Rathmichael house—"

"What? I thought we all agreed we wouldn't go back there! It's not safe." Jen looked up, alarmed, and Quinn told her, "My eejit of an uncle has only gone back to the house with the ghost who tried to kill us both."

"Ah now, you're not listening. Is that Jen you're talking to? Put me on speaker, she'll like to hear this."

Quinn was doubtful Jen would want to hear anything about the Rathmichael house, but he put the phone on speaker anyway and laid it on Jen's desk.

"Now, since you disappeared off the other day, not that I mind, I'm very glad you and Jennifer got together, I've been looking at all the data we had on the house. It's only been called Fairview since 1927, for one thing. Before that it was called Fairy View, and it's believed to be on a fairy fort."

"What's a fairy fort?" Jen asked.

"A hill fort," Quinn told her. "Ancient dwellings."

"Or, entrances to the world of the Good People," Kieran said. *Fairies*, Quinn mouthed at Jen. "It's terrible bad luck to disturb a fairy fort. And bad luck is something the house has had plenty of. Seven suspicious deaths, all unrelated to the best I can tell, and untold accidents. Now Jenny, I don't know if your man told you about Brónach Doyle?'

Jen tensed at the name. Quinn covered her hand with his. Her fingers were cold. "She disappeared in 1796. Lived alone in the house with her father, so she did. He said she'd run off with a young man but the locals said she'd met a terrible end."

"Well, it looks like they were right," said Kieran. His voice was heavy. "We looked at the older plans of the house. It was much smaller then and the stairs were a different shape. In Brónach's time, you'd have come right down the straight stairs and into the cellar."

"We know all this," Quinn said.

"Right, but here's what you don't know. Mrs Kelly arranged to have the cellar opened up this morning, and a team to start digging. There's nothing but rotten boards over the dirt down there."

Jen had gone very pale. One hand crept up to cover her mouth.

"We called the gardaí in half an hour ago," Kieran said.

Jen swallowed. Quinn squeezed her fingers and said, "What did you find?"

"Bones. Human. An adult, and," Kieran's voice shook, and then he righted himself. "And small bones. Children."

Quinn kept his eyes on Jen. She looked like she was about to be sick.

"I… ehm." Kieran sounded genuinely disturbed. "I'm not an expert on these things, but some of them were only half formed. Unborn. Others older. All in neat little rows, so they were. Jesus, Quinn, I couldn't stay down in that cellar."

Quinn gathered Jen into his arms and held her close. She let out a half sob and huddled against him as he tried to think.

"So… you think that was Brónach, and… what, her siblings? Or her children?"

"Well. The things Padraig told us…" There was a rustle of paper, and Kieran went on, "The spirit mentioned her babies. She would have vengeance, she said, and we all must know. She had to make us see. Jesus, son. If anything would keep an unquiet spirit around…"

"Right," Quinn said. He concentrated on stroking Jen's back, trying to comfort her. A sound to his left made him turn his head to see Tessa standing in her doorway, frowning. *Later*, he mouthed, and she retreated.

"Mrs Ní Dhomhnaill was of the opinion the remains should be laid to rest," Kieran was saying. "And that would calm the ghost, to see justice done and her babies given a decent Christian burial. I was wondering, does Jenny have any thoughts on that?"

Jen shook her head without lifting it from his chest.

"Ehm...not at present," Quinn said. "It's upset her a bit, Uncle."

"Ah, so it would. Well, I'll stop upsetting her now, and go and see what the gardaí have to say. Take care now, son."

"Thanks," Quinn said, and let go of Jen long enough to end the call. Then he held onto her for a while, trying not to turn those horrible revelations over in his mind and failing utterly. Brónach Doyle, who disappeared one day from her father's house, but who'd never left it. He wondered if she'd died in that cellar or if she'd lived there too, locked in and birthing malformed babies by herself. Raising those children she ended up burying in neat little rows. Who was the father of those wretched creatures? Did her father whore her out or keep her for himself?

He'd seen some terrible things as a garda, but nothing this awful.

Eventually Jen lifted her tear-streaked face, and when he looked down at her, Quinn realised his own face was wet.

"Alice says they should be buried. Brought out into the daylight and treated like human beings, and then buried like them too. That's what Brónach wants. For people to know what was done to her and to h-her babies."

Quinn nodded bleakly.

"God, who could do such a thing?" Jen hiccupped, her face crumpling.

Quinn hugged her close, his face pressed to hers. "Terrible people," he muttered. "People who are wrong on the inside."

Jen sniffed. "People used to say that about me."

Appalled, Quinn held her back so he could look at her. "You're not wrong, Jenny. There is nothing wrong with you."

She gave him a watery smile and laid her head back on his shoulder. Quinn wrapped his arms tight around her, needing to keep her safe, to comfort her and tell her he loved her, even if he didn't know how yet.

Quinn took her out for lunch to cheer her up, but Jen found her mind wandering back to Brónach Doyle whenever she got distracted, which was often. Apart from the appalling fascination of her story, there remained the question: could Brónach's spirit be laid to rest? If those terrible remains were brought to light, put in coffins and buried in sacred ground, would the spirit have anything left to claim vengeance over? Would she fade away, and go… where did they go?

"Jenny?"

She blinked, and looked across the pub table at Quinn sitting there, unfairly handsome in the sunlight.

"Another drink?"

She looked at her glass. "No. Better not. Got to go back to work."

"I won't mind," he said gently.

"I need something to do. I can't stop thinking about… you know."

He nodded. "I know. Me neither." He chewed his lip, then said, "Will it help, do you think? Bringing it to light?"

Jen shrugged. "I don't know. If that's what she

wants… I don't know what makes a ghost leave, or even if you can. It seemed to work for Max Robertson. Ellie says she hasn't had any more messages from him."

Because some secrets shouldn't stay buried, said a ghostly little voice inside her, and she covered her shiver with a gulp of wine.

"Then I guess we hope for the best," Quinn finished his Guinness, "and stay the hell away from Rathmichael. You know, I'd forgotten fairy forts were called raths," he added. "Whole place is probably built on one. What does Wirpness mean?"

Jen knew he was trying to distract her again, which was adorable of him. "I don't know. It's probably Viking or something. We're on the east coast."

"You reckon this is a Viking settlement?" He leaned forward, arms on the table, and grinned conspiratorially. "Seen any fellas about with horned helmets?"

"You know they didn't really wear those."

"Really? Disappointing. Mind you, though. Imagine trying to give your old mother a hug wearing one. You'd put her eye out."

Jen smiled, and allowed him to fetch her another drink, and tried not to think about how to lay a ghost to rest.

Hallowe'en fell on a Friday that year. Quinn told Jen she didn't have to come in to work if she didn't want to, but she gave him a Look, then added that it was better if she wasn't alone anyway.

"What happens?" he asked, lounging on the office sofa looking at her in lieu of doing any actual work.

Jen didn't look up from the scrawled notes she was typing up. "You're a big boy now, Quinn, you ought to know what happens on Hallowe'en."

"Big boy now, am I?"

Her cheeks went pink and her lips twitched in a

smile.

"What's this word? Your handwriting is terrible."

Quinn squinted at the piece of paper she held up, then used it as an excuse to move closer, leaning on the filing cabinet beside her desk. "Communication," he said. Jen nodded and carried on typing.

"Always used to hate Hallowe'en when I was on the Force. There's always some kids extorting money out of old grannies in the guise of trick-or-treating, people in costumes and masks knocking off banks, parties that get out of control…" Not to mention the wannabe Satanists and practitioners of the occult, some of whom did horrible things with entrails and some of whom just managed to set their student halls on fire.

"One year I had a dead trick-or-treater," Jen said. "Didn't realise until the satsuma went right through him and splatted on the front step."

"Satsuma? Aren't you middle class," Quinn teased.

"I was round at Charlotte's that year," Jen said gloomily. "I had to physically restrain her from handing out toothbrushes."

He smiled, but he could tell how tense she was. "Are the old stories true?" he asked softly. "About the walls between the worlds thinning and all the demons coming out to play?"

Jen gave a shrug that was too rigid to convince. "I don't know about stories," she said, "but it's the worst night of the year for ghosts. And people have got so much more convincing with their costumes. More than once I've tried to walk right through a person who was made of flesh and blood."

"Well then," he said, "you'll have to stick close to me, and I'll tell you if there's really someone there or not."

Jen stopped typing and looked up. "You don't have to babysit me," she said. "I know I've been a bit…

needy lately, but I really am fine. Alice will scare away any of the bogeymen."

Quinn rolled his eyes. "Have a care for my ego," he protested, "don't tell me a nine-year-old girl can look after you better than I can. Especially a dead one!"

Jen just smiled and went back to typing.

"Oh, thanks," he said, and she smiled. "Sorry, Alice," he added, feeling a bit of a fool for apologising to someone he still wasn't a hundred percent sure he believed in.

"She's not here." Jen frowned. "She's been a bit absent lately. I think you're putting her off. What's this bit? 107 something Road?"

He glanced at the notes. "Southwold Road. And it's 167. Why am I putting her off?"

Jen side-eyed him. "Something to do with all the snogging and nudity," she said dryly. "She might be old but she's also very young."

Tessa came out of her office, pulling on her coat. "Sure you're all right with me going early? Promised I'd be back to help the kids get into their costumes, they'll want to be out the minute it gets dark."

"No problem. Don't let them get too scary," Quinn said, glancing at Jen.

"Only if you're scared by a five-year-old Black Panther and a seven-year-old Wonder Woman," Tessa said, rolling her eyes.

"I thought you didn't like all those over-commercial superhero movies?" Quinn teased, and her cheeks went a bit pink.

"Yes, well, Laurel does."

Jen mouthed, 'Laurel?' at Quinn; Tessa hadn't divulged a lot about her new girlfriend and neither of them wanted to push her. Out loud, she said, "Well, have fun. Wakanda forever."

Tessa groaned. "See you Monday. Have a good

weekend."

"You too," Quinn said at the same time Jen did.

"You guys are so cute I could just throw up," Tessa said as she left.

"I am not cute," Quinn said, scowling.

"Yes you are, you're adorable," Jen said, and yelped as he yanked her out of her chair and into his arms.

"Now the grown-ups have gone," he murmured, "we can mitch off."

"We can what?"

"Go on the doss. Do a bunk."

"Oh, you mean skive," Jen said, winding her arms around his neck.

"You posh English people with your fancy words," Quinn said, and kissed her. She softened against him, and he slid his hands down to her lovely backside and scooped her up to sit on the desk.

"Now," he said, and she looked up at him with big blue eyes, "how about we make a new memory for Hallowe'en?"

She bit her delicious lip. "What did you have in mind?"

Quinn grinned wickedly. "This," he said, and showed her.

Jen left to shower and change, leaving Quinn to close up the office before meeting back at her place. He planned to go home first for his collection of takeaway menus and DVDs, and then he'd spend the night at hers. Maybe the whole weekend.

For the first time in a long time, he felt really, sublimely happy.

When his phone rang he reached for his pocket, before realising it wasn't his ringtone. Wasn't the office phone either. It was coming from the floor, so he knelt down and picked up Jen's phone where it appeared to have fallen under her desk.

The caller ID said Charlotte. He answered and said, "Charlotte, Jen's not here. She's left her phone in the office."

"Oh." Charlotte paused. "Is that James?"

He'd been plain Quinn for so long he'd almost forgotten his first name. "Indeed it is."

"Ah. Are you seeing her this weekend?"

He grinned to himself. "Sure. I'll take it over in a while. Is there a message I can pass on?"

"Oh… no, not really. I was calling about plans for Christmas."

"Christmas? Sure it's October!"

"Exactly, she's left it far too late, as usual."

Quinn rolled his eyes at that and picked up his keys. "October is too late to be planning Christmas? You've two whole months."

"Just under that, actually, and there's a lot to consider. You'll understand when you have children."

"When, Charlotte?" Quinn said mildly as he locked the door behind him and started down the steps.

"Oh. Yes, I was forgetting about Jen and those bizarre ideas she has. I mean, part of me thinks she's selfish, but then I suppose if she really believes this is all hereditary…"

Alarmed, Quinn said, "What's hereditary? Is she ill?" *And why aren't you alarmed at passing it on to your own kids?* part of him, the policeman part of him, wondered.

"No. Not unless you count… but I won't gossip about her," Charlotte said primly.

Understanding dawned. "You mean all that time she spent in clinics and institutions," Quinn said. "She's told me about that." *Including how you were usually the one to grass her up*, he didn't add. Walking out into the courtyard, he locked the outer door and turned towards the street. It was already half dark, and there was an electric pumpkin glowing in the shop opposite. Beth had an orange and black themed display in her shop.

"She has? And it doesn't bother you?" Charlotte asked, in a tone that implied it bloody well should.

"Well, of course it bothers me," Quinn said, "because it sounds terrible and I don't like to think of her going through it."

Charlotte sighed. "I'm half convinced she did it all for attention anyway. I mean, after she came out the last time she started dying her hair all those ridiculous colours, and if that's not a cry for attention I don't know what is."

Quinn forced himself to calm down. Charlotte didn't know about the White Lady. She had no idea of the shock and trauma Jen had gone through. And judging by her attitude it was no wonder Jen hadn't ever told her. Attention-seeking, for God's sake! Hadn't she seen the scars and asked herself—

Wait, no. She wouldn't have seen the scars. Unless Jen frolicked around in a bikini when she visited her newborn niece, Charlotte would have no idea those marks were there. And she'd presumably stopped dying her hair by then. Was that when she'd decided to settle down and stop colouring—

His footsteps slowed.

When she'd stopped colouring her hair and dressing like she didn't want to be seen. The bright underwear, the grey clothes, the sensible hair. And the scars.

When Ethan's body had been found, he carried bruises and scratches a few days old. They, combined with the bodily fluids found in his apartment and the blue hair found in his bed, had led the police to conclude he'd been conducting a violent sexual relationship with the woman seen exiting his apartment. But they'd never found her.

She'd been seen most days since the bomb. And then suddenly not at all. And then he'd killed himself. It didn't take a genius to figure out who'd driven him to it.

"James?" Charlotte's voice was impatient. "Are you still there?"

He found himself standing in the middle of the pavement, people scowling as they detoured around him. Strange to be standing still, when he felt like a freight train hurtling off its rails.

He looked up, and saw Jen hurrying towards him, still in the clothes she'd had on earlier.

A train hurtling off its rails into an abyss.

"Have you locked up?" she said. "I think I left my phone…" Her voice trailed off as she read his face. "Who're you talking to?"

An abyss above a stormy ocean.

"Is that her?" Charlotte said. "Hand me over, will you?"

Quinn's fingers clutched the phone so tightly he was amazed it didn't break.

"What's the matter?" Jen asked, and her voice and her face were just the same as they'd always been. She was the woman who'd saved his life in the White Lady five years ago and then fucked his brother and left him to hang and then made Quinn fall in love with her.

"Quinn, seriously, you're freaking me out. Has something happened? Is it Uncle Kieran? Your mother? My mother? What is it?"

Quinn's voice came out hoarse. "My brother," he said.

"What's going on?" said Charlotte in his ear. "I thought your brother was—"

Quinn ended the call and let the phone slip from his fingers. Jen darted forward and grabbed at it, fumbling it in her fingers and staring up at him, her face going pale.

"What about him?" she asked.

"You told me you didn't know him," Quinn said, and saw it hit her like a slap to the face.

"I-I didn't," she stammered. "Not before the bomb. I didn't lie to you about that. I never lied."

"But you didn't tell me about after," Quinn said, his gaze stuck on her. *It might not be true. I might have jumped to conclusions.*

She never told her family about the White Lady. Never came to the survivor's meetings. Freaked right the fuck out when she first saw Quinn's face. And she wouldn't talk about those self-harm scars.

Because she didn't inflict them. Ethan did. *They're the same scars.*

All the evidence was right there but he couldn't make himself believe it. Like a drowning man clutching at a lifebelt, he pleaded, "Tell me now. Did you know him after the bomb?"

Her mouth worked and no sound came out. The waves seemed to close over Quinn's head.

"Did you?" Quinn snarled at her, and she jumped.

"I—we met in the hospital," she whispered, and he had to lean close to hear. "We were the only ones who could walk away, and we…"

"You what?" Quinn said, as calmly as he could. It wasn't very calm at all. He was six fathoms deep, going down with the undertow, and above him Jen was smashing the lifebelt in two.

Standing there on the pavement, Jen was shaking. Her eyes filled with tears. Quinn told himself he didn't care.

She let out a sob, and suddenly the words vomited out of her. "We were both hurting each other. It was violent and unhealthy but… but we were alive, and… cutting myself, it felt kind of good, you know, like a good sting, and I wanted him to hurt me and he wanted me to hurt him, it was like we were using each other for self harm, and eventually I had to end it but I never thought he'd... he'd..."

Quinn couldn't move. *Please God make me a statue.* "That he'd kill himself?"

That he'd take an exercise rope and make a noose and hang himself from a beam, and swing there, alone and cold until Uncle Kieran persuaded the landlord to unlock the door—

Jen just shook her head violently, tears flying out at angles. Half an hour ago he'd been making love to her in his office and now she was destroying everything.

"How could you?" he whispered. Images of Paul Dunlop's sad hanging corpse flashed before his eyes, Ethan's face superimposed there. The protruding tongue, the bloodshot eyes, the clawed skin. That was how Ethan had died, hopeless and despairing, and Jen had pushed him to it.

"I didn't know that's what he'd do," Jen sobbed.

When you dumped him and left him vulnerable and depressed, what did you think he'd do? But it hurt too much, that train of thought. He'd be back underwater again, thinking that. So he pushed it aside and let his anger, that anger that had been there ever since he realised he'd sacrificed his leg for nothing, come right back up to the surface.

"No," said Quinn, advancing on her, "not him. Me. How could you do this to me? All this time working together, being friendly like, making me fall in love with you, making me vulnerable to you, and you never thought—you thought I'd never know, or you didn't care, or—do you like just going around, destroying men? Did you plan it? What is wrong with you? How can you live like this?"

He didn't realise how far he'd pushed her until her back came up against the railing outside the bank and she leaned back over it, away from him. She was frightened of him. Good, so she bloody well should be!

"Quinn, I'm sorry," she whispered. Her eyes were big and drowning in tears and she looked so damn convincing. "I never meant to hurt you."

A sharp laugh escaped him. "Then you should've let me bleed to death in that pub instead of—of letting me die of wounds now," he snapped. He stepped back, and hated himself when he saw her straighten in relief. *You're not the monster here, Quinn.*

"Get the fuck out of my life," he told her. "I never want to see you again."

Jen fled.

CHAPTER THIRTY-THREE

When Alice found Jen she was packing.

"That Brónach woman is terrifying," the little ghost said. "Still, she seems happy with the way things are going. As much as I could tell when she kept jabbering on in that heathen lingo. Are you going somewhere?"

"Away," Jen said shortly. "How do you know Brónach?"

Alice shrugged. "I thought I ought to go and see her. After all," she began, then appeared to change her mind about what she was going to say, and ended, "It's not as if she can hurt me. Where are you going?"

"I don't know." Jen shoved more winter clothes into her suitcase and sat on it to get the zip shut. That done, she reached for another case and started filling that.

Alice watched her silently for a moment. "You're leaving," she said.

"Yep."

"Why?" Her face lit up. "Are you eloping?"

Jen's hands curled into fists and she squeezed her eyes shut to keep the tears in. "No."

Alice seemed genuinely puzzled. "But... what about

Quinn? You two—"

"There is no 'us two'," Jen said, and the memories that invoked nearly made her choke. "It's over."

She balled up the shirt she'd worn that first night together, the shirt she'd removed to show Quinn her scars. *Should've kept it on.* Some secrets should be kept.

Should never have kissed him. Should never have gone away with him. Should have left the minute she found out who he was.

"But why?" Alice insisted. "Jenny, he was so good for you. So nice. Yes, he's a bit grumpy sometimes but he's a nice man, a good man. He won't hurt you."

He didn't need to. I did it all myself.

Jen flung down the boots she was carrying and they thundered on the bare boards. "Why are you so obsessed with men who'll hurt me? When has a man ever hurt me? I can take care of myself!"

"Well, you couldn't with Ethan," Alice blurted, and then her hands clapped over her mouth.

Jen's insides turned to ice. "What," she said, staring at the translucent figure, "do you know about Ethan?"

Alice looked mutinous, as if she was going to deny having said anything, and then she made an annoyed little noise and said, "I know he was hurting you. I saw, Jenny. I didn't want to, I wanted to leave you in peace while you... I mean, you can't accuse me of not moving with the times, but..."

"But?" Jen said, dread splintering through her veins.

Alice wrung her hands. "He was hurting you. You were bruised and bleeding. And you were miserable. I had to do something."

Jen's breathing suddenly sounded very loud. "Alice," she said. "What did you do?"

"It was an accident!" Alice shouted defensively. "I just wanted to scare him. I didn't know what I could do. I didn't think he'd actually let me finish it."

"Finish what?" Jen asked hollowly.

Alice's gaze darted about.

"Alice," Jen said. "Finish what?"

"I made him get the rope," Alice said. "And string it up, and put it round his neck, and…"

Jen found herself backing away. From Alice, her oldest and dearest friend, her protector, her guardian angel. Through the roaring in her ears she heard the words of an actor friend of Ethan's on the news. *I don't know what could have possessed him to do it…*

"You possessed him," she whispered.

"I just wanted to scare him."

"You killed him!"

"I didn't mean to," Alice repeated. "Well… maybe just a little. It never got so out of hand before."

"Before?" Jen's back hit the wall.

"It was only ever accidents before."

Before? But Jen had hardly had any boyfriends, and none of them… had…

Jon Blake and that terrible car crash, just after Jen found out he'd been seeing someone else. Arun from the home, who'd nearly died of an overdose not long after he tried to get Jen to take heroin. Ben, who'd been good with his hands and free with his affections, and who'd tripped on a speaker cable during a gig where he'd flirted with everyone…

Alice, what have you done?

For the first time in her life, Jen was afraid of a ghost.

Her hands trembled, and so did her voice when she said, "The White Lady. The girl—"

"She was just a troubled girl," Alice said. "A girl like…" Her gaze darted away.

"Like me?" Jen filled in. Her hands scrabbled ineffectually for something to defend herself with, as if a thrown book or a candlestick or even a knife would be any good against Alice.

"Not like you," said the little ghost vehemently. "You had me."

Jen's breath stuttered in front of her face. *She thinks I'd have killed someone. She thinks I was crazy too.*

"Alice, you've got to stop this."

"I would never hurt you," said the thing that used to be her friend.

"Me? You don't think it hurts me to know you've been going around murdering people on my behalf?"

"You weren't supposed to know," Alice said.

"That doesn't make it any better! No one was 'supposed to know' about Brónach Doyle, and look how that ended up! What else are you hiding from me? How many others have there been?" A terrible thought occurred to her. "Did you kill my father?"

Alice looked appalled. "No! He just died. Sometimes people just die."

"And sometimes you kill them."

"Only when they're nasty! Your mother chose a nice man, both times. Your sister did too, and I thought you…"

"Wait, you were watching them?" Another memory burst inside Jen's head. Years ago, her mother had fretted that Jen's 'problem' was hereditary. *Only think of Great Aunt Eloise…* "How many others?"

"As many as I could," Alice wailed. "My sister and her children, and then their children… You don't know the terrible things men can do."

"And you do?"

For a moment, Alice's childish features suddenly looked much harder and older. "I do," she said fiercely. "I pray you never do."

Jen stared at her for a long, awful moment. "Alice," she said, her voice as steady as she could make it. "I don't know who you really are or what was done to you but I never want to see you ever again." The distress on

Alice's face nearly made Jen's resolve crumble, but she carried on. "And if anything happens to Quinn, or anyone else in my life, I'm coming after you. I don't care if I have to find your grave and dig up your bones, I will find a way to banish you to hell. Do you understand me?"

Pearlescent tears rolled down Alice's little face. *She's not a child, she's a centuries-old murderer*, Jen told herself harshly.

"Do you understand me?" Jen repeated.

"I understand," Alice said, and then winked out of existence.

Jen stood for a long moment in her suddenly empty bedroom, then she turned and methodically got on with her packing.

Quinn spent the weekend getting blind drunk in the privacy of his own home. That way, no one could see him crashing about the place, ranting and screaming and sobbing uncontrollably. Three times he grabbed the pink scarf Jen had left hanging in his hallway, intending to set fire to it, and three times he clutched it and crumpled into a ball, breathing in her scent from it and howling with misery.

Ghost the cat took one look at him, flattened his ears, and scarpered.

The Angel of the White Lady was the Woman with Blue Hair, and they were both the girl he'd fallen in love with. Except that they weren't, they couldn't be, because how could he have fallen in love with a woman who'd betray him like that? How could he not see it?

How could Ethan still go on stealing girls from him when he'd been dead for five years?

By the time Monday rolled around Quinn's alcohol stream had very little blood left in it. He was woken by his phone ringing, and he focussed blearily on Tessa's name. The screen also showed him the time. Damn. Half past ten.

"I know you're busy shagging your little hearts out," Tessa said before he could speak, "but I have to go and meet a client and there's no one to hold the fort here."

Last night's liquid dinner threatened to make a reappearance. "I'll be there in half an hour," he mumbled, and ended the call, failing to hit the right button the first time around.

He was sweating alcohol. Ten minutes under a cold shower might help that, although whether it'd do much for the general air of wretched despair he was also sure he emanated, Quinn wasn't sure.

"You've faced worse," he reminded himself, but right now it didn't feel like it.

He made it into the office just over half an hour later, limping on a leg that just hadn't wanted to go on right this morning and squinting behind sunglasses despite the grey skies and drizzle.

"There you are," Tessa said brightly as he flinched from the bright overhead light. "Sorry to drag you from your love-nest, but this woman doesn't have a car so I said I'd meet her at the station in—" She broke off, peering at him. "Are you all right?"

"Fine," Quinn said, mooching towards his office.

"You look *awful*."

"Thanks."

"Where's Jen?"

Pain stabbed him in the chest. Quinn told himself it was probably just his heart restarting after all the stress he'd put it through. "Don't know. Don't care."

Tessa's face crumpled in sympathy. "Lover's tiff?"

Quinn leaned against the doorframe. 'Tiff' sounded like a playful little fight, possibly involving pillows. 'Tiff' was not how he'd describe this tearingly awful feeling that he'd had his soul torn into a million pieces.

"I don't want to talk about it," he said, and slammed the door behind him.

He flopped into his chair and rested his head on his hands. In the outer office, he heard Tessa get her things and leave, which at least meant he'd have some peace to sweat out this hangover.

On second thoughts...

He reached into the bottom drawer of his desk. Yep, still there, like the good old cliché it was. He took a swig of the whiskey, gagged for a second, then when he was sure his stomach wasn't going to empty itself, swigged some more.

There were some envelopes on his desk. He grabbed the opener and started slicing them open, which felt mildly therapeutic. Bill. Invoice. Something from the council he'd let Tessa deal with. Invoice. Bill. Typed letter with no masthead—

"Dear Quinn,

Please accept this letter as notice of my resignation. I expect you to understand why I will not be working my notice period.

Jennifer Hargrave.

PS: There's a ghost in your office. His name is Danny Jones. I believe he's your Uncle Kieran's father."

He read and re-read the letter. More of a note, really. Half a dozen lines, and she was out of his life.

Like hell she is. No more than Ethan.

You don't have to be a ghost to haunt someone.

He thought of that scarf hanging in his hallway. He really would burn it when he got home. Maybe it would exorcise her memory. And then he could move on. He could be his old self again, or maybe a new self, someone who didn't moon around over the things he missed. Someone who dated nice, normal girls, not sadistic freaks who cut out his heart and stomped all over it.

He looked at the whiskey by his elbow. *Maybe tomorrow.*

Tessa's meeting wasn't a long one, and she returned around lunchtime with a sandwich from the deli and a thoughtful expression.

"I just went by Jen's house," she said, opening Quinn's door without any preamble, "and there was no response. Is she ill?"

"Dunno." Quinn was a bit drunk now, and very tired. His stomach grumbled. Tessa regarded him with her head on one side.

"Where is she, then?"

He could pretend she'd had a family emergency. "Dunno," he said instead.

"All right, what's going on? On Friday you were almost frighteningly in love, and now... what happened?"

Quinn rubbed his forehead, which was starting to throb. "It just... didn't work out," he said.

"Bollocks." Tessa folded her arms. "She's the best thing to ever happen to you. I saw the way you looked at her. You can't go from madly in love to 'it just didn't work out'."

"Yeah, well, you can," Quinn said. His voice was starting to wobble and his eyes burned. He turned his face away, pretending to fuss with some papers. "And I don't want to talk about it."

"Tough," Tessa said, closing the door behind her and plopping down in the chair facing him. "You're going to talk about it. I want to know where Jen is. She's not answering her phone, she's not at home, and you look like death, so I'm sorry, but we're going to have to talk about it. What happened?"

Quinn risked a glance up at her. She was wearing the expression he'd seen on rare occasions when her kids were driving her up the wall. It said she'd better not hear any more excuses.

He flopped back in his chair with a groan. "Fine. You want to hear it? All right. Here's a little thing Jennifer didn't include on her CV. After the bomb hit the White Lady, she went home with my brother and fucked his brains out for three weeks."

Tessa's eyes went wide.

"And that's not all!" Quinn said with false brightness. "The two of them were apparently having some sort of contest to see who could beat up the other more, *whilst* they were having sex—" *dear God, how could I have thought she enjoyed what we did together?* "—which led to the charming development of him committing suicide when she left him."

Tessa stared.

"Now, I don't know about you, but I found that kind of hard to get past." He shoved Jen's resignation letter at her. "She's at least had the grace to get out of my life."

Tessa read the letter with an air of disbelief.

"But…"

Quinn waited, eyebrows raised.

"But it's so unlike her…"

He snorted. "Oh yeah? Miss bland and buttoned up? She was the Woman with Blue Hair. All this… grey stuff was a disguise! That's why she freaked out when she first saw me! She thought I'd figure her out! And I did. Lying, cheating, conniving little bitch…"

Tessa's frown interrupted his rant.

"What?"

She looked down at the letter again, then back up at him. "I'm sorry, but am I missing the part about her cheating and conniving? Lying, maybe, by omission, but who'd go around sharing a story like that?"

Quinn stared. "She's the reason my brother is dead," he yelled.

"Is she? Because it sounds to me…" Tessa pursed her lips as she thought about it. "It seems to me that after the bomb, Ethan and Jen were the only two people not badly injured, and they were probably feeling a lot of guilt over that. Especially Ethan, being that you were so badly hurt saving him. I'm no psychologist, but I strongly suspect that's the sort of thing that really messes a person up."

Quinn opened his mouth. He shut it again.

"To the extent that, maybe, yeah, they do some really stupid things. Like an ill-advised affair. You know he probably had PTSD. People look for avoidance techniques—sex, alcohol, self-harm. A violent sexual relationship fits the pattern. Did either of them seek help?"

Ethan would have been far too proud. And Jen had her own reasons…

"Don't defend them," Quinn said hoarsely.

"Them?"

"Her. She walked out on him and he killed himself."

"Gosh. A man suffering from post traumatic stress disorder kills himself?" Tessa said drily, then shook her head and apologised. "That was going too far. But look, if all this is true I don't think blaming Jen for it is going to help at all. If I found out my ex had killed himself after I left him I'd feel pretty terrible about it—and you know how I much I hate him," she added with feeling.

"But she…" Quinn began, his gaze darting about as if he was going to find the answer hidden in a corner of the ceiling. She what? Suffered a terrible trauma, did some stupid things, tried to fix herself and live with the consequences?

"She's probably feeling like hell right now," Tessa said, handing him the letter back. "I think you need to find her and apologise to her. Because I don't know what you've said or done, but she's left—left town left

—and it doesn't look like she's coming back."

Guilt slammed into him. *Once more a selfish bastard, Quinn.*

What if she started cutting herself again? What if she took it too far? What if he'd just done to her what he'd accused her of doing to Ethan?

Last time she took out all her pain on Ethan. This time she only had herself.

And Alice. But Alice hadn't been any help last time, had she? What if it was Alice encouraging Jen to hurt herself? What if Alice was lonely and wanted to keep Jen with her—

He shoved his chair back and nearly fell over in the process. "I've got to find her."

Tessa shook her head sadly. "You're not going anywhere until you sober up. Don't lie to me, Quinn. I can smell it on you. Go home, eat some food, get some sleep and for God's sake don't drink anything else unless it's water. You'll be no good to Jen if you're banged up for drink driving or wrapped around a tree somewhere."

She had a point. "But what if I'm too late?"

Tessa drummed her fingers on the table. Then she smiled. "Didn't you say she had a guardian angel?"

To say Quinn slept that night would be an exaggeration, since he spent most of it awake and in agonies of indecision. Where would Jen go? What would he say to her when he found her? How was he going to find her? What if he was too late?

He called DS Coulson, who simply said, "Yes, Tessa told me."

"She did?"

"Yes. I'll put the word out. And don't worry, I know how to be subtle."

Subtle. Quinn groaned as he put the phone down. DS

Laurel Coulson. Tessa had been dating her for weeks.

In the morning, early but not very bright, he downed a pint of tea, forced himself to eat some toast, and tried to make himself look like he hadn't spent the weekend pickling himself in Jameson's finest. He wasn't sure he succeeded.

Then he took a deep breath and walked round to Jen's.

Tessa had been right: the place looked empty. No answer at either the front door or the back, and no signs of recent habitation when he peered through the windows. No coffee cups or wineglasses, no washing up on the drainer. Everything was neat and tidy.

But when he looked through the glass in the back door, he saw the coat hooks and shoe rack were both empty.

Next on his list was a visit to the local taxi office, where they had a female dispatcher on today. Quinn wasn't feeling very charming at all, but he channelled his inner Ethan and she was all too eager to tell him whether they'd picked anyone up from Jen's address. Yes, on Sunday, and she'd headed to the station. Quinn didn't ask for the name and number of the driver, but picked it up from the computer screen and dialled it as soon as he was back outside.

"This is Detective James Quinn," he said, because half the time people didn't stop to ask whether that meant he was police or not. "I'm calling about a potential missing person who is in a vulnerable state. Can you confirm you picked up a Jennifer Hargrave from King Street on Sunday?"

The cabbie took a while to remember, but when Quinn prompted him, slightly desperately, to think about luggage, the man recalled she'd had a lot.

"Said she wasn't coming back," he said. "She asked if I knew any removals firms who'd pack up all her stuff."

"And did you?" Quinn asked. He got the name of the company the man recommended, but when he called them they had no information for him. *That would be too easy.*

According to the cabbie, Jen hadn't mentioned where she was going. Quinn looked at the train times and cross referenced them with her cab ride and concluded that she'd probably be heading to London, which was the least helpful information he'd had all day. All trains led to London. And all trains led back out of it again. All over the country, and even out of it. She could be quite literally anywhere.

Christ, if she had her passport she could be halfway across Europe.

Time for another approach. Quinn packed an overnight bag and looked up Charlotte's address. It wasn't likely Jen would have gone there, but unless Coulson came up with anything it was the best start he had. Hopefully Charlotte might let something slip, or there'd be a photo of a favourite childhood holiday or something. People who ran away usually went to ground in some recognisable way.

He tried to remember as he drove if Jen had mentioned any favourite places, but he couldn't think of any. She'd moved around so many times since the bomb that she'd barely put down roots anywhere.

He even called Emer to see if Jen had, by some miracle, checked back in to the hotel in Dalkey. She'd seemed so happy there, so in love with the place. Might she go back, or might the memories there be too painful?

"I haven't seen her," Emer said, "but we've a good deal on a honeymoon special if you wanted to book it."

Quinn managed not to swear at his cousin for that, and dialled his uncle instead. Kieran wouldn't be able to keep it to himself if he knew where Jen was.

But all he had to tell Quinn was news of the Fairview excavation. Archaeologists had been called in, and they reckoned they'd found seven individual human remains. Whether or not they were related, and how, would have to wait for DNA testing, which could take months since it was hardly a priority.

"Fascinated with the case, they are," Kieran said. "And the papers! It's like a good old gory murder mystery, but with the added bonus that it all happened so long ago no one is around to be hurt by it."

"Apart from Mrs Kelly and her family," Quinn added. "And myself and Jen."

"And yourself and Jen," Kieran repeated. "How is she?"

Quinn swallowed and glanced at the pink scarf lying on the passenger seat. "Fine," he lied. "Everything's grand."

He hung up, and concentrated on navigating the A12, which was being an unending joy this morning. Charlotte lived in Tunbridge Wells, which was about two and a half hours away from Wirpness. He'd still got the M25 to go, and then the town itself. He didn't even know what he'd do if she wasn't in.

You're a detective, man. Detect. He forced himself to think about it. He'd probably arrive too late for the school run, and he didn't know if Charlotte worked full time, only that she was an actuary. Next time he pulled in at a service station, he used his phone to look up firms in the town and see if she was listed as an employee. There, that one. So now he had two places to go, although Charlotte's office would be a lot less helpful than her home.

He also called Tessa to see if anything had turned up. It hadn't. "Do you know where her mother lives?" he asked.

Computer keys clicked. "In a village not far away. At

least, it's the right name, so it's probably her. I'll send you the address. How're you holding up?"

"Fine," Quinn said.

"Liar."

When he finally arrived at Charlotte's house, he wasn't surprised to find it a well-maintained Victorian semi on a street full of much larger houses. How like Charlotte to go for the smallest house on the best street in town.

Quinn parked on the street, which for some reason earned him a dirty look from a woman pushing a stroller approximately the same size as his car. Perhaps parking here was only for Range Rovers.

He sat at the wheel for a long moment, trying to work out what to say. Did he pretend he was just in the neighbourhood? Did he make up a story?

Ah, feck it.

Where other properties had off-road parking, Charlotte's house boasted a small, neat front garden with raked gravel and a couple of bay trees flanking the entrance. The front door was painted one of those heritage shades that Jen despised so much. Quinn rang the old-fashioned and deeply inefficient bell, and was surprised when Charlotte herself answered a few moments later.

"James?" she said, blinking at him. She had on a cashmere sweater and a retro-styled pinny. Both were pristine.

"People usually call me Quinn. Can I come in? I need to talk to you."

She frowned a bit, but stood back to allow him entry. The hall was painted a colour he could only call greige, and boasted an antique telephone table. He could smell something baking. "Is something wrong? Is Jen all right? Would you mind taking your shoes off?"

He gave her a sideways look. "Sure," he said, and sat

down on the stairs. He pulled one boot off, then deliberately unlaced the other one, easing it away from his moulded prosthetic foot and flashing a bit of metal ankle as he did.

Charlotte watched with wide eyes, but said nothing.

Quinn stood up and followed her into the kitchen, where she put the kettle on without asking what he wanted. "Do you know where Jenny is?"

She frowned, and moved aside a rack of half-iced cupcakes. "No. Why?"

"She's… gone. Left town. Got a cab to the station yesterday with lots of luggage and not a word as to why."

This at least seemed to alarm her. "She's run away? Again?"

"She's done it before?"

Charlotte took her time setting out mugs and teaspoons. The kitchen had an expensive, handmade look to it and all the appliances were discreetly branded. Quinn didn't need to look to see that the fridge was a Smeg and the toaster a Dualit. Charlotte bought social class from John Lewis, so she didn't have to make up her own mind what she liked.

"She moves on quite often," she said. "Never very good at making friends. Not even when we were children. It's why I was glad you and she seemed to be…" she waved a hand and Quinn tried not to feel pain. "I thought you might stabilise her."

Like a child's bicycle. "Do you know where she might have gone?"

Charlotte comforted herself with the rituals of making tea. "Offhand, no. I can call Mum and see if she knows. You have tried calling her, haven't you? Jen, I mean?"

"No, I thought I'd just drive all the way down here without even attempting that," Quinn snapped. "Sorry," he added. "It's been a bad couple of days."

"Did you fight?"

He nodded.

"Is it over between you?"

Quinn let out a harsh laugh. "Jesus, you don't soft-soap much, do you? I don't know if it's over. That's why I need to find her."

Charlotte handed him a mug of tea. He noticed she hadn't asked if he wanted sugar. She probably didn't allow any in the house. "Maybe she doesn't want to be found."

He nodded wearily, taking a seat at the scrubbed pine table. "I know that. But I need to find her. She's... vulnerable."

Charlotte paused in the act of picking up an icing bag and dealt him a sharp look. "In what way vulnerable?"

Quinn reminded himself that Charlotte didn't know about the White Lady and its aftermath. She didn't know her sister had wrecked herself, trying to survive without help because she was too frightened to ask for it.

"She's upset," he said. "It was a big fight."

Charlotte went back to the icing, but only managed one tiny blob before she said, "Maybe I should call Dr Wu." Glancing up, she coloured. "Uh. I don't know if Jen told you, but maybe in the circumstances, you should know…"

"You think your sister's crazy?"

"Not crazy!" Charlotte said hotly. "She's ill and needs help."

You have no idea how true that is, thought Quinn heavily. "But she'll never go for help, because of all that time she spent in institutions and clinics when she was a kid. Yes, she told me. She told me it was usually you who blew the whistle on her whenever she talked to Alice."

Charlotte's swift outrage quickly gave way to

surprise. "She told you about Alice?"

"She told me all of it. Charlotte, you don't have to believe in ghosts, you just have to believe your sister does. All you managed to do was make her distrust anyone trying to give her professional help, even when she really needed it."

So she cut herself and let an equally damaged man beat her up. But he couldn't tell her that.

Charlotte bit her lip. "I should go and see I've got Dr Wu's phone number," she said.

"No, that's not—" Quinn began, but he knew there was no point. Charlotte had decided her sister's delusions needed to be treated with pills and there was no way to change her mind. He watched her leave, heard her jog up the stairs and across the landing.

This wasn't helping in the slightest. He'd probably just made things worse. Now Charlotte would be off calling this doctor and they'd probably alert a bloody task force to search for Jen and she'd disappear like a rabbit down a hole, or even worse, she'd retreat inside herself and try to cut it all out again—

His horrible train of thought was interrupted by the sight of a small face peering round the door frame.

"You're Auntie Jen's boyfriend," it said.

Quinn winced. "Kind of," he fudged. "You're Millie, right?"

She nodded and stepped into the frame. "I have the pox," she said, pointing to a rash of itchy red bumps on her arm.

"Chickenpox? Poor thing."

Millie nodded, and then did the strangest thing. She looked to her left, and said, "No, not smallpox." Then she clapped her hand over her mouth, her eyes going wide, and ran away.

When Quinn got up to follow her, the air in the hallway felt very cold.

He walked slowly into the living room, where Millie was sitting on the floor pretending to watch cartoons. He could tell she was pretending, because her gaze crept over to him and then riveted itself on a pink pig in a dress.

"Millie?" said Quinn, taking a seat on the tastefully beige sofa. "What do you know about smallpox?"

Again, Millie glanced to her left. "Nothing. I don't think it exists any more."

"Hmm. Why doesn't it exist?"

A pause, and then Millie giggled behind her hand and said bossily, "Because of vaccinations, you silly man."

Right. Because every five-year-old knows about vaccination programmes, Quinn thought. He deliberately kept his gaze away from the empty spot next to Millie.

"Who told you about smallpox vaccinations, Millie?" he asked casually.

"No one," she said quickly, looking right at no one.

Quinn sighed. "All right. What's your name? No, not you," he added as Millie opened her mouth. "Your invisible friend."

Millie's eyes went very round. "You can see her?"

"No. But I know she's there. What's her name?"

Another pause, and then Millie said in a whisper. "Alice. But don't tell Mummy."

"Alice?" Quinn leaned forward, gobsmacked. "Jen's Alice?"

"Don't tell Mummy!" Millie said urgently. "You got to promise."

"I promise. Won't tell a soul," Quinn said distractedly. "Does your friend Alice know Auntie Jen?"

"Do you?" Millie asked the empty air, then frowned as she listened. "Why don't you like her any more?"

Quinn's heart pounded but he made himself wait for

the reply. Millie told him matter-of-factly, "Auntie Jen told Alice to go away, so she's my friend now."

Then who is taking care of Jen?

"Why did she tell her to go away?"

"I don't know. She's fun." Millie listened a moment, then frowned and said, "What does ungrateful mean?"

"It means you should have said thank you," Quinn said. "Who's ungrateful?"

"Auntie Jen. What should she have said thank you for?"

Quinn listened as hard as he could over the blood pounding in his ears, but got nothing.

"I don't need you to protect me," Millie proclaimed proudly to Alice. "I'm a big girl."

"Who did Auntie Jen need protecting from?" Quinn asked carefully.

Millie listened, then gave Quinn a dirty look. "She says there was a bad man and he looked like you. He hurt Auntie Jen. She says you're supposed to be different."

"Did you make her leave Eth—the bad man?" Quinn asked, staring at the place Alice was supposed to be.

"No, but she made sure he couldn't hurt her again."

"How?" Quinn managed. His heart felt like it was beating in his mouth.

"The same way," came the horrible answer, "she stopped the man from hurting Beth. Who's Beth?"

"A friend," Quinn murmured, the horror threatening to overcome him.

"Oh, there you are," Charlotte said from the doorway. "Sorry that took so long, Oliver reorganised the—"

Quinn held up a hand to silence her, and she must have read his face because she shut up. His mind was whirling. He felt sick.

Alice had killed Ethan and Paul. Or she'd made them kill themselves. Encouraged suicide carried a prison

402

sentence. Not that you could prosecute a bloody ghost.

"Alice," he said as calmly and steadily as he could, "do you know where Jen is?"

"Her name is Mildred," Charlotte said. Quinn glared at her.

Millie's gaze darted from Quinn to her mother, then back to Alice. She bit her lip.

"I need to find her," Quinn added. "It's very important."

"Is it a 'mergency?" Millie asked, looking up at her mother.

"Millie, what are you talking about? Who is Alice?"

Quinn kept his gaze steady on Millie. "It very much is an emergency," he told her. "I need your help."

He waited, desperate, for the response. When it came, it was with a giggle. Millie said from behind her hand, "She says she's in bloody heathen Cornwall."

"Cornwall?" Quinn said, exhaling sharply. She couldn't have gone further west without swimming.

"Millie, we don't say that word," Charlotte said, then added, "Who are you talking to?"

"Where in Cornwall?" Quinn demanded.

Millie waited, then shook her head. "She says you'll have to detect it. What does detect mean?"

"Discover," Quinn murmured. He leapt to his feet, insomuch as he was capable of leaping, and said in a rush to Charlotte, "We were just playing a game. Imaginary friends. You know kids."

Charlotte looked doubtful.

"Helps me think," Quinn added randomly. "Is that Dr Wu's phone number? Grand. I'll take it," and he snatched the piece of paper from her and buried in his pocket before she could stop him. *Let her go after that if she dares.* "What's in Cornwall? Any favourite childhood holidays?"

Charlotte looked immensely confused. "I think we

went to Penzance once," she said. "Why?"

"Gives me a place to start."

"It's a long way." Charlotte kept glancing at her daughter, who was pretending to watch cartoons again. "Millie, did you say your friend is called Alice?"

"I called her that," Quinn said before Millie could answer. "Just a random name. Popped into my head. Well, great to see you, Charlotte, Mildred, you take care now."

He darted for the front door, opened it, swore when he realised he was in his stocking feet, and retreated to the stairs to put his boots back on.

Millie skidded out into the hall, regarded him uncertainly for a moment, then leaned forward and whispered in his ear.

"Mummy says I'm not allowed imaginary friends."

"I bet she does," Quinn muttered.

"But Auntie Jen says they're harmless and I shouldn't be afraid. Alice has been friends with lots of girls in my family. She says she looks after them and stops bad men from hurting them."

Quinn's knuckles were white as he tied his laces.

"No one's going to hurt Auntie Jen, are they?"

"No," said Quinn, standing up and reaching for his jacket. "Not while I'm around they're not."

Millie paused, and said, "Alice says she's not allowed to hurt you, because Auntie Jen loves you."

"I love her too," Quinn said, his throat going thick.

"Alice says you should marry her and have babies."

He choked out a laugh. "We'll see." He put his hand on the doorknob, then looked back at the little girl standing there by the stairs. Behind her, her mother watched with a frown from the living room doorway.

"Take care of this one," he said, and he wasn't speaking to Charlotte. "And don't do anything I'll make you regret."

Then he slammed the door behind him and went on his way to Cornwall.

CHAPTER THIRTY-FOUR

She'd bought two bottles of wine at the village shop when she arrived. One of them was nearly empty now.

Jen stared unseeing at the TV, and tried not to think about the sharp objects in the cottage kitchen. She didn't do that any more. She didn't need to. She could get over heartbreak without carving up her own skin.

She poured more wine, and changed channels.

"*Previously, on Devilborn,*" said an achingly familiar voice, and she looked up to see Ethan smouldering at her.

Her hand gripped the wineglass very tight.

Thanks to traffic on the M25 and rush hour on the A303, it was dark by the time Quinn hit the A30 and he still had a couple of hours to go. The weekend was fast catching up with him, his head heavy and aching. He pulled into Exeter Services and loaded up on energy drinks, and was just walking back to the car when his phone rang.

A young woman looked over at the sound, and her eyes widened. "Oh my God, you look just like—"

"Fuck off," he said, and answered the call. "My favourite police officer," he said. "Tell me you've got something."

"She paid Cornish Cottage Holidays just over four hundred pounds yesterday. I shouldn't be telling you this and you'll have to take the next steps by yourself."

Quinn thought he might faint with relief.

"Laurel Coulson, I think I love you," he said, and she gave a dry laugh.

"Yes, it's me you adore. We didn't have this conversation," she reminded him, and hung up.

He got back into his car and dialled the cottage company. Lacking the energy to come up with a cover story, he told them he was a detective trying to trace a vulnerable woman. The ring of truth must have shone from his voice, because he was granted the address of a cottage in Mousehole, near Penzance.

Quinn reprogrammed his sat nav, downed another energy drink, and set off full of renewed purpose, rehearsing what to say. He'd start with an apology, obviously, and then maybe some begging. Maybe he should take flowers. Yes. Next time he saw a likely-looking place, he'd buy flowers.

The roads became increasingly narrow the further west he went, but Quinn had learned to drive on Irish roads, and Cornwall could hold no terrors for him. Desperately frustrated by the traffic around Penzance, he kept glancing at the clock. Nearly seven. He'd been on the go for far too many hours.

The cottage Jen had rented was at the top of the hideously appropriately named Love Lane. By the time he reached the top the road was little more than an unmade boreen. You'd never get two cows on this road, he thought, semi-hysterically.

And there was the cottage, small and grey, looking out over the dark bay. There were lights on in the downstairs windows.

Quinn parked up, took a few steadying breaths, then picked up the bunch of flowers lying on top of Jen's scarf, and made his way through the dark to the front door.

The blood welled up, shockingly red against her white skin. The knife was much sharper than she'd expected. Jen scored a neat line down her forearm, watching the red ooze up, and then a sudden sound broke the silence of the cottage and her head whipped around.

Someone was knocking on the door. Who the hell had come all the way up here? And why now?

Her hand throbbed, and she looked down, her stomach suddenly going hollow. The knife had slipped when she was startled.

The cut was a bit deeper than she'd intended.

She grabbed some kitchen roll and pressed it over the cut. The blood seeped through immediately. The knock came again.

"Really bad timing," she muttered despairingly, and went to the window to see who was there.

Quinn stared back in at her, white with shock. She saw his gaze travel down to the red mess on her arm and instinctively tried to hide it behind her back. Blood dripped onto the floor.

The front door suddenly crashed open and there he was, throwing some flowers on the sofa and grabbing her in his arms.

"Jesus, Jenny. Show me. How bad is it?"

She fought to keep her arm behind her back, but the jagged flesh caught on her t-shirt and she hissed in pain, straightening her arm away.

"What are you doing here?"

"I came to find you." He took hold of her arm, gently, carefully. "I've been worried about you."

"I'm fine," said Jen, and Quinn quite sensibly ignored that.

"Sit down," he urged, guiding her to the sofa and shoving the flowers away.

"I'll make a mess—"

"I don't care. Do you have a towel or anything?" He glanced wildly about, gaze alighting on the teatowel hanging neatly over the oven door handle. "Is this clean?"

"Yes, but—"

"It'll do." He folded it over and pressed it against the cut on her arm, kneeling down in front of her to do it. His attention was focused on what he was doing, not on her face, so he couldn't see the tears welling up. Why did he have to come now? Why not ten minutes ago, before she did this stupid thing?

"You should raise your arm," he said, holding it gently by the elbow. "Slow the bleeding. Do you feel dizzy? Faint?"

Jen shook her head, and he looked up at her. "I'm sorry," she said, her voice breaking on a sob, and Quinn looked like he was going to cry too.

"Don't, Jenny, please. You've nothing to be sorry for." With the arm not holding hers in the air, he gave her a fierce hug.

"I'm making such a mess," she sniffed against his shoulder.

"No one cares about the mess."

"Of everything. My job and my life and everything. You. I should've told you, Quinn, I'm so sorry. I was so stupid for thinking it could ever work."

"You're not stupid," Quinn said, pulling back and looking at her with such emotion she only cried harder. "I'm the idiot here. Jesus, the things I said to you... I'm so sorry, Jenny. Can you ever forgive me?"

She stared at him. He wanted her to forgive him?

After the things she'd told him, the things he knew about her? She wasn't sure she could forgive herself.

Blood dripped from her arm down his jacket, splatting on the floor. Quinn tore his gaze from hers to glance at it, then he looked back and said, "Okay, this needs a doctor."

"It's not that bad—"

Quinn gave her a look.

"I didn't mean it to be that bad," Jen amended.

He dug out his phone and swore at it. "No signal. Perfect. Come on, get in the car. There's got to be a hospital around here somewhere. Do you have another towel?"

The teatowel was soaked through with blood. She let him fetch another one from the bathroom and wrap her arm carefully in it, then he steered her out to the car and opened the door for her.

There was something pink on the passenger seat.

"That's my scarf," she said, staring at it. The one Millie had made for her. "Why do you have my scarf?"

"Because I'm a sentimental eejit," Quinn muttered, lobbing it on the back seat. "Get in."

He was silent as he reversed the car, putting his arm on the back of the seat in the way that made her feel light-headed. Or maybe that was the bleeding. The lane down to the village was dark, high-sided and uneven, and she let him concentrate on it, resting her head back against the seat.

"Is it true about Alice?" he said suddenly, and she blinked open eyes she didn't remember closing.

"Is what true?"

"That you told her to go away?"

Pain that had nothing to do with her arm washed over Jen. "I had to," she said. "Oh God, Quinn, if you only knew…"

"I think I do know," he said, and she'd never heard

him sound so grim.

He started talking about how he'd gone to Charlotte's house to try and find her, and about Millie's imaginary friend and the things she'd told him.

"Millie can see her?" *It's not just me. I'm not mad.*

"Millie, and I suspect quite a lot of other women in your family too. Jenny… the things she said about how she was protecting you. About Ethan…"

Jen shook her head rapidly, tears blurring the lights of the village as they came into view. "I know."

"She told you?"

The fingers of her right hand curled into a fist. Her left hand wasn't co-operating quite so well. She forced herself to breathe and speak calmly.

"You remember how Brónach took me over?"

Quinn shuddered. "Not likely to forget it."

"I think she did that with Ethan. Made him… do something he didn't want to do."

His hand left the steering wheel and found hers. "I know."

Relief brought tears pouring down her cheeks. "Quinn, I'm so sorry."

"It's not your fault. Jenny, it really isn't. I don't know what's driving Alice but what she did wasn't your fault."

"But if it wasn't for me…"

He squeezed her hand. "Don't think like that. Please. I know I said… some really stupid things, but I don't blame you for it. Even before I heard what Alice said."

Jen blinked, hope kindling inside her. "You don't?"

There was a catch in Quinn's voice as he spoke, but in the darkness she couldn't see his face. "He was damaged and unhappy. People do unwise things."

"Like me?" Jen hiccupped.

He stopped the car, flicked on the light and turned to face her. His eyes were wet with tears. He looked tired and pale and grim.

"How far did you mean to go with that?" he asked, troubled gaze flicking to her bloodsoaked arm.

"Not as far as I went." She searched his face. "Are you blaming yourself for this?"

He eventually nodded.

"Oh, Quinn." She reached out and touched his face, felt the wetness of his tears, the roughness of his stubble, the warmth of his skin. "Don't. I'm fine. It's just a cut. It doesn't mean... I didn't want to die. I don't want to. I just needed to..."

She looked down at the blood soaking through the towel, messy and shameful. She'd never been able to explain it, even to herself. To cut it out, as if all her unhappiness would flow away with the bad blood. To punish herself, perhaps. Not even herself. Someone needed to be hurt, she needed to hurt someone, but she didn't know who and it was no one else's fault, so she had to hurt herself.

"I just needed to cut," she said. "It helps, somehow, but... but not for long."

"And then you need to do it again?"

She shrugged, ashamed. "I know how it sounds," she said.

He covered her hand with his, expression bleak. "It sounds," he said slowly, "like why I drink. At first it helps—it stings and it numbs, but it doesn't last and then you need more."

She looked up at him, almost afraid to believe he understood.

"Jenny, why do you think I let people hit me?" he said, and fresh tears burned her eyes because he did understand.

"Oh God, we're both fuck-ups."

"We're not. We're not. We're people who've had too much to deal with."

Quinn's warm fingers wrapped around hers, safe and

secure, and she clung to him, her lifeline. "You're not alone, you know. If you ever feel like this again—you call me, and I'll be there to help. I know you don't want to see anyone about this, but I'm here. I love you, Jenny, even if... even if you don't..."

At that she nearly laughed. "James Quinn, you big Irish idiot. Of course I bloody do."

She reached over to kiss him, and he met her halfway, hot and urgent, his arms going around her. She only broke the kiss when he caught her arm and she flinched.

"Grand," he said, breath warm on her face. His eyes were dark and tender, and then he looked at the red seeping through the towel wrapped around her arm, and his expression sharpened. "Right. We were on our way to the hospital. You need stitches, and maybe some antibiotics, and there's got to be some phone signal around here somewhere."

He sat back in his seat and released the handbrake, but his gaze flicked over her and he gave a small smile. Jen smiled back, and then they were on their way.

She spent most of the morning thinking.

She'd woken late in Quinn's arms, barely remembering how they got back to the cottage last night. Her arm ached with the remnants of the anaesthetic and was now wrapped neatly in a white bandage, glowing bright as a reminder of how hateful her life had seemed only last night.

The bloodstained towel lay draped over the bathtub, red and white like a lifebelt. He'd saved her from drowning last night. Was that all it took? Just two people being honest with each other?

Now she looked down at Quinn lying there asleep, unreasonably handsome with his dark hair in careless disarray and his jaw bearded with a week's stubble, and wondered if he really had forgiven her last night. If he actually believed she wasn't responsible for Ethan's death.

She wondered if she believed it herself.

Funny how two men who looked exactly the same, who'd had the same upbringing and the same opportunities, could be so utterly different. Jen hadn't exactly been thinking about long-term plans when she'd known Ethan, but she'd known perfectly well he wasn't a long-term prospect.

If he hadn't died, what would she have done? Moved on, sure, got a new job, met her new niece and tried to avoid all the ghosts. That would all be the same. Would she ever have seen him again? Doubtful, even if she'd stayed in London. She couldn't see them staying friends, sending cheeky texts and meeting up for drinks every now and then. She'd have seen him on TV, watched him bloodsoaked and sexy in *Devilborn* and maybe tried to remember what that chest had felt like beneath her fingers, what those lips had tasted like. She'd have seen him in magazines and on websites, dating and making convention appearances and generally being a star in the ascendant.

She probably wouldn't have thought of him any more than any other ex. None of them had left scars on her psyche. Would Ethan have been any different, would the physical scars heal and fade and would he have been just another face from the past?

And if he'd gone on to have his career and she'd forgotten all about him and five years later she'd found herself working for his twin brother, would she tell him about Ethan? "We had a thing once, but it wasn't serious. Hope that won't make this weird!" Would Quinn have been attracted to her if he knew she'd been with his brother? Would she have pushed him away?

What if, what if?

Jen let her head fall back against the brass bedstead and let herself remember all the things she'd tried to forget. Before Quinn, before Ethan, before the White Lady, back when she'd been talked to softly and observed carefully and never allowed any shoelaces or sharp objects. When doctors had tried to fix her with drugs and counsellors had tried to fix her with words, and she'd tried to fix herself by closing her eyes tightly and pretending none of the things she shouldn't see were real.

She remembered kind, dark-eyed Arun, who'd taken refuge in drugs when his father beat him. She remembered hollow-cheeked Fiona, tipped into starvation by well-meaning relatives who told her the world wasn't kind to fat people. And she remembered pretty, fragile Shanti, who never said much but once tried to stab a boy who grabbed for her breast.

They'd all been broken, but it was Shanti who said they were like smashed plates.

"Hey," said Quinn, and she looked down to see him blinking away sleep, looking drowsy and irresistible.

"Hey yourself," she said back. Quinn smiled up at her, and for a moment she saw golden sunlight and heard birds singing and felt herself smile back, goofily, helplessly.

"How's your arm?" he asked, and she was back in the real world again, with fourteen stitches and a course of antibiotics.

"Fine. Aches a bit, but that's the—"

"—anaesthetic. I remember that," Quinn said, stretching in a manner that was quite distracting. He yawned, and even that looked good.

Last night, all they'd done was sleep together. He'd held her close, knowing without asking that it was what she needed more than anything. That his arms kept away the darkness and loneliness.

She wanted this to work so very badly.

"Did you sleep all right?" asked Quinn, and she nodded.

"Better for having you here." He smiled warmly at that, his eyes going all dark and soft, and Jen felt herself falling into them. He reached for her, and she leaned away.

The softness faded. Concern creased his brow. "What's wrong?"

"Nothing's wrong. It's just…"

He waited patiently, raising himself up on one elbow and regarding her in a way that was probably supposed to be helpful but instead just made her want to touch him.

"We're broken plates," she said, and Quinn just looked confused. "It's something someone said to me a long time ago. You can smash a plate on the floor, and it doesn't matter how much you apologise to it, it's still going to be broken."

"Okay," he said slowly.

"Apologising to it won't fix it."

"I see that," Quinn said, clearly wondering where this was going. "But glue will."

"Sure, for a given value of 'fix'. But if it's totally smashed there's no glue in the world that will put it back together again. And even if it's just a few pieces, and you're really careful with the restoration, you can still see the cracks. You'll always see the cracks. And the plate will never be as strong again. And if you subject it to any kind of stress…"

She ran out of steam there, because Quinn was looking at her very oddly. But then he reached out and took her bandaged hand, and looked up at her with those dark eyes, and said, "Then it breaks again."

She nodded.

"Is that what happened last night?"

Jen nodded again, and Quinn wrapped both arms around her. "Well then," he said. "We need better glue."

She luxuriated in the feel of his skin against hers for a moment, then she pulled back and looked up at him.

"Better glue?"

He looked sheepish. "I may have pushed the analogy too far there."

Jen gave him a squeeze, in love with him for trying. "Actually you might be right," she said.

"Really?" He didn't sound like he believed her.

"I need glue. I was just too scared of, um, asking for any." Talking to his chest, she explained, "I kept being treated like I was crazy—"

"You're not," Quinn said firmly.

"Right, and I knew that, but if you've been told you need help your whole life and then something happens when you do need help, when the plate smashes... I should've got proper help after the White Lady. I should have taken the counselling or gone back to Dr Wu or... well, anything but what I actually did. And instead I lied about it for years, pretended it had never happened. And then I didn't know how to deal with..."

"With being smashed again," Quinn said. He was silent a moment, then he said, "You're not a broken plate, you're a broken bone. You've got to heal from one trauma before you can face the next."

"Must there be a next?" Jen said.

"Sometimes you can't avoid it."

She knew he was right. Still, "Any more talk about broken legs and we're going to come up with a really terrible metaphor for you."

Quinn shifted his left leg under the sheets. His prosthetic leaned against the bedside table. "I'm missing a piece of me," he said simply. "But I'm still alive."

Which was as good as she was ever going to find.

"Speaking of pieces of yourself," Jen said,

disentangling herself and sitting up again, "we need to talk about Alice."

Quinn sat up too, rolling his shoulders as if preparing for a physical feat. "She appears to be haunting your niece."

Jen thought of all those ancestors, women confined to asylums and spoken of in hushed voices. How many had there been? How many would there be?

"Does Charlotte know?"

He made a fifty-fifty motion with his hand. "Millie said she's not allowed to have imaginary friends."

"She's petrified of the kid turning into me," Jen said glumly.

"Then she's an idiot," Quinn said. "You're amazing."

Despite all they'd been to each other, Jen still managed to blush. Quinn grinned at her and she leaned against him, bashing him lightly on the shoulder.

"The thing is, though," he said, draping an arm around her, "we do have a problem with Alice. And I think it's a problem that's been going on too long."

"She's done this before," Jen sighed.

"I think so. And take it from me, it's a damn sight easier to re-offend once you've got the hang of it."

"So how do we stop her?"

"Hey, you're supposed to be the expert."

"I can see ghosts, not psychoanalyse them."

She rested her head on his shoulder, and he propped his cheek against her hair. It felt right, comfortable. Companionable.

"Have you heard from Uncle Kieran what's going on with Brónach?"

Quinn shrugged. "No one's been attacked, so I assume she approves of the exhumations. Mrs Ní Dhomhnaill doesn't seem to have heard anything from her."

"Do you think she's... well, gone?"

"Gone where? Where do they go?"

"Heaven, or hell, or… I dunno. Not here."

Quinn was silent a moment. "Why do they become ghosts?" he asked. "Why some people and not others?"

She knew what he was asking. "I don't know," she said. "I don't think they do either."

She didn't say what she was thinking. That maybe the reason Ethan hadn't hung around to tell the truth about how he'd died was because he'd wanted to die. Or because maybe Alice had sent him on somewhere—

"Wait a sec," she said, straightening. "Brónach's moving on, apparently. At least she's not haunting anyone and pushing them down stairs any more. Because the truth about her life and her death have come out, right?"

"Right," Quinn said cautiously.

"Alice never wanted me to find her grave. I always figured it was because she felt uncomfortable about it, you know, like reminding me she was dead or something. But what if there's something she's been concealing?"

"Right," said Quinn, nodding. "Like the fact that Tessa couldn't find her in your family history?"

"But she clearly has a preference for my family, which can't be a coincidence. Maybe…" She tried to remember what Tessa had told her about a possible match, who'd turned out to be too old. "Oh God, I don't know, maybe she killed the original Alice and took over her life or something." She threw herself back against the headboard, annoyed.

"Or maybe," Quinn said, frowning, "she's not what she's been pretending to be. Millie said Alice had been protecting lots of other girls in your family. How old were you when you first saw her?"

Jen shrugged. "I don't even remember. She's always been there. Like a big sister."

"Exactly."

Their eyes met. "You think she's pretending to be a little girl to look more harmless?" Jen said slowly. Cold ran through her.

"Can they do that?"

"I don't know." She remembered Danny boasting about being a Spitfire pilot. "They can certainly lie. Quinn, remember how I told you there was a ghost in your office?"

A flash of something dark went across his face, and belatedly she remembered she'd told him this in the same letter that told him she was never coming back.

"I think he might be Uncle Kieran's father. He's an RAF pilot—his name is on the war memorial at Wirpness—and he once mentioned this Irish girl he fell for. It's possible he's just been hanging around to take care of them."

"He doesn't know Kieran is his son?"

Jen raised her palms. "He's not that bright. But look, do you think…"

"…if he knew…?"

"…he might…?"

"…go wherever he's going?"

Jen swallowed. "And he might take Alice with him."

CHAPTER THIRTY-FIVE

Charlotte appeared to have begun grumbling even before she got out of the car. From what Quinn could tell, she hadn't stopped since Jen had called her on the way back from Cornwall.

He thought how Uncle Kieran had simply said, "Grand plan, son. I'll bring your birthday card, and can you tell me how the buses are running?"

Quinn had, until that point, entirely forgotten that it was his birthday, which so far made it the most successful since Ethan had died.

His uncle was currently engaged in drinking all the tea in Quinn's kitchen and fussing over Ghost the cat, while Charlotte was complaining that no one really appreciated how busy she was.

"I've got to make two dozen more cupcakes for the PTA meeting," she said as she unbuckled Mildred from her car seat. "Do you know how long it takes to drive up here?"

"Two and a half hours, if the traffic's good," Quinn said. "Your sister's fine, by the way."

Charlotte at least had the grace to look slightly

shamefaced at this, but she quickly spoilt it by saying, "Well, she sounded fine when she called."

"And someone who sounds fine must be fine, eh Charlotte?" He didn't let her respond, but turned to greet Millie instead. The poor kid was wearing a gilet, for God's sake.

She beckoned him down to whisper in his ear. "Alice says she doesn't want to kiss and make up with Auntie Jen."

"No one's going to be kissing Alice," he replied, and straightened up. "Come on. Would you like a drink? I've some orange juice."

"Is it sugar-free?" Charlotte asked as her daughter skipped happily up the path.

"Sure," Quinn lied.

Jen, who'd been sitting at the kitchen table with Uncle Kieran, stiffened a little as her niece and sister came in. Quinn wasn't sure if it was Charlotte's presence that had that effect, or Alice's. Ghost jumped off the table with a squawk and rushed over to Millie, purring madly.

Uncle Kieran gave him a knowing look.

"Shall we get going?" Jen said, rising to her feet and avoiding looking at her family.

"Going where?" Charlotte said. "We've only just got here. Jen, don't you realise how inconvenient this is?"

"Well, with counselling I'm sure you'll get over it," Jen said briskly, and Quinn hid a smile as he handed her her coat.

She'd been nervous all day, ever since they'd left the cottage in Mousehole and driven back home. For his own part, Quinn was too terrified of the answer to ask if this really was home for her any more.

He took her hand as they walked down the dark street, the bandage rough against his fingers, and a sudden memory burst inside his head.

"What?" Jen asked.

"Five years ago," he said. "We did meet, didn't we?"

"If you can call tying a tourniquet 'meeting'," she said doubtfully.

"No. I thought I'd imagined this, but… did you come to the hospital?"

Her gaze shifted away. "Maybe."

"You touched my hand. I remember it, because no one ever bothered to do that. It was all medical and brusque. But you reached out and held my hand. The Angel of the White Lady."

She swallowed. "I just… wanted to see how you were. Ethan didn't mention you…"

"He never came," Quinn said softly. "But you did. I thought an angel was looking after me. Although that was probably all the drugs."

"Yeah, well, angels aren't all they're cracked up to be," Jen said, quite determinedly not looking in her niece's direction.

It was awful, seeing Alice but not talking to her. Like seeing your ex with another woman and pretending you hadn't. Jen clung onto Quinn's hand as they neared the office, and tried hard to ignore the little girl in the pinafore.

Beth was just closing up as they came by. "Haven't seen you for a couple of days," she said. "Everything all right?"

"Everything's fine," Quinn told her, and asked carefully, "And with you?"

"Oh, you know." She shrugged. "I get along."

"We should go out for a drink sometime," Jen said, wondering as she did if this was how you made friends.

Beth looked surprised, but pleased. "I'd like that," she said. "I really would."

Quinn smiled at her, and grinned at Jen as they went

up the stairs to the dark office. "That was nice."

"Well. It's about time I had friends who aren't dead."

"I heard that," muttered a peevish voice behind her, and she tried to ignore it.

Quinn switched on the lights as Charlotte, Millie and Kieran came into the office. Whilst Kieran wandered around making comments about the changes Quinn had made, Charlotte stood disapprovingly in the doorway. Jen could feel the weight of her gaze land on the cheap sofa and the not-quite magnolia paint. The carpet was the hard-wearing industrial kind and the desks made of plywood.

She lifted her chin and met her sister's gaze.

"What are we doing here?" Charlotte said. "If you just wanted to show me where you work you picked a very odd time to do it."

"Actually," Jen said, "I don't need you here at all. It's Millie I need." She took a deep breath. "And Alice."

At that point, Quinn came out of Tessa's office with a sheaf of paper in his hand, followed unseen by Danny. He was still in his bomber jacket and jaunty cap, and he cried a greeting to Jen and Alice. "And who are these lovely people?" he asked, glancing over the newcomers.

"This is Millie. She's my new friend," Alice said pointedly.

"This is my sister, Charlotte, and her daughter Mildred," Jen said, aware that they were watching her talk to the empty air.

"Er, yes, Jen, I think everyone knows that," Charlotte said with a forced laugh.

"Danny doesn't," Jen said, looking right at him. "Millie, this is my friend Danny. Say hello."

"'lo," Millie said shyly.

"Who are you talking to?" Charlotte said sharply. Her forehead was creased in the Jen Wrinkle.

"Ghosts," Jen said, and Quinn came to stand beside

her. He held up a piece of paper from Tessa's office, and she glanced at it and nodded. Quinn put it facedown on the desk.

"Danny is a ghost who haunts this office, and then of course there's Alice. You remember Alice, don't you? She's now attached herself to Millie, so if I were you I'd pay attention."

"Oh no, Jen, not again. Did you call Dr Wu?" Charlotte asked Quinn despairingly.

"I didn't need to," said Quinn calmly. He touched Jen's hand, and he gave his fingers a brief squeeze.

"Well, look, this isn't on. You shouldn't be encouraging her—"

"You don't believe in ghosts?" exclaimed Kieran.

"No. No sane person does," Charlotte said, glaring at Jen.

"Sure young Jenny here is perfectly sane."

"I can see him," piped up Millie.

"Can you, old thing?" Danny crouched down and held out his hand. Millie tried to shake it, giggling when her fingers passed right through it.

"Millie, stop that. There's no such thing as ghosts," Charlotte said, a tad desperately. She grabbed Millie's hand firmly, and took a step back. Danny just drifted upright and winked at the little girl.

"Why don't you believe in them?" Quinn said. "Because you've never seen them?"

"Well, of course! It's all made up."

"Like God is all made up? Perhaps you're not a church-goer. Let me ask you this then, Charlotte. Do you believe in kindness? In decency? In honesty?"

"What? Of course."

"Have you ever seen them?"

"Don't be ridiculous. They're concepts. You see their effects."

"Well, I've seen the effects of ghosts." Quinn pointed

427

to the healing cut on his cheek. "One did this to me, for example."

Charlotte's gaze darted between them.

"I was there, Charlotte," Uncle Kieran said. "Sure nobody was touching him at the time."

"Look, I don't know what sort of silly game you're all playing, but it needs to stop," Charlotte said in her Bossy Mother voice. "Millie and I are leaving—"

"Once again, Charlotte, this isn't about you," Jen said. She was amazed at herself for saying these things. "I know this might astonish you, but very little I do actually is. Like, for instance, I wasn't trying to upset you when I insisted my imaginary friend was real. I wasn't trying to make you look stupid when I talked to her in public. And I wasn't trying to embarrass you when I got sent to the home. Weirdly enough, that was all about me. And Alice."

Alice looked mutinous.

"Alice isn't real, Jen," said Charlotte through clenched teeth.

"Tell her, Mills."

Millie looked at Alice, then at Danny, and finally at Jen, who gave her a thumbs up. "I can see her."

"This isn't normal," Charlotte burst out. She looked like she was about to cry. "Why are you all just standing around like this is fine? My sister is ill!"

Jen opened her mouth to tell her sister she was actually feeling better than she had in a long time, but Quinn squeezed her hand and said to Charlotte, "Define normal?"

"Being like everyone else!"

"But why is that a good thing?" Kieran said.

"Well said, old chap," said Danny, and Jen smiled at that.

"Because it is! Look, I know you think it's all cool to be weird and quirky, but it's not, it's just embarrassing."

There was a silence while they all digested who was being embarrassing right now.

"It's embarrassing to you," Quinn said gently, in the sort of voice she imagined he'd use to talk someone off a ledge, "because you want to be normal. Just like everyone else. After your dad died, am I right?"

"Don't you dare," Charlotte said, her eyes bright and hard with tears. She clutched Millie even tighter and backed up until her legs hit the sofa.

"My da died when I was sixteen," Quinn said. "Maybe I know a little of what you went through. My brother, he went out looking for girls and drink. Me, I tried to become just like my da. My mother now, she turned inwards, and she's never really come back out again. What we all wanted was for things to become normal again."

Charlotte nodded, a tear escaping her.

"But here's the thing, Charlotte. You don't get to decide what's normal. And you don't get to impose your idea of it on someone else. Jenny was a little girl missing her dad, and you just told her she was crazy."

"I didn't—" Charlotte began, and crumpled onto the sofa. She picked Millie up and hugged her, as if she were a talisman. Perhaps she was. A normal child for a normal mother. 2.4 children in the suburbs. "If you could see ghosts, why couldn't you see him?" she sobbed.

"Because I don't get to choose," Jen said. Her own eyes were burning. "You don't know how hard I wished I could. Sometimes you can't avoid the trauma, Charlotte. You just have to heal up before the next one hits."

Charlotte just hugged her daughter and cried. Alice drifted over to hover near Millie and glare at Jen.

"Speaking of," Quinn murmured. He glanced at his uncle, who looked uncomfortable, and said, "There's a reason I asked you here."

"Ah, right," said Kieran, looking relieved. Then, "What is it?"

Quinn and Jen exchanged looks. Jen swiped at her damp eyes and cleared her throat. "I thought you might like to meet your father," she said. "Or more to the point, that he'd like to meet you."

Kieran looked around with an expression of comic disbelief.

"Ah, Jenny darlin', I think he's been gone a long time," he said.

She gave him a patient look and waited for the penny to drop.

"Jen, old thing?" Danny said, moving closer and peering at Kieran. "Are you telling me…?"

"What was her name, Danny? The Irish girl you loved."

Pain flickered across his features. "Rosie," he said quietly. "Róisín."

Jen repeated the names, and Kieran looked startled, then he said, "Ah now. Quinn must've told you…"

"Describe her to me, Danny," Jen said, and Danny did, his eyes on the old man who was his son.

"Blue eyes, like cornflowers. Long black hair. She liked to braid it over one shoulder. A big, wide, beaming smile, she used to light up the room. I couldn't stop looking at her when she smiled. And when she laughed, my God. The filthiest cackle you ever heard."

Kieran's eyes went wide as Jen repeated all this, but when she got to the cackle he gave a shocked laugh.

"Ah, she did. Face of an angel, laugh of a scoundrel, that's what my da used to say. My step-da," he amended.

"She married someone else?"

"She had to marry someone else," Jen said gently. "She was expecting Kieran when you died. But he was a good man, wasn't he?"

Kieran nodded, eyes bright with emotion. "He was a

legend. He took good care of her," he added to the empty air. "She was happy."

"Lived to a grand old age," Quinn added.

"Always remembered you," Kieran said, and started to cry. Quinn glanced at Jen, and left her to put his arm around his uncle, who hugged him fiercely.

Danny watched him longingly. "Is he really my son?"

Jen nodded. "Pretty sure he is."

"He's so old…"

She laughed a little at that. "It's been a long time. Danny, can I ask you something?"

Without looking away from Kieran, he nodded.

"Is that why you stayed? To make sure Róisín was all right? To watch over her?"

"I…" he tore his gaze away. "I don't know."

"You left her this house."

"So I did," Danny said, as if recalling a fond old jape.

"It's Kieran's now. All that time he worked here and you never knew him."

"I didn't know much until you came along. I stopped paying attention." Danny came closer, smiling. "Thank you, Jennifer."

"You're welcome." She leaned closer and whispered, "You weren't really a Spitfire pilot, were you?"

He looked panicked. "No, but don't tell my son that!"

She made a lip-zipping gesture. "Scout's honour." Her smile faded. She took a deep breath. "I need to ask you a favour, Danny. Now you've met Kieran, and you know your Rosie was all right, will you stay around, or will you… move on?"

"I—" He looked startled. "I don't know, old thing. I don't know what comes next."

"Something better than this," Jen said.

"How do you know?"

"I hope."

He nodded thoughtfully.

"And when you go," she said, and leaned forward to whisper the next bit as quietly as she could. Alice had hearing like a bat.

"Really?" Danny said.

"Really. Please. It's love that kept you here, isn't it? It's love that's keeping her too, but it's all got a bit… twisted."

"I heard that," said a shrill little voice. "I am not twisted."

"Alice, you've killed two people I know of."

"Jen, what are you saying?" said Charlotte from the sofa.

Jen looked down at Alice, and said, "I'm saying it's time to move on. I'm grateful for all the things you've done for me, I really am. Well, most things. You were my friend when I needed one, and you saved my life. And Quinn's life, and all those other people you helped me to help at the White Lady."

Alice, looking uncertain, nodded.

"But you can't go around hurting people because you think they've hurt me. I need to fight my own battles, Alice. You don't get to decide who deserves what."

"What is she talking about?" asked Charlotte, who seemed to have recovered somewhat.

"I'll explain later," Quinn said. "Just… whisht." When Charlotte looked mutinous, he added, "Fingers on lips!" and watched as Millie suited action to words and her mother reluctantly followed.

"Alice wouldn't hurt me," Millie said, and Jen's heart broke a little as she looked over at her, cuddled fiercely to her mother.

"No, darling, she wouldn't. But you can't rely on her."

"I won't go," Alice said. "Mildred needs me."

"She needs friends her own age, and a family who's not scared of her," Jen said. "Alice, what happened to you? What made you so determined to protect the girls in this family that you'd kill for them?"

Alice shook her head.

"Quinn can probably find out," Jen added, and Alice launched herself at him, murder in her eyes.

But Jen stepped in front of her, and Alice stopped. *She still wouldn't hurt me.* "Don't let him."

"Then tell me."

Alice shook her head, tears shining on her pale face. "You sent Brónach away," she blurted, and Jen understood.

"Brónach wanted people to know what was done to her. You don't?"

Alice shook her head fiercely.

"You just want to make sure it never happens again?"

This time a nod.

"It won't. Whatever it was, Alice, it won't happen. Not to me, not to Millie. We all look after each other."

As Alice stood and sniffed, Jen held out her hand to Millie, who scrambled off her mother's lap, much to Charlotte's distress. Jen crouched down and held her niece's hands.

"Now, Mildred," she said. "I promise to always look out for you, and keep you from harm as much as is possible. And so does your mummy, and your daddy too."

Millie looked puzzled, but she nodded.

"And Quinn will look after me, and I'll look after him, and Uncle Kieran, and if something bad happens then we'll all help each other. We'll be lifebelts, and we'll keep each other afloat. Right?"

"Right," Quinn said.

"Sure," Kieran said.

"I have no idea what you're talking about," said Charlotte.

"The dead don't need to look after the living, old

thing," said Danny, and Jen looked up to see him touching Alice's shoulder. No, not Alice. A young woman in a dark dress and pinafore, her weeping face hidden behind her hands. "They need to live their own lives."

"Alice Riley?" Jen said, and the woman her Alice had tried to forget shuddered. Her story was on the paper facedown on the desk. The youngest of seven, raised by a widow who married her lodger when Alice was nine. A few years later Alice was married to his cousin, a man twenty years her senior. The census showed six children born to the household, none of whom reached their second birthday. Alice had died aged 21, but Jen suspected her life had stopped when the lodger moved in.

I won't let the bad men hurt you.

"You need to move on, Alice," Jen said. "We've got this."

Alice looked up then, and her face was bruised, her eyes hollow. When she moved, it was with a limp. "I only wanted to help," she said.

"I know."

"I'm sorry, Jenny."

"I know."

"I loved you," Alice sobbed, and rushed forward to give Jen an icy hug, her arms passing right through. Jen hugged Millie instead, and said, "I loved you too."

She didn't realise she was crying until Millie said, "Auntie Jen, you're getting me all wet."

The cold had vanished. When she looked up, the ghosts were gone.

"Did someone just turn the heating up?" Charlotte said, and Jen released Millie to go back to her. She stood up, turned to Quinn, and held on to his warm, solid body as the last of the tears leaked out.

"She's gone," she sniffed. "They're both gone."

"It's for the best," he murmured, and she nodded against his chest. "You okay?"

"No," said Jen, lifting her head. "But I will be."

Quinn brushed a kiss across her lips, and she took a deep breath and turned to face her sister.

"Will someone please tell me what on earth is going on?" said Charlotte, smoothing down her cashmere sweater.

I just showed you all my demons and tore down all your petty issues and you're still behaving like it will all go away if you're bossy enough. For the first time, Jen felt sorry for Charlotte.

Jen glanced at Quinn, then back at her sister, and said, "Char, I couldn't begin to tell you."

Quinn grinned at her, and they walked together to the door.

"This is completely ridiculous," Charlotte said, following them. "And what in heaven's name was all that rubbish about the White Lady?"

"You might need to run a few bits by me again, son," Kieran said as he brought up the rear.

"We'll do an agency report," Quinn said, ushering them all past as he fished for his keys.

"It's a hell of a way to spend your birthday," Jen said to him.

"Hey, I said I wanted to spend it with you, so."

"I'm going to call Dr Wu," Charlotte said as she stomped down the stairs, dragging her daughter with her.

"No, you're not," Jen said calmly. "Now, who's hungry?"

"The pub does good burgers," Quinn added.

"Me!" cried Millie.

"No burgers," Charlotte said. "I've got rice crackers in the car."

"I'm starving," said Jen. "Apparently banishing ghosts takes it out of you."

"Maybe you need gin," Quinn said as he locked the door, and she laughed.

"I think I've had enough of spirits," she said, and she took his hand and walked out into the empty night.

AUTHOR'S NOTE

Some things in this book were researched in person. Some were researched through articles and documentaries, and simply asking questions. And some came from experience.

There's no simple explanation for self-harming, and no simple solution either. I wish there was. The mental health charity Mind has a section on their website that might help you—or someone else—to understand it a little better, and some advice for coping: www.mind.org.uk > Information & support > Types of mental health problems > Self-harm.

I hope I've done this very subjective subject justice, and that if you need help, you can find it. Take care of yourselves, and each other.

Love, Kate.

KATE JOHNSON

ACKNOWLEDGEMENTS

Writing is a very solitary thing, but publishing requires a lot of people. As ever, the amazing women of the Naughty Kitchen have been indispensable throughout all my Ghost Book related wobbles.

Thanks especially to Jan for proofreading, and to Ruth & Pat for showing me around Dalkey and Dublin and helping with Irish translations: it's not a simple language to get a hold of! Any errors are entirely my own.

Everyone who helped me choose a title. You wouldn't believe how many there were before I even narrowed it down. Jean, I hope you're right about this one. Jan, you can still call it *The Ghost Book* if you like. Al, it's *All My Friends Are Dead* to you. And if I could remember who wanted to call it *Icy Dead People* I'd be very happy.

And finally, everyone who turned this book down (and oh boy were there a lot of you). It wasn't ready yet. I hope it is now.

ABOUT THE AUTHOR

Kate has a second cousin who held a Guinness World Record for brewing the strongest beer, and once ran over herself with a Segway scooter. Despite this, she is the author of over a dozen critically acclaimed novels and has been shortlisted for a Romantic Novel of the Year Award three times, winning in 2017 with **Max Seventeen**, a sci-fi action romance. She has also written over thirty erotic romance titles under the name Cat Marsters.

Kate loves cats and lives with several of them in southeast England. Her interests include books, quizzes, and dyeing her hair, and she can often be found Being A Professional Author at conferences, workshops and panels.

You can follow Kate online:
www.twitter.com/K8JohnsonAuthor
www.facebook.com/K8JohnsonAuthor
https://www.pinterest.co.uk/k8johnsonauthor/little-haunting-by-the-sea
or find out more on www.KateJohnson.co.uk

Want to be first to hear about new releases? Sign up here: http://etaknosnhoj.blogspot.co.uk/p/newsletter.html

ALSO AVAILABLE

All books: http://author.to/KateJohnsonAuthor

Royal Wedding romance series
Not Your Cinderella
Not Your Prince Charming
Not Your Knight in Shining Armour (2019)

Sci-fi action romance series
Max Seventeen
Max Seventeen: Firebrand
Max Seventeen: Empire of Dirt (2019)

The Sophie Green Mysteries: chick-lit mystery
I, Spy?
Ugley Business
A is for Apple
Still Waters
Run Rabbit Run
Worth a Shot: a Luke Sharpe novella

The Untied Kingdom: alternate history romance
Impossible Things: a fantasy romance

For more information please visit KateJohnson.co.uk

Keep reading for an excerpt from *Max Seventeen...*

EXCERPT FROM MAX SEVENTEEN
Paranormal Romantic Novel of the Year 2017

Max was running.

The day was hot and bright, because days were always hot and bright on this crappy planet at the arse-end of the universe. Cheaply terraformed, barely able to support the dreg ends of life, farted at by the sun on a regular basis. Nobody lived here if they didn't have to.

At this moment, Max was sincerely considering how much 'have to' there was about living on Zeta Secunda, a planet so shitty it didn't even have a proper name. There was a spaceport a few clicks away, but spaceports required ID and security, and Max was fresh out of both. Well. Fresh out might be a stretch. Probably that last ID had ended up in the same place as that last decent pair of boots: inside those fecking sand-beasts. Ten feet long, and that was just the jaw. Max had been lucky to get out alive.

For a given value of luck, anyway. That bunch of culchies were still mad at Max for something. Hard to figure out what. Might've been the card sharping. Might've been the fake money. Might've been that fella left with his pants hanging out the window.

Either way, Max was running.

Sand fountained up ahead, and a whine whistled past. Grand, so they'd found their guns. At least here in the badlands they were the cheap old kind with bullets, which required aiming and accuracy, neither of which this lot seemed to have. Quite probably they were hungover. Possibly also still drunk. Not that Max could judge, brain still throbbing with last night's poteen.

Max was running on empty.

"I see you, kid!"

Max ignored that, and leapt over some low rocks to

the sand below. Ahead, there was nothing but more rocks and more sand. So much more sand.

"Ain't nowhere to hide!"

Yeah, *obvs*. Sand, rocks, more sand. Max was dark with dirt and sun and vaguely sand coloured, but not nearly enough. There was nowhere to go, no shelter, no respite. Sooner or later they'd catch up.

Another smash. Another whine. Closer this time.

Max stumbled, foot rolling on a stone, knee thudding into the sand. Hell of a day to have fallen out the window with no clothes on.

The sun was fierce punishing. The desultory government advisories for Zeta Secunda included not going outside without solar protection. They meant proper pharma grade sunscreen. They didn't mention the fucking sand. Max didn't even have a shirt.

"Run, punk, run!" Those yahoos were getting closer. Some terrible little land buggies, or maybe horses. They used both around here, and it wasn't as if the wind was giving away any clues. No bugger was rich enough for a heavy-air vehicle. The HAVs and the HAV-nots, Max thought hysterically, stumbling on.

Smash, whine. Closer together. Sound and sand hitting at the same time.

Shit, not this time, don't let me die like this! I've got no fucking pants on!

The ground shook with the vehicles, pounded with the hooves of the horses. Closer, closer. Max kept on running. The sand gave way, shelving and sliding. Burned like the lava it once had been, grinding and grating, raw against raw skin. Max slid, the sand like waves made out of grit, desperate not to scream.

Sand fountained, the herald of impeding doom, and Max scrambled to bleeding feet, limping on over unforgiving dunes. The shadows closed in.

Max kept on running.

The engines of the Dauntless hummed smoothly, at a frequency that seemed perfectly calculated to grate on Riley's nerves.

Just four more years, then you can quit this fascist popsicle stand.

Fantasies of ripping out that Service chip they'd implanted and hurling it at the captain made up quite a lot of Riley's downtime.

"Sir?"

The captain gave no indication she'd heard.

"Sir, it's about Pherick. Pherick Green, the coolant engineer? It's just, he's been gone three standard weeks now, and—"

The captain tapped something on her tablet and didn't look up. "Green is on personal leave."

"Yes, sir, I know. But we're not allowed personal leave longer than—"

"The Service is capable of making exceptions," said the captain coolly.

Really? thought Riley. In whose favour? Eleven bloody years I've been committed to the Service, and when was the last time I got any leave?

The dark thought occurred that on Sigma Prime, you could commit murder and still get out of jail in less than eleven years.

"I understand you are friends," said the captain, and there was something in the way she said it that made Riley uneasy.

"We work together."

"I see. And Ensign..." she tapped her tablet, "Yakira is not an acceptable substitute?"

"Ensign Yakira is doing a fine job."

"Then what is the problem?"

The problem? Riley wanted to say. The problem is that Pherick just disappeared one day, barely a few hours after telling me he'd uncovered something really disturbing but he couldn't tell me what. The problem is that his brother Jameson went AWOL on an away mission three months ago and he's not even supposed to be part of away missions. The problem is I think something very strange is going on here and I'm kind of scared that if I start asking questions about it, I'll be the next one to disappear.

Out loud, Riley said, "I just wondered when Pherick would be back, sir. I owe him a drink."

"I'm sure you'll be buying it soon. Was there anything else?"

You'll be watching every single thing I do on this ship from now on, won't you? thought Riley, but said, "No, sir. Thank you, sir."

The cool, neutral corridors of the ship closed in like a jail as Riley strode away, plotting escape.

Max Seventeen is available in ebook and paperback:
http://mybook.to/Max17

Did you enjoy this book? Please consider leaving a review!

This book is enrolled in Kindle's Matchbook program. For more information, see Amazon.com

Printed in Great Britain
by Amazon